*Hidden Histories of Unauthorized Migrations
from Europe to the United States*

STUDIES OF WORLD MIGRATIONS

Marcelo J. Borges and Madeline Y. Hsu, editors

*For a list of books in the series, please see our website
at www.press.uillinois.edu.*

Hidden Histories
of Unauthorized Migrations
from Europe to the United States

Edited by

DANIELLE BATTISTI and

S. DEBORAH KANG

UNIVERSITY OF ILLINOIS PRESS

Urbana, Chicago, and Springfield

© 2025 by the Board of Trustees
of the University of Illinois
All rights reserved
1 2 3 4 5 C P 5 4 3 2 1
♾ This book is printed on acid-free paper.

Library of Congress Cataloging-in-Publication Data
Names: Battisti, Danielle editor | Kang, S. Deborah,
    1970– editor
Title: Hidden histories of unauthorized migrations
    from Europe to the United States / edited by Danielle
    Battisti and S. Deborah Kang.
Description: Urbana : University of Illinois Press,
    2025. | Series: Studies of world migrations | Includes
    bibliographical references and index. |
Identifiers: LCCN 2024046672 (print) | LCCN
    2024046673 (ebook) | ISBN 9780252046469
    (cloth) | ISBN 9780252088551 (paperback) | ISBN
    9780252047770 (ebook)
Subjects: LCSH: Illegal immigration—United States—
    History—20th century. | Europeans—United
    States—History—20th century. | Europe x Emigration
    and immigration—History—20th century. | United
    States—Emigration and immigration—History—20th
    century.
Classification: LCC JV6455 .H5 2025 (print) | LCC
    JV6455 (ebook) | DDC 364.1/3709730904—dc23/
    eng/20250225
LC record available at https://lccn.loc.gov/2024046672
LC ebook record available at https://lccn.loc.gov/2024046673

Contents

Acknowledgments

We owe many thanks to the individuals and institutions that have supported this project since its inception. Perhaps first and foremost, we are immensely grateful to our contributors who agreed to join us in this venture during the COVID-19 pandemic. Despite the profound uncertainties of that moment, they found the grace to share their scholarly expertise and create a sense of collaboration and community that has only grown these past several years.

We would also like to thank the Karsh Institute of Democracy, the European Studies Program, and the Department of Sociology at the University of Virginia. As the pandemic ended, these institutions made it possible for our contributors to convene in Charlottesville for a manuscript workshop during the fall 2022 semester. We are grateful to Peter Debaere, Amanda Frost, Walter Kamphoefner, Kristina Poznan, and Yael Schacher for reading our contributors' draft chapters and participating in the workshop; their keen insights were critical to the completion of this anthology.

Anonymous reviewers and the editors of the Studies of World Migration series at the University of Illinois Press prepared detailed reports that proved invaluable in the revision of this work. We would also like to extend our gratitude to Megan Donnan for guiding us through the production process and Sandra Getuba for preparing the index. Allison Torres Burtka has made this volume materially better thanks to her excellent editorial work on our chapters. Finally, the support of Alison Syring, our editor at the press, has been indispensable; we are deeply indebted to her for helping us to navigate the practical and intellectual challenges presented by the publication of a multi-author work.

Introduction
Pulling Back the Curtain

Unauthorized European Migrations to the United States

DANIELLE BATTISTI AND S. DEBORAH KANG

When we told family members, friends, and colleagues that we were preparing an anthology on undocumented European migration, we were met with a variety of responses ranging from confusion to curiosity. Thanks to popular and scholarly depictions, many people we talked to had come to develop strong associations with European immigration. Those included references to iconic storylines in American history, beginning with individuals and families disembarking on Ellis Island to start their journeys in pursuit of social and economic mobility in the United States Some went on to connect European immigrants with New York's Little Italies, Chicago's *Polonia*, or Detroit's Greektown, where scenes of cultural pluralism and immigrant assimilation seemed to mix together in equal parts as they imagined those spaces as ethnic weigh stations of a sort. Yet still others recalled romanticized fictional accounts like *The Godfather*, where even problematic Euro-American characters figured into popularized narratives of immigrants getting ahead by hard work, ingenuity, and sacrifice.

It had not occurred to most of them to question the tacit assumptions regarding European legality and belonging embedded in such narratives, let alone consider the possibility that many European migrants might have entered through unauthorized channels or lived and worked for portions of their life without legal status in the United States. Yet, as we presented aspects of this work to audiences throughout the country, we also met people who did know this history. Along with other scholars who had begun to think through these issues, descendants and relatives of unauthorized European migrants occasionally shared their own family's clandestine history with us. They wanted to know more. Were their family histories unique or part of a larger trend in American immigration history? And if so, why wasn't it generally a part of the shared narratives we tell about European immigration—why had the history of unauthorized European immigration been hidden for so long?

This anthology addresses these questions by highlighting emerging scholarship on the subject of unauthorized European migration to the United States, thereby exposing an otherwise hidden history. In the process, we narrate a more complex portrait of the Ellis Island cohort and their descendants than the narratives that are generally acknowledged in selective re-imaginations of European immigration. Immigrants and ethnic groups who are now lauded by some policymakers and pundits as the nation's quintessential legal immigrants for "waiting their turn" to come to the United States, entering through the proper channels, and "pulling themselves up from their bootstraps" to make it in America obscure a messier historical reality.[1] Not only were their migration experiences far more diverse than those presented by commonly shared narratives, but also, the erasure of illegality from those accepted plotlines constitutes part of the long process by which European immigrants and their children have benefited and continue to benefit from their legal and social status as white persons.[2]

Rosaria Baldizzi's story exemplifies the often-unseen complexities underlying the accounts of European immigrant experiences. Her migration journey is one of the several immigration histories reconstructed at the Lower Eastside Tenement Museum in New York City. Since the opening of the popular historic site in 1988, millions of visitors have been able to step into the European immigrant past by touring an exhibit of immigrant households at 97 Orchard Street, designed by museum curators to help us better understand the lives of "typical" immigrant families. One display features the Baldizzi family apartment, where married Italian immigrants Adolfo and Rosaria Baldizzi and their two American-born children, Josephine and Johnny, lived from 1928 to 1935. A stroll through the Baldizzi apartment enables visitors to learn about the family's journey from Italy and glimpse into their home life, workplace experiences, and social interactions in New York City.

It was not until 2016, however, that the museum mentioned the fact that Rosaria Baldizzi was an unauthorized immigrant.[3] Guided by shifts in scholarship rather than the discovery of new archival material about the family, the Tenement Museum developed a more nuanced retelling of Rosaria's journey for its tours and website. Both the museum's in-person and virtual exhibits now prominently feature Rosaria as an undocumented immigrant, detailing how she did not possess an immigration visa at the time of her entry in 1923.[4] Yet Rosaria lived and worked without harassment or punishment in the United States for many years thereafter. In fact, the U.S. government legalized Rosaria in 1945, when she was allowed to adjust her status to become a legal permanent resident; by 1948 she had been granted U.S. citizenship.

Figure 0.1. Naturalization Certificate of Rosaria Baldizzi, May 18, 1948.
Collection of Tenement Museum.

Rosaria's "irregular" pathway into the United States was not as irregular as
many may think, however. Although exact numbers are difficult to ascertain, it
is safe to say that hundreds of thousands of European immigrants came to the
United States through unauthorized channels beginning in the late nineteenth
century, and they continue to do so today.[5] Whether it be a German migrant
laborer who contracted to work in the United States after the Foran Act (Alien
Contract Labor Law) was passed in 1885, a Greek economic migrant who stowed
away on a ship without a visa in violation of the national origins quotas of 1924,
a Russian refugee who crossed the U.S.-Mexico border without an immigration
inspection in the 1930s, an Italian commercial sailor who deserted his vessel at
an American port in the 1950s, a Polish migrant who overstayed a tourist visa
in the 1980s, or many other examples we could cite, unauthorized European
immigrants long have made their way to the United States between 1885 and
the start of the twenty-first century.

In *Hidden Histories*, we seek to reinsert the history of unauthorized European migrants into the scholarly literature and contemporary policy debates.
The authors featured here unpack how the phenomenon of European illegality

largely emerged in response to the passage of laws in the late nineteenth and early twentieth centuries that restricted European migration.[6] They further illustrate how European migrants' "entry into illegality"—that is, the specific strategies by which Europeans skirted immigration controls in the United States and abroad—was often contingent on race, nationality, gender, and class, among other factors.[7] The volume also provides new insights into the development of the nation's immigration enforcement architecture by tracing how Europeans were policed abroad, at the borders, and within the country itself. The attribution of legal status to any given individual is a social as well as a legal process; to underscore this point, *Hidden Histories* traces the role of cultural representations in the construction of illegality.[8] Finally, and perhaps most important, our authors stress how the longstanding ascription of legality, belonging, and citizenship to European migrants mediated the experiences of unauthorized Europeans in the United States. These assumptions generally enabled unauthorized Europeans to pass as legal immigrants. They were also created and reinforced by state actions that forgave, and even erased, European immigrants' illegality by extending numerous opportunities for European immigrants to adjust their legal status and become U.S. citizens.

By revealing these little-known histories, our aim is not to collapse the distinctions between the experiences of undocumented Asian, Latin American, African, and European migrants. Instead, this volume traces the continuities and discontinuities among the experiences of these immigrant groups. Due to pervasive racism in the United States and the drive to conquer and settle the American West, Europeans were afforded many more opportunities for "legal" admission than other migrant groups and faced much less pressure to enter "outside of the law" for much of the nation's history. Our volume stresses that enduring conceptions of European belonging gave unauthorized European migrants advantages by shielding them from various forms of legal violence.[9] As our contributors demonstrate, immigration officials repeatedly minimized detentions and deportations for European migrants even as they constructed a "deportation machine" that targeted non-white immigrants.[10] While undocumented status constituted a pathway to detention and deportation for some, it opened the doors to American citizenship for others. The uneven policing of unauthorized Europeans, moreover, enabled them to live outside of the shadows and establish families, homes, and livelihoods in the United States and abroad. Several chapters in this collection further highlight that unauthorized European migrations have been cloaked from public view, in large part because of state and non-state practices that normalized those irregular migrations. These erasures have been central in the creation of narratives that enabled many unauthorized European migrants to elude negative characterizations as lawbreakers and national security threats that have frequently been applied to non-white immigrants. In short, *Hidden Histories* complements the work of historians and sociologists of unauthorized Asian, Latin American, and African migration by underscoring the vast racialized inequities in the perceptions and policing of undocumented immigrants.[11]

In the pages that follow, we situate *Hidden Histories* in the scholarly literature on American immigration history, explaining how and why scholars long neglected the study of unauthorized European migrations to the United States. We then trace the development of federal laws and policies from the late nineteenth century to the early twenty-first century that created the conditions for European illegality and also afforded unauthorized Europeans numerous opportunities to adjust their status and become legal immigrants. The last section supplies an overview of the collection's nine chapters, highlighting our contributors' unique approaches and insights into the history of European illegality.

Dismantling the Myths of European Immigrant Belonging, Citizenship, and Legality

Hidden Histories addresses a major gap in the scholarly literature on American immigration history. While work on European illegality is now an emerging field, that was not the case until quite recently.[12] Indeed, as the recent revision of Rosaria's story at the Tenement Museum attests, many took for granted the legality of European migrants. These assumptions were grounded in scholarly and vernacular narratives that associated the European immigrant experience with the nation's history and identity. To this day, these narratives have had remarkable staying power because they have become integral to our sense of imagined community. Thus, even as scholarly interpretations of the European immigrant experience changed, the ascription of legality and belonging to European migrants has persisted. By unearthing the histories of unauthorized European migration, this anthology aims not only to enrich our understanding of undocumented migration but also dismantle the myths surrounding the European immigrant experience.

Despite the ubiquity of unauthorized European immigrants in the United States, the first practitioners in the field of immigration history constructed narratives that ignored their stories. Focusing on the study of European migrants, these scholars, operating in the mid-twentieth century, established a paradigm by which European immigrants were viewed as "normative." In contrast, African, Asian, and Latin American migrants, when they were examined, were compared to Europeans, relegated to the background, or dismissed entirely as outside of the scope of inquiry.[13] Drawing on widely circulated theories of assimilation and ethnicity articulated by sociologists, who also took a Eurocentric focus in their practice, they were generally not guided by questions about Europeans' right to migrate, and they rarely questioned the European immigrant's *eventual* path toward incorporation.[14]

The most widely disseminated work of this cohort was historian Oscar Handlin's *The Uprooted: The Epic Story of the Great Migrations that Made the American People*. Even though Handlin viewed certain European immigrant groups with skepticism and saw their integration into American society as a process fraught with challenges, in *The Uprooted* he famously declared that "immigrants were American history."[15] That Pulitzer Prize–winning book, and Handlin's corresponding public notoriety, helped to popularize the notion of America as a "nation of immigrants." The phrase was touted by influential voices in society, ranging from public school teachers to President John F. Kennedy.[15] As a form of "popular nationalism," the nation of immigrants narrative celebrated the assimilation of European migrants into the polity, credited their economic and cultural contributions with the building of the nation, and rendered their success stories a synecdoche for American history as a whole.[17]

The nation of immigrants paradigm has been extensively challenged, if not rejected, by immigration scholars for masking multiple dimensions of the migration experience. Often first- or second-generation European immigrants themselves, early critics shirked the nationalist predilections of their predecessors and advanced culturally pluralist accounts of American immigration history. Popularly referred to as "salad bowl theory," these studies traced the formation of ethnic identities and explored how immigrant communities diversified American culture and society.[18] The continued Eurocentric focus of this work, however, led practitioners of the New Social History to further assail the disciplinary conventions in the field. Informed by the civil rights movement and the demographic changes generated by the Immigration and Nationality Act of 1965, historians such as Rudolph Vecoli argued that the "*blight* of assimilationist ideology" had prevented scholars from exploring the "multicultural character of the American people."[19] At the same time, increasing numbers of Asian American and Latinx historians who were often interested in their families' overlooked or misunderstood histories played foundational roles in creating more racially diverse accounts of the nation's immigrant past.[20] By the 1970s and 1980s, the exclusion of non-Europeans from U.S. immigration history was no longer considered a "viable intellectual strateg[y]."[21]

In addition to decentering European migration histories, late twentieth-century scholarship demonstrated how the association of European immigrants with citizenship and belonging was not inevitable but instead the product of the exclusionary forces that drove the nation's development. Scholars studying Asian, African, and Latinx migrants explored the roles of race and racism in the American immigrant experience, demonstrating how non-white immigrants experienced forms of *de jure* and *de facto* discrimination analogous to those endured by non-white citizens in the United States.[22] Building on the findings of whiteness studies, immigration scholars also traced the formation and attribution of a white racial identity to European newcomers and how perceptions of whiteness conferred on European immigrants and their children social and legal advantages denied to non-white migrants.[23] Taken together, these studies have compelled scholars to adopt a more critical perspective on our imagined community and the ways its citizenry was largely constructed "by design."[24]

Studies of American immigration law and policy that have proliferated since the late 1990s continue to rewrite the nation of immigrants myth by framing immigration history as a process of racial gatekeeping. Applying the earlier advances in the field to a study of the nation's immigration laws and policies and immigration enforcement agencies, immigration scholars have examined how non-white immigrants historically experienced significant barriers to the right to immigrate, remain in the United States, and obtain the same economic opportunities and political rights as European immigrants and their children.[25] By the late twentieth century, the escalation in immigration law enforcement, which manifested in the criminalization of immigration law infractions, the historic increases in formal deportations, and the dramatic expansion of the nation's immigration detention system, led immigration scholars to draw powerful connections between the history of immigration law enforcement and the rise of the carceral state.[26] At the same time, immigration historians made visible the human costs of immigration policing on undocumented immigrants, particularly Latinx migrants who have been disproportionately affected by immigration law enforcement from the early twentieth century to the present.[27]

The history of European illegality is an integral component of this broader history of racial gatekeeping. It illuminates how our nation's immigration system effectively developed two separate and unequal tracks for the policing of undocumented Europeans and undocumented Latinx immigrants. Yet, despite the significance of this history to our understanding of immigration law enforcement in the United States, scholars largely have left assumptions regarding European legality intact. In the past half century, our portrait of the European immigrant experience has undergone a radical transformation. Our anthology contributes to this ongoing effort by tracing the making and unmaking of European illegality from the nineteenth century to the present.

Racial Gatekeeping and the Creation
of European Legality and Illegality

Since the nation's inception, racial gatekeeping practices and policies have frequently worked to the advantage of European noncitizens. Settler colonial practices, beginning with the European colonization of North America and continued by the United States, resulted in the violent dispossession of land from native peoples, the removal of Indigenous peoples from American territory, and the rendering of natives as "foreign" in their own land. U.S. property law, land-grant policies, laws governing slavery and freedom of movement, and antebellum legislation designed to prevent Black migrants from entering the country and obtaining citizenship rights all worked together in complementary ways that legitimized Euro-American membership in the nation and the exclusion of others understood as non-white. As a result, European peoples *alone* enjoyed opportunities to freely immigrate to the United States, the unencumbered ability to move without threat within its territories, the relative right to remain in places that they chose for resettlement, and liberal opportunities for property ownership and political rights—including naturalization.[28]

The Civil War ushered in a more liberal and racially inclusive understanding of national citizenship in theory, but in reality, citizenship remained highly circumscribed by laws and practices that ultimately upheld the link between whiteness and full membership in the nation.[29] Over the course of the late nineteenth and early twentieth centuries, Jim Crow laws and practices stripped African Americans throughout the country of hard-fought-for and short-lived access to equal rights. Native peoples were relegated to federal reservations, where they were treated as childlike wards of the state not yet ready for citizenship. The state also increasingly identified groups of foreigners judged to be unfit for citizenship in this period. Asian and Latinx migrants were the primary targets of restrictionist policies and nativist violence built on racialized constructions of membership and citizenship, but federal immigration laws also began to put significant restrictions on European immigration for the first time starting in the 1880s.[30] By the late nineteenth and early twentieth centuries, increased economic anxieties, concerns linking radical politics and national security, and evolving ideas about racial, ethnic, and religious distinctions began to significantly challenge European migrants' theretofore assumed access to resettle in the United States.[31]

However, even while racialized worldviews, particularly toward Southern and Eastern European immigrants, constrained European immigrants in various ways, they never affected white immigrants to the extent experienced by their non-white counterparts.[32] The uneven application of restrictionist laws and the civil and criminal penalties for unauthorized entry spared European immigrants from various forms of state violence commonly experienced by Asian and Latinx migrants. In addition, by the early twentieth century, a framework emerged that afforded European migrants multiple avenues to adjust their immigration status. In short, the history of European illegality was characterized by not only the transgression of the nation's immigration laws but also its paradoxical erasure from public consciousness via formal and informal legal mechanisms.

Congress passed the Foran Act (also known as the Alien Contract Labor Law) in 1885 in an attempt to clamp down on agricultural and industrial exploitation of unfree immigrant labor, in the wake of a public outcry against the employment of so-called Chinese "coolies." The legislation made it illegal to immigrate to the United States with a preexisting contract of employment, and it further empowered the federal government to exclude and deport immigrants in violation of the law.[33] Like their Chinese counterparts, southern and eastern Europeans sought work via global labor markets, and they too sometimes lacked the economic and social capital to emigrate and find work independently. As a result, tens of thousands of Italian, Greek, and other European workers came to the United States indebted to a *padrone,* or labor boss, who ensured their cheap and compliant labor for major agricultural and industrial enterprises in exchange for providing overseas passage, job placement, resettlement loans, and a host of other services. Although Americans generally didn't stigmatize them the way they stigmatized "coolies," and even showed sympathy for their exploited condition, European contract workers nevertheless threatened white American workers' notions of economic and political independence.[34]

The passage of the Foran Act, the ways that it shaped the state's immigration enforcement regime, and its impact on immigrant workers deserve much further attention. The most comprehensive research to date suggests that the Foran Act was largely ineffective in stopping contract labor practices for southern and eastern European immigrants who continued to immigrate via the padrone system in what Gunther Peck characterizes as "sufficiently clandestine" ways through the 1910s.[35] Moreover, because federal judges attempted to mitigate against the legislation's anti-contract implications, they gutted key aspects of the law by calling on the U.S. Immigration Bureau to distinguish between voluntary and coerced migrants at inspection points. Consequently, enforcement of the Alien Contract Labor Law became a highly racialized practice. On the whole, immigration inspectors gave European laborers the benefit of the doubt that they were able to freely migrate. Contract laborers from Europe therefore quickly adopted the simple strategy of concealing their work arrangements to commercial or state inspectors at points of disembarkation and entry. When asked by an inspector if they had a job waiting for them in the country, labor agents, shipping companies, peers, and other parties involved in labor schemes instructed European migrants to reply with some variation of: "No, but my prospects look good. My cousin, uncle, friend, etc. will help me find work."[36] Chinese and South Asian laborers who made similar claims were rarely believed and were subject to much greater scrutiny. In fact, the Chinese Exclusion Act's prohibition on *all* Chinese labor reflected American assumptions that all Chinese immigrants were operating under exploitative labor contracts that undercut competition from free American laborers.[37]

Again, numbers are difficult to ascertain, but Peck's work suggests that tens of thousands of European immigrants successfully evaded the Foran Act from 1885 to 1914, when World War I disrupted global labor markets. By contracting employment and migrating under indebted circumstances where they were subject to the coercion of a padrone and their business partners, vast numbers of European immigrants successfully immigrated in violation of the law at the turn of the century. Yet, the state overwhelmingly failed to recognize such behaviors, thus helping to establish a pattern in which irregular European immigration became normalized, tolerated, and not subject to significant penalty.

Congress passed a host of other federal immigration laws in the late nineteenth and early twentieth centuries, including omnibus immigration acts in 1882, 1891, and 1903 that expanded the categories under which European immigration could be restricted. Those acts thereby created the conditions in which the law could, and would, be violated. Poor immigrants were known to stow away on vessels to avoid paying the head tax on entry or being found "likely to become a public charge." Others did so because they feared being refused entry for having committed a crime of "moral turpitude." Yet still others evaded formal inspection points because they worried that a poor physical bearing, chronic health condition, or communicable disease might bar their admission. Immigrants (and migrants from the country's colonial possessions) espousing radical political beliefs were increasingly excluded at the gates or detained and deported as a form of post-entry social control. All told, European immigrants were increasingly subject to exclusionary policies by the turn of the century, and they could also be detained at holding centers like Ellis Island while receiving medical care, facing an extended investigation, or awaiting expulsion or deportation.[38] European immigrants therefore adopted several evasion strategies in response to these selection policies.[39]

It was in the aftermath of World War I when nativist attitudes toward European immigrants reached their zenith. The "One Hundred Percent Americanism" campaigns during the war, fallout from the communist revolution in Russia, and the corresponding Red Scare in the United States all heightened fears about national security and immigrant radicalism spreading from Europe to America. But the notion that "new" immigrants were fundamentally different from "older stock" immigrants had already taken root before the interwar period. Employing the pseudo-scientific discourse of eugenics to legitimize cultural prejudice and structures of white supremacy, influential groups like the Immigration Restriction League had already identified southern and eastern European immigrants (along with non-European immigrants) as a problem that needed to be solved and called on the federal government to stem the flow of undesirable foreigners. In large part due to these groups' advocacy and influence, Congress responded by organizing the Dillingham Commission's "scientific" study (1907–1911) of the immigration problem, and subsequently passing major restrictionary laws, including the 1917 literacy test, the 1921 Emergency Quota Act, and the 1924 Johnson-Reed Act.[40]

Such legislation, particularly the Johnson-Reed Act, represented a monumental shift in the country's position toward European immigration. Among other restrictions, the law set relatively low annual ceilings on immigration, enacted paltry national origins quotas for southern and eastern European sending states, and restricted legal entry to immigrants who had cleared a range of security and health checks to secure an immigration visa before they departed for the United States.[41] While the Johnson-Reed Act went far in achieving one of its goals to reduce the flow of immigration from southern and eastern Europe, it correspondingly expanded the number of European immigrants who would now immigrate outside of the law. Economic opportunities, family ties, political persecution in sending states, and other "push and pull" factors continued to draw hundreds of thousands of European immigrants who were willing to run the risks associated with irregular migration in the years that the national origins system was in operation. Some migrants were able to defraud consular agents with false information and documents to obtain an immigration visa. Immigration to Canada or Mexico with the express intent of a clandestine crossing into the United States, often with the assistance of an organized smuggling ring, became an increasingly common tactic after 1924.[42] Still others gained entry through non-immigrant visa categories that emerged as a byproduct of the new immigration regime established in the 1924 act. Tourists, students, temporary workers, commercial seamen, and others who overstayed the allotted windows of time granted via a non-immigrant visa became de facto illegal immigrants.[43] Finally, when the state discovered, arrested, and sanctioned unauthorized migrants with deportation orders, it was not uncommon for an individual to ignore that order in a further attempt to remain in the United States.[44]

In response to the growing problem of unauthorized European migration, immigration advocates, ethnic organizations, and policymakers pressed the government for, and often received, various forms of bureaucratic relief and special legislation. Two days after Congress passed the Undesirable Aliens Act of 1929, a measure that would be employed to criminalize undocumented Mexican migrants, it passed the Registry Act, enabling unauthorized immigrants who met certain criteria to adjust their legal status.[45] Yet by explicitly excluding people ineligible for citizenship, the act foreclosed the possibility that unauthorized Asian migrants could adjust their status. Although Mexicans could technically normalize their status under the measure, the state erected bureaucratic and financial hurdles that significantly limited their ability to take advantage of the provision in practice, thereby achieving ethnic selection through what appeared to be a racially neutral law.[46] Ultimately, the Registry Act intentionally prioritized the adjustment of status of unauthorized European migrants, and it signaled the state's tacit approval for irregular pathways of European immigration.

During the interwar period, unauthorized Europeans continued to be afforded multiple avenues of redress. The most significant involved the pairing of the pre-examination and voluntary departure procedures. Employed as one strategy for the removal of undocumented Mexican migrants, voluntary departure has been rightfully characterized as one of the most punitive enforcement tools deployed by federal immigration agencies.[47] Yet voluntary departure assumed a dramatically different guise as part of an underappreciated two-step administrative process that legalized unauthorized Europeans. As Mae Ngai explains, the process cobbled together voluntary departure with an existing innocuous administrative practice whereby the Canadian government granted temporary stays to immigrant visitors from the United States. In the mid-1930s, bypassing congressional roadblocks, executive branch officials allowed unauthorized "pre-examined" immigrants to also cross into Canada so they could perform a legal reentry into the United States and thereby obtain relief from removal. The scholarship shows that the racial requisites of the immigration statutes, administrative discretion, and judicial decisions all combined to render European immigrants as the primary and intended beneficiaries of this mode of status adjustment once again.[48]

By mid-century, clear cleavages had emerged between the experiences of unauthorized Europeans and, in particular, out-of-status Mexican nationals. These disparities resulted not only from the various forms of regularization created for European migrants but also the disparate application of the civil and criminal penalties for illegal entry. The deportation and criminal prosecution of undocumented Mexicans during the Great Depression created an enduring negative stereotype of Mexican nationals as the nation's iconic illegal immigrant; at the very same time, policymakers created new legal openings that allowed migrants from Russia and the Near East to enter or remain in the United States as stateless persons and refugees.[49] In the ensuing decades, immigration officials regularly carried out mass deportations of Mexican migrants while the majority of individuals criminally prosecuted under the Undesirable Aliens Act of 1929 were Mexican nationals.[50] By 1950, a study commissioned by Senator Patrick McCarran (D-NV) concluded that between 1924 and 1948, Mexicans constituted 90 percent of deportation and voluntary departure cases.[51] The passage of the McCarran-Walter Act of 1952 only magnified these trends by enhancing the Border Patrol's legal authority to apprehend Mexican migrants and streamlining their deportation hearings.[52]

World War II and its aftermath eventually proved to be a watershed moment that unleashed forces compelling the United States to open its doors to immigrants from all over the world. Shifting foreign relations also created opportunities for Asian immigrants to adjust their unauthorized status for the first time. However, European immigrants remained the primary beneficiaries of various forms of immigration relief, and, in particular, major refugee relief legislation passed in the late 1940s and early 1950s.[53] Furthermore, by 1965 national origins quotas that adversely affected certain European immigrant groups were ultimately abolished and replaced with an immigration regime largely premised on selection for family ties and immigrants' economic contributions to the nation.[54] Therefore, in the latter half of the twentieth century, many Europeans who had long wanted to immigrate to the United States could more easily do so through legal channels.[55] However, European migrants who lacked close family ties to an American citizen, those who didn't bring a specialized set of skills to the economy, and migrants with a questionable moral record continued to employ evasive strategies to resettle in the United States. Overstaying a non-immigrant visa was the most common, but certainly not the only way that irregular European immigrants attempted to work around the country's gatekeeping apparatus. Yet, as our contributors' research reveals, large sectors of the American public generally tolerated or willfully ignored their unauthorized entries and presence. For example, the same vitriol that was unleashed on unauthorized Mexican immigrants in the 1980s and 1990s hardly targeted large numbers of illegal Irish or Polish immigrants living and working in the United States in a similar manner. On the contrary, sympathetic lawmakers and enforcement agents once again responded to white ethnic lobbies with social support and legislative relief for out-of-status European migrants in the late twentieth century.[56]

In the 1990s, with the growth of the internet and the fall of the Soviet Union, Eastern European and Russian "mail order brides" began to receive a great deal of media attention as a potential source of fraudulent immigration.[57] Certain segments of the public had already begun to vilify non-white (primarily Southeast Asian) women who engaged in international marriage markets as fraudulent visa seekers whose true intent was to exploit lonely American men for financial gain, access to the country, and the creation of a new stream of immigration visas for their relatives.[58] Although mail-order brides hardly figure into most scholarship on the modern movement against illegal immigration, the drafters of the 1996 Illegal Immigration Reform and Responsibility Act devoted a section of the legislation to "international matchmaking organizations" that subjected those businesses to stricter INS regulation and established substantial financial penalties for noncompliance.[59]

European immigrants continue to arrive and remain in the United States outside of the law. However, we take the turn of the century as an end point for this collection. Terrorist attacks on the World Trade Center and Pentagon on September 11, 2001, reshaped American society in fundamental ways. The discovery that several visa overstayers perpetrated those attacks prompted a major reorganization of the country's gatekeeping bureaucracy, with the creation of the Department of Homeland Security in 2003. That agency has since been granted unprecedented authority, financial resources, and technology to monitor, police, and punish migrants abroad, at the border, and within the country's interior. The September 11 attacks also unleashed a new racialized discourse of national or "homeland" security and contributed significantly to the resurgence of a fierce movement that has moved beyond a critique of illegal immigration to encompass a wide range of attacks on immigrants in general, and sometimes even their American-born children.[60]

Collection Overview

In compiling *Hidden Histories,* our aim has not been to generate a comprehensive history of unauthorized European migration to the United States. Instead, we sought to explore the state of the field by identifying scholars in the United States and the world who shared our scholarly interest in this topic. To that end, we issued a call for papers resulting in the body of work collected herein. Because we did not want readers to come away from this collection with a false sense that we had provided them with a complete narrative of all irregular European migrations to the United States, we chose to organize the volume thematically rather than chronologically.[61] Moreover, in arranging the contributions in this manner, we aim to highlight numerous conceptual points illuminated by the scholarship. The anthology's three sections afford a layered rather than strictly linear account of European illegality that begins with a focus on the domestic legal mechanisms that made and unmade European illegality; continues with an exploration of how constructions of race, gender, class, disability, and, more broadly, respectability mediated the experiences of unauthorized Europeans in North America; and ends with studies regarding the global production of illegality through formal policing mechanisms and cultural representations of unauthorized European migrants. Taken together, the chapters in this volume illustrate the variety of themes and approaches adopted by scholars in studying unauthorized European migration, and they serve as a generative starting point for future research.[62]

In Part I, our authors trace the making and unmaking of European illegality in the United States throughout the twentieth century. In case studies featuring undocumented Russian, Italian, and Irish immigrants, combinations of ethnic advocacy, cultural constructions of "deserving" migrants, and public sympathy came together to produce various forms of relief for irregular European immigrants. That relief was ubiquitous. It was proffered amid changing geopolitical dynamics and disparate economic environments in the 1930s, 1950s, and 1980s. It came in the form of executive actions, congressional legislation, creative administrative maneuverings, prosecutorial discretion, and judicial rulings, among other means. In each instance, the American people and the U.S. government demonstrated tolerance for unauthorized European immigrants and sanctioned the creation of pathways to normalize them. In this context, we use the term *normalize* holistically. Here it connotes a process of legalization, as well as a cultural acceptance of unauthorized European migrants as "normal" immigrants whose legal resettlement was barred by a mere technical barrier or a provision of the law that was meant to target other immigrant groups but unfairly affected European migrants.

In Chapter One, S. Deborah Kang recounts the history of a 1934 measure that legalized the status of undocumented Russian refugees in the United States. Its passage hinged on several factors that Russian exiles and their allies used to their benefit. White Russians and their advocates not only crafted benign representations of European illegality that sharply contrasted with popular characterizations of other migrant groups during the Great Depression, but they also played on the emigres' anti-communist credentials to draw further distinctions between Russians and other, less worthy, groups of undocumented migrants. Advocates also made pragmatic political decisions during an era of heightened nativist sentiment that proposed humanitarian relief only for a small contingent of migrants who had already, clandestinely, found refuge in the United States. As a result, restrictionary immigration practices based on racial selection were largely kept in place for other migrants, even while legislative and enforcement fissures allowed undocumented Russians and eventually other unauthorized European migrants a path for normalization.

In the following chapter, Danielle Battisti traces Italian migrants' use of unauthorized migration strategies to circumvent restrictions imposed on southern and eastern Europeans by the national origins system in 1924. Battisti's case study of merchant seamen who continued to "jump ship" decades after the Johnson-Reed Act was passed illuminates an enduring route Italians employed to bypass immigration restrictions. In addition, Battisti argues that the state largely accepted those migrants because of their status as white male heads of household. Special legislation passed by Congress and procedures created by administrative bodies, namely the pairing of voluntary departure with the practice of pre-examination, overwhelmingly permitted Italian men to adjust their status, even while other migrant groups were excluded from doing so. Permissive decisions from enforcement agents and judicial bodies also prevented the permanent removal of Italian seamen at a time when similar behavior from Asian and Mexican migrants triggered detentions and deportations.

In Chapter Three, Carly Goodman narrates the experiences of Irish migrants who, unable to meet the new bars for admission after the immigration reforms of

1965, built new lives in the United States by overstaying temporary tourist visas. However, Irish migrants quickly came to resent their undocumented status and even felt entitled to immigration privileges that had historically been conferred upon them. Therefore, by the 1980s, ethnic organizations mobilized to fight their cause and successfully lobbied for the passage of laws that created new legal pathways for both the future admission of Irish immigrants abroad and the adjustment of status for those unauthorized Irish already in the United States. Irish advocacy groups were successful in convincing sympathetic lawmakers, many of whom could imagine themselves or their family members in the place of the Irish, in large part because they drew on the "nation of immigrants" trope. They advanced a nostalgic narrative that placed Irish immigration history as a foundational part of the nation's past, and implied the need to preserve its future in a country with a rapidly changing demographic composition.

In Part II we call on our readers to reimagine how they think about the stereotypical European immigrant and the immigration experiences we associate with them. Not only does this section illuminate Europeans' continued use of irregular modes of entry when other options were closed to them, but it also highlights the varied experiences of sojourners, temporary workers operating within global labor markets, and people occupying borderlands and transnational spaces—underscoring the point that immigration was not necessarily the end goal of all peoples on the move. Featuring the migration experiences of individuals hailing from Canada, Syria, and Poland, the chapters in this section also stress how public performances of whiteness and respectability helped make it possible for irregular migrants to remain hidden, thereby avoiding legal censure, removal, or social stigmatization. However, ascriptions of whiteness alone failed to shield some from exclusion and deportation. As our authors explain, perceptions of whiteness and respectability were often mediated by assumptions regarding gender, class, religion, and disability; hence, women and religious minorities officially classified as white faced heightened scrutiny by state officials at the border and interior spaces of the nation.

In Chapter Four, Randa Tawil examines the state's attempt to police the mobility of pregnant immigrants and noncitizen visitors in the early twentieth century. Those efforts were part of a general attempt to control women's access to health and welfare services and, more broadly, arbitrate social morality and family household dynamics. Tawil's research points to the ways that the state and its private-sector partners, particularly medical professionals, used mechanisms of post-entry social control to transform pregnant women who had entered the country legally into illegal aliens after they violated established social norms and/or were thought to become an economic burden to society.

In Ashley Johnson Bavery's chapter, we see the state similarly employing public health precautions, and charges that certain migrants would become an undue burden on society, to restrict the entry of Muslim Syrian migrants who defied easy classification in racial schemas of the early twentieth century. Fearing rejection at Ellis Island, migrants from the Mahjar (Syrian-Lebanese diaspora) therefore developed transnational networks in Europe, the United States, and Mexico to skirt official border checkpoints while crossing into the United States from Mexico. Bavery's research shows how those transnational networks were not only critical in circulating information and establishing trafficking rings that sustained irregular migration patterns, but also that they were important in their own right as communities whose financial and social supports enabled migrants to endure the precarity surrounding their legal status.

Finally, Mary Patrice Erdmans and Polina Ermoshkina's study of undocumented Polish home care workers in the 1980s complements the other chapters in this section by demonstrating how educated and economically secure Poles who overstayed visitor visas were largely able to avoid criminalization and punishment during an era of increased public attention to the "problem" of illegal immigration. Their presentation as white, as well as their claims to middle class respectability, made them attractive candidates to individuals and families looking for in-home care workers. Those desirable positions subsidized the migrants' cost of living, allowed migrants to elude public scrutiny in the workplace, and ultimately increased migrants' ability to adjust their status or return home with financial and social capital.

In Part III, our contributors chart the global production of illegality, reminding readers that the construction of so-called legal and unauthorized subjects often began abroad. Gatekeeping regimes do not occur in isolation. They reflect complex relations between states, and sometimes non-state actors like NGOs or corporations, that produce international systems governing migration. In some cases, like-minded regimes develop parallel and complementary gatekeeping mechanisms. In other instances, a negotiation balances the needs of sending and receiving nations. At still other times, less powerful nations acquiesce to the demands of a more powerful party. That last point is particularly true when an individual state's reach extends beyond its borders through remote control mechanisms.

Torsten Feys's research expands our understanding of immigration policing by revealing how transatlantic shipping companies assumed much of the responsibility for gatekeeping in Europe and the United States. As an integral component of American immigration law enforcement between 1819 and 1914, the controls exerted by shipping lines challenge long-held notions that America's borders were open to European migrants in the nineteenth century. They were, however, porous. Shippers' attempts to regulate migrant movements were riddled with conflicts between shippers and the state. These conflicts, as Feys illustrates, created a paradoxical situation in which shippers simultaneously advanced the restrictionist goals of American policymakers, even while they exploited legal loopholes that facilitated illicit entries from Europe.

In Chapter Eight, Kyle Romero underscores the uneven development of American remote controls in Europe. His study of Russian refugees in post–World War I Constantinople reveals how, despite widespread xenophobia at home, representatives of the American Relief Administration (ARA) based in Europe developed an irregular channel for refugee admission into the United States. In this instance, Russian refugees greatly benefited from the resourcefulness of their American champions who had powerful connections in Washington, DC, and the support of transnational ethnic and humanitarian organizations. Yet, the very processes by which the ARA selected Russians for admission to the United States exposed the class, gender, status, and ableist fault lines that would inform the shaping of American refugee policy well into the twenty-first century.

In our final chapter, Joanna Wojdon explores the cultural production of illegality through a reading of Polish film, fiction, and press representations of the so-called "vacationers," or unauthorized Poles living and working in the United States during the late twentieth century. Wojdon demonstrates how those accounts served the geopolitical interests of the then communist state, which adopted a strategically ambivalent position toward emigrants and sojourners abroad. While Polish media tended to denigrate vacationers and depicted American life in negative terms, the state simultaneously looked the other way as it issued permissions for "tourist" travel, and derived benefits from remittance dollars that made their way back to Poland. That delicate balance was adopted to serve the state's political and economic interests during the turbulent last decade of communist rule in the country.

Notes

1. Along with unauthorized entries, more accurate and complex migration narratives take account of transnationalism, return migrations, and seasonal labor migrations. Samuel L. Baily, *Immigrants in the Lands of Promise: Italians in Buenos Aires and New York City, 1870–1914* (Ithaca, NY: Cornell University Press, 1999); Donna Gabaccia, *Italy's Many Diasporas* (Seattle: University of Washington Press, 2000); Linda Reeder, *Widows in White: Migration and the Transformation of Rural Italian Women, Sicily, 1880–1920* (Toronto: University of Toronto Press, 2003).

2. For pivotal works on European immigrants' claims to whiteness, see Thomas A. Guglielmo, *White on Arrival: Italians, Race, Color, and Power in Chicago, 1890–1945* (New York: Oxford University Press, 2004); Matthew Frye Jacobson, *Whiteness of a Different Color: European Immigrants and the Alchemy of Race* (Cambridge, MA: Harvard University Press, 1998). For a rebuttal of the "bootstraps" myth, see Cybelle Fox, who has meticulously documented how Euro-American immigrants and their children benefited more than virtually any other social group in the United States from welfare assistance

provided by New Deal programming; Gary Gerstle and Lizabeth Cohen similarly illustrate how claims to whiteness enabled the children and grandchildren of the Ellis Island cohort to take advantage of state welfare benefits. Cybelle Fox, *Three Worlds of Relief: Race, Immigration, and the American Welfare State from the Progressive Era to the New Deal* (Princeton, NJ: Princeton University Press, 2012); Lizabeth Cohen, *A Consumers' Republic: The Politics of Mass Consumption in Postwar America* (New York: Knopf 2003), 193–256; Gary Gerstle, *American Crucible: Race and Nation in the Twentieth Century* (Princeton, NJ: Princeton University Press, 2001).

3. Lana Dublin, email to Danielle Battisti, Baldizzi 1948 C-File, September 14, 2021. See also Tenement Museum, "An Updated History of the Undocumented Immigrant," accessed December 10, 2023, https://www.tenement.org/blog/an-updated-history-of-the-undocumented-immigrant/; and Tenement Museum, "I Would Cross a Million Borders," accessed December 12, 2023, https://www.tenement.org/podcast-i-would-cross-a-million-borders/.

4. Adolfo is also sometimes featured as a stowaway in Tenement Museum accounts, although whether he actually entered the country without inspection is less clear. Tenement Museum, "Rosaria Baldizzi: A Complicated Path to Citizenship," accessed December 10, 2023, https://www.tenement.org/development_news/rosaria-baldizzi-a-complicated-path-to-citizenship/.

5. Reliable estimates of the number of unauthorized immigrants in the United States in recent years alone show about 4 percent of the total number as originating from Europe. Randy Capps, Julia Gelatt, Ariel G. Ruiz Soto, and Jennifer Van Hook, "Unauthorized Immigrants in the United States: Stable Numbers, Changing Origins," Migration Policy Institute Fact Sheet, December 2020, https://www.migrationpolicy.org/sites/default/files/publications/mpi-unauthorized-immigrants-stablenumbers-changingorigins_final.pdf. See also Phillip Connor, Jeffrey S. Passel, and Jens Manuel Krogstad, "How European and U.S. Unauthorized Immigrant Populations Compare," Pew Research Center, November 13, 2019, https://www.pewresearch.org/short-reads/2019/11/13/how-european-and-u-s-unauthorized-immigrant-populations-compare/; and Jeffrey S. Passel and D'Vera Cohn, "Mexicans Decline to Less Than Half the U.S. Unauthorized Immigrant Population for the First Time," June 12, 2019, https://www.pewresearch.org/short-reads/2019/06/12/us-unauthorized-immigrant-population-2017/. Such data does not, however, record racial classification for said migrants. Racial categorization makes up a critical part of our analysis.

6. While most of the scholarship here focuses on U.S. immigration laws, laws governing emigration in Europe also played a role in this process and are discussed in several chapters. See also Tara Zahra, *The Great Departure: Mass Migration from Eastern Europe and the Making of the Free World* (New York: Norton, 2016).

7. In an effort to understand the making and unmaking of illegality, sociologists Sofya Aptekar and Amy Hsin argue for a "stratified" understanding of migrants' "entry into illegality." Their empirical study demonstrates how factors such as nationality, race, and socioeconomic status shape the specific ways that migrants become unauthorized immigrants and "in turn, shape opportunities to adjust legal status." Sofya Aptekar and Amy Hsin, "Stratified Entry into Illegality: How Immigration Policy Shapes Being Undocumented," *Social Forces* 102, no. 1 (2023): 45–62.

8. On the social and legal processes that construct illegality, see René D. Flores and Ariela Schachter, "Who Are the 'Illegals'? The Social Construction of Illegality in the United States," *American Sociological Review* 83, no. 5 (2018): 839–68.

9. Sociologists Cecilia Menjívar and Leisy J. Abrego explain that for migrants, legal violence pertains not only to the penalties stipulated by the law and the immigration enforcement practices of state officials but also to a broad and lasting set of harms—in their words, forms of "social suffering," set in motion by immigration laws and policies. Their study of Central American migrants, for example, demonstrates how the criminalization of immigration infractions has harmed migrants' "quotidian practices" at home, work, and school. Moreover, these harms are often transnational, affecting migrants and their families in the United States as well as their countries of origin. Thus, a legal system that "purports to protect the nation," they write, "instead produces spaces and the possibility for material, emotional, and psychological injurious actions that target an entire group of people with a particular set of shared social characteristics." Cecilia Menjívar and Leisy J. Abrego, "Legal Violence: Immigration Law and the Lives of Central American Immigrants," *American Journal of Sociology* 117, no. 5 (March 2012): 1380–421, 1414.

10. Adam Goodman, *The Deportation Machine: America's Long History of Expelling Immigrants* (Princeton, NJ: Princeton University Press, 2020).

11. On the ways that legal status functions as an axis of stratification, see Cecilia Menjívar, "Liminal Legality: Salvadoran and Guatemalan Immigrants' Lives in the United States," *American Journal of Sociology* 111, no. 4 (2006): 999–1037.

12. Despite the ubiquity and significance of unauthorized immigration from Europe, the literature on this topic is emerging. The most significant studies to date include Mae M. Ngai, *Impossible Subjects: Illegal Aliens and the Making of Modern America* (Princeton, NJ: Princeton University Press, 2004); Libby Garland, *After They Closed the Gates: Jewish Illegal Immigration to the United States, 1921–1965* (Chicago: University of Chicago Press, 2014); Ashley Johnson Bavery, *Bootlegged Aliens: Immigration Politics on America's Northern Border* (Philadelphia: University of Pennsylvania Press, 2020); Carly Goodman, *Dreamland: America's Immigration Lottery in an Age of Restriction* (Chapel Hill: University of North Carolina Press, 2023). Less comprehensive but significant work also includes Kathleen Lopez, "Gatekeeping in the Tropics: U.S. Immigration Policy and the Cuban Connection," in *A Nation of Immigrants Reconsidered: US Society in an Age of Restriction, 1924–1965,* eds. Maddalena Marinari, Madeline Y. Hsu, and Maria Cristina Garcia (Urbana: University of Illinois Press, 2019), 45–64. While he does not explicitly interrogate the issue of unauthorized migration strategies, Gunther Peck certainly demonstrates the continued use of contract labor systems for European migrants to gain entry to the United States after Congress banned the practice in 1885. Gunther Peck, *Reinventing Free Labor: Padrones and Immigrant Works in the North American West, 1880–1930* (New York: Cambridge University Press, 2000). Claudia Sadowski-Smith examines the fictionalized narratives of visa overstayers from post-Soviet states since the 1990s but notes the lack of sociological or historical scholarship on this cohort of irregular migrants. Claudia Sadowski-Smith, *The New Immigrant Whiteness: Race, Neoliberalism, and Post-Soviet Migration to the United States* (New York: New York University Press, 2018), 112–32.

13. For an extended historiographic essay on this topic see, Jon Gjerde, "New Growth on Old Vines—The State of the Field: The Social History of Immigration to and Ethnicity in the United States," *Journal of American Ethnic History* 18, no. 4 (1999): 49–50. For influential early practitioners of immigration history, see Marcus Lee Hansen, *The Atlantic Migration, 1607–1860: A History of Continuing Settlement of the United States* (Cambridge, MA: Harvard University Press, 1940); Oscar Handlin, *The Uprooted: The Epic Story of the Great Migrations That Made the American People* (Philadelphia: University of Pennsylvania Press, 1952); Frank Thistlethwaite, "Migration from Europe Overseas in the Nineteenth and Twentieth Centuries," *Rapports*, vol. 5, *Histoire Contemporaine*, Comite International Des Sciences Historiques, XIe, Congres International Des Sciences Historiques: Stockholm, 1960, 21–28.

14. The first major study of migrants examined working-class Polish immigrants in Chicago who were perceived to be struggling with urbanization and modernization in the first half of the twentieth century. Models positing a cycle of old-world organization, followed by immigrant disorganization, and an ultimate reorganization of assimilated communities emerged out of the Chicago School of Sociology and laid the foundation for theories of assimilation generated by sociologists and historians for the rest of the century.

15. Handlin, *The Uprooted*, 3.

16. David A. Gerber, "What Did Oscar Handlin Mean in the Opening Sentences of The Uprooted?" *Reviews in American History* 41, no. 1 (March 2013): 1–11.

17. Matthew Frye Jacobson, "More 'Trans-,' Less 'National,'" *Journal of American Ethnic History* 25, no. 4 (2006): 74–84; Wendy L. Wall, *Inventing the 'American Way': The Politics of Consensus from the New Deal to the Civil Rights Movement* (New York: Oxford University Press, 2008); Diana Selig, *Americans All: The Cultural Gifts Movement* (Cambridge, MA: Harvard University Press, 2008).

18. Kathleen Neils Conzen, David A. Gerber, Ewa Morawska, George E. Pozzetta, and Rudolph J. Vecoli, "The Invention of Ethnicity: A Perspective from the U.S.A.," *Journal of American Ethnic History* 12, no. 1 (1992): 3–41; Philip Gleason, *Speaking of Diversity: Language and Ethnicity in Twentieth-Century America* (Baltimore: Johns Hopkins University Press, 2019), 14.

19. Rudolph J. Vecoli, "Ethnicity: A Neglected Dimension of American History," in *The State of American History*, ed. Herbert J. Bass (Chicago: Quadrangle Books, 1970), 80; Rudolph J. Vecoli, "The Resurgence of American Immigration History," *American Studies International* 17, no. 2 (1979): 44–66. Vecoli's earliest critique of assimilation theory offered a class-based approach, Rudolph J. Vecoli, "Contadini in Chicago: A Critique of the Uprooted," *Journal of American History* 51, no. 3 (December 1964). See also Bill Ong Hing, "Beyond the Rhetoric of Assimilation and Cultural Pluralism: Addressing the Tension of Separatism and Conflict in an Immigration-Driven Multiracial Society," *California Law Review* 81, no. 4 (1993): 863–925.

20. Mae Ngai, "Asian American History—Reflections on the De-centering of the Field," *Journal of American Ethnic History* 25, no. 4 (2006): 97–108; Sucheng Chan, "The Changing Contours of Asian-American Historiography," *Rethinking History* 11, no. 1 (2007): 125–47; Moon-Ho Jung, "Beyond These Mythical Shores: Asian American History and the Study of Race," *History Compass* 6, no. 2 (2008): 627–38; Ernesto Chávez,

"Chicano/a History: Its Origins, Purpose, and Future," *Pacific Historical Review* 82, no. 4 (2013): 505–19.

21. Gjerde, "New Growth on Old Vines," 50.

22. George J. Sanchez, "Race, Nation, and Culture in Recent Immigration Studies," *Journal of American Ethnic History* 18, no. 4 (1999): 68.

23. Alexander Saxton, *The Indispensable Enemy: Labor and the Anti-Chinese Movement in California* (Berkeley: University of California Press, 1971); David Roediger, *The Wages of Whiteness: Race and the Making of the American Working Class* (New York: Verso, 1991); Noel Ignatiev, *How the Irish Became White* (New York: Routledge, 1995); Jacobson, *Whiteness of a Different Color*; Guglielmo, *White on Arrival*; Russell A. Kazal, *Becoming Old Stock: The Paradox of German-American Identity* (Princeton, NJ: Princeton University Press, 2004).

24. Aristide R. Zolberg, *A Nation by Design: Immigration Policy in the Fashioning of America* (Cambridge, MA: Harvard University Press, 2006).

25. Other influential developments in the field include the decentering of the nation-state; emphasizing the circular, return, or multidirectional paths of migration; and the integration of transnational approaches into migration studies. See John Bodnar, *The Transplanted: A History of Immigrants in Urban America* (Bloomington: Indiana University Press, 1985); Nina Glick Schiller, Linda Basch, and Cristina Szanton Blanc, "From Immigrant to Transmigrant: Theorizing Transnational Migration," *Anthropological Quarterly* 68, no. 1 (1995): 48–63; Donna Gabaccia, "Is Everywhere Nowhere? Nomads, Nations, and the Immigrant Paradigm of United States History," *The Journal of American History* 86, vol. 3 (December 1999), 1115–34; David Gerber, "Forming a Transnational Narrative: New Perspectives on European Migrations to the United States," *The History Teacher* 35, no. 1 (2001): 61–77; Reeder, *Widows in White*.

26. For an overview see Torrie Hester, "Deportability and the Carceral State," *The Journal of American History* 102, no. 1 (2015): 141–51. For just some of the many significant works on this topic, see Kelly Lytle Hernández, *City of Inmates: Conquest, Rebellion, and the Rise of Human Caging in Los Angeles, 1771–1965* (Chapel Hill: University of North Carolina Press, 2017); Patrisia Macias-Rojas, *From Deportation to Prison: The Politics of Immigration Enforcement in Post-Civil Rights America* (New York: New York University Press, 2016); Carl Lindskoog, *Detain and Punish: Haitian Refugees and the Rise of the World's Largest Immigration Detention System* (Gainesville: University of Florida Press, 2018); César Cuauhtémoc García Hernández, *Migrating to Prison: America's Obsession with Locking Up Immigrants* (New York: The New Press, 2019); Goodman, *The Deportation Machine*, 164–96; Kristina Shull, *Detention Empire: Reagan's War on Immigrants and the Seeds of Resistance* (Chapel Hill: University of North Carolina Press, 2022).

27. Again, the literature is vast. For a sampling on this subject, see Ngai, *Impossible Subjects*; Goodman, *The Deportation Machine*; Francisco E. Balderrama and Raymond Rodríguez, *Decade of Betrayal: Mexican Repatriation in the 1930s* (Albuquerque: University of New Mexico Press, 2006); Kelly Lytle Hernández, *Migra! A History of the U.S. Border Patrol* (Berkeley: University of California Press, 2010); Ana Raquel Minian, *Undocumented Lives: The Untold Story of Mexican Migration* (Cambridge, MA: Harvard University Press, 2018); Jessica Ordaz, *The Shadow of El Centro: A History of Migrant

Incarceration and Solidarity (Chapel Hill: University of North Carolina Press, 2021); S. Deborah Kang, *The INS on the Line: Making Immigration Law on the US-Mexico Border, 1917–1954* (New York: Oxford University Press, 2017); Menjívar and Abrego, "Legal Violence"; Joanna Dreby, *Everyday Illegal: When Policies Undermine Immigrant Families* (Berkeley: University of California Press, 2015); Jason De León, *The Land of Open Graves: Living and Dying on the Migrant Trail* (Berkeley: University of California Press, 2015).

28. Gerald Neuman, *Strangers to the Constitution* (Princeton, NJ: Princeton University Press, 1996); Daniel Kanstroom, *Deportation Nation: Outsiders in American History* (Cambridge, MA: Harvard University Press, 2007); Eric Foner, *Gateway to Freedom: The Hidden History of the Underground Railroad* (New York: W. W. Norton, 2015); Kunal M. Parker, *Making Foreigners: Immigration and Citizenship Law in America, 1600–2000* (New York: Cambridge University Press, 2015); Martha S. Jones, *Birthright Citizenship: A History of Race and Rights in Antebellum America* (New York: Cambridge University Press, 2018); Michael A. Schoeppner, *Moral Contagion: Black Atlantic Sailors, Citizenship, and Diplomacy in Antebellum America* (New York: Cambridge University Press, 2019); Samantha Seeley, *Race, Removal and the Right to Remain: Migration and the Making of the United States* (Chapel Hill: University of North Carolina Press, 2021); Kevin Kenny, *The Problem of Immigration in a Slaveholding Republic: Policing Mobility in the Nineteenth-Century United States* (New York: Oxford University Press, 2023); Llana Barber, "Anti-Black Racism and the Nativist State," *Journal of American Ethnic History* 42, no. 4 (Summer 2023): 5–59.

29. Hiroshi Motomura, *Americans in Waiting: The Lost Story of Immigration and Citizenship in the United States* (New York: Oxford University Press, 2006).

30. Barber argues for the significance of antebellum laws restricting Black mobility and citizenship as the origin point for state gatekeeping and nativist policies. Barber, "Anti-Black Racism."

31. The literature generally argues that even while there were broad-based anti-immigrant movements in the early nineteenth century, they never produced legislation that significantly affected European migrants' immigration opportunities en masse, constructed barriers to citizenship, or gave up on the viability of assimilating European immigrants. At most, European immigration and resettlement options were subject to class and gender constraints. John Higham, *Strangers in the Land: Patterns of American Nativism, 1860–1925* (New York: Atheneum, 1967); Tyler Anbinder, *Nativism and Slavery: The Northern Know Nothings and the Politics of the 1850s* (New York: Oxford University Press, 1992); Neuman, *Strangers to the Constitution*; Hidetaka Hirota, *Expelling the Poor: Atlantic Seaboard States and the 19th-Century Origins of American Immigration Policy* (New York: Oxford University Press, 2017); Erika Lee, *America for Americans: A History of Xenophobia in the United States* (New York: Basic Books, 2019).

32. Ngai, *Impossible Subjects*; Katherine Benton-Cohen, *Inventing the Immigration Problem: The Dillingham Commission and Its Legacy* (Cambridge, MA: Harvard University Press, 2018).

33. Peck notes the passage of a little-known and generally unenforced congressional law in 1874 to "prevent the enslaving, buying, selling, or using Italian children" for the purposes of labor exploitation. However, his overall argument is that these laws were

much more concerned with the impact of coerced labor competition on American workers. The law also sanctioned the imposition of fines on individuals and companies found to be importing laborers under contract. Peck, *Reinventing Free Labor*, 84–93. See also Torrie Hester, "'Protection, Not Punishment': Legislative and Judicial Formation of U.S. Deportation Policy, 1882–1904," *Journal of American Ethnic History* 30, no. 1 (2010): 11–36.

34. Peck, *Reinventing Free Labor*. For the evolving understanding of the "coolie" trade in the United States and legislation surrounding it, see Moon-Ho Jung, "Outlawing 'Coolies': Race, Nation, and Empire in the Age of Emancipation, *American Quarterly* 57, no. 3 (2005), 677–701.

35. Peck, *Reinventing Free Labor*, 89–93. Peck notes Italians in particular continued to operate via padrone networks well through the 1910s. He also argues that the system flourished for Greek, Turkish, Bulgarian, Mexican, and Hungarian immigrants to North America in this period. The role that governments in emigrant nations played in the padrone system also warrants much further scrutiny.

36. Ronald H. Bayor, *Encountering Ellis Island: How European Immigrants Entered America* (Baltimore: Johns Hopkins University Press, 2014), 50–51. See also Peck, *Reinventing Free Labor*, 86–87. Peck and Chang both note the transnational character of the lax enforcement against padrones and contract laborers in the United States and Canada. Both discuss how Canada became a largely tolerated backdoor route for European contract laborers to enter into the United States. The same did not hold for South Asian laborers. See also Kornel Chang, *Pacific Connections: The Making of the U.S.-Canadian Borderlands* (Berkeley: University of California Press, 2012).

37. Jung, "Outlawing 'Coolies.'" The 1875 Page Act was also built on assumptions that Chinese immigrant women were brought to the United States for the purposes of prostitution. Erika Lee and Judy Yung, *Angel Island: Immigrant Gateway to America* (New York: Oxford University Press, 2010); Chang, *Pacific Connections*; Erika Lee, *At America's Gates: Chinese Immigration during the Exclusion Era, 1882–1943* (Chapel Hill: University of North Carolina Press, 2003).

38. Numerous scholars have shown that distinctions of class, gender, sexuality, and other factors significantly affected the likelihood of an individual immigrant's exclusion, detention, or deportation. We should also note that while Lee and Yung cite a 70 percent detention rate for alien arrivals at Angel Island and note that those detentions lasted for weeks on end, only about 2 percent of arrivals who entered through Ellis Island were detained at all; the vast majority were permitted entry within five hours of arrival. Lee and Yung, *Angel Island*, 17–20; Bayor, *Encountering Ellis Island*, 39–40.

39. Just some of the significant works outlining factors that could prevent immigrants from entry at ports, and deportation after entry was granted, include Bayor, *Encountering Ellis Island*; Vincent J. Cannato, *American Passage: The History of Ellis Island* (New York: Harper Collins, 2009), 191–215; Margot Canaday, *The Straight State: Sexuality and Citizenship in Twentieth-Century America* (Princeton, NJ: Princeton University Press, 2009); Alan M. Kraut, *Silent Travelers: Germs, Genes, and the "Immigrant Menace"* (Baltimore: Johns Hopkins University Press, 1994); Martha Gardner, *The Qualities of a Citizen: Women, Immigration, and Citizenship, 1870–1965* (Princeton, NJ: Princeton University Press, 2005); Kanstroom, *Deportation Nation*; Deirdre M. Moloney, *National*

Insecurities: Immigrants and U.S. Deportation Policy since 1882 (Chapel Hill: University of North Carolina Press, 2012); Douglas C. Baynton, *Defectives in the Land: Disability and Immigration in the Age of Eugenics* (Chicago: University of Chicago Press, 2016); Torrie Hester, *Deportation: The Origins of U.S. Policy* (Philadelphia: University of Pennsylvania Press, 2017); Julia Rose Kraut, *Threat of Dissent: A History of Ideological Exclusion and Deportation in the United States* (Cambridge, MA: Harvard University Press, 2020); Moon-Ho Jung, *Menace to Empire: Anticolonial Solidarities and the Transpacific Origins of the US Security State* (Berkeley: University of California Press, 2022).

40. Matthew Pratt Guterl, *The Color of Race in America, 1900–1940* (Cambridge, MA: Harvard University Press, 2001); Benton-Cohen, *Inventing the Immigration Problem*; Maddalena Marinari, *Unwanted: Italian and Jewish Mobilization against Restrictive Immigration Laws, 1882–1965* (Chapel Hill: University of North Carolina Press, 2020).

41. Ngai, *Impossible Subjects*, 21–55; Zolberg, *A Nation by Design*, 243–92.

42. Bavery, *Bootlegged Aliens*. In 1929 Congress criminalized unauthorized border crossings in response to nativist calls to restrict Mexican immigration, as national origins quotas did not apply to western hemisphere nations. Eric S. Fish, "Race, History, and Immigration Crimes," *Iowa Law Review* 107, no. 3 (2022): 1051–106.

43. The 1952 Immigration and Nationality Act standardized non-immigrant visas for temporary foreign workers for certain fields where the Department of Labor certified there was a shortage of American labor. Most of these (H-2) visas were granted to Mexican nationals for farm work. However, the program expanded and eventually spawned guest worker programs for agricultural (H2A) and professional (H2B) fields in the Immigration Act of 1990. Hiroshi Motomura, *Immigration Outside the Law* (New York: Oxford University Press, 2014).

44. Ngai, *Impossible Subjects*, 56–64. Unauthorized immigrants discovered by the state often were offered the opportunity to "voluntarily depart" by a certain date. It was, of course, a coercive rather than voluntary order. The main distinctions between voluntary departure and deportation were financial (travel costs paid by the migrant vs. the state) and legal (if ordered deported, a migrant could not apply for an immigration visa at a future date; those who voluntarily departed could do so).

45. Elizabeth F. Cohen, *Illegal: How America's Lawless Immigration Regime Threatens Us All* (New York: Basic Books, 2020), 104–6.

46. Ngai, *Impossible Subjects*, 75–90.

47. Goodman, *The Deportation Machine*.

48. Ngai, *Impossible Subjects*, 75–90. See also Battisti's discussion in Chapter Two.

49. Ngai, *Impossible Subjects*; S. Deborah Kang, "Sovereign Mercy: The Legalization of the White Russian Refugees and the Politics of Immigration Relief," *Journal of American Ethnic History* 43, no. 1 (2023): 5–42.

50. Hernández, *Migra!*; Kang, *The INS on the Line*. These mass deportations transpired over the course of the 1940s and 1950s; the most prominent, known as Operation Wetback, took place in 1954 and resulted in the forced removal of about 1 million ethnic Mexicans.

51. *The Immigration and Naturalization Systems of the United States*, Report of the Committee on the Judiciary pursuant to S. Res. 137, S. Rpt. No. 1515, April 20, 1950, 635. On the disparate criminal prosecution of Mexican nationals in the 1930s, see Hernán-

dez, *City of Inmates,* 139; and in the 1950s, see *Brief of Professor S. Deborah Kang as Amicus Curiae in Support of Defendants-Appellants,* United States of America v. Jorge Cesar Ferretiz-Hernandez, Ignacio Felix-Salinas, and Elias Chiroy-Cac, No. 22–13038-JJ, 22–13039-AA, 22–13307-JJ (11th Cir. October 6, 2023), 19.

52. The act granted immigration officials the authority to search private property within twenty-five miles of the border without a warrant and released INS officials from search and seizure requirements within a reasonable distance from any external boundary of the United States. Kang, *The INS on the Line,* 143–49. By exempting deportation proceedings from compliance with the 1946 Administrative Procedure Act (APA), the 1952 law deprived Mexican nationals of the APA's procedural protections. The law also reenacted the criminal penalties for unauthorized entry and reentry first passed under the 1929 Undesirable Aliens Act. *Affidavit of Dr. S. Deborah Kang, Associate Professor, University of Virginia, United States v. Hernandez-Perez,* No. 23-cr-81-GRB, ECF No. 41–1 (E.D.N.Y. filed Oct. 12, 2023). For more on the combination of anti-Semitism, racism, and xenophobia that informed the preservation of national origins quotas under the McCarran-Walter Act, see Maddalena Marinari, "Divided and Conquered: Immigration Reform Advocates and the Passage of the 1952 Immigration and Nationality Act," *Journal of American Ethnic History* 35, no. 3 (2016): 9–30; Jane Hong, "A Cross-Fire between Minorities," *Pacific Historical Review* 87, no. 4 (2018): 667–701.

53. Because of China's allied status during the war, the U.S. government actively sought to normalize Chinese "paper sons" as a diplomatic gesture to China and a means of ensuring national security at home. Ngai, *Impossible Subjects,* 202–24. For the extension of asylum, parole, and other forms of relief to Chinese diplomats, students, professionals, and non-immigrants in the United States following the 1949 communist revolution, see Madeline Y. Hsu, *The Good Immigrants: How the Yellow Peril Became the Model Minority* (Princeton, NJ: Princeton University Press, 2015). Importantly, relief for irregular Asian immigration occurred as processes of racialization began to position Asian Americans culturally as model minorities, in contrast to African Americans, in the postwar period. See also Ellen D. Wu, *The Color of Success: Asian Americans and the Origins of the Model Minority* (Princeton, NJ: Princeton University Press, 2015); Uzma Quraishi, *Redefining the Immigrant South: Indian and Pakistani Immigration to Houston during the Cold War* (Chapel Hill: University of North Carolina Press, 2020). For the Eurocentric focus of the Displaced Persons Act and the Refugee Relief Act, see Carl J. Bon Tempo, *Americans at the Gate: The United States and Refugees during the Cold War* (Princeton, NJ: Princeton University Press, 2008). See also Danielle Battisti, *Whom We Shall Welcome: Italian Americans and Immigration Reform, 1945–1965* (New York: Fordham University Press, 2019) for intent to allow traditional immigrants entry to the United States via family reunification provisions in the 1953 Refugee Relief Act.

54. Although the 1965 Immigration and Citizenship Act eliminated national origins quotas, Ngai argues that the new law paradoxically imposed new restrictions on Mexican immigrants and other Western Hemisphere migrants in ways that reinforced a racialized view of those groups as exploitable laborers. Ngai, *Impossible Subjects,* 227–64. Zolberg, *A Nation by Design,* 293–336.

55. Italy, Greece, Portugal, and the United Kingdom sent the most legal immigrants from Europe to the United States from 1968 to 1980. U.S. Department of Justice, Immigration and Naturalization Service, *1985 Statistical Yearbook of the Immigration and Naturalization Service*, September 1986, 6.

56. The most notable of such legislation was the creation of the Diversity Visa Lottery as an avenue of relief for unauthorized Irish immigrants, as well as the law's preferential distribution of visas for Irish applicants. See Goodman, *Dreamland*. Congress also granted amnesty to millions of unauthorized immigrants, the vast majority from Mexico, in the 1985 Immigration Reform and Control Act. However, backlash to the law from the right was immediate and intense. That reaction helped to spawn, among other things, restrictionist activism from institutions such as John Tanton's Federation for American Immigration Reform and the Center for Immigration Studies, and a new crop of "law and order" anti-immigration lawmakers in the GOP. See Goodman, *The Deportation Machine*; Sarah R. Coleman, *The Walls Within: The Politics of Immigration in Modern America* (Princeton, NJ: Princeton University Press, 2021); Carly Goodman, "Unmaking the Nation of Immigrants: How John Tanton's Network of Organizations Transformed Policy and Politics," in *A Field Guide to White Supremacy*, eds. Kathleen Belew and Ramon Gutiérrez (Berkeley: University of California Press, 2021), 203–19; Nicole Hemmer, *Partisans: The Conservative Revolutionaries Who Remade American Politics in the 1990s* (New York: Basic Books, 2021); Gary Gerstle, *The Rise and Fall of the Neoliberal Order: America and the World in the Free Market Era* (New York: Oxford University Press, 2022).

57. Amy L. Elson, "The Mail-Order Bride Industry and Immigration: Combating Immigration Fraud," *Indiana Journal of Global Legal Studies* 5, no. 1 (1997): 367–74; Polina Levchenko and Catherine Solheim, "International Marriages between Eastern European-Born Women and U.S.-Born Men," *Family Relations* 62, no. 1 (2013): 30–41; Emily Starr and Michele Adams, "The Domestic Exotic: Mail-Order Brides and the Paradox of Globalized Intimacies," *Signs* 41, no. 4 (2016): 953–75.

58. First Session on Fraudulent Marriage and Fiancé Arrangements to Obtain Permanent Resident Immigration Status: Hearing before the Subcommittee on Immigration and Refugee Policy of the Committee on the Judiciary, 99th Cong. (1985).

59. Illegal Immigration Reform and Immigrant Responsibility Act of 1996, Pub. L. No. 104–208, 110 Stat. 3009 (1996).

60. A. Naomi Paik, *Bans, Walls, Raids, Sanctuary: Understanding U.S. Immigration for the Twenty-First Century* (Berkeley: University of California Press, 2020).

61. For example, there are entire national groups, such as unauthorized Greek migrants, who are not featured in this collection.

62. Questions for future research include but are not limited to the role of sending states in producing European illegality; how the devolution of European empires influenced migrant resettlement strategies; the role of smuggling networks and shipping lines in facilitating unauthorized European migrations; the scope and methods of domestic and international policing organizations that were formed to address unauthorized European migration; the role of legalization policies in providing relief for refugees

and asylum seekers and, more broadly, shaping U.S. refugee and asylum policies: the impact of the Refugee Act of 1980 in creating new groups of unauthorized European migrants; cultural representations of European illegality in the United States and the world; the impact of immigration status in shaping family memory and group identity construction; comparative studies of unauthorized European migration in the United States and the world; and social and cultural histories of unauthorized European migration experiences. On this last point, see the migrant-centered work of Ana Minian and Beth Lew-Williams as a point of reference. Minian, *Undocumented Lives*; Lew-Williams, "Paper Lives of Chinese Migrants and the History of the Undocumented," *Modern American History* 4, no. 2 (2021): 109–30.

PART I

Making and Unmaking
Unauthorized Entries

1 A Pathway to Citizenship

Russian Refugees and the Politics of
Immigration Relief during the Great Depression

S. DEBORAH KANG

In 1934, the Immigration and Naturalization Service (INS) legalized the illegal immigration status of Nicholas Krivitsky, a native of Russia. When he was nineteen, Krivitsky decided to desert his ship, the S.S. *Polonia*, where he served as a crew member.[1] Like Krivitsky, Percy Wolinsky was an undocumented immigrant. In 1921, Wolinsky, a Russian Jew, crossed the U.S.-Canadian border without an official immigration inspection. Yet, by November of 1934, the INS adjusted Wolinsky's status.[2] In a similar vein, the immigration agency legalized Aksinia Dorofeevna Timofeeff, who evaded inspection by mingling with a "big crowd" as she crossed the line in 1925 San Ysidro.[3] Krivitsky, Wolinsky, and Timofeeff were only a few of the roughly 2,000 undocumented immigrants who were the beneficiaries of a federal law—the Act of June 8, 1934—that halted their deportations, adjusted their immigration status, and gave them a pathway to U.S. citizenship.[4]

Drawing on the nearly 2,000 case files of the so-called White Russian[5] beneficiaries of the Act of June 8, 1934, this chapter supplies a new history of undocumented migration, immigration legalization, and refugee law and policy in the United States.[6] The history of these Russian émigrés resides at the intersection of these themes insofar as they were simultaneously defined under law as refugees and unauthorized immigrants. With the collapse of the Russian empire and the rise of Soviet Russia, hundreds of thousands of soldiers and civilians fled political persecution and crossed multiple national borders in search of safety, shelter, and sustenance.[7] By 1921, the League of Nations implemented a series of measures that offered the exiles some degree of protection and then designated them as refugees under international law. Although their refugee status enabled them to resettle in countries throughout the world, many believed that a better life was to be found in the United States. Through illicit crossings of the nation's land borders and as visa overstays and stowaways, they made their way into the country and rebuilt their lives. Yet, the onset of official diplomatic relations between the United States and the Soviet Union in 1933 raised the possibility that these once stateless persons could be deported to the USSR. The efforts of refugee advocates and sympathetic policymakers saved the exiles from this fate; by successfully lobbying for the passage of the Act of June 8, 1934, they afforded the Russians the means to legalize their immigration status and apply for U.S. citizenship.

This history of the Russian refugees illuminates the conditions under which various forms of immigration relief, such as legalization and the grant of refugee status, emerged in American immigration law.[8] Grants of relief from the restrictions and penalties imposed by the immigration laws have a long history. Indeed, the Alien and Sedition Acts of 1798, one of the very first federal immigration statutes, authorized the president to exercise their discretion to stay the deportation of suspected enemy aliens.[9] Since the late eighteenth century, additional types of relief became available to noncitizens at each stage of the immigration process, including admissions at the nation's land and sea ports of entry and deportation from the interior spaces of the nation.[10] These relief provisions, as legal historian Allison Brownell Tirres explains, were analogous to the exercise of "sovereign mercy" in American criminal law. Designed to "relieve suffering in some form," official acts of mercy were a familiar feature of the legal landscape and included the dispensation of pardons and clemency.[11] Sovereign mercy was no less essential to the immigration laws; its manifestations reflected the ways that altruism and humanitarian norms have resided "at the core of the nation's immigration system."[12]

While legal scholars have supplied much important commentary on the kinds of relief available to immigrants today, we know very little about their history or the social, economic, cultural, and political forces that led to their incorporation into our immigration system.[13] The few historical references to acts of immigration relief frame them as adjuncts or exceptions to the immigration exclusion laws, antecedents of U.S. refugee and asylum policies, or as expressions of resistance by immigrants and their advocates.[14] Although this essay builds on these interpretations, it also departs from them by centering the history of immigration relief and piecing together the specific conditions under which forms of relief made their way into the immigration laws. In the case of the White Russians, I argue that their experience illustrates how state interests in border control tempered the grant of any humanitarian relief. Indeed, even though international law defined the White Russians as refugees, their American advocates assiduously refused to pursue a domestic refugee law on their behalf. At the height of the Great Depression, they recognized that widespread anti-Semitism and xenophobia had already vitiated several attempts to pass immigration and refugee measures, particularly for the benefit of European Jews fleeing Nazi Germany, that might open the gates to new immigrant inflows.[15] Thus, the defenders of the White Russians made the novel, yet tactical, choice to represent the refugees as unauthorized immigrants who deserved legalization and U.S. citizenship. In short, the rescue of the White Russians hinged on their recasting as undocumented immigrants under law.

The Act of June 8, 1934, not only enabled policymakers to maintain control over the nation's external boundaries but also allowed them to reinforce multiple social boundaries—or the dividing lines between non-European and European undocumented immigrants, Red and White Russians living in the United States, and poor and well-to-do White Russian émigrés.[16] Underscoring the profound contingencies surrounding the conceptions of illegality and legality in the United States, the Act of June 8, 1934, was explicitly reserved for individuals "not ineligible to citizenship." As such, the new legalization procedure distinguished European undocumented immigrants from non-European undocumented immigrants. The former were often characterized as innocents who had made a careless error that was deserving of forgiveness; the latter were perceived as lawbreakers who constituted a threat to the nation and merited imprisonment and/or expulsion. Indeed, at the very same time that Congress debated the White Russian legalization bill, anti-Mexican racism led to the forcible removal of nearly a half million ethnic Mexicans from states and localities throughout the United States.[17]

Yet, ideological anxieties unsettled the neat racial boundaries created by the Act of June 8, 1934. Longstanding fears about the rise of a communist state abroad and the undetected crossings of communist sympathizers along the nation's borders informed the care policymakers took to reassure the American public that the legalization measure would only assist the so-called good Russians—the Whites, rather than the Reds. With the latter, many of whom were also undocumented, the U.S. government sought every possible means of deportation to any country, including the USSR.[18] In a similar fashion, concerns about class—about the economic burdens posed by undocumented immigrants on the dole—led the INS to favor the legalization applications of self-sufficient White Russian refugees. In short, while the Act of June 8, 1934, might have defined white, anti-communist, and middle-class White Russians as quintessential insiders, at the same time, it made quite clear that people lacking these racial, ideological, and class characteristics not only fell outside the bounds of the polity but also merited removal from the nation altogether.

Since the political, legal, and social identities of the Russian migrants changed across time and space, this essay begins by tracing the journeys of the Russian émigrés from Soviet Russia to the United States in the 1920s. I then discuss how a humanitarian movement to reform or soften the penalties against undocumented European immigrants laid the political and rhetorical groundwork for the passage of the Act of June 8, 1934. The next section relates how the congressional debates on the measure stressed the Russians' status as undocumented immigrants. In so doing, sympathetic lawmakers ensured that any provision of immigration relief served the border control interests of the state, as well as the Russians' humanitarian needs. Finally, I describe INS implementation of the act and how the process worked to erase the Russians' identities as exiles and ethnics so as to transform them into Americans.

*   *   *

The history of the Russian refugees is complex and even troubling; over the course of the twentieth century, they would be the victors and the vanquished and the persecutors and the persecuted. While the term "White Russian" principally refers to the military units that remained loyal to the tsar during the March Revolution and then opposed the Bolsheviks during the Russian Civil War, it also refers to a broader group, principally the nobility and the propertied classes, that shared the military's anti-Bolshevik orientation.[19] They, especially the officers and infantrymen, also were intensely anti-Semitic; their racist attitudes were expressed in the 1919 massacre of about 100,000 Jews in Ukraine.[20] Many members of the White Russian military would go on to join the Nazis and participate in the genocide of the Jews.[21] Yet, with the defeat of the White armies in 1923, they became enemies of the Soviet Union and the targets of state-sanctioned repression and violence. Hundreds of thousands of soldiers and civilians fled the new Soviet state seeking refuge primarily in Europe and Asia; by the mid-1930s, an estimated 315,000 Russian refugees were in Europe and 130,000 in the Far East.[22] For much of the 1920s, many clung to the belief that the new Soviet state would be short-lived and that they would be able to return home.[23] These aspirations led Russians to construe their exile as a temporary condition and resist identifying themselves as immigrants and refugees.

While nostalgia and loss informed the Russians' self-perception, their humanitarian plight led the international community to define them as refugees. To meet their immediate subsistence needs, international organizations and European nations tried to provide the Russians with shelter and sustenance.[24] But the scope of the emergency exceeded the ability of these organizations and states to assist them. The League of Nations intervened by appointing Dr. Fridtjof Nansen, a Polar explorer and humanitarian, as the High Commissioner for Refugees on June 27, 1921. Initially, Nansen tried to work with the Soviet government to repatriate or return the refugees, but this effort ultimately failed. By the end of 1921, the Soviet government had passed a set of migration-related decrees that revoked Soviet citizenship for those who lived abroad for more than five years and those who left Russia after November 7, 1917, without the USSR's authorization.[25] As a result, the Russians were rendered stateless peoples.

In response to the 1921 decrees, Nansen and the league created an International Certificate of Identity, or what became known as the Nansen Passport.[26] The document specifically defined refugees as "any person of Russian origin who does not enjoy the protection of the Government of the Union of Soviet Socialist Republics and who has not acquired any other nationality."[27] Accepted by fifty-four countries by the end of the decade, it was valid for only a year and allowed the bearer to cross the growing number of national borders that had emerged after World War I and, in turn, find work and reunite with family members. It also gave signatories a means of keeping track of Russian refugees in their midst, whether for the purposes of removal or refugee recognition.[28] Nansen's own goal with respect to the passport was to enable the Russian (and later Armenian and Assyrian) refugees to cross national borders as they searched for jobs; in so doing, he hoped to spread the burden of supporting the Russians among the member states of the League of Nations.[29] While many problems would emerge with the passport, it is credited with laying the foundation for an international refugee law regime.[30]

For more than a decade after the Civil War, Russians led a peripatetic existence, repeatedly relocating and resettling throughout the world.[31] For many, the United States "represent[ed] the promised land."[32] Here, they hoped to achieve greater social mobility and escape the political and economic discrimination they encountered in their countries of first flight.[33] Others had tired of being perpetual refugees, as Michael Honig (formerly Mendel Honigman) observed: "It was very difficult to become a citizen [of Romania] and being a refugee it was hard . . . so I decided to come to the United States."[34]

Yet, for all the exiles, the passage of the 1921 and 1924 quota systems created significant barriers to their admission. Reflecting contemporary American biases against southern and eastern Europeans, the systems decreased the quotas for immigrants from these nations while increasing them for arrivals from northern and western Europe.[35] As one Russian journalist wrote in a Russian-language newspaper published in Harbin, China—where Russian refugees thirsted for news about Russian immigrant life in the United States and any loosening of its immigration laws: "[Russians, Poles, and Italians] are the nationalities which assimilate poorly and who give few or poor 'Americans.' For British, Germans, and Scandinavians, who easily come under the influence of Americanism the respective quotas have been lowered but slightly. America does not fear these."[36] For the hundreds of thousands of Russian refugees around the world, reducing the quota from 20,000 to about 2,000 effectively closed the gates to America; thus, for example, in 1926, a Russian refugee seeking a quota visa would need to wait ten to fifteen years for 18,000 other applicants to receive their visas first.[37]

Instead of waiting, most Russians pursued alternative modes of entry. According to one 1934 estimate, half of the Russian refugees in the United States managed to gain admission as visitors, entertainers, and students on temporary visas.[38] The other half made the conscious choice to enter in violation of the immigration laws as deserting seamen or through a surreptitious border crossing from Canada or Mexico.[39] Many of the former, however, eventually became unauthorized immigrants by failing to renew their temporary visas. In short, as they themselves would openly admit to immigration inspectors during their legalization proceedings, they were undocumented immigrants in America.[40] The case files attest to the relative ease of their illicit entries. Russians crossing the nation's land borders with Canada and Mexico explained that they simply walked past immigration officials at the border inspection stations.[41] Others recalled how they escaped detection by crossing the line with large crowds[42] or walking around, rather than through, the immigration inspection office.[43] Some accepted rides casually offered by American tourists in exchange for a few dollars.[44] Russians who took jobs as seamen or stowed away on ships recounted their anxieties about being discovered but consistently reported few difficulties in deserting ship upon reaching dock in the United States.[45]

Other Russian refugees adopted a more risk-averse approach to their crossings and took great pains to plan them in advance. Some tried to dress and speak like American nationals to pass as ordinary border crossers along the nation's southern line.[46] The migrants also relied on established smuggling rings that accompanied them as they walked,[47] drove,[48] or rode trains[49] across the Canadian and Mexican borders; or stowed them away on small boats that crossed the Rio Grande,[50] the Niagara River,[51] or the waters between Cuba and Florida.[52] Due to immigration inspectors' gender biases, single and divorced women also carefully planned their journeys. To evade the scrutiny of immigration officials, they adopted various ways of posing as dependents of men: Aniela Perechadk, a Polish Russian, explained that she remained silent during her immigration inspection as "the priest with me did the talking for both of us."[53] Divorcée Jenny Turchin (formerly Jenny Chechelnitzkaia) and her daughter posed as the U.S. citizen wife and child of a marine captain. Taking the names of the captain's actual wife and child—Celestina and Catalina, the three left Cuba together on the SS *Parismina* and were admitted in New Orleans as U.S. citizens.[54]

Yet, despite their illicit migrations, the Russian exiles largely escaped the stigmas applied to other undocumented immigrant groups. In the mind of the American public, their flight from political and religious persecution rendered them refugees, or humanitarian migrants deserving of aid and forbearance, rather than economic migrants or lawbreakers. By 1934, this view was largely accepted due to the extensive humanitarian aid that had been supplied to Russians abroad by the U.S. government, advocacy organizations, and ordinary individuals in the 1920s.[55] The press generated further sympathy for the Russians by publishing engaging accounts about the danger and drama surrounding their global journeys—their secret escapes from the Soviet Union, temporary residence in cosmopolitan communities in Europe, Asia, Canada, and Mexico, and surreptitious entries into the United States.[56] Neglecting to mention the atrocities committed by the anti-Bolshevik Russian armies in Europe, these narratives enabled the migrants to paper over any troubling elements of their past, present themselves as stateless persons, and generate American support for their cause.

Perhaps most important, the American press, policymakers, and public embraced the refugees for their anti-communist political ideology.[57] Even though the formation of the Popular Front and FDR's New Deal softened animosities toward collectivist ideologies, anxieties regarding the rise of the Soviet Union and communism at home continued to be an undercurrent in American life and politics.[58] Indeed, the Act of June 8, 1934, was passed in the same year that federal officials first attempted to deport labor leader Harry Bridges.[59] Moreover, at the very same time that Department of Labor and INS officials lobbied for the legalization of the Russian exiles, they initiated talks with Moscow regarding the deportation of 900 Russians who failed to demonstrate the same political ideals.[60] Described as "undesirables" and "political 'agitators,'" they lived in the United States under orders of deportation but enjoyed "free harbor" because of the lack of diplomatic relations between the United States and Soviet Union until 1933.[61] Underscoring the distinction between these Russians and those they frequently dubbed "the Whites," the INS informed the *New York Times* that among this group of deportees, "there were no '"White Russian' refugees nor others who might face political persecution in Russia."[62]

The Russians also won acceptance due to their social status. Although most had lost everything in their flight from the Soviet Union, by the time they applied for registry in 1934, the majority had climbed the socioeconomic ladder to become members of the lower middle and middle classes.[63] Living in the United States for an average of 7.7 years, the applicants rarely faced scrutiny and surveillance by immigration officials; their undocumented immigration status did not prevent them from attending school, finding jobs, purchasing homes, raising families, and becoming well-respected members of their communities. By external standards, the Russians appeared no different from many Americans; indeed, during the economic crisis, they—insofar as almost all were employed, rented or owned their own homes, and held bank accounts and insurance policies—were faring better than the average American.

Given the perceived positive qualities of the Russians—their structural integration and even cultural assimilation into American society, several immigration advocacy organizations came to their aid as panic spread through many Russian immigrant communities with the news that the United States and Soviet Union would commence diplomatic relations.[64] In its March 1933 plea to President Roosevelt, the Consolidated Committee of the Russian National Organizations in California (CCRNO) stressed that the Russians were different from other immigrants insofar as they were political and religious refugees forced to leave their homes. If deported to the Soviet Union, the CCRNO continued, the refugees would most likely be executed. This outcome, the organization exhorted, would vitiate the nation's reputation as a "friend to the Political Refugees."[65]

*   *   *

As immigration advocates and policymakers worked to prevent the Russians' deportation, hundreds of thousands of undocumented Mexican and European migrants found themselves bereft of relief in the 1930s. Shortly after the onset of the Great Depression, President Hoover launched a nationwide deportation campaign to remove all unauthorized immigrants as a solution to the economic crisis.[66] Although the campaign quickly ended due to domestic and international protests, states and localities followed the Hoover administration's example by launching their own expulsion campaigns. Perhaps most famously, the city of Los Angeles devised a so-called repatriation drive that resulted in the forced departure of nearly a half-million ethnic Mexicans.[67] On both sides of the Canadian border, as historian Ashley Johnson Bavery has emphasized, Windsor and Detroit officials took the initiative to deport unwanted Europeans.[68] Taken together, these local, state, and federal campaigns powerfully reinforced emerging conceptions of illicit entry as a crime that merited harsh punishments such as detention and deportation.

Yet, widespread criticism of the Hoover-era deportation drives led a set of progressive policymakers to explore a more humanitarian approach to immigration law enforcement.[69] As a part of this effort, INS leaders, in conjunction with the Department of Labor, launched internal and external investigations into the nation's immigration system. Conducted by a group of prominent citizens known as the Ellis Island Committee, one of these inquiries called for more humanitarian approaches to deportation, undocumented immigration, and refugee admissions.[70] With respect to the latter, the committee urged legislators to protect racial and religious refugees and stateless persons and reminded them of the nation's asylum tradition.[71] Cognizant of the widespread anti-immigrant sentiment in Congress, however, the committee adopted a cautious stand on refugee relief, recommending that refugee admissions abide by numerical limits set by the national origins quota system. For refugees and stateless persons, such as the White Russians, already in the United States, the committee similarly advised lawmakers to employ existing legislation to avert their deportations. But, in the process, the committee's final report reframed popular conceptions of unauthorized European migrants and articulated a powerful set of arguments for their legalization.[72]

Throughout its *Report,* the committee firmly defended the importance of immigration law enforcement, but, at the same time, it directly challenged the conflation of illegality with crime. Repeatedly characterizing illegal entry as a benign infraction, the committee wrote, "illegal entry is not an offense which can be classified as *malum in se*"[73]—that is, "a wrong in itself . . . [or] inherently and essentially evil."[74] Such a designation was reserved for acts, such as murder, considered to be immoral regardless of their definition under law. In contrast, undocumented entry was often the product of administrative error; for instance, the committee observed that for decades along the Canadian border, Bureau of Immigration officials failed to keep thorough admission records. On many other occasions, individuals were unable to produce evidence of their legal entry because immigration officials incorrectly recorded their names on manifest sheets. In sum, the committee concluded, "Aliens who entered at such points during these years have suffered consequently through no fault of their own but as a result of the negligence of the Government."[75]

In those cases where illegal entry was the result of human error, the committee argued that many immigrants simply did not know that they were violating the immigration laws. Pleading on behalf of immigrant sailors, the committee explained, "Thousands of seamen had left their ships in American ports and remained there, often without realizing they were guilty of illegal entry."[76] Finally, the very complexity of the nation's immigration laws and the fact that the laws had changed several times in the 1920s made it difficult for ordinary immigrants to understand when they were breaking the law.[77] From the Ellis Island Committee's perspective, illegal immigration bore none of the hallmarks of crime but rather administrative error and human ignorance.

The committee also argued that the punishments for illegal entry were out of proportion to the infraction itself. Its 1934 report posed a direct challenge to the Act of March 4, 1929, one of the first federal measures to criminalize illicit entry. It argued that the offense of a first illicit entry did not merit the penalty—a $1,000 fine and a one-year prison term—dictated by the 1929 law. The prison term was especially reprehensible because the INS detained violators in local prisons that, as the *Report* explained, "have no facilities for segregating prisoners according to sex, age or type of criminal offense, and are unsuited for detention of these aliens, many of whom enter illegally through ignorance of the law or because of youth and recklessness."[78] In a move that likely raised the ire of nativists, the committee recommended that *no criminal penalties* be applied to first-time offenders.[79]

The committee's final report also scrutinized the civil, as well as criminal, penalties for illegal entry. In so doing, it called for the reinstatement of a statute of limitations on deportation. Under the 1917 immigration law, immigration officials could only deport individuals within five years of their entry into the United States.[80] By 1924, Congress eliminated this time limit, making it possible for people to be deported at any point after their entry into the country. To highlight the unfairness of the new deportation provisions, the committee reminded readers of the relatively harmless character of illegal entry:

> Deportation without time limit seems too harsh a penalty for an act which is not wrong in itself. . . . We are dealing, after all, with human beings—men and women who in most cases have been promoted to come here against our law, either to join relatives or family, to escape persecution, or to find some better answer to the economic riddle which confronts us all.[81]

Yet, without a statute of limitations on deportation, undocumented immigrants would live in "perpetual jeopardy."[82] Both the criminal and civil penalties for undocumented immigration were overly harsh. Just as worrisome to the committee, the laws also prevented too many of these undocumented immigrants from becoming citizens.

According to one estimate, in 1929 there were 1.3 million undocumented immigrants in the United States.[83] To provide these migrants an opportunity to become citizens, Congress passed the Act of March 2, 1929, popularly known as the Registry Act of 1929.[84] The measure was specifically designed to benefit two groups of undocumented immigrants: first, those who lacked an official record of entry due to an administrative error; and second, undocumented persons deemed to be of good moral character.[85] The benefits of the Registry Act and the Act of June 8, 1934, however, were not universal but instead reserved for those who were not racially ineligible for citizenship.[86] As such, these measures would extend the racial dividing lines that informed the admission of legal immigrants at the borders to the legalization of undocumented immigrants within the nation itself.

In its 1934 report, the Ellis Island Committee revisited the Registry Act of 1929. In so doing, it called not only for the softening of the nation's laws with respect to deportation and illegal entry but also an expansion of immigration legalization—an expansion of the Registry Act of 1929. It specifically asked Congress to amend the 1929 law so that more undocumented European immigrants could be eligible for an adjustment of status. Among these individuals were stateless persons or those migrants who, due to shifts in national boundaries, could not return to their homelands.[87] Citing the case of the Russian refugees, it also recommended that those who faced political or religious persecution upon their deportation to their home countries be allowed to regularize their status. Without these amendments, these undocumented immigrants would be "condemn[ed] to a permanent state of alienage," creating an underclass that

> profits neither the country nor the alien and his family. It hinders his assimilation. It bars him from many professions and vocations. It exposes him and his family

to all the disabilities and prejudice to which aliens are subject, to discriminations in respect to employment, old age pensions, the benefits of public works legislation. It excludes him from the fullest and most useful participation in the life of the country.[88]

Based on the findings of the Ellis Island Committee, the INS, with the approval of Secretary of Labor Frances Perkins, prepared five bills pertaining to deportation and undocumented immigration.[89] Ultimately, none of the bills passed congressional muster. Yet, along with the Ellis Island Committee's final report, they supplied the rhetorical framework for the numerous legalization bills that were proposed in the 1930s.[90] Perhaps most prominently, as explained by historian Maddalena Marinari, the sponsors of the Kerr-Coolidge bill articulated a cautious defense of legalization by stressing that it would preserve family unity without compromising the restrictionist tenets underlying U.S. immigration policy. The opposition of congressional restrictionists, however, proved too strong, and the Kerr-Coolidge bill failed to pass.[91] The Act of June 8, 1934, was one of the few legalization measures to survive the scrutiny of Congress in the 1930s. Unlike the Kerr-Coolidge bill, the June 8 law proposed to assist a group of migrants whose race, class, and, in particular, political ideology more clearly served the American state's geopolitical interests. Underscoring the extensive support for the Russians, the *Washington Post*, in a story about the work of the Ellis Island Committee, explained that changes to U.S. deportation law were necessary because "Upon no class of immigrant perhaps, has the mailed fist [of deportation law] fallen harder than it has upon the White Russian."[92] Only a few months after the publication of the *Report*, Congress passed the Act of June 8, 1934.

*   *   *

Two noted immigration liberals, Sen. Royal Copeland (D-NY) and Rep. Samuel Dickstein (D-NY) led the fight to pass S. 2692 (Act of June 8, 1934). Both had staunchly opposed the discrimination against southern and eastern Europeans wrought by the 1921 and 1924 quota systems and worked to mitigate the impacts of these laws. For the benefit of European migrants, Copeland sponsored the Act of March 2, 1929, and strongly supported the Kerr-Coolidge bill.[93] Meanwhile, Dickstein succeeded Rep. Albert Johnson (R-IL), the author of the 1924 Immigration and Nationality Act and one of the most zealous xenophobes of his day, as the chair of the House Committee on Immigration and Naturalization. In this role, Dickstein was unable to overcome the opposition of anti-immigration forces to pass major immigration reforms but, nevertheless, managed to block even more restrictive bills.[94] As the son of Russian orthodox Jews who emigrated to America when he was two, Dickstein also championed the cause of Jewish migrants and refugees abroad and served as the most vocal defender of the Russian exiles during the debates on S. 2692.[95] Keenly aware of congressional objections to the creation of various forms of immigration and refugee relief, Copeland and Dickstein, like the Ellis Island Committee, cast the Russian refugees as unauthorized immigrants who deserved to have their deportations suspended and to be legalized and become U.S. citizens.

When the debates began in the spring of 1934, Copeland and Dickstein drew attention to the plight the exiles faced: without some form of legal relief, the Russians might be deported to the Soviet Union where, by law, they would be subject to the death penalty. In introducing S. 2692 on the floor of the Senate, Copeland explained: "Mr. President, this is a bill to take care of certain Russian refugees who are in this country . . . they cannot go back to Russia. They would meet death, I suppose, if they did so."[96] As further evidence of their humanitarian plight, Dickstein recounted the hardships these Russian refugees faced:

> . . . Helen Haritonoff, who is a widow, her husband having been killed in the Russian Army at the beginning of the World War. Two of her brothers perished during the civil war in Russia and her parents died of starvation during the revolution. She herself escaped with her life during the anti-Bolshevik revolts of 1921–22; and after walking for several miles across ice to Finland, she picked up two of her nieces, the daughters of her brothers who perished during the civil war.[97]

Yet, both Copeland and Dickstein recognized that their appeals to compassion would not sway restrictionist lawmakers. Indeed, the very representation of the Russians as refugees created an opening for their opponents to argue that the exiles demanded assistance when the nation had to prioritize native-born citizens in providing Depression-era relief.

In anticipation of these objections, lawmakers minimized their characterization of the Russians as refugees and, instead, foregrounded their identity as undocumented immigrants. For example, Dickstein repeatedly insisted that the measure legalized only a small group of migrants[98] after one member threatened, "we will oppose the bill" because it "confus[ed] the question of granting favors to a few hundred Russians whose lives may be at stake with a far-reaching question of who might be political or religious refugees."[99] Moreover, in classifying the Russians as undocumented immigrants, the sponsors of S. 2692 adopted the tone of the Ellis Island Committee *Report* and held the Russians harmless. As Rep. Cochran (D-MO) explained, their undocumented presence was not a result of any ill intent but instead circumstances beyond their control.[100]

To win further support for the undocumented Russian exiles, Dickstein stressed their affinity for citizenship by describing how many had already integrated both culturally and socioeconomically into American society. On the floor of the House, he praised the Russians as "people who speak the English language perfectly. Some of them are professors in our colleges, some of them in our universities, some of them experts in airplanes and some of them are in our Coast Guard."[101] As a further indicator of their adjustment, Dickstein noted that many had U.S. citizen spouses and children: "Ninety-five percent of these aliens are of a high type and are good prospective citizens. In most cases the men have married American women and have American children."[102] Dickstein also promoted the achievements of the so-called Russian Battery of the New York National Guard; composed of at least thirty undocumented Russians, it had received a prize from the War Department for its "discipline and morale."[103] Finally, in an argument that reflected contemporary eugenicist thought, Dickstein referred to their biology, "And, as I said a moment ago, in 95 percent of the cases, many . . . were found to be all fine specimens of manhood."[104]

Dickstein's attempt to Americanize the Russians also constituted one moment in a longer effort to win for southern and eastern Europeans the same forms of racial inclusion and acceptance accorded to northern and western Europeans. By stressing their "Americanness," Dickstein aimed to "whiten" the Russian émigrés.[105] His strategy, however, entailed reproducing racial dividing lines. As he lobbied on behalf of the Russian exiles, he also called for the repatriation of Filipinos and Hawaiians and Puerto Ricans living on the U.S. mainland.[106] A decade earlier, he had backed the exclusion of Japanese immigrants under the Immigration Act of 1924.[107] As historian Gary Gerstle explains, the congressman from New York elected to "play America's racial game" because "Whenever talk focused on the Japanese, the racial standing of the southern and eastern Europeans seemed to rise. The latter were no longer racially despised peoples, but simply Europeans, racially and culturally indistinguishable from the Germans, English, and Scandinavians."[108]

Further reflecting the complexities and contradictions of immigration policy formation, two longstanding restrictionists, Rep. Thomas A. Jenkins (R-OH) and Rep. Thomas L. Blanton (D-Tex) joined congressional liberals in urging the embrace of the Russian exiles. Jenkins supported the national origins quota system of 1924,[109] and by the late 1930s, he would call for the detention of unauthorized immigrants in "camps where their liberty would be restricted drastically." These deprivations, Jenkins argued, would drive undocumented immigrants out of the country.[110] Yet, in the case of the Russian émigrés, their anti-communist ideology seemed to erase all his anxieties about their alleged racial inferiority and illegality. Indeed, during the debates, Jenkins differentiated the Russian refugees not only from other southern and eastern Europeans but also other Russians, declaring:

> It is a bill to run the Reds out of the United States and keep the "white people" in, and by "white people" is meant those people who are not Reds, but people who believe in orderly government, people who believe that the Government of the United States ought to be run according to a constitution and not according to anarchy and force under a red flag. That appeals to me.[111]

Despite the paradoxes in Jenkins's defense, it foreshadowed the posture immigration restrictionists would take in their own advocacy of anti-communist refugees after World War II and during the Cold War.[112]

Blanton also staunchly supported the 1924 act and the application of severe civil and criminal penalties to undocumented Mexican migrants.[113] Yet, like Jenkins, he spoke in favor of S. 2692 for ideological reasons and pronounced, "It is a bill for Americanism and against bolshevism. It is a bill for lovers of constitutional government instead of Russian Bolsheviks, and this is why I am for it."[114] Recent events, moreover, imbued his defense of the Russians with racial significance. Only months before, a group of Howard University students protested to end the segregation of the public restaurants inside the U.S. Capitol; Blanton accused them of being communists and demanded their expulsion from Howard.[115] Through this incident, Blanton fused together arguments about ideology and race to define insiders and outsiders within the body politic.[116] For the congressman, loyal Americans did not challenge the racial status quo as the Howard University students did. Instead, they, like the Russian exiles, helped to maintain it, leading politically quiescent lives that exemplified the putative virtues of American democracy and conformed to mythic notions of immigrant incorporation in the United States.

Finally, even though Congress recognized that the White Russians were refugees and made the determination of their "bona fide" refugee status a requirement of the 1934 law,[117] they consciously drafted the measure in ways that avoided creating a general refugee policy. Thus, there was much opposition when the bill was amended to include the following phrase: "or (b) who was in the United States as a bona fide political or religious refugee."[118] Jenkins objected to the change, arguing that it could be read as creating a formal refugee policy.[119] Concurring with Jenkins, Rep. McFadden (R-PA) argued that the wording resulted in the "establishment of a new principle that was proposed here to let into the United States political and religious refugees." In response, the Senate adopted another amendment that ensured that the law would apply only to the Russians.[120] To further diminish the number of beneficiaries of the law, it expired after only one calendar year.

*   *   *

Given the widespread support for the Russians and the rapidly approaching expiration of the law, INS officials expedited its implementation despite its burdensome requirements. The legalization procedure required the payment of a $10 fee, the completion of many forms, investigations into the migrants' criminal, employment, property, and immigration records, correspondence with foreign officials regarding applicants' claims to refugee status, and interviews with the applicants and their witnesses. In its intricacies, this process resembled those the agency applied to other classes of immigrants seeking entry into the United States. Yet, whereas the INS, particularly in its administration of the Chinese exclusion laws, had earned a reputation for presuming that immigrants were excludable rather than admissible, in the case of the Russians, immigration inspectors adopted the opposite approach.[121] Approving 83 percent of the applications, INS inspectors chose not to probe too deeply into any problematic features of the files and, instead, sought every possible reason to adjust the Russians' status.

In this effort, the INS continued the work begun by immigration advocates, the Ellis Island Committee, and congressional lawmakers to transform the Russians into Americans. Even though the refugees provided rich accounts of their lives, immigration inspectors ignored these nuances and compressed the voluminous details of their life stories to ensure that they met the requirements of the law. Thus, for example, inspectors asked the Russians to enumerate their "color" and their "race" on several forms included in the registry application. Some Russians struggled to respond, filling the blanks with answers such as "White Russian,"[122] or "Russia."[123] Their uncertainty demonstrated not only the instability surrounding notions of race but also Russians' lack of familiarity with American approaches to race thinking. As scholars have emphasized, their displacement introduced the Russians to different forms of racialization during their sojourns in Europe, Asia, Africa, and Latin America and, in turn, destabilized their sense of ethnic, racial, and national identities.[124]

Despite their confusion regarding American ideas of race, the Russians, in ways both witting and unwitting, facilitated the INS's work in reshaping their national identities. With respect to the latter, when asked to list their places of birth and nationality, nearly all the applicants used an older, pre-Soviet nomenclature. They uniformly wrote "St. Petersburg," rather than "Petrograd" or "Leningrad" and "Russia" rather than the "Soviet Union."[125] Throughout the case files, anonymous editors, likely immigration inspectors, crossed out the defunct place names and penciled in the Soviet-era designations. So many national boundaries and place names had shifted after World War I and the Civil War that immigration inspectors working on registry cases from Eastern Europe and Russia asked for the latest version of a world atlas so that they could properly correct the application forms.[126] Even though the INS brought the files into conformity with contemporary world maps, they must have recognized that the émigrés' responses, grounded in their own cartographic memories of Tsarist Russia, signaled their longstanding antipathies toward the Soviet Union and, perhaps, their ideological affinity for American citizenship.

The Russians also made a conscious effort to present themselves as Americans. In particular, the vast majority carefully chose their words when answering questions regarding their political loyalties. Almost all knew that it was in their best interest to say "no" when immigration inspectors asked whether they adhered to communist forms of government. Many more also expressed their admiration of American democracy; Nicolas Grushko, for instance, shrewdly declared, "I think it is the best government. I traveled all over Europe."[127] Often, the Russians and their witnesses described their commitment to the United States in strong and even nationalistic terms. Thus, for example, even though Vadim Fedoolov, as the son of a high-ranking government official in imperial Russia, was more likely than not to obtain registry, the CCRNO testified that he was "a person inherently loyal to the best political, religious and civil traditions of our national past and entirely devoid of any red subversive influences and private convictions."[128]

As they proclaimed their suitability for U.S. citizenship, the refugees rarely discussed their identity as ethnics at home and abroad even though voluminous evidence of their ethnicity appeared in their case files. In the United States, for example, Russian nationals received the support of ethnic advocacy groups such as the CCRNO, launched anti-Bolshevik organizations, worked for and even founded Russian-language newspapers, joined ethnic veterans' organizations, attended ethnic Russian churches and synagogues, and lived in Russian immigrant neighborhoods, which provided a plentiful supply of naturalized Russians who often served as witnesses for the registry applicants.[129] Before becoming Russian Americans, many, as indicated in their case files, self-identified as members of ethnic and national minorities, specifically Jews, Germans, Poles, Latvians, Lithuanians, Ukrainians, and Armenians, who had been absorbed into the Russian Empire over the course of two centuries of war and conquest.[130]

Immigration inspectors openly expressed their preferences for those they dubbed "desirable" migrants, specifically those applicants who met the racial, ideological, economic, and social requirements of the law. They were especially effusive in their admiration of Russians who had enrolled at elite schools such as Harvard, Columbia, Bryn Mawr, and Yale and became university professors.[131] The agency also defined as "desirable" those migrants able to support themselves financially. These included Princess Stephanie, a member of the Russian nobility who managed to retain her wealth and, during her immigration inspection, talked about the founding of her interior design company and the imminent launch of her eponymously named cosmetics line.[132] Inspectors also praised applicants for displaying their loyalty to the United States and, in contrast to the Reds, remaining politically quiescent. As they wrote of Nigoghos Nigoghosian, an Armenian-Russian, "He is alert, pleasing in appearance and manner, has continued to earn his living and has conducted himself in a manner not objectionable to his neighbors."[133]

Yet, in pursuing adjustments of their immigration status, the Russians did not have to be perfect. During his inspection, Samuel Brody (originally Zabrodsky) took few pains to establish his refugee status and blithely admitted that he wanted to stay in the United States simply because he liked it here; his application was approved.[134] Many who openly admitted entering without inspection across the Canadian and Mexican borders were permitted to adjust their status.[135] Despite his fraudulent documents and fake name, Serge Nikolaievitch Borisoff faced little difficulty in gaining registry.[136] Walter Kosteen (originally Wadin de Kostin) was fined for wrestling on the beach at Coney Island and committed numerous traffic violations while working as a chauffeur at a school for girls.[137] His application was approved. As further evidence of the solicitude demonstrated toward these applicants, the INS suspended the deportation orders of those Russians whose registry cases were pending.[138]

As the final arbiter of the Russian applications, Commissioner General MacCormack overruled 58 percent of the denials. Although he facilitated the legalization of additional White Russians, McCormack's stance on European refugees was complex. While he personally sympathized with their plight, he defended the restrictionist principles underlying the nation's immigration laws, fearing that any attempt to liberalize the laws would "backfire" and provide nativist lawmakers with a pretext to restrict immigration admissions even further.[139] Thus, when he faced the dilemma of assisting a group of German Jewish children abroad or the White Russians at home, he prioritized the latter. Concerned that Congress would defeat a Russian legalization bill if the INS admitted the children, in April 1934, MacCormack decided to delay for a year the implementation of a measure that would bring the children to the United States.[140] MacCormack's choice poignantly illustrates the obstacles to creating broad and enduring forms of immigration relief.

Passed during a high point in the history of American xenophobia, the Russian legalization law marks a significant moment in the history of immigration relief. It was a significant humanitarian gesture, sparing nearly 2,000 people from deportation to the Soviet Union, where they faced an uncertain fate. Yet, the measure also reflected the limits of sovereign mercy by maintaining the state's interests in immigration exclusion at the borders and social control within the nation's interior spaces. Recognizing that anti-Semitism and xenophobia precluded the creation of broad humanitarian measures, such as a formal refugee and asylum system, the law's sponsors vigorously represented the Russians as undocumented immigrants deserving of legalization and downplayed their status as refugees. At the same time, the June 8 law powerfully reaffirmed existing social boundaries. It retained the longstanding racial requisites for registry, drew hard ideological dividing lines between desirable and undesirable Russian immigrants, and underscored the importance of class status to belonging and membership in the polity. As a form of sovereign mercy, the legalization of the White Russians served as an ongoing reminder of the state's power to define insiders and outsiders under law.

Notes

An earlier version of this chapter was published in the *Journal of American Ethnic History* 43, no. 1 (Fall 2023): 5–42.

1. National Archives, RE-18, Entry 12, RG 85, Washington, DC. I have replicated the names of the Russian refugees as they were recorded by the INS and recognize that agency officials adopted unconventional and erroneous spellings in many cases.

2. RE-127.

3. RE-181.

4. An Act Relating to the Record of Registry of Certain Aliens, Pub. L. 73–299, 48 Stat. 926 (1934). (Hereinafter referred to as the "Act of June 8, 1934" or the "Registry Act of 1934.")

5. Policymakers, the press, and the American public routinely referred to the exiles as the "White Russians." Yet, to avoid confusing the refugees with Belarusians, who are also called "White Russians," I will largely refer to the Russians as émigrés, exiles, or refugees.

6. In 2019, I took two random samples of the case files at the National Archives; this essay relies on my sample of the general population, which is composed of 350 case files.

7. Sir John Hope Simpson, *The Refugee Problem: Report of a Survey* (London: Oxford University Press, 1939).

8. Allison Brownell Tirres, "Mercy in Immigration Law," *BYU Law Review* 2013, no. 6 (2014): 1563–612.

9. Tirres, "Mercy in Immigration Law," 1563 (citing Act of June 1798, 1 Stat. 570).

10. Tirres, "Mercy in Immigration Law," 1569–89.

11. Tirres, "Mercy in Immigration Law," 1570, 1582.

12. Hiroshi Motomura, *Immigration Outside the Law* (New York: Oxford University Press, 2014), 191.

13. On the legal scholarship, see, for example, Tirres, "Mercy in Immigration Law"; Richard Boswell, "Crafting an Amnesty with Traditional Tools: Registration and Cancellation," *Harvard Journal on Legislation* 47, no. 1 (2010): 175–208; Motomura, *Immigration Outside the Law.*

14. See, for example, Paul Kramer, "Imperial Openings: Civilization, Exemption, and the Geopolitics of Mobility in the History of Chinese Exclusion, 1868–1910," *The Journal of the Gilded Age and Progressive Era* 14, no. 3 (2015): 317–47; Madeline Yuan-Yin Hsu, *The Good Immigrants: How the Yellow Peril Became the Model Minority* (Princeton, NJ: Princeton University Press, 2015); Maddalena Marinari, *Unwanted: Italian and Jewish Mobilization against Restrictive Immigration Laws, 1882–1965* (Chapel Hill: University of North Carolina Press, 2020); Danielle Battisti, *Whom We Shall Welcome: Italian Americans and Immigration Reform, 1945–1965* (New York: Fordham University Press, 2019); Libby Garland, *After They Closed the Gates: Jewish Illegal Immigration to the United States, 1921–1965* (Chicago: University of Chicago Press, 2014); Julian Lim, "Immigration, Asylum, and Citizenship: A More Holistic Approach," *California Law Review* 101, no. 4 (2013): 1013–78; Yael Schacher, "Exceptions to Exclusion: A Prehistory of Asylum in the United States, 1880–1980" (PhD diss., Harvard University, 2015).

15. Richard Breitman and Alan M. Kraut, *American Refugee Policy and European Jewry, 1933–1945* (Bloomington: Indiana University Press, 1987); Daniel J. Tichenor, *Dividing*

Lines: The Politics of Immigration Control in America (Princeton, NJ: Princeton University Press, 2002), 150–75.

16. On the transformation of deportation law from a form of border control into a form of post-entry social control, see Daniel Kanstroom, *Deportation Nation: Outsiders in American History* (Cambridge, MA: Harvard University Press, 2010), 91–131.

17. Francisco Balderrama and Raymond Rodríguez, *Decade of Betrayal: Mexican Repatriation in the 1930s* (Albuquerque: University of New Mexico Press, 1995); Abraham Hoffman, *Unwanted Mexican Americans in the Great Depression: Repatriation Pressures, 1929–1939* (Tucson: University of Arizona Press, 1974); Adam Goodman, *The Deportation Machine: America's Long History of Expelling Immigrants* (Princeton, NJ: Princeton University Press, 2020).

18. Emily Pope-Obeda, "Expelling the Foreign-Born Menace: Immigrant Dissent, the Early Deportation State, and the First American Red Scare," *Journal of the Gilded Age and Progressive Era* 18 (2019): 49–51.

19. Peter Kenez, "The Ideology of the White Movement," *Soviet Studies* 32, no. 1 (1980): 58–83.

20. Kenez, "The Ideology of the White Movement," 79.

21. Kenez, "The Ideology of the White Movement," 79; Simpson, *The Refugee Problem*, 90, 92.

22. If one includes the Russians displaced by World War I, it is estimated that there were 1 million to 1.5 million Russian refugees by 1921. Isabel Kaprielian-Churchill, "Rejecting 'Misfits:' Canada and the Nansen Passport," *The International Migration Review* 28, no. 2 (1994): 283.

23. Simpson, *The Refugee Problem*, 62, 107–8; Marc Raeff, *Russia Abroad: A Cultural History of the Russian Emigration, 1919–1939* (New York: Oxford University Press, 1990).

24. A. Balawyder, "Russian Refugees from Constantinople and Harbin, Manchuria Enter Canada (1923–1936)," *Canadian Slavonic Papers/Revue Canadienne des Slavistes* 14, no. 1 (1972): 15–30; Louise W. Holborn, "The Legal Status of Political Refugees, 1920–1938," *American Journal of International Law* 32, no. 4 (1938): 680–703; James E. Hassell, "Russian Refugees in France and the United States between the World Wars," *Transactions of the American Philosophical Society* 81, no. 7 (1991): 22–31; Peter Gatrell, *The Making of the Modern Refugee* (Oxford, UK: Oxford University Press, 2015), 50, 54–55, 57, 76; Simpson, *The Refugee Problem*, 180–84. See also E. Kyle Romero's chapter in this anthology.

25. Kaprielian-Churchill, "Rejecting 'Misfits,'" 283; George Ginsburgs, "The Soviet Union and the Problem of Refugees and Displaced Persons, 1917–1956," *The American Journal of International Law* 51, no. 2 (1957): 332, 336; Peter Gatrell, *A Whole Empire Walking: Refugees in Russia During World War I* (Bloomington: Indiana University Press, 2005), 188–96.

26. John Torpey, *The Invention of the Passport: Surveillance, Citizenship, and the State* (New York: Cambridge University Press, 2000), 127–29; Simpson, *The Refugee Problem*, 239–43.

27. Kaprielian-Churchill, "Rejecting 'Misfits,'" 283–84.

28. Kaprielian-Churchill, "Rejecting 'Misfits,'" 283, 285; Torpey, *Invention of the Passport*, 128. On the ways the certificate met the needs of member states, see Holborn, "The Legal Status of Political Refugees," 684.

29. Gatrell, *The Making of the Modern Refugee*, 56; Simpson, *The Refugee Problem*, 203–5.

30. Torpey, *Invention of the Passport*, 129; Holborn, "The Legal Status of Political Refugees," 684–85.

31. Simpson, *The Refugee Problem*, 84. As the case files indicate, they often did so with the assistance of immigration advocacy organizations; see RE-105, RE-405, RE-592, RE-1231.

32. Gatrell, *The Making of the Modern Refugee*, 52.

33. For the Russians seeking greater socioeconomic mobility, see RE-159, RE-177, and RE-1615, RE-763. For those seeking to escape discrimination, see RE-153, RE-154, RE-155, RE-156, and RE-159.

34. RE-191.

35. John Higham, *Strangers in the Land: Patterns of American Nativism, 1860–1925* (New Brunswick, NJ: Rutgers University Press, 1955); Mae M. Ngai, *Impossible Subjects: Illegal Aliens and the Making of Modern America* (Princeton, NJ: Princeton University Press, 2004).

36. G. C. Hanson, American Consul, Harbin, China, to Secretary of State, July 7, 1924, RG 59, Box 140, 150.616/290 (enclosing "America for Russians: Impressions of one who returned," *Novosti Zhizni*, July 3, 1924). See also RE-1361.

37. J. Butler Wright, Assistant Secretary of State, to Senator Jesse H. Metcalf [Rhode Island], August 25, 1926, RG 59, Box 140, 150.616./297; Unsigned, undated memo, "Irene Roudakoff's Case," RG 174, Folder 2, Immigration General, 1933, 1934, 1935; see also Marinari, *Unwanted*, 80.

38. Read Lewis, Foreign Language Information Service, to Colonel MacCormack, March 20, 1934, RG 59, Box 140, 150.616/355.

39. Read Lewis, Foreign Language Information Service, to Colonel MacCormack.

40. Serge M. Iserguin, President, and Basil P. Antonenko, Executive Secretary, Russian National Organizations in California to the President, March 31, 1933, RG 59, Box 140, 150.616/340.

41. See, for example, RE-127, RE-249, RE-429, RE-645, RE-924, RE-1321, and RE-1615.

42. RE-181.

43. RE-485 and RE-360.

44. RE-1510. Frequent border crossers, whether Mexican nationals, Mexican Americans, or Anglo Americans, appear to have assisted the Russians. See RE-1242 and RE-360.

45. See, for example, RE-41, RE-298, RE-312, RE-380, and RE-479.

46. RE-302.

47. RE-177 and RE-439.

48. RE-662.

49. RE-47, RE-1130, RE-374, and RE-1361.

50. RE-298.

51. RE-233.

52. RE-1473 and RE-592.

53. RE-425.

54. RE-498. See also RE-1627 and RE-1628.

55. The charitable work U.S. citizens and organizations undertook created personal networks that led to a wide array of commercial, cultural, and intellectual exchanges between Americans and Soviets from the early 1920s to the early 1930s. Until the late 1930s, when Stalin adopted a series of anti-foreign policies and signed the German-Soviet Nonaggression Pact, these ties made possible some degree of openness and understanding between Americans and the Soviets. Jimmy Dwain Parks, "Culture, Conflict and Coexistence: American-Soviet Cultural Relations, 1917–1958" (PhD diss., University of Oklahoma, 1988), 6–22.

56. "Bill Permitting Russians Here to Stay Urged: Deporting 4,000 Royalists Would Mean Execution, Committee Told," *Washington Post*, March 23, 1934, 9; "Russian Exiles, Other Lands Barred, Told to Quit Baltimore," *Washington Post*, May 16, 1934, 15; Florence Finch Kelly, "Refugees from Russia's Revolution: *SANDRIK: Child of Russia*," *New York Times*, September 30, 1934, BR5; "Refugees from Russia Ask for Sanctuary Here," *Los Angeles Times*, October 22, 1934, A3; "Refugee of Noble Birth Here: Young Princess Retells Her Escape from Reds," *Los Angeles Times*, May 29, 1935, A3; Helen Yakobson, *Crossing Borders: From Revolutionary Russia to China to America* (Tenafly, NJ: Hermitage Publishers, 1994). See also RE-342, RE-348, RE-333, RE-405, and RE-424.

57. On the aversion to leftist political parties among the Russian refugees in the United States, see Hassell, "Russian Refugees in France and the United States between the World Wars," 37–38, 63–64.

58. Gary Gerstle, *American Crucible: Race and Nation in the Twentieth Century* (Princeton, NJ: Princeton University Press, 2001), 129–86.

59. Stanley Kutler, *American Inquisition: Justice and Injustice in the Cold War* (New York: Farrar, Straus & Giroux, 1984).

60. Department of State to American Embassy, Moscow, Telegram, July 27, 1934, RG 59, Box 140, 150.616/358SA; John Farr Simmons, Chief, Visa Division, State Department, to C. D. Beebe, August 27, 1934, RG 59, Box 140, 150.616/361; and D. W. MacCormack, Commissioner General, Immigration and Naturalization Service, to Secretary of State, August 1, 1934, RG 59, Box 140, 150.616/362. See also Pope-Obeda, "Expelling the Foreign-Born Menace," 49–51.

61. "U.S. to Ask Soviet to Take Back Reds: We Seek Pact to Permit the Expulsion of 'Undesirables' Now in This Country," *New York Times*, August 1, 1934, 4.

62. "U.S. to Ask Soviet to Take Back Reds," 4.

63. The case files undermine stereotypes that the Russians were members of the nobility and demonstrate that they hailed from a variety of social classes. No matter what their class standing was in Russia, however, most arrived in the United States with few material resources. On the class status of the Russian expatriate community, see Svetlana V. Onegina, "Postrevolutionary Political Movements in the Russian Expatriate Community in the 1920s and the 1930s (Toward a History of Ideology)," *Russian Studies History* 41, no. 1 (2002): 38–39.

64. James Grafton Rogers, Dean, School of Law, University of Colorado at Boulder, October 25, 1933, RG 59, Box 140, 150.616/343. On Russian advocacy organizations in the United States, see Hassell, "Russian Refugees in France and the United States," 36, 61.

65. Serge M. Iserguin, President, and Basil P. Antonenko, Executive Secretary, Russian National Organizations in California, to the President, March 31, 1933, RG 59, Box 140, 150.616/340. Formed in 1926 by members of the so-called Russian colony in San Francisco, the CCRNO functioned as an umbrella organization for at least twenty different Russian associations in the city. Its support was particularly critical to the non-Soviets in the community who lacked consular support. Antonina von Arnold, "Organization of the Russian Community in San Francisco," April 29, 1938, 9–14, Antonina R. von Arnold Papers, Box 12, Folder 13, Hoover Institution Library and Archives, Stanford University, Stanford, CA.

66. Abraham Hoffman, "Stimulus to Repatriation: The 1931 Federal Deportation Drive and the Los Angeles Mexican Community," *Pacific Historical Review* 42, no. 2 (1973): 204–19.

67. Balderrama and Rodríguez, *Decade of Betrayal*.

68. Ashley Johnson Bavery, *Bootlegged Aliens: Immigration Politics on America's Northern Border* (Philadelphia: University of Pennsylvania Press, 2020).

69. Ngai, *Impossible Subjects*; S. Deborah Kang, *The INS on the Line: Making Immigration Law on the US-Mexico Border* (New York: Oxford University Press, 2017).

70. Ngai, *Impossible Subjects*; Kang, *The INS on the Line*.

71. Ellis Island Committee, *Report of the Ellis Island Committee* (New York, 1934), 5, 98–99, https://hdl.handle.net/2027/uiug.30112056692970.

72. Yuki Oda, "Family Unity in U.S. Immigration Policy, 1921–1978" (PhD diss., Columbia University, 2014), 174.

73. Ellis Island Committee, *Report*, 97.

74. "Malum in se," *Black's Law Dictionary* (St. Paul, MN: West Publishing Co., 1990), 959.

75. Ellis Island Committee, *Report*, 92.

76. Ellis Island Committee, *Report*, 92.

77. Ellis Island Committee, *Report*, 97.

78. Ellis Island Committee, *Report*, 87–88.

79. Emphasis added. Ellis Island Committee, *Report*, 88.

80. An Act to Regulate the Immigration of Aliens to, and the Residence of Aliens in, the United States, Pub. L. 64–301, 39 Stat. 874 (1917). Undocumented Russians who applied for registry were governed by at least three different legal regimes with respect to deportation. If they entered after 1917 but before 1921, they were subject to deportation for three years after their entry. If they entered after 1921 but before 1924, their deportation was possible within five years of their entry. Upon the passage of the Immigration Act of 1924, undocumented Russians could be deported at any point after entry. By 1934, those undocumented Russians who had entered under the 1917 and 1921 legal regimes were most likely not subject to deportation, particularly if they could demonstrate continuous residence in the United States for three or five years. Yet, they still applied for registry under the 1934 law because their undocumented status prevented them from becoming naturalized citizens. Ellis Island Committee, *Report*, 96; "Russian Exiles, Other Lands Barred, Told to Quit Baltimore," *Washington Post*, May 16, 1934, 15.

81. Ellis Island Committee, *Report*, 97.

82. Ellis Island Committee, *Report*, 97.

83. By mid-1933, applications for registry fell far short of the initial projections; while Congress anticipated 1.3 million applicants, only 55,200 certificates of registry had been issued. Ellis Island Committee, *Report*, 92.

84. An Act to Supplement the Naturalization Laws, and for Other Purposes, Pub. L. 70–962, 45 Stat. 1512 (1929).

85. In both cases, individuals had to have entered the country before June 1921 and lived continuously in the United States since their entry. Over the course of the twentieth century, the entry deadline date was advanced to allow more undocumented immigrants to regularize their status. Elizabeth F. Cohen, *Illegal: How America's Lawless Immigration Regime Threatens Us All* (New York: Basic Books, 2020), 104, 122; Ellis Island Committee, *Report*, 92.

86. Since Mexican Americans were defined as white under law by 1929, they were not formally excluded from the registry procedure. Nevertheless, the 1929 act benefited Europeans to a greater extent than Mexican migrants because few were informed of their eligibility for the procedure. Ngai, *Impossible Subjects*, 82.

87. Ellis Island Committee, *Report*, 99.

88. Ellis Island Committee, *Report*, 96.

89. For a discussion of these bills, see S. Deborah Kang, "Sovereign Mercy: The Legalization of the White Russian Refugees and the Politics of Immigration Relief," *Journal of American Ethnic History* 43, no. 1 (Fall 2023): 18.

90. Forty-one bills were proposed during the seventy-fourth and seventy-fifth Congress. Natalia Molina, "Deportable Citizens: The Decoupling of Race and Citizenship in the Construction of the 'Anchor Baby,'" in *Deportation in the Americas: Histories of Exclusion and Resistance*, eds. Kenyon Zimmer and Cristina Salinas (College Station: Texas A & M University Press, 2018), loc. 3719 of 5514, Kindle.

91. Marinari, *Unwanted*, 93.

92. Robert T. DeVore, "Congress Asked to Revise Abusive Deportation Laws," *Washington Post*, May 13, 1934, B1.

93. Marinari, *Unwanted*, 90, 93.

94. Oda, "Family Unity," 67; Marinari, *Unwanted*, 83.

95. Samuel Dickstein, interview by Professor Allan Nevins and Dean Albertson, December 1949-June 1950, transcript, Columbia University Oral History Collection, Columbia University, New York, 19–21; Marinari, *Unwanted*, 83, 87. On the subsequent discovery of Dickstein's role as a Soviet spy, see Peter Duffy, "The Congressman Who Spied for Russia," *Politico Magazine*, October 6, 2014, https://www.politico.com/magazine/story/2014/10/samuel-dickstein-congressman-russian-spy-111641.

96. 78 Cong. Rec. 7286 (1934).

97. 78 Cong. Rec. 10434 (1934).

98. Dickstein specifically stated, "this bill does not do anything except to enable a number of Russian refugees who are in this country, to adjust their status under our immigration laws through registration under the act of March 2, 1929." 78 Cong. Rec. 10433 (1934).

99. 78 Cong. Rec. 10433 (1934).

100. 78 Cong. Rec. 10435 (1934).

101. 78 Cong. Rec. 10433 (1934).

102. 78 Cong. Rec. 10433 (1934).

103. 78 Cong. Rec. 10434 (1934).

104. 78 Cong. Rec. 10433 (1934).

105. On whiteness and Russian immigrants in the United States, see Susan L. Carruthers, "Between Camps: Eastern Bloc 'Escapees' and Cold War Borderlands," *American Quarterly 57* no. 3 (2005): 928.

106. Roger Daniels, *Guarding the Golden Door: American Immigration Policy and Immigrants since 1882* (New York: Hill and Wang, 2004), 71.

107. Oda, "Family Unity, 119; Gerstle, *American Crucible,* 120.

108. Gerstle, *American Crucible,* 120–21.

109. For Jenkins's restrictionist views, see "Immigration Cut Favored: House Votes to Cut Immigration Ninety Per Cent for Two Years," *Marysville Journal-Tribune* (Marysville, Ohio), March 2, 1931, 1; "Plug Holes in Immigration Laws: Congressman Advises Reunion Association—Too Many Foreigners Come In, Jenkins Says," *Cincinnati Enquirer,* November 17, 1933, 12; "Immigration Plank Sought by Jenkins," *Akron Beacon Journal,* June 9, 1936, 8; "Urges Limit on Mexican Aliens," *Evening Independent* (Massillon, Ohio), June 11, 1930; "Philippines Freedom Legislation Sure to Pass Senate," *Honolulu Advertiser,* April 5, 1932, 8.

110. "To Urge Enforcement: To Drive to Restrict Immigration at Junior Order Meeting Today—Aliens to be Discussed," *Cincinnati Enquirer,* August 30, 1939, 24.

111. 78 Cong. Rec. 10437 (1934).

112. See, for example, Carl J. Bon Tempo, *Americans at the Gate: The United States and Refugees during the Cold War* (Princeton, NJ: Princeton University Press, 2008); Gil Loescher and John A. Scanlan, *Calculated Kindness: Refugees and America's Half-Open Door, 1945-Present* (New York: Free Press, 1986).

113. Eric S. Fish, "Race, History and Immigration Crimes," *Iowa Law Review* 107, no. 3 (2022): 1051–106.

114. 78 Cong. Rec. 10437 (1934).

115. Blanton declared: "We saw a bunch of them [communists] right here in this Capitol last Saturday, when 20 or 25 colored students from Howard University marched on this Capitol in a body insisting on violating the rules and regulations." 78 Cong. Rec. 4939–40 (1934); Elliott W. Rudwick, "Oscar DePriest and the Jim Crow Restaurant in the U.S. House of Representatives," *The Journal of Negro Education* 35, no. 1 (1966): 77–82; "Blanton Wants President of Howard Dismissed with 30 Students," *New York Age,* March 31, 1934, 1.

116. On the racialization of communists and their sympathizers in the 1930s, see Gerstle, *American Crucible,* 162–63.

117. Act of June 8, 1934, § (b).

118. 78 Cong. Rec. 7286 (1934).

119. 78 Cong. Rec. 10436 (1934).

120. 78 Cong. Rec. 10436 (1934).

121. Erika Lee, *At America's Gates: Chinese Immigration during the Exclusion Era, 1882-1943* (Chapel Hill: University of North Carolina Press, 2003).

122. RE-865.

123. RE-1159, RE-1212, RE-1515, and RE-1020.

124. Laurie Manchester, "How Statelessness Can Force Refugees to Redefine Their Ethnicity: What Can Be Learned from Russian Émigrés Dispersed to Six Continents in the Inter-War Period?" *Immigrants & Minorities* 34, no. 1 (2016): 70–91; Laurie Manchester, "Colonial Impulses among First-Wave Russian Émigrés in Africa, China and South America" (Seattle: NCEEES Working Paper, 2013).

125. RE-926, RE-927, and RE-953.

126. Byron H. Uhl, Assistant Commissioner of Immigration, Ellis Island, to Commissioner General, February 16, 1931, file 55598/496B, RG 85. P. A. Baker, Acting Commissioner of Immigration, New York District to Commissioner General, February 26, 1931, file 55598/496B, RG 85.

127. See, for example, RE-26 and RE-311.

128. RE-509.

129. See, for example, RE-112, RE-114, RE-811, RE-365, RE-366, RE-1079, and RE-1714.

130. A handful of applicants drew attention to their refugee status by declaring that they were citizens of the world or citizens of no country. See RE-24, RE-137, RE-194, and RE-253.

131. See, for example, RE-20, RE-29, RE-31, RE-123, RE-298, RE-345, RE-391, and RE-427.

132. RE-263.

133. RE-253.

134. RE-123.

135. See for example, RE-29, RE-23, RE-105, RE-127, RE-161, RE-177, RE-181, RE-182, RE-191, RE-253, RE-298, RE-302, RE-201, RE-387, RE-425, RE-429, RE-439, RE-463, and RE-471.

136. RE-970. Borisoff used at least two aliases: Sarkis der Kevorkian and Serge Jean de La Scase.

137. RE-280.

138. RE-112 and RE-114.

139. Breitman and Kraut, *American Refugee Policy*, 225.

140. Breitman and Kraut, *American Refugee Policy*, 223–24.

2 Privileges of Illegality?

*Italian Seaman Deserters and Adjustment
of Status in the Twentieth Century*

DANIELLE BATTISTI

In March 1941 Umberto B., an Italian citizen and crew member of an Italian commercial vessel, the SS *Colorado,* began a perhaps strange but not altogether anomalous journey on a path toward a new life in the United States.[1] World War II was well underway and although the United States had not yet entered the war, there were strong signs that the Roosevelt administration was preparing for the possibility that the United States would soon enter the conflict. One such indication came that year when the Department of Justice issued arrest warrants for 100 German and 775 Italian seamen serving on twenty-eight hostile vessels known to be in American waters. Under the 1917 Espionage Act, the government was authorized to arrest suspected saboteurs in the interests of national security. Acting under that authority, the U.S. Coast Guard set out to seize dozens of foreign vessels and took hundreds of alien soldiers into protective custody. As the Coast Guard closed in on the crew of the *Colorado* sailing off the coast of San Juan, Puerto Rico, in March 1941, Umberto and dozens of other seamen onboard decided to sabotage their own ship. Whether they were acting on orders or of their own volition is not clear, but they ultimately decided it was their duty to keep the U.S. government from seizing a vessel that could then presumably be used against Italian interests.[2]

Federal officials, of course, took a dim view of such actions. They charged Umberto and hundreds of other Italian seamen who perpetrated similar acts on the *Colorado* and other ships with "conspiracy to tamper, and attempt to tamper, with the motive power of vessel while it was in the jurisdiction of the United States and with the intent to injure and endanger the safety of the vessel."[3] Umberto and his fellow sailors were quickly convicted and sentenced to serve up to three years in a federal prison in Danbury, Connecticut. During the course of Umberto's imprisonment, Japan's attack on Pearl Harbor prompted the country's declaration of war on Japan, which in turn pulled the United States into conflict with Germany and Italy. Following American entry into the war and the passage of corresponding national security measures at home, Umberto was reclassified by the U.S. government as an enemy alien with naval experience living in the United States, and he was transferred from prison to an internment camp at Fort Missoula, Montana, where he remained until he was ordered deported after the war ended in 1945.

Umberto's imprisonment, internment, and deportation order did not detract from his desire to remain in the United States, however. Umberto violated his deportation order in 1945 and remained in the country without authorization, ultimately making his way to New York City, where he met and married an American citizen in March 1947. Once married, Umberto applied to Immigration and Naturalization Service to adjust his status, but the petition was denied on the basis that his criminal record demonstrated evidence of "moral turpitude," and he was again instructed to leave the country. Rather than appeal the decision, probably because his marriage quickly fell apart, Umberto again chose to violate his deportation order and remain in the country without authorization for months. However, sometime between 1947 and 1949, Umberto returned to Italy. He didn't stay long, though. Umberto quickly sought and secured work on a commercial shipping vessel only to once again reenter the United States and desert his ship at Newport News, Virginia, in 1949. Umberto was then found out and arrested by the INS the following year. This time he fought the deportation order and while released on bond and awaiting appeal, Umberto married for a second time, again to an American citizen in New York City.[4]

Umberto hardly cut the figure of an ideal immigrant. He had arguably shown his dedication to a fascist regime and demonstrated "moral turpitude" by sabotaging the *Colorado* when it was about to be seized by the United States.[5] He had violated U.S. immigration laws when he repeatedly overstayed in the country on non-immigrant visas and failed to comply with court-ordered deportations. Finally, Umberto's two quick marriages suggested strategic unions rather than love matches. Committing only one of those acts was enough to warrant removal or deportation as far as the state was concerned. But after two years and a series of hearings, immigration courts were increasingly tolerant of Umberto's appeals because of his growing family responsibilities. In his 1954 appeal, Umberto's legal representative focused his argument on the "economic detriment" Umberto's wife would suffer if he was deported. When the couple had their first child the following year, the defendant's case was strengthened further. The Board of Immigration Appeals ultimately suspended Umberto's deportation order in 1956 and granted him permission for "voluntary departure" from the country and "pre-examination" for a legal reentry. By exercising those privileges, Umberto was able to adjust his status to that of legal permanent resident and was put on a path toward acquiring citizenship.[6]

Although the contours of Umberto's story probably aren't the first that come to mind when picturing Italian immigration to the United States, they also weren't as atypical as they might appear at first glance. This chapter explores the scope and nature of unauthorized Italian immigration to the United States from 1924 to 1965 with a special focus on the postwar period.[7] It will show how the state—via laws passed by Congress, practices of government agencies, and decisions made in immigration courts—generally permitted the legalization of unauthorized Italian migrants, especially seamen deserters like Umberto, through obscure but enormously consequential legal practices. The most important and least understood route for the legalization of those migrants was through pre-examination and voluntary departure procedures in the mid-twentieth century. Understanding the process of pairing pre-examination and voluntary departure helps contribute to the literature on American immigration law, which most commonly cites voluntary departure as one of the exclusionary and punitive measures in the state's toolbox to remove "undesirable" or irregular migrants. It is rarely cited as a privilege and route to inclusion, as it was for most of the unauthorized Italians in this study.[8] It is also important to acknowledge that "loopholes," including the wielding of pre-examination and voluntary departure practices, overwhelmingly benefitted white migrants by design. Although it was never a straight or guaranteed path, the state put mechanisms in place to adjust, accommodate, and ultimately absolve many unauthorized European migrants of their marginalized status at the very same time that the state was actively targeting unauthorized migrants from Latin America and elsewhere for removal.

Italian seamen deserters were largely able to normalize their status because state actions in this period tended to recognize the familial and community ties established during the immigrant's residency in the United States as elements that bound newcomers to the nation. According to legal scholar Hiroshi Motomura, conceptualizing of immigration as a process of "affiliation" increasingly became the basis for immigrant (lawful or unlawful) integration into the nation throughout the twentieth century.[9] Immigration laws that had long prioritized concepts of family reunification, and that became a pillar of U.S. immigration policy from 1924 through the late twentieth century, reflected such thinking.[10] However, the legitimacy of an immigrant's affiliation with the United States continued to be highly circumscribed by racialized and gendered constructions of citizenship. The result was, irregular Italian immigrants in the postwar period were overwhelmingly accepted by both the state and the public as members of American society on a path toward future citizenship, at a time when domestic minorities and other marginalized newcomers to American society were not accorded the same understanding. Enduring constructions of American citizenship that idealized white heteronormative families, with men understood to be the economic and social head of household, played a major role in determining the fate of the men, and their families, examined in this study. Italian immigrants, and their lawyers, were thus able to use ideas about the nature of economic productivity in the United States, religious and cultural beliefs reinforcing family unity as an unquestioned positive good, and their racial presentation as white to successfully prevent their removal from the country at various stages on their path toward legalization.[11]

To make these arguments, I draw upon government documents and the case records of about 600 Italian immigrants who received pro bono legal aid from the Italian Welfare League (IWL), an immigrant aid organization operating in New York City.[12] There is only so much information that scholars can derive from aggregate statistics on unauthorized migrants collected by the Immigration and Naturalization Service (INS) and other government agencies. I therefore sampled data from the IWL's legal records from 1950 to 1960 to better understand processes of immigration and naturalization for unauthorized migrants in the postwar period. Most of the IWL's pro bono cases in the 1950s involved irregular migrants, thus demonstrating the ubiquity of unauthorized migration in the greater New York City area among working-class migrants who could not afford private legal services. Although it would be misleading to make the case that this sample is representative of *all* irregular Italian immigration cases in the period, it does provide rich statistical and contextual information that is not accessible in annual INS reports alone, or other government documents, and is therefore worthy of analysis.

An examination of unauthorized Italian immigration to the United States in the 1950s is significant for several reasons. National origins quotas were in place to stem the tide of southern and eastern European migration to the United States from 1924 to 1965. Those quota restrictions went far in reducing Italian immigration (through both legal and irregular channels) in the 1930s and 1940s. But it was also external events, including the onset of the Great Depression, Mussolini's restrictions on emigration and his regime's rerouting of migrants to colonial possessions, and the outbreak of World War II that limited international migration. However, those forces gave way in the postwar period and Italian emigrants not only sought entry to the United States and other receiving nations in large numbers once again, but also, they were actively supported by their government in their quest to do so.[13] Emigration pressures were so great in postwar Italy that tens of thousands of Italians migrated without authorization to numerous receiving states in both Europe and the Americas in the postwar years.[14] Therefore, the decade from 1950 to 1960 provides us with a window in which to examine unauthorized Italian immigration to the United States in an era of immigration restriction yet continued demand and feasibility for immigration on the part of Italian migrants.

Making and Unmaking the "Illegal" European Immigrant

In the late nineteenth-century United States, the federal government asserted its control over the process of restricting immigration to the United States. Before the Civil War, both the federal government and the individual states simultaneously, and often inharmoniously, regulated foreigners, newcomers, and other denizens' migration rights and status as citizens.[15] However, that system of dual governance largely came to an end when the Civil War and Reconstruction-era constitutional amendments regarding citizenship signaled the primacy of the federal government over the states to regulate the boundaries of citizenship. Therefore, in the late nineteenth century, several federal immigration laws, rulings by the Supreme Court asserting the state's right to defend its sovereign borders, and the establishment of federal regulatory institutions asserted the primacy of federal control over immigration and citizenship laws in the United States.[16]

Certain migrants became illegal as increasingly restrictionist legislation was put in place to govern immigration and citizenship in the United States. By the turn of the century, a host of federal laws banning particular classes of foreigners from immigrating and ultimately naturalizing had taken root in American life and law. Correspondingly, the concepts of both *legal immigrant* and *illegal alien* also came into being.[17] For much of the nineteenth century, racial minorities, political radicals, impoverished women, and people with physical or mental defects bore the brunt of restrictionist impulses.[18] However, conservatives anxious about domestic social change, as well as national security concerns in the wake of World War I and the Bolshevik Revolution, stoked nativist impulses and dramatically expanded the scope of restrictionist legislation in the early twentieth century. The crowning achievement of resurgent nativist forces was the passage of the Johnson-Reed Act in 1924. That comprehensive immigration law reaffirmed bans already in place on Asian immigration and completely barred Asian naturalization. It set annual caps on immigration totals and systematized selection for immigrants on the basis of racial desirability by establishing national origins quotas that heavily favored European immigration—especially immigration from northwestern European nations. Although the establishment of the quota system indeed ushered in a sea change in the governance of American immigration, it hardly departed from past precedent in many respects. The new law expanded and more sharply systematized long-established practices—especially those for racial and ethnic selection of migrants. It did, however, codify for the first time exclusionary sentiments that had been growing toward southern and eastern European peoples—who were now targets of restriction, if not outright exclusion like non-white immigrants.[19] But as Mae Ngai aptly points out, the national origins system drew dividing lines "around," rather than "through," Europe in delineating southern and eastern Europeans as still white enough to immigrate, naturalize, and claim citizenship rights—albeit in more limited numbers.[20]

Those privileges of whiteness that arguably existed in even the restrictionary elements of the national origins system were also reflected in the ways that the state responded to southern and eastern European immigrants who subsequently began to enter into the country in an unauthorized manner after 1924. As we know from Ashley Johnson Bavery's work, Italian and other southern and eastern European migrants who were determined to make it to the United States quickly found multiple ways to circumvent quota restrictions.[21] In this way, they pursued migration strategies that were not unlike those of other immigrant groups who were barred before them. What was different in the 1920s and 1930s, however, was the remarkable speed with which Congress acted to provide relief for unauthorized European immigrants. In 1929, Congress passed the Registry Act. Among other things, the law allowed "honest law-abiding alien[s] who may be in the country under some merely technical irregularity" to adjust their legal status by permitting those who fell under its remit to register with the INS. For a fee of twenty dollars, demonstration of one's "good moral character," and proof of continuous residency in the United States since 1921, the applicant could then obtain legal permanent residency.[22]

There was, in fact, nothing written into the law to favor European immigrants; nor was any single national group explicitly mentioned in the bill. However, Asian immigrants were ineligible to register by virtue of their exclusionary status, and although most Mexicans were eligible to adjust their status, few knew about the law, understood it, or could afford the fee.[23] That was not the case in eastern seaboard and midwestern cities where southern and eastern European associational life and kinship-based networks facilitated the spread of information about the law, where immigrants and their kin had economic resources to take advantage of the policy, and where ethnic groups exercised the political influence to make laws like the Registry Act a practical reality in the first place.[24] It is also notable that Congress had never before taken any comparable measures to normalize the status of other groups that pursued irregular migration strategies before European migrants were widely affected by the new restrictionary legislation of 1924. The result was a policy that clearly intended to, and did, provide relief to European migrants. According to Ngai, of the 115,000 immigrants who registered with the INS between 1930 and 1940 to take advantage of the normalizing provision, 80 percent were European or Canadian (the latter of whom were overwhelmingly recent European arrivals seeking a back door into the United States).

The Roosevelt administration followed up the 1929 legislation with even further action. The Roosevelt coalition was much beholden to southern and eastern

European immigrants and their children, who formed formidable voting blocs in several areas of the country, and who had become particularly influential in urban political machine politics by the 1930s.[25] The illegal status borne by tens of thousands of individuals in their communities became an important political issue to many of those ethnic groups, which began to lobby for even more relief opportunities for their unauthorized kin. But legislative efforts were blocked by southern conservatives in the Democratic Party that had not only come to oppose relief for European migrants but also increasingly called for the addition of Mexico and other countries of the Western hemisphere to be added to the national origins system of quotas.[26]

Facing such opposition, the Roosevelt administration maintained the political favor of white ethnic groups through more creative means. It employed administrative discretion in the INS to construct policy changes that offered relief to European migrants. In 1935, the Secretary of Labor created a two-step administrative process that paired the practices of voluntary departure and pre-examination to adjust the status of unauthorized immigrants.[27] It drew upon a previously inconsequential provision of the Immigration Act of 1917 that allowed the U.S. Attorney General to grant an illegal alien a waiver of deportation—originally intended only for aliens who entered under some technical irregularity.[28] It also expanded a courtesy practice in place since 1933 where the INS granted *legal* aliens leave and reentry permission to go on short visits to Canada if they were first examined and found admissible by immigration inspectors.[29] The INS borrowed from both procedures and essentially created the practice of pre-examination and voluntary departure whereby an *illegal* alien who was in the United States and found otherwise admissible for entry could be "pre-examined" by the INS for legal admission, voluntarily leave the country, proceed to the nearest American consulate, obtain a new visa for permanent residence from officials there, and reenter the United States as a legal immigrant.[30] This procedure manufactured a legal entry into the country for its beneficiaries.

Once again, those beneficiaries were almost exclusively of European origin, and the measure was created with sympathy toward politically influential white immigrant constituencies in mind. Asian immigrants were not admissible as citizens under the national origins system and were therefore totally excluded from the program. Mexicans were not formally excluded from taking part in this practice, and some tried to do so in the late 1930s, but American consulate officials in Juarez stalled in processing cases until the INS rewrote the rules in 1940 to limit pre-examination cases to be processed only in Canadian consulates. Exceptions on the southern border were made for European immigrants, however—even ostensibly undesirable ones. German engineers, who were loyal members of the Nazi party at the time of their arrest, were brought to Alabama as prisoners of war to work on aeronautic projects for the U.S. military during

World War II. Those enemy aliens, officially in the country without immigrant visas, were allowed to adjust their status and become legal immigrants by a process of expedited security checks and through using pre-examination and voluntary departure proceedings via U.S. consulates in Mexico in a special agreement between the war, state, and justice departments in what became known as "Operation Paperclip" in 1946.[31] Finally, the Eurocentric intent of the program was affirmed in 1945 when the INS banned citizens of Canada, Mexico, and "islands adjacent to the United States" from taking advantage of pre-examination provisions.[32]

Other aspects of the state's immigration regime also provided additional means of relief. The Alien Registration Act of 1940, enacted as a matter of national security to enable the federal government to identify, surveil, and potentially arrest and deport enemy aliens living in the United States during World War II, once again affirmed the U.S. Attorney General's discretion to suspend the deportation of "aliens of good moral character if deportation would result in serious economic detriment to the alien's immediate family."[33] It was within this legislative, juridical, and cultural framework that unauthorized Italian immigrants carved out an inclusionary position for themselves, and their co-ethnics, within American society after World War II. If all else failed, unauthorized migrants and their families could, and did, appeal to their congressional representatives for private relief bills.[34]

Irregular Italian Migrants in New York City, 1950–1960

With thriving ethnic enclaves on the Lower East Side of Manhattan, East Harlem, and neighborhoods in Brooklyn, Queens, and farther afield, Italian Americans composed one of the largest and most visible ethnic groups in New York City at mid-century. Adding to pre–World War II Italian immigrants and their descendants were as many as 150,000 Italians who immigrated and settled in the greater New York City area from 1945 to 1973.[35] Thousands of those postwar newcomers were unauthorized migrants. Many of their experiences have been preserved in the records of the Italian Welfare League.

The IWL is an immigrant aid and social welfare organization that began operating in New York City in 1920 "to promote the interests of, and (to) look after the needy Italians in New York."[36] It was led by a handful of Italian American women who were active with the American Red Cross, other war relief organizations, and veterans organizations focused on humanitarian relief during World War I.[37] The organization was most active from 1920 through the mid-1970s in providing various services to Italian immigrants, including offering logistical support in the immigration and resettlement process, supplying material assistance to immigrant families, and tendering legal aid to newcomers. From the sample decade 1950 to 1960, the IWL granted pro bono legal representation to roughly 600 Italian immigrants and their families. Because the IWL provided free legal assistance, and because of the occupational histories and financial disclosures found in archival case records, it is reasonable to conclude that the IWL overwhelmingly represented working-class individuals and families. About 80 percent of the cases in the sample dealt with individuals who were at one point classified by the state as illegal immigrants.[38]

Italians could enter the United States through several irregular modes, including stowing away on a vessel and overstaying a visitor, student, or temporary work visa.[39] However, the vast majority of unauthorized Italian immigrants represented by the IWL came to the United States as "seamen deserters."[40] Commercial seamen entered the country legally on D-1 visas. This visa granted a non-immigrant crew member of a marine vessel or aircraft who will depart on

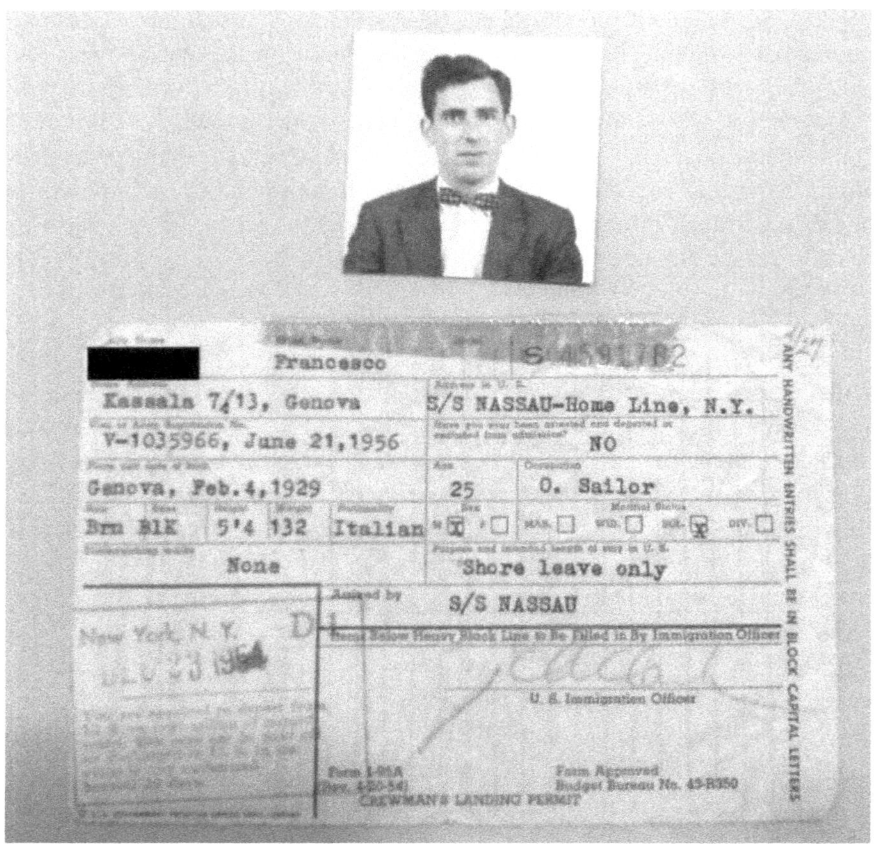

Figure 2.1. An IWL case file for an Italian migrant who entered the United States as a commercial seaman and overstayed his D-1 visa. Center for Migration Studies of New York; Italian Welfare League, Collection 003, Box 134, Folder Francesco A.

the same vessel on which they arrived within twenty-nine days permission for a temporary stay in the United States. But deserters never left. They chose to overstay their visa and remain in the United States after their designated date of departure. Typically, deserters abandoned their vessels at American ports to seek alternative employment, meet up with family already in the United States, and/or build new relationships within and outside of already established ethnic communities where they largely resettled.

Several thousand seamen deserted their vessels and stayed in the United States without permission from the state each year. The practice began shortly after the passage of the Johnson-Reed Act in 1924 and had become a tried-and-true route for Italians and other southeastern European migrants to circumvent the national origins system by the 1950s.[41] In 1936, former Commissioner of Immigration Edward Corsi estimated that at least 400,000 unauthorized aliens had gained entry to the country by "jumping ship." Yet, despite the ubiquity of the practice, and ship jumpers' intentional violation of the law, Corsi expressed public sympathy for the group as a whole and advocated for relief on their behalf. Drawing a distinction between seamen deserters and "those who had criminal tendencies," Corsi argued it would be a waste of the state's fiscal resources to deport them and to break up the many families they had established with American-born citizens.[42]

Of course, restrictionists were less sympathetic to the practice, and they periodically shined a public spotlight on seamen deserters. Throughout the 1950s, the INS regularly highlighted desertion rates and the agency's efforts to police desertion in their annual reports.[43] The INS conducted a series of high-profile raids on immigrant enclaves in New York and New Jersey in the summer of 1951, resulting in the arrest of 1,350 seamen deserters.[44] However, flashy arrests didn't necessarily result in deportations or other modes of expulsion. They did help to generate support for increasing restrictions on commercial seamen when Congress passed the McCarran-Walter Act the following year. The omnibus legislation, which was primarily meant to reform and update the national origins system, also placed new penalties and fines on seamen deserters, or people who facilitated desertion. It also denied crewmen who were ineligible for an immigration visa the right to disembark from docked vessels.[45] However, INS statistics suggest the new rule was not effectively enforced and failed to significantly affect desertion rates—particularly for Italian nationals. Italy was regularly identified by the INS as one of the top sending states for seaman deserters during the 1950s.

Despite the government's awareness and targeting of seamen deserters, both INS records and the IWL's caseload for the 1950s show that, on the whole, Italian deserters rarely faced significant reprisals for their actions. On the contrary, the IWL records paint a picture of a cohort of unauthorized migrants that did not face extreme economic hardship resulting from their arrests for immigration violations, social stigmatization for their actions from members of their

Table 2.1. Alien Crewmen Total Arrivals and Desertions, 1950–1960

	Total Alien Crewmen Arrived by Sea	Number of Deserting Alien Crewmen
1950	530,209	2,410
1951	532,463	3,591
1952	635,902	3,021
1953	565,056	2,317
1954	603,264	1,963
1955	671,563	NA
1956	1,533,249*	2,968
1957	1,688,749*	2,880
1958	1,673,475*	2,622
1959	1,692,893*	2,225

*Air and sea vessels. After 1955, INS reports no longer distinguished between the two.
Source: U.S. Immigration and Naturalization Services, Annual Report, Washington, DC: U.S. Department of State, 1950–1960.

Table 2.2. Top Sending States for Seamen Deserters (with total numbers), 1950–1960

	1st	2nd	3rd
1950	NA	NA	NA
1951	**Italy (705)**	British Empire (361)	Spain (274)
1952	**Italy (468)**	Norway (308)	Greece (207)
1953	British Empire (310)	**Italy (275)**	China (186)
1954	**Italy (295)**	Spain (233)	British Empire (209)
1955	Greece (491)	British Empire (474)	**Italy (286)**
1956	Greece (837)	**Italy (448)**	British Empire (313)
1957	Greece (924)	**Italy (454)**	British Empire (251)
1958	Greece (871)	**Italy (349)**	British Empire (244)
1959	Greece (747)	British Empire (275)	**Italy (261)**

Source: U.S. Immigration and Naturalization Services, Annual Report, Washington, DC: U.S. Department of State, 1950–1960.
Note: Scholarship suggests that most seamen deserters from the British Empire were ethnic Chinese migrants embarking from Hong Kong (See Lee, "Hunting for Sailors, 107–22).

communities, or negative legal outcomes in their quest to remain in the United States and ultimately obtain citizenship. In fact, an overwhelming majority of Italian deserters were allowed to stay in the United States, legalize their status, eventually seek citizenship, and therefore achieve a level of political and social inclusion denied to other unauthorized migrant groups at the time.[46]

The typical profile of an Italian seaman who overstayed his visa and was represented by the IWL in the 1950s is that of a man in his twenties who hailed from southern Italy, or a northern province heavily reliant on maritime commerce (i.e., Liguria or Veneto). He deserted his vessel in New York City, Baltimore, Norfolk, or another eastern seaboard city to ultimately settle in a predominantly Italian American neighborhood in Brooklyn, the Bronx, or elsewhere in or near New York City.[47] He was working class and typically found employment as a longshoreman, in service sectors of the economy, or in a skilled-trade industry. Men who became chefs, bakers, waiters, contractors, masons, garment workers, and industrial laborers were also well represented among the ranks of those who ultimately came to the IWL for aid.[48]

At some point while those men lived, worked, and established social and familial networks in their neighborhoods, they came to the attention of immigration authorities and faced arrest for their immigration violations. Those arrests sometimes happened as the result of INS raids on workplaces, or when a migrant came in contact with the state for other reasons. Very rarely do IWL records indicate that arrests resulted from community tips to the INS.[49] Although most of these men lived in legal shadows until their arrest, it was also not uncommon for former seamen to voluntarily come forward and self-report to the IWL so that they might proactively register their status as an alien in the country and seek an adjustment to their legal standing in the United States with the INS.[50] The passage of the Alien Registry Act in 1940 surely entered into their calculations. Failure to register was sometimes cited by the INS and the courts as evidence of "moral turpitude" and intent to violate the laws and rule of the United States in deportation cases. Yet, the very act of coming forward to a legal authority and self-reporting is telling. It indicates the existence of ethnic networks circulating knowledge not only of the nation's immigration policies, but also of the overwhelmingly positive outcomes for other unauthorized Italian migrants who had already been allowed to normalize their status. We do not see similar rates of self-reporting in ethnic communities where deportation was the normative outcome in the same period.

Of the hundreds of Italian deserters who sought IWL assistance, the vast majority were allowed to stay in the United States and become legal permanent residents on a path toward citizenship. Although almost all seamen deserters in the IWL sample were initially issued pro-forma orders of deportation when they were arrested, those orders were systematically appealed before the Board of Immigration Appeals (BIA), an independent body within the Justice Department with the authority to review and adjudicate immigration cases. Most deserters represented by an IWL attorney who appealed their deportations achieved a suspension of deportation from the U.S. Attorney General's office or a normalization of their status through the pairing of voluntary departure privileges and pre-examination grants from the BIA.[51] An individual could apply for pre-examination if "he believes that he will be admissible to the United States under all the provisions of the immigration laws," and that "he is a person of good moral character."[52] By granting the appellant the privileges of voluntary departure and pre-examination, the BIA all but guaranteed the migrant's re-entry as a legal permanent immigrant.

When voluntary departure and pre-examination privileges were granted, migrants typically had a six-week window to make their way to Canada. It was relatively easy for most Italian men to secure one or multiple extensions to that timeline if life circumstances got in the way, though. In practice, the men in the IWL sample often had months at their leisure to act. Most migrants in the sample made the trip due north from New York City to the small border town of Rouses Point, New York, where they disembarked from their train to cross the border and head to the U.S. consulate in Montreal (Quebec). Crossing at Vanceboro, Maine, and heading to the consulate at St. John's Bay (New Brunswick) was another popular route for Italian migrants on the eastern seaboard.[53]

Migrants left the United States as unauthorized migrants but legalized their status in Canada, where their documents were examined by consular officials and they were authorized legal reentry to the country on an official immigration visa. Since the migrants in question had already been pre-examined as "admissible for entry" via their BIA hearings, applicants only needed to secure a clean bill of health from the U.S. Public Health Service before leaving the country to add to their dossier. Those who did so were given a sealed letter by the INS addressed to the Canadian immigration officer at the checkpoint through which the migrant entered Canada. The purpose of the document was to guarantee "the purpose of the applicant's visit to Canada and guarantee that if admitted to Canada he will be readmitted to the United States" on parole.[54] Once in Canada, the pre-examination process continued at an American consulate, where a consular agent once again determined that the individual could be granted an immigration visa (usually by virtue of his status as the spouse of a citizen or legal permanent resident). Once that process was complete, the migrant then crossed back into the United States as a legal permanent resident. Almost all the IWL's clients were in and out of Canada within a day, suggesting there was, in fact, very little scrutiny placed on pre-examination applications by consular agents.[55] If the BIA had authorized a voluntary departure and pre-examination order, then going through the actual motions of physical exit and reentry were largely acts of legal theater.

The legalization of Italian immigrants via reentry through the country's northern border in the 1950s took place on well-trodden ground. Historian Kornel Chang points out that the development of informal and formal agreements on the policing of the U.S.-Canadian border in the late nineteenth and early twentieth centuries primarily focused on policing and restricting the movement of Asian migrants. While there was increased bilateral policing of Asian migration by both nations, Chang argues, "U.S. and Canadian officials . . . treated the cross-border flow of white Americans, Canadians, and European immigrants mostly with benign neglect and in some cases outright support." The result of that "served to distance ethnic Europeans from the so-called status or category of 'illegal aliens,' facilitating their national and racial assimilation as 'white' Americans and Canadians."[56] Even at the high point of nativist sentiments toward southern and eastern European immigrants in the interwar period, attempts to ramp up policing of the northern border to prevent unauthorized entries and smuggling of trade goods by those migrant groups never quite altered the porous nature of the border for European migrants, nor its cultural significance as a gateway to the United States.[57]

Acts of discretionary relief, including pre-examination and voluntary departure, largely depended on the applicant's status as a husband, father, and breadwinner for his citizen wife and children. In IWL records, if a seaman deserter had managed to marry an American citizen and produce at least one American-born child with her before he was arrested and ordered deported, 97.5 percent of the time, he was allowed to normalize his status. In cases where the former seaman was married to a U.S. citizen but there were no children, he was still granted an adjustment of status in 87 percent of cases. However, only about a third of all seamen deserters represented by the IWL were married to American citizens *before* their initial arrest by immigration authorities.[58] Most of the IWL cases show that single men who had deserted hastily married and started a family when they were free on bond *after* their initial immigration-related arrest. Because they were not detained while awaiting state action on their immigration status, the men in the sample commonly went to their local courthouse in the days and weeks after their arrests to get married to U.S. citizens. A small percentage of IWL records show couples subsequently taking part in a second ceremony at their local church after their city hall wedding, to further demonstrate the legitimacy of the match as a reflection of romantic love and sacramental devotion. That was not the case in most IWL records, though.[59] In some instances, marriages occurred years into a migrant's legal proceedings, even as some defendants chose to violate the court's voluntary departure or deportation orders multiple times, continuing to flout the state's legal authority before establishing family ties with an American citizen. Because the state afforded these men a degree of freedom following their apprehension, a privilege that was increasingly being denied to unauthorized Mexican immigrants who were apprehended by the INS in both urban centers and more rural locales in this period, about 84 percent of all seamen deserters in the sample ultimately married by the time their immigration cases had closed.[60] Ninety-five percent of those once single, eventually married, men were ultimately able to normalize their status.[61]

Thus, the overwhelming majority of Italian deserters who were arrested by the INS, taken to immigration courts, and represented by the IWL were not ordered deported but were instead allowed to adjust their status to permanent resident alien. The highest rates of deportation for Italian seamen involved single men who were arrested within just a few weeks or sometimes months of their desertion and had not yet set down roots in the United States. However, only thirty-three of the seamen deserters in the IWL sample remained unmarried for the duration of their trials. Of those thirty-three men, one-third were middle-aged bachelors who had been in the country since the 1920s or 1930s and were only recently arrested. Those financially solvent individuals "of good moral standing" who had resided continuously in the United States for seven years or more were also allowed to adjust their status. Because the state recognized the social and economic ties that bound even single white men to the country, they were permitted discretionary relief.[62]

Even so, the determining factor for granting relief to Italian sailors generally hinged on the establishment of familial ties and the gendered economic responsibilities that came with them. If a former sailor had married, and better yet, fathered at least one child before the date of his immigration proceedings, it was almost a matter of course that discretionary relief would be granted—and granted swiftly. Most IWL cases concluded within a twelve-month time span. A positive outcome was almost always assured, even for those men who hastily got married and established families after the INS arrested them.

One is also struck by the permissive or even positive attitudes that state agents and the general public held regarding those behaviors. Rather than charge deserters with fathering "anchor babies," to use a contemporary term with negative connotations that is applied to migrant families with mixed legal standing in the United States, IWL records and BIA transcripts reveal the state's widespread concern for maintaining the family as an economic and social unit.[63] The white male heads of household represented in the IWL sample needed to make only a cursory argument that their removal would cause "undue economic hardship" to their wife (usually American citizens either by birth or naturalization) and/or children to successfully avoid deportation. The success of this tactic reflected a racialized understanding within the American mainstream of white family unity as a fundamental human right, and underlying concerns for the social and economic welfare of white women and children.[64]

Scholarship on South Asian and Chinese seamen reveals markedly different outcomes in this period. The state came down hard on those groups, curtailing Chinese sailors' rights to disembark while at port, imposing greater surveillance on those who did disembark, and targeting enforcement against overstayers. Moreover, exclusion, detention, and ultimately expulsion became the norm for Asian sailors despite American desires to court better relations with China, and notwithstanding the fact that many South Asian seamen lived for decades in the United States, married American citizens, and fathered American children by the time of their arrests and deportations.[65]

In fact, when we think of enforcement against illegal immigration in this period, the most notorious episode to come to mind has to be Operation Wetback in 1954, in which the INS proactively sought to raid farms and other sites of employment for hundreds of thousands of unauthorized Mexican migrants. Those actions resulted in the INS actively incarcerating Mexican migrants en masse in immigrant detention centers in Texas and elsewhere after their arrest, therefore barring migrants from fleeing authorities or seeking to legalize ties to American citizens (as unauthorized Italian immigrants did that vary same year) before they could be swiftly deported by the state. Moreover, the state actively publicized the massive military-style operation the INS undertook to rid American citizens of those unworthy and criminal "illegal aliens" in the name of both national and economic security.[66]

Evidence of racial privilege in the case of Italian deserters is striking. In fact, privilege is so clear that immigration officials regularly overlooked numerous factors that one would think would disqualify Italian migrants for relief. In theory, seamen deserters were not supposed to show their intent in their decision to overstay in the United States. However, in plenty of IWL cases, a seaman's intent to overstay in the United States was clear, and it had no negative effect on the outcome of their cases. Ercole B., a twenty-three-year-old seaman from Campania, jumped ship only after his love interest from home had secured her own immigration visa and moved to the United States before him. The couple married about one year after Ercole's arrival and later came forward to officials to adjust his status. Another seaman, Matteo B., clearly intended to join his father and younger brother, who secured legal permanent residency in the United States via the Displaced Persons Act preceding Matteo's arrival. Leonardo L., a crewman who had entered the United States at least twenty times before deserting in 1959, courted his future wife during those visits before making the calculated decision to overstay. Those men, and many more Italian migrants, were nevertheless allowed to adjust their status with little attention paid to their "criminal" intentions to violate U.S. immigration laws.[67]

Both authorized and unauthorized immigrants might also be denied entry or continued residency in the United States if immigration officials deemed an individual guilty of demonstrating "moral turpitude." That highly malleable charge had been used since the late nineteenth century to deny various undesirable migrants access to the United States. The behaviors that constituted acts of moral turpitude were always subjective and selectively applied.[68] However, a criminal record was ostensibly one of the clearest demonstrations of one's poor moral character. And yet, over a dozen Italian seamen represented by the IWL had one or more convictions for bootlegging, theft, forgery, assault, and other offenses when they applied for relief. Not one of those men was ultimately barred from normalizing his status.[69]

Acts of an "immoral" sexual nature also were commonly invoked as proof of a flawed character and evidence of moral turpitude. However, some Italian seamen had bigamous marriages with wives in the United States, Italy, Bermuda, Brazil, Mexico, and elsewhere. Sometimes bigamy occurred as a technicality of sorts. Giuseppe F., for example, married an Italian American woman (who was a recent migrant but held derivative citizenship) the day after his January 1958 arrest by the INS, even though he was already married years before in Bari. By April of the following year, however, Giuseppe had managed to divorce his Italian wife by proving the couple had been legally separated for several years; appealed his original deportation order (in which the courts questioned the legitimacy, as well as the legality, of his post-arrest marriage in the United States); and secured normalization through the processes of voluntary departure and pre-examination.[70] In other cases, the immorality of the bigamous party in question was more egregious—as was the case with Arcangelo S. Arcangelo had a criminal record and an estranged wife in Campania before entering the country as a stowaway. He then lived and worked without papers in the United States from 1947 to 1952. He bigamously married an American woman sometime after 1949 and then deserted, but did not divorce, that second wife when he returned to Italy on his own accord in 1952. Arcangelo shows up in the records again in 1956 as a commercial seaman who deserted the SS *San Felice* in Norfolk, Virginia. Arcangelo was somehow able to marry a third woman (also an American citizen), but that marriage quickly failed and by 1958, he was living in New York City with yet another Italian American woman. At Arcangelo's BIA hearing in 1959, he claimed to financially support the woman with whom he currently cohabitated, as well as two illegitimate American-born children produced from his previous relationships. Financial obligations to both his current partner and American-born offspring succeeded in swaying BIA officials to suspend Arcangelo's deportation order, questions of moral turpitude and his dubious devotion to family values notwithstanding.[71]

"Ship-Jumper Given First Visa by U.S. Under Day-Old Law"

On December 3, 1965, the *New York Times* ran a profile of the first immigrant to be granted an immigration visa under the newly liberalized Immigration and Nationality Act—best known for abolishing the national origins system.[72] The feature reported on Salvatore E., a twenty-nine-year-old man from Naples, as en route to join his wife and young son who were already living in Brooklyn. Salvatore's wife had immigrated lawfully in 1961. When Salvatore couldn't secure an immigration visa for himself at the same time, he pursued other options. He ultimately found a position as a commercial seaman on a vessel bound for the United States and jumped ship in 1963. While we don't have all the details of Salvatore's case, beginning with his overstay and culminating with his voluntary departure a few months later, we do know that Salvatore self-reported to the INS—perhaps expecting to adjust his status as so many other Italian sailors had done before him, but Salvatore was ordered to leave the country. It appears that Salvatore did not attempt to appeal that decision, left the country voluntarily, and pursued other modes of entry. His wife's congressional representative, John Rooney (D-NY), introduced a private relief bill on the family's behalf, but before it went to the floor, the family found relief of sorts when Salvatore became the first recipient to be granted an immigration visa after changes from the Immigration and Nationality Act of 1965 went into effect.[73] What are the chances that a one-time seaman deserter from Italy would use the first immigration visa issued under the newly liberalized system? While we can't actually calculate an answer to that question, it is fair to say that stories like Salvatore's, and many others featured in this chapter, were far more common than we generally acknowledge.

The Italian seamen deserters discussed in this chapter became unauthorized migrants when they overstayed their commercial visas to live, work, and establish familial and social connections in the United States. Although they represent only a fraction of postwar Italian immigration, and an even smaller number of the overall number of unauthorized migrants residing in the United States in the 1950s, their numbers were not insignificant. Nor were their experiences as unauthorized migrants. The Italian men in this study were overwhelmingly able to integrate into American society. Even more significantly, they were able to do so with the assistance of an indifferent, if not sympathetic, state. The Italian men who sought help from the IWL were only minimally policed within their communities. They were allowed to live in ways that facilitated their continued social and economic integration while they navigated their legal status. Finally, the vast majority were able to normalize their position as legal residents on the path toward becoming full-fledged citizens by the enforcement actions, legal decisions, and policy structures that prioritized their status as white male husbands, fathers, and breadwinners over their status as unlawful immigrants.

Notes

1. Last names have been dropped to protect anonymity. Many thanks to Matthew Sutton for assistance in compiling Italian Welfare League data.

2. Some seamen were also charged with overstaying their commercial sailing visa within the jurisdiction of the United States. Immigration Case Files and Allied Social Welfare Cases, 1950s, *The Italian Welfare League Records, 1916–1987* (CMS 003), the Center for Migration Studies, New York, Box 136 B-Bis, Folder: Umberto B. (Collection hereafter cited as *IWL Records*). See also "Warrants Issued for 875 Seamen," *New York Times,* April 1, 1941; "Hearings at Ellis Island," *New York Times,* April 2, 1941; "Sabotaged Ships Ordered Moved," *New York Times,* May 6, 1941; "Italian Seamen Arrive," *New York Times,* July 15, 1941.

3. *IWL Records,* Box 136 B-Bis, Folder: Umberto B. Along with the *Colorado,* media coverage cited acts of sabotage on the SS *Aussa, Villaperosa, Ida Z.O., Alberta, San Leonardo, Brennero, Conte Biancamano, Euro, Pietro Campella, Arsa, Ircania,* and *Confidenza.* See "Ten Found Guilty in Ship Sabotage," *New York Times,* June 19, 1941; "Italians Get Three Years," *New York Times,* May 9, 1941; "Sentences 16 Italian Seamen," *New York Times,* July 25, 1941; "Italian Seamen Guilty," *New York Times,* July 30, 1941; "39 Italian Seamen Guilty, *New York Times,* May 6, 1941; "Shifted as Saboteurs," *New York Times,* April 23, 1941; "Seized Seamen Assigned," *New York Times,* April 13, 1941; "20 More Italian Seamen Held," *New York Times,* April 15, 1941; "Italians Convicted of Sabotaging Ship," *New York Times,* May 2, 1941; "479 Italians Excluded," *New York Times,* April 17, 1941.

4. *IWL Records,* Box 136 B-Bis, Folder: Umberto B.

5. In a similar case involving sabotage on the SS *Aussa,* the general manager for the liner was reported to have "provoked a patriotic demonstration from the defendants by raising his hand in the Fascist salute," in "Ten Found Guilty in Ship Sabotage," *New York Times,* June 19, 1941.

6. *IWL Records,* Box 136 B-Bis, Folder: Umberto B.

7. I prefer to use the term *unauthorized* immigrant or migrant to *illegal* alien or *undocumented* immigrant and try to use it or similar nomenclature in most cases. For an excellent discussion on the use of such terminology, see Hiroshi Motomura, *Immigration Outside the Law* (New York: Oxford University Press, 2014), 1–18.

8. For the use of voluntary departure statistics as an instrument of expulsion, see Adam Goodman, *The Deportation Machine: America's Long History of Expelling Immigrants* (Princeton, NJ: Princeton University Press, 2020), 1–72.

9. Hiroshi Motomura, *Americans in Waiting: The Lost Story of Immigration and Citizenship in the United States* (New York: Oxford University Press, 2006).

10. Catherine Lee, *Fictive Kinship: Family Reunification and the Meaning of Race and Nation in American Immigration* (New York: Russell Sage Foundation, 2013); Yuki Oda, "Family Unity in U.S. Immigration Policy, 1921–1978," (PhD diss., Columbia University, 2014).

11. For a more extended discussion of some of these concepts, see, Danielle Battisti, *Whom We Shall Welcome: Italian Americans and Immigration Reform, 1945–1965* (New York: Fordham University Press, 2019). Grainne McEvoy, "American Catholic Social Thought and the Immigration Question in the Restriction Era, 1917–1965" (PhD diss., Boston College, 2014).

12. The IWL is a nonprofit immigrant aid organization that began operating in the 1920s and continues to serve Italian American families today. The agency historically offered Italian immigrants a wide variety of resettlement assistance, social welfare aid, language and citizenship training, and pro bono legal aid. While the IWL primarily operated in New York City, it also kept offices in Brooklyn and Ellis Island. Today the IWL primarily provides services to Italian American families with special needs children. Nicholas Falco, ed., *A Guide to the Archives: Records of the Italian Welfare League Inc.* (Staten Island, NY: Center for Migration Studies, 1988).

13. For Italy's long history of supporting international migration as a strategy of national advancement, see Donna Gabaccia, *Italy's Many Diasporas* (Seattle: University of Washington Press, 2000). Mark I. Choate, *Emigrant Nation: The Making of Italy*

Abroad (Cambridge, MA: Harvard University Press, 2008). For governmental support of Italian emigraticn in the postwar period, see Michele Colucci, *Lavoro in movimento, l'emigrazione italiana in europa, 1945–1957* (Rome: Donzelli, 2008); Andreina De Clementi, *Il Prezzo della ricostruzione. L'emigrazione italiana nel secondo dopoguerra,* (Rome: Laterza, 2010); Enrico Pugliese, *L'Italia tra migrazioni internazionali e migrazioni interne* (Bologna: Il Mulino, 2002); Elia Morandi, *Governare l'emigrazione: Lavoratori italiani verso la Germania nel secondo dopoguerra* (Torino: Rosenberg & Seller, 2011); Franca Iacovetta, "Ordering in Bulk: Canada's Postwar Immigration Policy and the Recruitment of Contract Workers from Italy," *Journal of American Ethnic History* 11, no. 1 (Fall 1991): 50–80; Fabiana Idini, "L'accordo di emigrazione assistita tra Italia e Australia (29 marzo 1951)," *Altreitalie* 45 (2012): 74–94.

14. Sandro Rinauro, *Il Cammino della Speranza, l'Emigrazione clandestine degli Italiani nel Secondo Dopoguerra* (Torino: Einaudi, 2009).

15. For conflicts over the regulation of immigrants, runaway slaves, Native Americans, and other denizens of states in the antebellum period, see Daniel Kanstroom, *Deportation Nation: Outsiders in American History* (Cambridge, MA: Harvard University Press, 2007), 21–9c; Hidetaka Hirota, *Expelling the Poor: Atlantic Seaboard States and the Nineteenth-Century Origins of American Immigration Policy* (New York: Oxford, 2017); Aristide R. Zolberg, *A Nation by Design: Immigration Policy in the Fashioning of America* (Cambridge, MA: Harvard University Press, 2006), 24–166; Eric Foner, *Gateway to Freedom: The Hidden History of the Underground Railroad* (New York: W.W. Norton, 2016); Martha S. Jones, *Birthright Citizens: A History of Race and Rights in Antebellum America* (New York: Cambridge University Press, 2018); Samantha Seeley, *Race, Removal, and the Right to Remain* (Chapel Hill: University of North Carolina Press, 2021).

16. Motomura, *Americans in Waiting.* Similar consolidations of national power occurred throughout the West in the late nineteenth and early twentieth centuries. John C. Torpey, *The Invention of the Passport: Surveillance, Citizenship, and the State* (New York: Cambridge University Press, 2018).

17. Mae Ngai, *Impossible Subjects: Illegal Aliens and the Making of Modern America* (Princeton, NJ: Princeton University Press, 2014).

18. Erika Lee, *At America's Gates: Chinese Immigration during the Exclusion Era, 1882–1943* (Chapel Hill: University of North Carolina Press, 2003); Kanstroom, *Deportation Nation*; Margot Canaday, *The Straight State: Sexuality and Citizenship in Twentieth-Century America* (Princeton, NJ: Princeton University Press, 2009); Douglas Baynton, *Defectives in the Land: Disability and Immigration in the Age of Eugenics* (Chicago: University of Chicago Press, 2016).

19. Zolberg, *A Nation by Design*, 199–336; John Higham, *Strangers in the Land: Patterns of American Nativism, 1860–1925* (New York: Atheneum, 1967); Desmond King, *Making Americans: Immigration, Race, and the Origins of the Diverse Democracy* (Cambridge, MA: Harvard University Press, 2000). For works that challenge a Eurocentric view of the origins of immigration restriction in the 1920s, see Ngai, *Impossible Subjects,* 1–55; and Lee, *At America's Gates.* For the anti-Asian roots of the Dillingham Commission, see Katherine Benton-Cohen, *Inventing the Immigration Problem: The Dillingham Commission and its Legacy* (Cambridge, MA: Harvard University Press, 2018).

20. Ngai, *Impossible Subjects,* 24–27.

21. Ashley Johnson Bavery, *Bootlegged Aliens: Immigration Politics on America's Northern Border* (Philadelphia: University of Pennsylvania Press, 2020).

22. Act of March 2, 1929 (45 Stat. 1512).

23. Ngai, *Impossible Subjects*, 82. S. Deborah Kang also discusses pressure from agribusiness leaders to regularize unauthorized Mexican immigration under the Registry Act, as well as nativist impulses to limit those provisions and other permissive elements of Mexican migration to the United States in the interwar period. S. Deborah Kang, *The INS on the Line: Making Immigration Law on the US-Mexico Border, 1917–1954* (New York: Oxford University Press, 2017), 54–58. Ngai, however, argues that the state primarily used administrative discretion to restrict Mexican immigration, adjustment of status, and naturalization, *Impossible Subjects*, 54–55.

24. Maddalena Marinari, *Unwanted: Italian and Jewish Mobilization against Restrictive Immigration Laws, 1882–1965* (Chapel Hill: University of North Carolina Press, 2020); Bavery, *Bootlegged Aliens*.

25. Gary Gerstle, *American Crucible: Race and Nation in the Twentieth Century* (Princeton, NJ: Princeton University Press, 2001), 256; Cybelle Fox, *Three Worlds of Relief: Race, Immigration, and the American Welfare State from the Progressive Era to the New Deal* (Princeton, NJ: Princeton University Press, 2012); Lizabeth Cohen, *Making a New Deal: Industrial Workers in Chicago, 1919–1939* (New York: Cambridge University Press, 1990).

26. The primary architect behind such efforts was Congressman John C. Box of Texas, who proposed a ban on Mexican immigration in 1926 (H.R. Bill 6741) and legislation to include Western Hemisphere nations within the national origins system in 1928. Natalia Molina, *Fit to Be Citizens: Public Health and Race in Los Angeles, 1879–1939* (Berkeley: University of California Press, 2006), 118–19.

27. The INS was housed in the Department of Labor until it was transferred to the State Department in 1938.

28. These agreements originated during World War I, when the United States and Canada, as wartime allies, were concerned about managing the flow of temporary labor between the two countries to keep the supply of labor for war production steady. Torrie Hester, *Deportation: The Origins of U.S. Policy* (Philadelphia: University of Pennsylvania Press, 2017), 164–65.

29. For more on the policing of the U.S.-Canadian border, see Kornel Chang, *Pacific Connections: The Making of the U.S.-Canadian Borderlands* (Berkeley: University of California Press, 2012), 147–78; Lee, *At America's Gates*, 147–88; Patrick Ettinger, *Imaginary Lines: Border Enforcement and the Origins of Undocumented Immigration, 1882–1930* (Austin: University of Texas Press, 2009); Bavery, *Bootlegged Aliens*.

30. Ngai, *Impossible Subjects*, 84–85. For more on voluntary departure, see Kang, *The INS on the Line*, 65–67.

31. Monique Laney, *German Rocketeers in the Heart of Dixie: Making Sense of the Nazi Past during the Civil Rights Era* (New York: Oxford University Press, 2015), 28–36.

32. Ngai, *Impossible Subjects*, 75–90.

33. Act of June 28, 1940 (54 Stat. 670). The INS suspended the deportations of several thousand aliens per year from 1941 through the late 1950s. The overwhelming majority were of European (mostly German and Italian) origin. Ngai, *Impossible Subjects*, 88.

34. *IWL Records,* Boxes 134–168.

35. Joseph Sciorra, *Built with Faith: Italian American Imagination and Catholic Material Culture in New York City* (Knoxville: University of Tennessee Press, 2015); Simone Cinotto, *The Italian American Table: Food, Family, and Community in New York City* (Urbana: University of Illinois Press, 2013); Robert A. Orsi, *The Madonna of 115th Street: Faith and Community in Italian Harlem, 1880–1950* (New Haven, CT: Yale University Press, 1985); Salvatore J. LaGumina, *New York at Mid-Century: The Impellitteri Years* (Westport, CT: Greenwood Press, 1992); Salvatore J. LaGumina, *From Steerage to Suburb: Long Island Italians* (New York: Center for Migration Studies, 1988).

36. Center for Migration Studies, Guide to the Italian Welfare League Records: CMS.003 (March 1988), https://cmsny.org/wp-content/uploads/2016/07/cms_003.pdf, last accessed February 22, 2024.

37. For more on those subjects, see Julia F. Irwin, *Making the World Safe: The American Red Cross and a Nation's Humanitarian Awakening* (New York: Oxford University Press, 2013).

38. The 1950–1960 sample contains 603 cases in total. A small number of IWL cases (in addition to the 603 referenced here) involved non-Italian foreign nationals. I did not include those cases in my data set. I did, however, include ethnic Italians from disputed territory, such as Venezia-Giulia—a former Italian territory that was transferred to UN trusteeship and/or Yugoslavian control by 1954 as part of Italy's World War II peace settlement. Roberto G. Rabel, *Between East and West: Trieste, the United States, and the Cold War, 1941–1954* (Durham, NC: Duke University Press, 1988). *IWL Records,* Boxes 134–168.

39. Temporary work visas in IWL records were often granted for Italian artists such as singers, composers, and craftsmen in the fine arts or building trades. *IWL Records,* Boxes 134–168.

40. The IWL represented 239 seamen deserters in the 1950s, out of a total of 347 unauthorized male Italian migrants. *IWL Records,* Boxes 134–168.

41. For more on European sailors working on commercial lines and migration, see Torsten Feys, "Bounding Mass Migration Across the Atlantic: European Shipping Companies between Border Building and Evasion 1860–1920s," *Journal of Modern European History* 14, no. 1 (2016): 78–100. For the antebellum roots of American policing of seamen's mobility, see Michael A. Schoeppner, *Moral Contagion: Black Atlantic Sailors, Citizenship, and Diplomacy in Antebellum America* (New York: Cambridge University Press, 2019).

42. The "anti-alien bloc" in Congress might go as high as estimating 1,000,000 seamen deserters. "Restrictions Urged on Illegal Aliens," *New York Times,* November 11, 1936.

43. U.S. Immigration and Naturalization Services, Annual Report, Washington, DC: U.S. Department of State, 1950; 1951; 1956. Sometimes those concerns were linked to anti-racketeering efforts, as was the case in 1953, 1954, and 1957. U.S. Immigration and Naturalization Services, Annual Report, Washington, DC: U.S. Department of State, 1953; 1954; 1957. For longtime concerns about immigrant smuggling rings (of alcohol, narcotics, and people) via merchant vessels, see Bavery, *Bootlegged Aliens.* Lisa Lindquist Dorr, *A Thousand Thirsty Beaches: Smuggling Alcohol from Cuba to the South during Prohibition* (Chapel Hill: University of North Carolina Press, 2018), 127–57. For press

coverage, see "City Called Haven for Illegal Aliens," *New York Times*, December 21, 1949; "Deportations Rise to 580,000 a Year," *New York Times*, May 6, 1951; "11 Arrested Here in Illegal Entries," *New York Times*, February 1, 1952.

44. "4 Aliens Taken in Newark," *New York Times*, July 16, 1951; "101 Seized in Area for Illegal Entry," *New York Times*, July 18, 1951; "40 More Aliens Seized," *New York Times*, July 20, 1951; "40 Aliens Seized in a Day," *New York Times*, July 21, 1951.

45. U.S. Immigration and Naturalization Services, Annual Report, Washington, DC: U.S. Department of State, 1953. The denial of a D-1 visa provision was primarily meant to target Asian crewmen and former members of "totalitarian" organizations (which in practice in the 1950s meant targeting former or current communists; U.S. authorities did not target former fascists in the same way that they attempted to restrict communist entry to the country during the Cold War). See Senator McCarran's public comments on the "ready-made fifth column" in the United States represented by illegal aliens of a certain political bent. "McCarran Charges Alien Infiltering," *New York Times*, August 21, 1951. In a somewhat contradictory measure, Congress did take up a bill that would make it easier for deserting seamen to lay claim to their lost wages and effects. Sen. Report No. 2350, *Disposition of Seamen's Effects* (83rd Congress, 2nd Session, August 5, 1954).

46. With the possible exception of Greek seamen deserters, more scholarship is needed. For a preliminary investigation, see Alexander Kitroeff, "Ship Jumpers: An Unspoken Chapter of Greek Immigration to the United States," Pappas Post, April 16, 2024, https://pappaspost.com/ship-jumpers-an-unspoken-chapter-of-greek-immigration -to-the-united-states/.

47. Deserters from Campania and Sicilia constituted more than 40 percent of the overstay cases found in the IWL records. Sailors hailing from the coastal regions of Liguria and Veneto came in third and fourth, respectively, in the IWL's files. *IWL Records,* Boxes 134–168. About 30 percent of the sample where records indicate the port of arrival, IWL clients jumped ship in New York City, followed by about 15 percent and 12 percent in Baltimore and Norfolk, respectively. Data is missing for port of arrival in about 15 percent of cases.

48. IWL dossiers included detailed work histories for each client. The IWL provided free legal assistance to migrants. That service may have skewed the data toward an overrepresentation of working-class migrants who entered through irregular channels. *IWL Records,* Boxes 134–168. See also "101 Seized in Area for Illegal Entry," *New York Times,* July 18, 1951, for coverage of a suspected smuggling ring involving kickbacks to the Longshoreman's Association for employing unlawful immigrants as longshoremen in New York City and New Jersey.

49. *IWL Records,* Boxes 134–168.

50. For more on the Alien Registry Act, see Julia Rose Kraut, *Threat of Dissent: A History of Ideological Expulsion and Deportation in the United States* (Cambridge, MA: Harvard University Press, 2020).

51. *IWL Records,* Boxes 134–168. For more on the procedural evolution of deportation hearings, see Hester, *Deportation.*

52. Federal Register, Part 485-Prexamintion of Aliens within the Continental United States, May 19, 1955. The National Catholic Welfare Conference Collection, the Center for Migration Studies, New York. Box 76, Folder: Pre-examination.

53. Although I have complete data on crossing points for only about 50 percent of pre-examination/voluntary departure cases, Rouses Point/Montreal adjustments led the way, followed by Vanceboro/St. John's Bay, then Niagara Falls and Toronto. *IWL Records,* Boxes 134–168.

54. Federal Register, Part 485-Prexamintion of Aliens within the Continental United States, May 19, 1955. The National Catholic Welfare Conference Collection, the Center for Migration Studies, New York. Box 76, Folder: Pre-examination.

55. *IWL Records,* Boxes 134–168.

56. Chang, *Pacific Connections,* 147–78.

57. Bavery, *Bootlegged Aliens.*

58. Out of 239 seamen deserters in the sample, 96 were married pre-arrest. Only 67 of those 96 were married to American citizens. The rest were married to immigrants with green cards or maintained transnational family networks. The rest in the sample who married did so after their initial arrest. *IWL Records,* Boxes 134–168.

59. Those who did try to demonstrate pre-arrest intent to marry also included family testimony of an engagement, receipt of an engagement ring, written evidence of an engagement announcement, etc. *IWL Records,* Boxes 134–168.

60. For the turn toward detention of Mexican migrants in jails, detention centers, and other facilities in the 1950s (especially following Operation Wetback in 1954), see Kelly Lytle Hernández, *Migra! A History of the U.S. Border Patrol* (Berkeley, University of California Press, 2010), 196–217; Jessica Ordaz, *The Shadow of El Centro: A History of Migrant Incarceration and Solidarity* (Chapel Hill: University of North Carolina Press, 2021); Sarah Lopez, "From Penal to 'Civil': A Legacy of Private Prison Policy in a Landscape of Migrant Detention, *American Quarterly* 71, no. 1 (March 2019): 105–34; Mike Amezcua, *Making Mexican Chicago: From Postwar Settlement to the Age of Gentrification* (Chicago: University of Chicago Press, 2022), 19–60.

61. *IWL Records,* Boxes 134–168.

62. *IWL Records,* Boxes 134–168.

63. For the racial, class, and gender dynamics of the construction and evolution of the term or racial script "anchor baby," see Natalia Molina, "Deportable Citizens: The Decoupling of Race and Citizenship in the Construction of the 'Anchor Baby,' in *Deportation in the Americas: Histories of Exclusion and Resistance,* eds. Kenyon Zimmer and Cristina Salinas (College Station: Texas A&M Press, 2018).

64. Such racialized notions of citizenship and belonging were also found in Italian American campaigns for immigration reform in the postwar era. Battisti, *Whom We Shall Welcome*; Marinari, *Unwanted.*

65. Anna Pegler-Gordon, *Closing the Golden Door: Asian Migration and the Hidden History of Exclusion at Ellis Island* (Chapel Hill: University of North Carolina Press, 2021); Heather Lee, "Hunting for Sailors," in *A Nation of Immigrants Reconsidered: US Society in an Age of Restriction, 1924–1965,* eds. Maddalena Marinari, Madeline Y. Hsu, and Maria Cristina Garcia (Urbana: University of Illinois Press, 2019), 107–22. Vivek Bald, *Bengali Harlem and the Lost Histories of South Asian America* (Cambridge, MA: Harvard University Press, 2013), 94–136. Bald points out that many South Asian men partnered with African American women and produced multiracial families in this period.

66. Kang, *The INS on the Line*; Hernández, *Migra!*; Ngai, *Impossible Subjects*, 127–66; Lopez, "From Penal to 'Civil.'" Raids against Mexican migrants in cities were similarly publicized for using military precision to root out criminal activity. Amezcua, *Making Mexican Chicago*, 19–60.

67. *IWL Records*, Boxes 134–168. In Matteo B.'s case, he had turned twenty-one and was therefore ineligible to apply for refugee relief under a family application that had been years in the making. *IWL Records*, Box 138, Matteo B.

68. Canaday, *The Straight State*; Gardner, *The Qualities of a Citizen*; Kraut, *Silent Travelers*. For much of the early twentieth century, deportations for prostitution were second only to deportations for those likely to become a public charge; both of these disproportionately affected women. Hester, *Deportation*, 83.

69. The same could not be said of Italian women (regardless of their legal status). *IWL Records*, Boxes 134–168.

70. The records are unclear as to whether Giuseppe and his first wife had been separated since 1953 or 1956. *IWL Records*, Box 147, Folder: Giuseppe F.

71. *IWL Records*, Box 163, Folder: Arcangelo S. Other cases involve documented cases of adultery, divorce, and legal fights over financial support for wives and children. For example, see *IWL Records*, Box 158, Folder: Natale P.

72. "Ship-Jumper Given First Visa by U.S. Under Day-Old Law," *New York Times*, December 3, 1965.

73. "Ship-Jumper Given First Visa by U.S. Under Day-Old Law."

3 Irish Immigrants in the 1980s

Immigration Narratives, Whiteness, and Diversity

CARLY GOODMAN

"We've come to this great country / Like our fathers in the past / To build a better future / Nail our colours to the mast / But the shackles of bureaucracy / They hold my people down / And so I'm classed illegal alien / As I move from town to town." In the archives of the Irish Immigration Reform Movement (IIRM) are the handwritten lyrics to a song that describes the plight of undocumented Irish immigrants in New York in the mid-1980s. An ocean now separates the narrator from his home, from his very heart. Despite earned credentials such as "diplomas and degrees," the lack of opportunities at home has driven him into exile and to the dirty, exploitative jobs available to people called "illegal alien." Now in the United States, he is a stranger alone in a crowd of a hundred thousand others just like him. The problem, as he identifies in the song, is that this crowd of strangers has been made "illegal" and denied status in a land they are ready to embrace. Unable to remain at home, but unwelcome in the United States, "God's chosen land," the narrator pleads for policy change. "Legalize the Irish, give us status, set us free / To be a part of what is truth / A part of your democracy."[1]

By the mid-1980s, several million noncitizens were living without status in the United States, and while most were originally from Mexico and Central America, this group included the Irish as well. During that decade, hundreds of thousands of Irish people—as much as 10 percent of Ireland's population—fled a long recession at home.[2] Of those who came to the United States, many settled in New York—Woodside, Queens, was the destination for the song's narrator—while others flocked to Irish American communities in Boston, Philadelphia, Connecticut, and elsewhere.[3] The "strange Manhattan skyline" and noise didn't feel like home. But generations of Irish immigrants had made lives in the United States, making it a clear destination for young people in the 1980s. The IIRM, a grassroots organization representing these newcomers, would soon capitalize on the deeply felt roots of Irish immigrants to push for meaningful policy reform and access to legal status for the undocumented Irish.

In the mid-nineteenth century, Irish immigrants came by the millions, in some years constituting a third or half of all U.S. immigrants. Although Irish American contributions to the country were later understood as foundational, at the time, New York City and state officials often treated these newcomers as a problem. Some argued that Irish poverty, Catholicism, and drinking made them un-American and unassimilable. Such practices of nativism and immigrant exclusion later became embedded in federal policies of immigration restriction and regulation.[4] But the Irish gradually gained acceptance, especially when subsequent arrivals of Eastern European, Jewish, Italian, Chinese, and other Asian immigrants became new targets for xenophobia. Eugenic theorists placed white northern and western Europeans near the top of their ethnic hierarchies, sweeping Irish Americans into whiteness, while castigating other groups as degenerate and harmful to the polity.[5]

When the United States thoroughly restricted immigration in the 1920s, Ireland was afforded a relatively generous quota of 28,000 visas annually. That decade, 200,000 Irish came as immigrants to the United States. The number would plummet during the Great Depression and World War II; only 15,000 came in the 1940s.[6] The 1950s, deemed a kind of "lost decade," would see half a million people departing Ireland, 70,000 of them as immigrants to the United States, before the Irish economy began to rebound and the flow of Irish immigrants slowed to a trickle by the mid-1960s.[7] Economic improvements and opportunities allowed more people to stay home. As the IIRM put it, "an entire generation of young people raised and educated outside the shadow of the emigrant ship" had benefited from the boom.[8] Only 10,000 immigrated to the United States between 1976 and 1985.[9]

But when opportunities disappeared again, a new generation sought exit. The United States seemed a natural destination: "Today it's one-way traffic / Out of Shannon to New York," the song went. In 1980, when the U.S. decennial census asked people about their ancestry, 40 million Americans reported Irish ancestry, the third most cited group.[10] There were more Americans claiming Irish descent than there were Irish citizens, fueling the idea that the Irish formed a core part of the American story—and thus a place for Irish exiles remained.[11]

But the New Irish, as those who immigrated in the 1980s were called, faced bureaucratic challenges because they could not access green cards, and many were undocumented. As a *Philadelphia Inquirer* article put it in 1987, "[R]aised on Irish-American success stories and convinced that Ireland has a special relationship with America, the new immigrants are often surprised to find they are treated much like other illegal aliens. They, too, are underpaid, overworked and subject to arrest and deportation."[12] It seemed unfair that the Irish who arrived in the 1980s were understood to be "illegal," when their counterparts earlier in the century had been welcomed and incorporated into the United States, and had made lasting contributions.

To address this injustice, the IIRM and others joined together to advocate for changes to U.S. immigration policy that would allow unauthorized Irish immigrants living and working in America to gain legal status, and to enable future legal Irish immigration. They succeeded by building empathy for their plight through media coverage and by working with sympathetic policymakers. They were able to change public perceptions and state policies on immigration, something that was unusual in a context of rising nativism and renewed focus on cracking down on unauthorized immigration. Yet the scripts they deployed to build empathy and create new access simultaneously reproduced ideas about belonging along lines of race.

Restriction

To understand the push for reform in the 1980s, look back to the Hart-Celler Act of 1965, which marked the end of restrictive national origins quotas that had determined and limited admissions since the 1920s. The abolition of the national origins quotas was important to Cold War liberals hoping to win hearts and minds across the non-white world. The 1965 law created uniform per-country limits for immigrants from every nation, in the interest of leveling the playing field. Rejecting the explicitly racist quota system, the law created a system that emphasized close family ties and skilled work in selecting immigrants, as well as a provision for refugees. What was a neutral set of criteria on paper, however, was at least partially an effort to reinforce Eurocentrism in immigration policy through other means.

The end of a system that explicitly privileged the Irish still stung, however. Irish American groups had lodged complaints about the 1965 act's effect on Irish immigration promptly. "We shouldn't become extinct," the chairman of the St. Patrick's Day Parade told the *New York Times* in 1966. Most of the Irish seeking to come to the United States, he said, "are not skilled. But 'unskilled Irishmen' have helped build our country."[13] In the 1968 St. Patrick's Day parade in New York, marchers wore buttons that read "Immigration or die," with an image of a shamrock. "We've made this country," said Donald M. O'Callaghan of the Ancient Order of Hibernians, one of the sponsors of the protest buttons.[14] John P. Collins of the American Irish National Immigration Committee testified frequently before Congress, attesting to how immigration law was unfairly limiting Irish immigration.[15] Collins's organization put ads in the *Times* showing how the 1965 act echoed historical discrimination in U.S. history: "No Irish Need Apply"—for visas.[16] But early efforts to redress this problem that would have made visas available to the Irish were weakened because of worries that they would be seen as reinstating the now-discredited national origins quotas system.[17]

But Congress did little on the immigration issue until the 1980s. Congress passed the Refugee Act of 1980, revamping the refugee admissions system. In 1981, the Select Commission on Immigration and Refugee Policy, which had been created in 1978, published its report with recommendations. In the decade and a half since 1965, the issue of undocumented immigration had become more potent. The commission weighed in in its report: "most U.S. citizens believe that the half-open door of undocumented/illegal migration should be closed."[18]

As Mae Ngai and others have pointed out, unauthorized immigration in the 1970s and 1980s was an outcome of the restrictions placed on legal migration. Work, family, the need for safety, and histories of imperial entanglements continued to draw people to the United States. When legal pathways were foreclosed, illicit migration became the only choice. But limits were not equally distributed. The immigration system had long encouraged white immigration and settlement, while working to exclude immigrants of color. This longer history had helped create and reinforce racial hierarchies and categories of belonging. Although the 1965 law had liberalized immigration admissions by abolishing racist quotas, it also kept and imposed immigration restrictions. In particular, the imposition of numerical limits on Western Hemisphere immigration, including a 1976 amendment setting per-country caps, and the termination of the Bracero guest worker program in 1964, made ongoing migration from Mexico, Central America, and elsewhere more likely to be unauthorized. Simultaneously, legal immigration increased after 1965, with a shift to immigration from outside of Europe. Increased racial diversity in the United States coincided with rising conservatism and a politics of backlash against perceived gains by African Americans, women, and others. Much of the debate about immigration was shaped by perceptions that too many immigrants of color were in the United States and were changing the country. But framing unauthorized immigration as a matter of "law and order" or a system "out of control" allowed policymakers to avoid analysis of how racism was shaping the conversation.

In the early 1980s, policy leaders like Sen. Alan Simpson (R-WY) held hearings, met with experts, wrote op-eds, and worked to build support for what eventually became the Immigration Reform and Control Act (IRCA). This 1986 legislation blended punitive elements—border security, and sanctions on employers who hired unauthorized immigrants—with legalization programs that its proponents believed would bring people out of the shadows. Restrictionists and reformers pushing for IRCA amplified immigration issues in the national media, fostering a sense of urgency, and nationalizing a topic that had once been more of a local and regional issue.

Like other unauthorized immigrants in the 1980s, the Irish lacked access to a legal channel for admission to the United States. Most came as visitors on temporary visas. The IIRM cited a statistic showing some 30,000 coming annually on tourist and other short-term visas, most of them unable to obtain the permanent residency status they sought. Although the Select Commission recommended investigations into "overstays and student visa abusers," it acknowledged that fiscal constraints and border enforcement priorities meant that the Immigration and Naturalization Service (INS) had few resources to devote to "interior enforcement on a broad scale."[19] Furthermore, as Anna O. Law shows, Congress appeared aware that Irish immigrants were continuing to come without authorization but "seemed to look the other way."[20]

On the one hand, the Irish continued to be able to access short-term visas, and to travel to the United States with relatively little scrutiny. That access and trust was likely grounded in their whiteness—because the figure of the "illegal immigrant" was understood to be an immigrant of color, most likely Latino and coming over the U.S.-Mexico border. Settling in Irish American neighborhoods, they blended in.

Being undocumented was particularly difficult for immigrants of color, who were subject to exploitation, surveillance, and racial discrimination. But the threat of deportation hung over the Irish as well. As the immigration debates of the 1980s continued, and IRCA became law, undocumented people worried about greater scrutiny and attention. As one immigrant quoted in the *Boston Globe* put it, "It's just a constant fear at work. You don't know. Is it the IRS, is it Immigration, is it Social Security? . . . It never leaves you; you never forget."[21] The new exiles, so much like their Irish predecessors in spirit and connection to the United States, were being forced to live "lives in an illegal limbo, shut out in the cold by unfeeling, uncaring and emotionless bureaucracy," as Patrick H., identified as an "undocumented Irishman," wrote in an editorial in 1987.[22] How could a bureaucracy as uncaring as the U.S. immigration system be made to feel for the plight of the Irish?

Reform

The Irish sought a way to both adjust immigrants' status—something like legalization or amnesty for those present in the United States—and ensure an open door for Irish immigrants going forward. Before 1965, the Irish had enjoyed a more generous admissions quota and plenty of access outside of the quotas for those without close family ties. But with the system now prioritizing close family ties—which few unauthorized Irish immigrants possessed because of timing and attenuation of relationships to American relatives—it appeared to disadvantage Europeans. Without close family members or employers to sponsor them, the Irish couldn't qualify for the visas theoretically allocated to Ireland. As much as nostalgia for the old days of more open Irish immigration fueled people's advocacy, however, a return to the pre-1965 system was not in the cards. The 1920s restrictions that had favored the Irish but reinforced noxious eugenic ideas about who should be welcomed were broadly understood to be shamefully racist.

Yet something needed to be done, especially with the growing weight of immigration enforcement hanging over people's heads. In Boston, Bill McGowan convened a group of Irish immigration advocates, forming a group called the Massachusetts Immigration Committee (MIC) in 1985.[23] Appealing to established groups like the Ancient Order of Hibernians, the MIC gained the support of Boston philanthropist and Irish immigrant Thomas Flatley, who also contributed to the campaigns of Rep. Brian Donnelly (D-MA) and Sen. Ted Kennedy (D-MA). As Flatley would testify before Congress in July 1986, "There is something radically wrong in a system that penalizes, no matter how inadvertently, a nation and a people who have contributed so uniquely to America's growth and prosperity."[24] The sense that the restrictions preventing the Irish from living freely were harmful, discriminatory, and unjust permeated the debate. In this instance, policymakers could recognize and understand the pain that the immigration bureaucracy inflicted.

Groups lobbied Donnelly, who represented the eleventh district in Massachusetts—the most Irish district in the country—to create "non-preference visas," that is, visas outside of the family and employment preference system, specifically for the Irish.[25] In 1985 Donnelly proposed a bill that gained support from Boston-area groups representing white ethnic Americans and immigrants; Sen. John Kerry (D-MA) introduced companion legislation. Although these bills didn't move forward, their idea was included in IRCA, passed in the autumn of 1986. IRCA contained a legalization program for unauthorized immigrants who had been in the country since before January 1, 1982. Unfortunately, most Irish immigrants arrived too late to qualify. But they were in luck; Donnelly's idea would be implemented through another IRCA provision.

The Donnelly visa program, known as "NP-5," authorized 10,000 non-preference visas over two years, 1987 and 1988, to go to nationals of countries that were "adversely affected" by the Hart-Celler Act of 1965—those that saw their numbers drop after the national origins quotas were eliminated. The State Department calculated a list of thirty-six adversely affected countries, including Ireland and Northern Ireland, that had lower immigration between 1966 and 1985 than during the period 1953 through 1965.[26] Over one week in January 1987, over 1 million NP-5 visa applications were submitted.[27] Sean Benson, a member of the IIRM, later recalled that he sent in over 400 applications for himself.[28] Publications like *Irish America* and the *Irish Echo*, and the Adrian Flannelly radio show, publicized the program, and aid groups encouraged people to apply.[29]

Over 250,000 Irish people reportedly applied, and of the 10,000 visas issued, the Irish received a plurality—3,112, more than nationals of any other adversely affected nation.[30]

The Donnelly visa program demonstrated that the United States could easily make visas available to "independent" immigrants, those without family ties to the United States or particularly needed skills. In doing so, it tapped into rhetoric that had long animated liberal reformers of the immigration system, especially those attuned to the plight of "unskilled" European immigrants. Efforts to restrict low-wage workers were understood by midcentury reformers as efforts to restrict immigration of undesirable people from southern and eastern Europe. In turn, Rep. Emmanuel Celler had spoken up about the place of "new seed" immigrants, those who were "the type of immigrant that built up our country . . . those who built our railroads, ships, and planes, tunneled our mountains and our subways, erected our bridges and roads."[31] Later, the Select Commission recommended expanding the category of "independent" immigrant admissions—immigrants without close family ties to the United States. As historian John Higham testified before Congress in 1986, the system's focus on family ties "is giving admission to followers rather than leaders. . . . Let us open the door to more people who want to come here on their own."[32]

Honoring the Past

In 1987 the Irish Immigration Reform Movement (IIRM) formed in New York to advocate for more visas for the Irish.[33] In a letter to the editor in *Irish America*, Patrick Hurley framed the problem in terms that would become the basis of the group's messaging. "The United States has long been the sanctuary for the Irish in times of oppression and economic difficulty," he wrote. "That right of sanctuary was earned by the contributions of countless Irishmen in the building of this great country. We are no different in nature to the immigrants who came before us. We cherish the same hopes and dreams you once cherished. However, for us, no welcoming sanctuary any longer exists." That, he recognized, was because of the restrictions imposed through the Hart-Celler Act, along with ramped-up immigration enforcement measures, including through IRCA. He also urged Americans of Irish descent to put themselves in the shoes of the newcomers, and to think of themselves as "immigrants of the past." He charged: "Irish Americans do not forget us. Do what you can to help change the immigration laws not only for us, but for many more Irish who will surely follow. You owe it to yourselves, as well as us."[34] As Flatley had warned in his 1986 testimony, "The traditions that have been built up perhaps through the years between the Irish and the United States will fade eventually unless something is done in this area."[35]

The IIRM organized chapters in Boston, Philadelphia, Chicago, San Francisco, Connecticut, New Jersey, and elsewhere.[36] The group actively engaged the Irish government, which sent officials to meet with policymakers in the United States. At the IIRM's urging, the Irish government appointed an immigrant liaison officer for the consulate's New York office. Jerry Tinker, a legislative aide for Sen. Kennedy, credited the Irish Embassy as being "far more important" than any other group during the legislative battle.[37] The IIRM also hired professional lobbyist Harris Miller to support its Hill advocacy, and they began to meet with Congress members of Irish heritage.

When the IIRM testified before Congress in 1988, it focused on preserving "the continuity of history—American-Irish history."[38] Donald Martin urged Congress to "take into account the contributions which have been made to American culture by the Irish and other Europeans." He cited the number of Irish immigrants granted the Medal of Honor for their American military service. He proudly mentioned the number of Irishmen who died fighting the Confederacy in the U.S. Civil War, even quoting in his written testimony General Robert E. Lee's statement praising his Irish opponents, who "ennobled their race by their splendid though hopeless assaults on our lines."[39]

"There were Irish people on this continent long before there was a United States of America and their descendants are in every State," Martin said.[40] "If those immigrants could speak to you now," he added, "we are certain they would argue for fairness and diversity."[41] Such messages were clear examples of what scholars have called "immigrant contributionism," the logic that certain groups have earned their place of belonging in the United States.[42] Of course, this narrative's effectiveness depends on a group's acceptance, something that has long been more attainable for white European immigrants than others.[43]

Proponents of visas for the Irish needed to ask for them without suggesting that the system favor white immigrants—something that likely wouldn't be politically palatable in post-civil rights America. Rev. Joseph A. Cogo, testifying on behalf of the American Committee on Italian Migration, suggested that the immigration system should be reformed in service of "protecting our cultural heritage," a phrase he didn't define.[44] But the implication, shared by some proponents of programs that would allocate more visas to "independent immigrants," was that the system's recent shift to admitting Asian and Latin American immigrants rather than Europeans had created "imbalance." Donnelly had described how the 1965 law unintentionally disadvantaged Europeans. "The cumulative effect of the policy of the last 20 years has been to discriminate against many of the peoples who have traditionally made up our immigrant stock," he said, urging Congress to correct the resulting disparities.[45] Martin said the IIRM was seeking a modest change that would "allow new seed immigrants from the traditional sources of American immigration"—meaning European countries.[46] In a 1989 letter to Rep. Bruce Morrison (D-CT), the IIRM's Connecticut chapter wrote that ensuring future visa access to Irish people was critical for continuing the Irish American heritage of the country. "Without a continuing influx of legal immigration from those countries [Irish, Polish, Europeans shut out of the 1965 legislation] and Canada, we as Americans stand to lose our cherished heritage, the fabric of which is the contributions and cultures of the very countries we are presently closing our doors to."[47] Without new immigration from primarily white countries, some fundamental element of U.S. culture would be diminished. Unlike restrictionists who had made similar arguments in the 1920s, the 1980s advocates were careful to frame that heritage as cultural rather than racial. But the idea that the ongoing flow of white immigrants was needed to stem demographic change must have informed some policymakers' thinking.

In addition to testifying before Congress and meeting with policymakers, the IIRM took its message to the public. They plastered "legalize the Irish" stickers everywhere, held dances to raise funds, and marched prominently in St. Patrick's Day parades. They convinced the Ancient Order of Hibernians to carry a banner reading "Immigration Reform Now," instead of the traditional "England Get Out of Ireland," at New York's parade.[48] A march of 1,800 people garnered media coverage by ABC, CBS, and NBC television networks.[49] Instead of shrinking into the shadows, the Irish and their allies felt empowered to be visible. Members of the IIRM credited their boldness to being well educated and coming of age in an Ireland where they had high expectations for themselves. They didn't feel they had done anything wrong by being unauthorized; instead, something harmful had been done to them.

But their message also resonated because of their racial and ethnic identity. As Patrick Hurley, an undocumented IIRM leader, said, the public "didn't conceptualize illegal aliens as being like Irish people." The novelty of the illegal Irish immigrant proved an appealing subject for media attention, which the IIRM capitalized on to build its public case. The media, Hurley said, was obsessed with "the illegal Irish immigrant" and interviewed him often.[50] As *Irish America* reported, David Boeri, a reporter with Channel Two News in Boston, said, "When the IIRM came about they had much more in common with the people they represented. They are also smart, savvy and likeable guys." The fact that they were white and spoke English was clearly an advantage.[51] As Rep. Romano Mazzoli (D-KY) said after Martin's 1988 testimony, "The renown of Irish people to be eloquent I think was already demonstrated, even today."[52] Congress extended the Donnelly visa program, providing 15,000 additional visas per year in 1989 and 1990 for nationals of the adversely affected countries. But the IIRM wanted more, and a compelling theme was emerging to help them achieve it.

Independent Immigrants

The broad debate about both how to reform the immigration admissions system and how to address the specific grievances of the Irish focused on the centrality of family unification to the post-1965 immigration system. The family-based system, adopted in part to perpetuate the existing majority-European makeup of the immigration stream, had produced unexpected results, thanks to geopolitical shifts. By the 1980s, most immigrants came through the family system, and most came from Asian or Latin American countries. But the family system and the imposition of numerical per-country limits on most visa categories had caused large backlogs. This meant that people from certain countries could qualify for an immigrant visa, but then wait years, or even decades, to receive it.[53] This was painful and led to criticisms that the system was broken. Some policymakers were hoping to address and reduce these long waiting times, perhaps by eliminating certain visa categories, like the one for siblings of U.S. citizens.[54]

Additionally, some wondered if the emphasis on family ties was putting the United States at a disadvantage in terms of its global economic competitiveness. Shouldn't the country try to attract immigrants with the most to contribute to a dynamic economy, especially looking toward the new millennium? As the IIRM testified before Congress in November 1987, to gain advantage in the global market, the United States should want to attract "the resourcefulness and drive of the skilled, independent immigrant"—not exclude it.[55]

The Irish shared frustration with the system's emphasis on family ties, which they lacked. "Family reunification is a goal we all support," testified Sen. Al D'Amato (R-NY). "But what about those who have no immediate relatives in the United States? The law shuts them out because they are from countries like Ireland or Italy, whose great days of immigration are long in the past."[56] D'Amato described his own grandparents arriving through Ellis Island with no relatives to sponsor them. They came, he said, with "an unquenchable thirst for freedom and the strong belief in the American dream."[57] The idea that there should be a new channel for legal immigration not based on family relationships, specific employment, or on humanitarian need, but on something else, was potent.

Voices in support of the idea emphasized that what they wanted to honor was a model of immigration that depended on strivers. Such imagery gained traction in the individualistic 1980s, when mythologies about bootstrapping high achievers succeeding on their own talents, merit, and hard work dovetailed with anti-statism and capitalistic excess. But of course, the idea of making space for this type of immigrant also depended heavily on the historical narratives summoned to support it. In these narratives, the strivers were almost exclusively white, European immigrants who were welcomed into the American story in the mid-twentieth century.

In this discussion, policymakers and others who supported the admission of independent immigrants sometimes elided the fact that many people in the 1980s *did* come to the United States in ways strikingly similar to those of earlier waves of now-celebrated immigrants—Haitians, Salvadorans, Mexicans, and others came seeking haven, safety, and economic mobility. They encountered restrictions, denials, and discrimination, even as lawmakers waxed poetic about the "classic" immigrant of the past.[58]

Congress created another small program for "independent immigrants," seeing this as an admirable idea. Rep. Howard Berman (D-CA) disagreed with proposals that emphasized the importance of restoring European immigration to its former dominant level, but he was moved by the argument that there were imbalances in the current system. Immigrants from just a few countries in Asia and Latin America tended to get the lion's share of visas.[59] Berman's visa program would be open not only to those countries deemed "adversely affected," like Ireland, but to 162 "underrepresented countries" from beyond Europe.

Again, the program was popular and effective. Some 3 million people submitted entries for the 20,000 visas.[60] The countries that won the most visas were Bangladesh, Pakistan, Poland, Turkey, and Egypt. Ireland trailed behind, garnering only 362 visas. That disappointing result motivated the Irish to continue their advocacy. To win sufficient visas in a global visa program, the IIRM realized they needed a leg up. As they wrote, "50% or more of the visas must be targeted toward lottery winners from the 36 countries adversely affected by the 1965 Act."[61] But as Kennedy staffer Michael Myers put it, "You can't just have an Irish provision, because that would never pass Congress."[62]

Diversity

The key to creating a permanent provision to enable independent immigration was "diversity." Diversity had been articulated as one of the goals for the U.S. immigration system.[63] The United States remained "the world's number one magnet," not only because of the dynamism of its economy but also, the Select Commission had written, because of American values: "freedom, equality under the law, opportunity and respect for diversity."[64] Americans liked to project "diversity" backwards as a goal of their forebears, because it made sense of a country founded by enslavers and settlers espousing freedom, and it brushed histories of violent conquest under the rug. The country was becoming more racially diverse. Celebrating cultural pluralism as a strength rather than casting it as a weakness might help address the demographic and political challenges of the next decades. The idea that the United States was a diverse country forged through waves of migration—a nation of immigrants, a country shaped by people coming from elsewhere, united by creed—was compelling to many.

It seemed to the IIRM and others that prioritizing the admission of Irish immigrants could contribute to a more diverse immigration stream. That message drew criticism from people who pointed out that admitting more white immigrants in the name of diversity seemed cynical. But it worked. The framework of diversity helped garner support from unlikely corners for creating a new visa category. On the right and among restrictionists across the spectrum, some were clearly concerned about the fact that people of Asian and Latin American origin constituted most immigrants. But now they could disavow racism, even as they created more opportunities for European immigration. Instead, they could say they were in favor of more diverse immigration. More immigrant diversity, in this context, could aim to address and break up the concentration of immigrants coming from just a handful of countries. Framed in this way, high levels of Mexican immigration, for example, actually undermined diversity. The concentration of immigrants coming from specific countries—stemming from the system's emphasis on family ties and its per-country limits—could contribute to ethnic enclaves and perhaps ethnic separatism and disunity.

Questions about unity and assimilation undergirded a contemporaneous "English only" movement. White, English-speaking Americans could mask their anxieties about demographic change behind colorblind language and practical concerns about immigrant integration and the adoption of English. Language policy proved one of the more potent wedge issues in the immigration policy debate in the 1980s. John Tanton, who had founded the restrictionist organization Federation for American Immigration Reform in 1979, also launched U.S. English to advocate for official English or English-only policies. Like the IIRM, the English-only crowd *also* framed its policy desires in terms of "E. Pluribus Unum." But it aimed for assimilation to a culture defined as English-speaking and European-descended—and wanted large reductions in immigration as well.[65]

The Irish had no problem with policies that would favor English-speaking immigrants—something briefly considered—but the IIRM didn't seek to cut or restrict immigration of non-white, non-English speaking people. As Miller wrote in a letter, "Unlike some of the other ethnic groups which frequently try to inject racism and fear into the debate (a leader of a major ethnic organization recently was quoted, I hope incorrectly, as saying the Senate debate this year has 'racial undertones'), IIRM has always stayed positive."[66] Yet anxiety about pluralism promulgated by restrictionists ironically helped build support for diversity in immigration admissions. Diversity would preserve the "nation of immigrants" model and prevent any one ethnic or national group from dominating. As Higham had testified in 1986, "Just as the national origins quota system in the early twentieth century suppressed variety in the interest of favored ethnic groups, so the current law does that in the interest of family chains."[67] Around 80 percent of immigrants came via family ties and 80 percent of immigrants were Asian and Latin American. The implication that the family-based system limited variety was directly related to what observers might have felt was the overrepresentation of immigrants of color coming to the United States in the 1980s. Building on this point, IIRM lobbyist Harris Miller stated in a memo, "Everyone agrees that in order to encourage diversity in the immigration pool, countries such as Ireland and Italy need a chance to have more immigrants come to this country."[68]

The group was careful in its messaging to say that diversity provisions should not take away from other groups. They did not want to suggest that space should be made for the Irish at the expense of Mexican or Chinese immigrants. "Immigration diversity can be achieved without harming the countries that now send the bulk of our immigrants," as Sen. Paul Simon (D-IL) wrote to IIRM chairman Sean Minihane in 1989, agreeing with a talking point the group embraced.[69]

Critically, the Immigration Act of 1990, which contained the diversity program, rejected zero-sum thinking and negotiations. Because of the legislation's relative generosity, the needs of the Irish were not pitted against those of other groups. The IIRM was careful to position diversity admissions as additive rather than a substitute for existing visa categories—and this helped prevent fracture and conflict between the advocacy groups hoping to shape the legislation.

Policymakers created two different diversity/independent immigrant programs in the 1990 law. The diversity visa lottery followed an IIRM proposal. The group proposed distributing diversity visas in inverse proportion to family-based preference admissions and using regional weights to determine allocations. Because Asia and Latin America received about 87 percent of preference admissions, they should be allocated 13 percent of diversity admissions. After dividing the world into the two highest-sending regions (Asia and Latin America) and four lowest-sending regions (Europe, Africa, North America, and Oceania), Miller's math would grant the most diversity visas to Europe— nearly 47 percent of them—with Africa receiving 37 percent, followed by Asia receiving 12 percent, and the other regions receiving less than 2 percent each: Latin America, North America, and Oceania.[70] Within regions, the visas would be distributed by lottery. The diversity visas would complement the other visa categories, producing more diversity in terms of immigrants' national origins.

Finding an ally in Rep. Bruce Morrison (D-CT), the IIRM also wanted more visas for people from adversely affected countries, like a continuation of the Donnelly program. Morrison lauded the 1965 act for spreading the "promise of immigration opportunity to people from areas of the world from which they in the past were not able to come."[71] But it had also created problems, he argued. It had "cut the ties that we have traditionally had to other parts of the world that have provided another measure of our diversity," referring to the "adversely affected" nations like Ireland.[72] Morrison's decision to run for governor in 1990 provided an opening for the IIRM to organize support while pushing him to act boldly on immigration from his position as chair of the House subcommittee. Morrison's "transition lottery," included in the final legislation, made 40,000 visas available per year for three years, for nationals of adversely affected countries.[73] A special provision reserved at least 40 percent of the visas for "the foreign state the natives of which received the greatest number of visas issued under section 314 of the Immigration Reform and Control Act,"—a.k.a. the Donnelly visa program. Since Ireland had won the most Donnelly visas, the Irish would receive at least 40 percent of the 120,000 transition visas. At the law's passage, Sen. Daniel P. Moynihan (D-NY) acknowledged in the record the role the IIRM played in "bringing this legislation to fruition. Probably no organization has been as diligent, or played such a helpful role in moving the Congress forward, as the IIRM and they deserve great thanks and hearty congratulations."[74]

The Irish created their own luck by lobbying effectively, garnering sympathy, and shifting their messaging from nostalgia and immigration contributionism to a broader argument about the centrality of independent immigration and diversity to the American story. They sustained their campaign by speaking boldly about their plight, and by showcasing the harms that befell them because of the cruelty of limits, restrictions, and bureaucracy. Forced to leave home only to encounter a gate slammed shut by a country that celebrated itself as welcoming genuinely stung. The pains of immigration restriction and living without legal status were deeply felt. The media and policymakers were moved to action because they could see restriction and even illegality itself in the case of the Irish, as inhumane, even un-American.

They were afforded much of the patience and dignity they demanded because of their savvy, but also because of their whiteness and their careful, colorblind appeals to a shared past. They had helped amplify the idea that a "classic" model of American immigration—which had long served white immigrants—might be worth reviving for the twenty-first century. "It is difficult to see this as anything but a veiled tilt away from current immigrant source regions," wrote INS Commissioner Doris Meissner in an op-ed criticizing the law their lobbying helped craft.[75] It was self-serving and even cynical to tout the Irish contribution to immigrant diversity.

But the outcome, which served the Irish well for the moment—soon the Celtic Tiger would slow emigration from Ireland, and new restrictions in the United States after 1996 would continue to bedevil those who did immigrate—would also create a new path for independent immigrants who looked nothing like them. The language the IIRM had marshaled, which depended on a set of racial assumptions to gain support, also helped create a policy that considerably broadened access to immigration for Black African immigrants who were otherwise all but shut out, who faced even more stringent restrictions on their mobility. It is striking to remember that gatekeepers hold the power to create genuine access and opportunities for people—as they did in creating the lottery. But except for the lottery, it may be unclear whether such openings, which depend on images and assumptions that frame the nation of immigrants as white, can be truly inclusive.

Notes

1. Kevin Molloy, Handwritten Lyrics, Irish Immigration Reform Movement Records, AIA 016, Box 10, Folder 9, Archives of Irish America. The material in this chapter draws from work in my book *Dreamland: America's Immigration Lottery in an Age of Restriction* (Chapel Hill: University of North Carolina Press, 2023) and in the chapter "Legislating Diversity in the Immigration Act of 1990," in Maria Cristina Garcia and Maddalena Marinari, eds., *Whose America? U.S. Immigration Policy Since 1980* (Urbana: University of Illinois Press, 2023).

2. About 360,000 Irish citizens left between 1981 and 1991. Linda Dowling Almeida, *Irish Immigrants in New York City, 1945–1995* (Bloomington: Indiana University Press, 2001), 61.

3. Almeida estimates that around 10 percent of these emigrants (40,000) went to America, while some advocates claimed the figure was as high as 150,000 to 200,000. Almeida, *Irish Immigrants in New York City*, 61. See also Matthew O'Brien, "Ethnic Legacy and Immigrant Mobility: The New Irish and Irish America in the 1990s," *Etudes Irlandaises* 28, no. 2 (2003): 119–33; Íde B. O'Carroll, *Irish Transatlantics 1980–2015* (Cork, Ireland: Cork University Press, 2018).

4. Hidetaka Hirota, *Expelling the Poor: Atlantic Seaboard States and the Nineteenth-Century Origins of American Immigration Policy* (New York: Oxford University Press, 2017).

5. Mae M. Ngai, "The Architecture of Race in American Immigration Law: A Reexamination of the Immigration Act of 1924," *The Journal of American History* 86, no. 1 (1999): 67–92.

6. U.S. Department of Homeland Security, "Table 2: Persons Obtaining Legal Permanent Resident Status by Region and Selected Country of Last Residence, Fiscal Years 1820 to 2019," in *2019 Yearbook of Immigration Statistics*.

7. Sean Benson, interview, November 29, 2005, Ireland House Oral History Collection, AIA 030, Archives of Irish America, New York University.

8. IIRM, "The Story of the IIRM," Irish Immigration Reform Movement Records, AIA 016, Box 9, Folder 3, Archives of Irish America.

9. Marvine Howe, "Working to Help Irish Immigrants Stay, Legally," *New York Times*, November 27, 1988, http://www.nytimes.com/1988/11/27/nyregion/working-to-help-irish-immigrants-stay-legally.html.

10. "Ancestry of the Population by State: 1980" (Supplementary Report PC80-S1–10), U.S. Department of Commerce, Bureau of the Census, April 1983, accessed at https://www.census.gov/content/dam/Census/library/publications/1983/dec/pc80-s1–10.pdf.

11. "Census: Americans More Irish Than Irish," *Philadelphia Daily News*, June 1, 1983.

12. Inga Saffron, "Well-Traveled Irish Now among the Illegals," *Philadelphia Inquirer*, May 2, 1987.

13. Paul Hofmann, "Irish-Americans Organize to Assist Visa Seekers Barred by Immigration Law as Unskilled Workers," *New York Times*, November 15, 1966, 20, https://www.nytimes.com/1966/11/15/archives/irishamericans-organize-to-assist-visa-seekers-barred-by.html.

14. Paul Hofmann, "Curbs on Irish Immigrants Protested," *New York Times*, March 16, 1968, 37, https://www.nytimes.com/1968/03/16/archives/curbs-on-irish-immigrants-protested.html.

15. "Irish Immigration Declines, House Subcommittee Told," *New York Times*, December 14, 1969, 31.

16. American Irish National Immigration Committee, "No Irish Need Apply," *New York Times*, accessed at http://www.jscjohnpcollinsret.com/uploads/3/4/6/1/34611293/ny_times_ad.pdf.

17. See, for example, a bill introduced in 1968 by Dominick V. Daniels (D-N.J.). Tichenor cites this memo: Andrew Biemiller to George Meany, July 19, 1968, Papers of the legislative department of the AFL-CIO, Box 27, Folder 33. Daniel J. Tichenor, *Dividing Lines: The Politics of Immigration Control in America* (Princeton, NJ: Princeton University Press, 2002), 235.

18. U.S. Congress Select Commission on Immigration and Refugee Policy, "Immigration Policy and the National Interest," March 1, 1981, 63, https://files.eric.ed.gov/fulltext/ED211612.pdf.

19. U.S. Congress Select Commission on Immigration and Refugee Policy, "Immigration Policy and the National Interest."

20. Anna O. Law, "The Diversity Visa Lottery: A Cycle of Unintended Consequences in United States Immigration Policy," *Journal of American Ethnic History* 21, no. 4 (2002): 3–29, 9, http://www.jstor.org/stable/27501196.

21. Peter Anderson, "The Twilight Society," *Boston Globe*, December 14, 1986.

22. Patrick H., an undocumented Irishman, "Editorial—A Statement of Intent," *New Irish: Published By and For the Irish*, June 21, 1987. Irish Immigration Reform Movement Records, AIA 016, Box 14, Folder 2, Archives of Irish America.

23. Michael P. Quinlin, *Irish Boston: A Lively Look at Boston's Colorful Irish Past* (Guilford, CT: Globe Pequot, 2004), 155.

24. U.S. Congress, House Committee on the Judiciary, *Legal Immigration*, July 30, 1986 (Statement of Thomas Flatley), 66.

25. Niall O'Dowd, "Visa Man," *Irish America*, May 1989, Irish Immigration Reform Movement Records, AIA 016, Box 162, Folder 11, Archives of Irish America; "The Year of the Illegal Aliens," *Irish America*, December 1988, Irish Immigration Reform Movement Records, AIA 016, Box 13, Folder 19, Archives of Irish America.

26. "Nonpreference Immigration Visa Availability under Section 314 of the Immigration Reform and Control Act of 1986: Determination of Areas 'Adversely Affected' by the Enactment of Public Law 89–236," Box 369, Folder 3, Alan K. Simpson papers, Collection 10449, American Heritage Center, University of Wyoming. The nations identified as "adversely affected" were Albania, Algeria, Argentina, Austria, Belgium, Bermuda, Canada, Czechoslovakia, Denmark, Estonia, Finland, France, the Federal Republic of Germany, German Democratic Republic, Great Britain and Northern Ireland, Guadeloupe, Hungary, Iceland, Indonesia, Ireland, Italy, Japan, Latvia, Liechtenstein, Lithuania, Luxembourg, Monaco, the Netherlands, New Caledonia, Norway, Poland, San Marino, Sweden, Switzerland, and Tunisia. No. 92, 52 Fed. Reg. 17948 (May 13, 1987). Irish Immigration Reform Movement Records, AIA 016, Box 12, Folder 35, Archives of Irish America.

27. "Over a million seek U.S. visas," *Irish Echo*, January 31, 1987, Irish Immigration Reform Movement Records, AIA 016, Box 26, Archives of Irish America.

28. Sean Benson, interview.

29. "10,000 Non-Preference Visas to Be Issued by U.S.," *Irish Echo*, January 10, 1987, Irish Immigration Reform Movement Records, AIA 016, Box 26, Archives of Irish America.

30. "Irish Win 3112 Visas in Lottery," *Irish America*, April 1987, Irish Immigration Reform Movement Records, AIA 016, Box 162, Folder 9, Archives of Irish America.

31. Quoted in Philip E. Wolgin, "Beyond National Origins: The Development of Modern Immigration Policymaking, 1948–1968" (PhD diss, University of California Berkley, 2011), 103.

32. U.S. Congress, House Committee on the Judiciary, *Legal Immigration*, July 30, 1986 (Statement of John Higham, historian), 3.

33. Sean Benson, interview. The group adopted a thorough constitution by early spring 1988. IIRM Constitution, Robin O'Brien Hiteshew Collection 3059, Box 11, Folder 10, Historical Society of Pennsylvania, Philadelphia.

34. "Patrick," letter to the editor, "Undocumented Alien from County Cork Now Resident in Queens," *Irish America*, June 1987, Irish Immigration Reform Movement Records, AIA 016, Box 162, Folder 9, Archives of Irish America.

35. U.S. Congress, House Committee on the Judiciary, *Legal Immigration*, July 30, 1986 (Statement of Thomas Flatley), 63.

36. "The Year of the Illegal Aliens," *Irish America*, December 1988, Irish Immigration Reform Movement Records, AIA 016, Box 13, Folder 19, Archives of Irish America.

37. "The Year of the Illegal Aliens."

38. U.S. Congress, House Committee on the Judiciary, *Reform of Legal Immigration*, September 7 and 16, 1988 (Statement of Donald Martin on behalf of IIRM).

39. U.S. Congress (Statement of Donald Martin on behalf of IIRM), 560.

40. U.S. Congress (Statement of Donald Martin on behalf of IIRM), 550.

41. U.S. Congress (Statement of Donald Martin on behalf of IIRM), 548.

42. Robert L. Fleegler, *Ellis Island Nation: Immigration Policy and American Identity in the Twentieth Century* (Philadelphia: University of Pennsylvania Press, 2013). Danielle Battisti details how contributionism led to demands for immigration opportunities for specific groups. Danielle Battisti, *Whom We Shall Welcome: Italian Americans and Immigration Reform, 1945–1965* (New York: Fordham University Press, 2019), 219–34.

43. Battisti, *Whom We Shall Welcome*, 220–22.

44. U.S. Congress, House Committee on the Judiciary, *Reform of Legal Immigration*, September 7 and 16, 1988 (Statement of Rev. Joseph A. Cogo), 504.

45. U.S. Congress, Senate Committee on the Judiciary, *Legal Immigration Reforms*, October 23 and December 11, 1987 (Statement of Rep. Brian J. Donnelly), 52.

46. U.S. Congress, House Committee on the Judiciary, *Reform of Legal Immigration*, September 7 and 16, 1988 (Statement of Donald Martin on behalf of IIRM), 561.

47. Letter, January 24, 1989, Robin O'Brien Hiteshew Collection 3059, Box 11, Folder 12, Historical Society of Pennsylvania, Philadelphia.

48. IIRM Newsletter, Volume III, Number 2, March 1990, Irish Immigration Reform Movement Records, AIA 016, Box 12, Folder 2, Archives of Irish America.

49. IIRM Newsletter, Volume III, Number 2.

50. Patrick Hurley, interview, October 31, 1997, Ireland House Oral History Collection, AIA 030, Archives of Irish America.

51. "The Year of the Illegal Aliens," *Irish America*, December 1988, Irish Immigration Reform Movement Records, AIA 016, Box 13, Folder 19, Archives of Irish America.

52. U.S. Congress, House Committee on the Judiciary, *Reform of Legal Immigration*, September 7 and 16, 1988 (Statement of Rep. Romano Mazzoli), 562.

53. Mae M. Ngai, "The Civil Rights Origins of Illegal Immigration," *International Labor and Working-Class History* 78 (October 2010): 93–99.

54. For example, a 1988 bill proposed by Simpson and Kennedy reduced the fifth preference category (siblings) by disqualifying married people from these visas. Immigration Act of 1988, S. 2104, 100th Cong. (1988). See also John M. Goering, *Legal Immigration to the United States: A Demographic Analysis of Fifth Preference Visa Admissions: A Staff Report Prepared for the Use of the Subcommittee on Immigration and Refugee Affairs, Committee on the Judiciary, United States Senate*, 100th Cong., 1 (April 1987), vol. 4.

55. IIRM Congressional Testimony, November 7, 1987, cited in IIRM "In the News" newsletter, Robin O'Brien Hiteshew Collection 3059, Box 11, Folder 11, Historical Society of Pennsylvania, Philadelphia.

56. U.S. Congress, Senate Committee on the Judiciary, *Legal Immigration Reforms*, October 23 and December 11, 1987 (Statement of Sen. Alfonse D'Amato), 43.

57. U.S. Congress, Senate Committee on the Judiciary, *Legal Immigration Reforms*, October 23 and December 11, 1987 (Statement of Sen. Alan K. Simpson), 10. Alan K. Simpson papers, Box 369, Folder 4.

58. U.S. Congress (statement of Sen. Alan K. Simpson), 5.

59. Marvine Howe, "Immigrants to Get Visas by Lottery," *New York Times*, March 1, 1989, http://www.nytimes.com/1989/03/01/us/immigrants-to-get-visas-by-lottery.html.

60. "3 Million Win a Chance to Enter U.S. 'Visa Lottery,'" *Los Angeles Times*, May 10, 1989, http://articles.latimes.com/1989-05-10/news/mn-2797_1_visa-lottery-immigrant -visa-state-department.

61. "3 Million Win a Chance to Enter U.S. 'Visa Lottery.'"

62. Michael Myers, interview, August 28, 2006, Edward M. Kennedy Oral History Project, Miller Center, University of Virginia.

63. "U.S. Immigration Policy and the National Interest: Staff Report of the Select Commission on Immigration and Refugee Policy," Supplement to the Final Report and Recommendations of the Select Commission on Immigration and Refugee Policy, April 30, 1981, 358.

64. U.S. Congress Select Commission on Immigration and Refugee Policy, "Immigration Policy and the National Interest."

65. John Tanton, "A Skirmish in a Wider War," interviewed by Otis Graham Jr., April 20–21, 1980, Oral History Project for the Federation for American Immigration Reform, 41, Box 1, John Tanton Papers, Bentley Historical Library, University of Michigan; S. I. Hayakawa, "Common Language, Common Sense," *New York Times*, February 21, 1990, https://www.nytimes.com/1990/02/21/opinion/common-language-common-sense.html.

66. Harris Miller to Werner Brandt, Office of the Speaker, June 20, 1989, Irish Immigration Reform Movement Records, AIA 016, Box 9, Folder 2, Archives of Irish America.

67. U.S. Congress, House Committee on the Judiciary, *Legal Immigration*, July 30, 1986 (Statement of John Higham, historian), 2.

68. Harris Miller to IIRM Members, re Lobbying Effort, June 21, 1989, Irish Immigration Reform Movement Records, AIA 016, Box 13, Folder 5, Archives of Irish America.

69. Letter from Paul Simon to Sean Minihane, March 17, 1989, Robin O'Brien Hiteshew Collection 3059, Historical Society of Pennsylvania, Philadelphia.

70. James S. Holt and Harris N. Miller, Holt Miller & Associates, to Sean Minihane, IIRM, October 30, 1989, Irish Immigration Reform Movement Records, AIA 016, Box 7, Folder 4, Archives of Irish America.

71. U.S. Congress, House Committee on the Judiciary, *Immigration Act of 1989*, September 27, 1989 (Statement of Chairman Bruce Morrison), 2.

72. U.S. Congress (Statement of Chairman Bruce Morrison), 2.

73. Negotiators cut the House bill's allocation of 15,000 additional transition visas for Eastern Europeans and Africans.

74. Congressional Record Proceedings and Debates of the 101st Congress, Second Session, Volume 136, Part 24, October 26, 1990 (GPO, 1990), Statement of Sen. Moynihan, 35619.

75. Doris Meissner, "Yes to Immigrants, No to Quick Fixes Immigration: The Bill Should Pass on Its Merits, Not Under the Delusion That It Will Solve America's Problems," *Los Angeles Times*, Oct 26, 1990.

PART II

Reimagining the European Migrant

4 Time Difference

*Pregnancy and Deportability in
Early Twentieth-Century United States*

RANDA TAWIL

In October 1907, Medical Superintendent Dr. Edgar Gilray examined Anna Metan, a patient who had arrived at Erie County Hospital earlier that week to deliver her baby.[1] She was probably the first in her family to give birth in a hospital, but alone in a new country, she had few other options. Metan did not have extended family to look after her and help her with delivery and recovery. Moreover, hospitals and the male doctors who staffed them had gained reputations as safe and modern care facilities that could offer better care than traditional services such as female midwives. Turn-of-the-century Protestant reformers in the United States also promoted hospital use as they advocated for maternal and newborn health—particularly among the white ethnic immigrants they served in settlement houses and other outreach centers. For all these reasons, Anna Metan may have thought the hospital was the best place to receive care for her and her child.[2]

Shortly after arriving, Anna Metan most likely regretted her decision to enter Erie County Hospital. It had been labeled by the local press as the "worst hospital in the state," and in one account was accused of being as unhygienic as a tenement house.[3] Furthermore, it seemed Dr. Gilray was less concerned with caring for Metan and her child than securing payment of her bill. Overseeing both the almshouse and the hospital, Superintendent Gilray routinely dealt with immigrants who could not pay for their care, and forwarded the bill to Robert Hill, Buffalo's Superintendent of State and Alien Poor. Buffalo was home to a booming migrant population: by the first decade of the twentieth century, three out of four residents of Buffalo were foreign born.[4] The rapidly industrializing city offered myriad employment opportunities to newcomers and was close to the Eastern Seaboard port cities where Metan and other European immigrants typically arrived. It had been a destination for Eastern European immigrants like Metan since the 1880s. By the first decade of the twentieth century, 80,000 ethnic Polish people lived there, and most were from Metan's region of Galicia.[5]

In Metan's case, however, the city would not pay her bill. Instead, Superintendent Robert Hill wrote to the U.S. Commissioner of Immigration, John F. Clark to call for Metan's deportation. "If this case is acted upon promptly," he wrote, "she can be returned to Poland before her time of lying-in."[6] By entering the hospital, Anna Metan had unknowingly exposed herself and her baby to state bureaucracy and its consequences.

Metan had landed at Ellis Island seven months earlier after a month-long journey. According to the Immigration Act of 1903, immigrants who used public funds within their first two years in the United States could be deported.[7] Immigrants like Metan could face deportation for using public hospitals for "causes existing prior to arrival": if they landed in the United States with a condition they would later need public funds to manage, then they could be deported. Metan was eight months pregnant when she was treated at Erie County Hospital but had been in the country for only seven months. It was that timeline, and interpretation of Metan's body, that enabled Gilray to claim that her pregnancy existed before she arrived in the United States. Gilray tried to fill out the government form the best he could; he wrote that Metan's disease was pregnancy and the cause was sexual intercourse. He also made sure to scribble an S in front of the "he" on the sheet, since the standard form was created for male patients. Because Metan visited the hospital to give birth, her pregnancy had been interpreted through emerging legal and medical terms that retroactively rendered her entry into the United States as problematic, and her body deportable.

The week before Metan left Galicia, she had had sexual intercourse with Francziszek Jaskowiec. She decided to leave her homeland to "better her condition"—surely a difficult choice for a twenty-two-year-old woman. However, she had reasoned, there was not much left for her in Galicia. The region was the most diverse and the poorest in the Austro-Hungarian Empire. It had been annexed from the Polish-Lithuanian Commonwealth in 1772, and the seizure caused the region to lose many of its traditional trade routes, increasing poverty and precarity for the already poor population. By the nineteenth century, Galician peasants dubbed their region "the Kingdom of Bareness and Starvation."[8] Metan had been born out of wedlock, her mother had died when she was a child, and her stepfather had already emigrated to somewhere in the Americas years earlier. As Metan made her journey to the United States, she may not have known she was pregnant. The trip could have caused several physical changes or maladies. When she arrived at Ellis Island, public health officials also did not detect her pregnancy (even though some officials claimed they could tell a pregnant woman by the shine of the hair on the left side of her face).[9] After they stripped her, prodded her eyes, and examined her body, they determined Anna Metan was fit for entry.[10] Yet seven months later in Buffalo, her body was

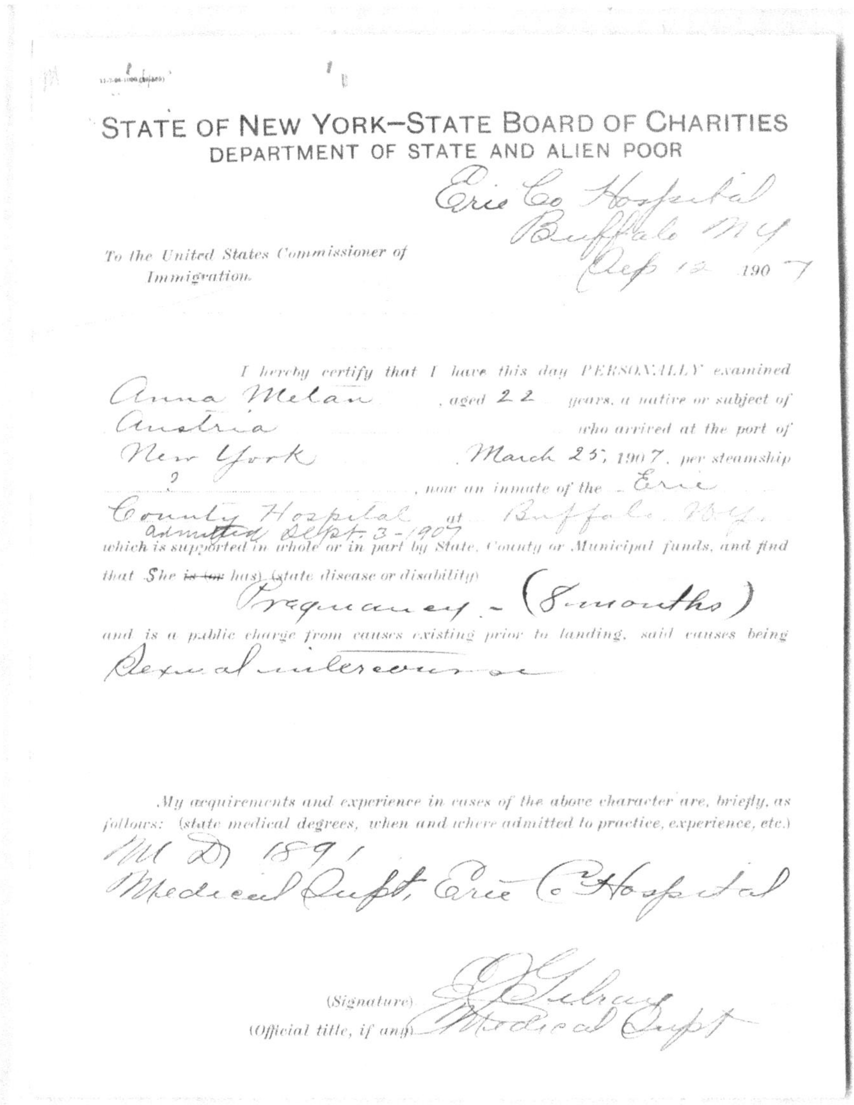

STATE OF NEW YORK—STATE BOARD OF CHARITIES
DEPARTMENT OF STATE AND ALIEN POOR

Erie Co Hospital
Buffalo N Y
Sep 12 190 7

To the United States Commissioner of
Immigration.

I hereby certify that I have this day PERSONALLY examined *Anna Metan*, aged *2 2* years, a native or subject of *Austria* who arrived at the port of *New York* March *25*, 190 *7*, per steamship ______, now an inmate of the *Erie County Hospital* at *Buffalo N.Y.* *admitted Sept. 3 - 1907* which is supported in whole or in part by State, County or Municipal funds, and find that *She* is (or has) (state disease or disability) *Pregnancy - (8 months)* and is a public charge from causes existing prior to landing, said causes being *Sexual intercourse*

My acquirements and experience in cases of the above character are, briefly, as follows: (state medical degrees, when and where admitted to practice, experience, etc.)

M D 1891
Medical Dept, Erie Co Hospital

(Signature) *Gilray*
(Official title, if any) *Medical Dept*

Figure 4.1. Dr. Gilray's report on Anna Metan. Courtesy of the National Archives and Records Administration, Washington, DC.

pathologized by medical professionals, immigration inspectors, and legislators. She was a poor, immigrant woman. The intersection of her gender, sexuality, and class made her into a problematic body to the state, and thus deportable by U.S. law. Her body's reproductive capabilities put into question her status in the country and threatened the social and economic mobility she desired to "better her condition" by migrating to the United States. For Anna Metan, the U.S. border expanded both geographically and temporally, affecting what it meant to live as an impoverished white, ethnic, immigrant woman in the country.

Today, as pregnant people's reproductive intentions and capabilities continue to be monitored and interpreted through a collaboration between doctors and the state, Anna Metan's situation seems as instructive as it is upsetting. Her pregnancy and treatment were given new meaning through advances in obstetrics that ostensibly made her birth experience safer; but at the same time, these advances were weaponized against her through the legal system. Historically and today, Black and brown women have faced the brunt of the medical system's collaboration with the state through sterilization campaigns, welfare restrictions, and what Ruth Gilmore has called "organized abandonment."[11] In Metan's case, her whiteness could not protect her from gendered and classed laws created to monitor the bodies of people deemed by the state to be undeserving of care. Her predicament was harrowing but not unique. Many women who entered the country "legally" could still be rendered deportable by government officials and doctors' perceptions of sexuality and reproduction. By working together, doctors and immigration officials could enact control over the single, pregnant, poor women they termed "undesirable." The stories of Anna Metan and others remind us how policing mobility and sexuality are historically linked and have at times been bolstered by health workers. Their entanglements enable the state to control its migrants well after they gain entrance to the country.

In this chapter, I chart the ways that immigration law, medical science, and progressive reform movements worked together in the early twentieth century, at times haphazardly and in contradictory ways, to categorize and police pregnant migrant women after their entrance into the United States. Deportations of heavily pregnant women in the early twentieth century were relatively rare—as were deportations in general. As Torrie Hester reminds us, 95 percent of deportations from the United States occurred after 1970.[12] The early twentieth century, however, marked an important transformation in the concept of deportation. Daniel Kanstroom has argued that the logic surrounding deportation changed from enforcement at the moment of border crossing to enforcing certain aspects of social control across both time and space. The former uses deportation to remove those who were considered inadmissible by regulatory legislation, or migrants who had clearly broken the law upon entry, while the latter "uses deportation as a method of continual control of the behavior of noncitizens."[13] In cases of pregnancy, the difference between these concepts is muddied: if someone did not know they were pregnant, had they broken the law? Was pregnancy a "cause [of disease] existing prior to arrival" or just a normal function of women's reproductive systems? And who decided? The meaning of reproduction butted heads with new forms of migration regulation and surveillance, affecting women's independence and livelihood. By studying how cases were decided, we can better understand the ways different social, medical, and governmental organizations produced ideas of women's bodies and their sexuality in concert. Immigration agents arbitrated deportations due to pregnancy, and in doing so worked to define sexuality, race, reproduction, and class in the United States.

The New Timekeepers

Anna Metan confronted a system of immigration restriction preoccupied with racialized sexuality and new legal frameworks of time. Beginning with the Page Act of 1875, the first federal immigration restriction, the U.S. government passed laws prohibiting women's mobility largely based on the government's perception of her racialized sexuality.[14] The act restricted the "importation of women for the purposes of prostitution." In practice, the law allowed migration agents to criminalize and police poor and Asian women, categorizing them as "prostitutes" and prohibiting their entry to the country.[15] The act was a precursor to the explicit restriction of Chinese labor migration in 1882. The Chinese Exclusion Act, passed largely due to white workers' economic anxieties and organized racial violence against Chinese people in California and the Pacific Northwest, prohibited Chinese laborers from migrating to the country.[16] Constructions of gender and sexuality were central to this legislation as well. Portrayals of working-class male Chinese migrants vilified their "bachelor" lifestyle as a threat to heteronormative social structures, and their acceptance of subpar living conditions were thought to depress the wages of white men who supported their families.[17] In 1892, the Geary Act furthered restrictions by requiring Chinese laborers who had already migrated to the United States to apply for a government certificate approving their status in the country. The process was intentionally difficult, and Chinese laborers' failure to obtain certification resulted in some of the first formal deportation hearings in the country. Two landmark Supreme Court cases, *Fong Yue Ting* and *Yamataya vs. Fisher,* cemented U.S. federal power to deport noncitizens.[18] In this way, anti-Chinese racism, tied to fears of Chinese sexuality and mobility, marked the beginning of the deportation regime that women like Anna Metan, although regarded as white, would face.

Lawmakers continued to pass laws to restrict migration as well as expand causes for deportation. By the end of the nineteenth century, the combined migration from Asia, southern and eastern Europe, and the Ottoman Empire surpassed that from northern and western Europe. At the same time, eugenicists began to actively spread theories of "race suicide," the idea that Anglo Americans would be replaced by "lesser" races who would slowly erode the country.[19] In 1891, the government introduced public charge laws requiring deportation for a migrant who sought public funds within a year of their arrival into the United States for a condition that existed before landing.[20] Importantly, the cost of deportation was to be borne at the expense of the steamship company. The law was put in place partly to regulate the steamship industry by incentivizing shipping agents to restrict people they believed to be inadmissible.[21] In doing so, the law created new temporal and geographic forms of inspection and surveillance that stretched to the entire migrant's journey and well after they landed in the United States. Migrants were inspected by health officials abroad before they entered a ship to the United States, before stepping off the ship into the United States, and as stipulated by the Immigration Act of 1903, up to two years afterward. By the year that Anna Metan arrived in the country, the time after entrance that one could be deported had been extended to five years.[22] Also that year, the government passed the Mann Act, a law that supposedly fought sex trafficking of white women, but in fact largely policed their mobility and independence.[23] The new laws stretched the time within which a migrant could be surveilled, enforcing social control through deportation. In doing so, the laws formed racialized, gendered, and ableist ideas of who was fit to enter the country.

To enforce the new immigration laws, the federal government relied on partnerships with professions and institutions that had their own concepts of racialized sexuality and the body. Before the twentieth century, immigration enforcement agents rarely interacted with institutions like hospitals and alms-houses, and when enforcement officials did try to gain information, what they received was usually unhelpful. For example, until the first decade of the twentieth century, few hospitals kept records of their patients' nationality, making it impossible to know who had broken the law by using public funds.[24] The long tradition of almshouses and public care in the United States had traditionally followed state residency requirements, so doctors rarely interacted with the federal government. To enforce the new immigration laws, the Bureau of Immigration issued an annual booklet of rules and regulations for doctors and medical facilities to follow. The 1907 booklet instructed facilities on how to implement the immigration act passed that year. It stipulated that every hospital administrator was required to ask for the nationality of the patient and their date of arrival into the United States. If the patient was discovered to be breaking the law, the hospital administrator was required to notify the nearest immigration agent.[25] The collaboration changed state hospitals into sites of health inspection, often to the patient's detriment.

It would have been in Dr. Gilray's discretion not to report Anna Metan to immigration authorities. According to the rules and regulations the bureau provided, doctors were required to report immigrants who were inflicted with "insanity, idiocy, imbecility, feeble-mindedness, epilepsy, tuberculosis, or a loathsome or contagious disease." When a migrant came in for care, the doctor was the authority who decided whether a "disease" had been dormant but still part of the migrant when they entered the country. In this way, doctors had authority over the interpretation of immigration laws.[26] For example, in 1910, Adele Taussig was deported to Austria after she sought care for an ovarian cyst, which the doctor concluded started growing before she arrived in the United States.[27] Pregnancy was not listed explicitly in rulebooks, and its beginning date was not always agreed upon. Into the twentieth century, most women considered their pregnancy legitimate at the time of the "quickening" (when they felt a kick or movement). At the same time, the new field of obstetrics was defining its own measurement of pregnancy. Doctors began to record pregnancy beginning the day after a woman's last menstrual cycle and progressing linearly until delivery.[28] Dr. Gilray's prognosis made no space for his patient's understanding of her pregnancy. Indeed, the fields of obstetrics and public health imposed a new temporality on childbirth and child rearing, usurping women's authorities over their bodies and sometimes pitting mother and child against each other.[29]

Dr. Gilray's actions fit within the history of his field, which developed not from collaboration with women but rather from domination over them. As Deirdre Cooper Owens has shown, early obstetric research in the United States was made through coordination with enslavers who wanted to ensure their enslaved female population produced healthy babies.[30] In this way, medical interventions into childbirth and maternal care started through racialized notions of reproduction, as interpolated through the value of both mother and child. Within this logical framework, it made sense that Dr. Gilray might have aligned with the government's financial interest over the interests of a single, poor, immigrant woman.

By the early twentieth century, cultural ideas about birth and maternity were quickly changing. Feminist scholars of medicine have pointed to 1900 as a turning point in the medicalization of pregnancy. American and European doctors developed interest in antenatal care, placing new importance on the fetus's development from the moment of conception.[31] Just five years after Anna Metan checked in to Erie County Hospital, for example, the first display of the stages of fetal development was shown in Scotland. While the temporalization by doctors was, as Sara DiCaglio has asserted, "radically at odds with dominant understandings of a fundamentally precarious and uncertain state," they could use their medical authority to dominate poor immigrant women's understanding of fetal development.[32] Doctors and patients could differ on the meaning of pregnancy. Many women and midwives viewed it as a routine life event, and part of a women's overall biology; male doctors fought against that notion. The Wyoming Health Department went so far as to suggest that pregnancy should be treated as "nine months of sickness."[33] Thus when Metan could not pay, Gilray treated her as if her pregnancy were an illness subject to state intervention.

Doctors' interest in fetal care and pediatrics aligned with larger social movements of the nineteenth and early twentieth centuries concerned with the population's moral and physical health. With the stated goal of helping women, new professions like social work and philanthropy also often policed female independence and blamed women for their own misfortunes. As Mariana Valverde has written, social reformers "sought to rehabilitate the poor, and make altruism into a science."[34] In their belief, almshouses like the one Metan entered gave indiscriminately, which hindered rather than helped the poor. Unmarried pregnant women like Metan were at the center of public discourse on the dangers of charity without positive and progressive rehabilitation. To scientifically help society, money could not be spent on cases like hers; neither could time.

Many scholars have examined the way that time has been used as a tool of social control to impose rhythms, timelines, and social formations that ignore preexisting realities. As Elizabeth Freeman notes, state time "converts historically specific regimes of asymmetrical power into seemingly ordinary bodily tempos and routines, which in turn organize the value and meaning of time."[35] Anna Metan's body was judged based on a duration of time over which she had no control. Elizabeth Cohen urges us to see time as "lived consent" in a liberal democracy. For example, by waiting until the age of eighteen to vote, a U.S. citizen consents to the law, or by stepping down from office after the end of a term, a citizen consents to democratic norms.[36] But how could Metan consent to a law enacted retroactively? Immigration officials created a legal apparatus that would ensure control over her even after she entered the country. Indeed, Megan Burke reminds us that this new temporality "operated as both a structure and an experience of gendered subordination."[37] Immigrants were an easy target for government intervention because of their direct interaction with state officials. As Eithne Luibhéid has argued, the mechanisms of migration enforcement allowed the government unprecedented access to the bodies of its potential populace.[38]

Officials tried to hurry Metan's deportation so that she would not give birth in the United States; however, by the time the order was secured, doctors determined she was too close to delivery for her to travel safely. Two months later, Metan was sent to Ellis Island with her child (an American citizen) to await deportation. She and her child were put on a ship back to Galicia.[39] While Anna Metan's time in the United States ended with deportation, the vast majority of women did not meet the same fate. Uncovering the reasons behind who was deported and who was allowed to stay reveals the logics around sexuality, race, class, medicine, and immigration law in the early twentieth-century United States.

What we know of the women's lives was not documented in their own terms. Sources often can tell us more about the power women faced than they can reveal about their interior worlds. Even their characterization as women may erase lived experiences of gender, which limits our understanding of the past. Most of the women in this study seemed to use mobility to navigate their patriarchal home environments, and their cases show how laws around mobility extended their policing even as they traveled. Each woman's removal was handled differently, betraying the malleability of law, its enforcement, and also the limits of the archive. The women's voices have been ventriloquized by state agents, and the archive offers us only glimpses into their lives, thoughts, and desires. Their agency was made precarious and ultimately based on their relationship to men, and each woman used what limited power she may have had to her advantage. The rest of this chapter focuses on two sites of immigration and its enforcement: East Coast public hospitals and "lying-in homes" in Detroit. Each site of immigration enforcement targeted women for different reasons, but ultimately both harnessed immigration law to target and police their presence as poor, single, pregnant women migrants. Their experiences expose the way that law produced pregnant women as illegal, and in doing so, put in danger the bodily autonomy of all traveling women. Their stories present a complex answer to Martha Gardner's poignant question, "when does a migrant cease to arrive and begin to reside?"[40] Immigrant women often needed to travel to the United States to escape patriarchal communities in their own country, but that very same mobility ensured they could be policed in the United States.

After Ellis Island

The vast majority of immigrants who arrived at Ellis Island were allowed into the country.[41] The United States wanted "able-bodied" workers who could grow the U.S. economy through factory work in the North and Midwest, and aid in expropriating Indigenous populations in the Plains and Southwest. As one immigration inspector put it, "immigration looms so largely in the prospect of our country that it may be said, without giving just cause to charge exaggeration, that all other questions of public economy, relating to things rather than to human beings, shrink into comparative significance."[42]

Karolina Pryk arrived at Ellis Island in 1908 four months pregnant. She came to the United States to work as a maid while her fiancé, Wladislaw Kwiatkowski, finished his mandatory army service in Austria.[43] Most visibly pregnant and unmarried women were not permitted entrance after the passage of the Immigrant Act of 1891, which extended exclusion to a person "likely to become a public charge" (LPC). Immigration officers usually placed single pregnant women into the LPC category, assuming they could not be self-sufficient as single mothers. We can therefore surmise that although Pryk was thoroughly scrutinized, inspectors must have not detected her condition, and she was allowed entry.[44]

As Amy Fairchild has argued, health inspectors at Ellis Island served more as a disciplining mechanism for migrants than rigorous medical practitioners. Officials forced migrants to obey orders, wait in lines, consent to surveillance, and even strip in front of strangers. The process modeled the expectations society had for them to be obedient citizen-workers. In this way Ellis Island was a productive space where immigrants learned how to adapt for the jobs that lay ahead.[45] The facility stood in contrast with other ports like Angel Island, and those developing on the U.S.-Mexico border, which were built around exclusion and containment. Angel Island was constructed with the specific purpose of controlling and detaining the mostly Chinese people who traveled through it.[46] In the early twentieth century, the U.S. government became apprehensive of any non-Mexican migrant who crossed the U.S.-Mexico border, suspicious that they traveled to the border through Mexico to circumvent Ellis Island.[47] Angel Island and the U.S.-Mexico border were built to manage exclusion; Ellis Island was policed to manage inclusion.

After Ellis Island, Pryk continued her journey to Philadelphia, where she intended to live close to her aunt and cousin while she awaited her fiancé's arrival.[48] She quickly found a job and settled into her own apartment on Front Street. At eight months pregnant, she entered the Philadelphia Almshouse Hospital. The attending doctor immediately called immigration inspectors: she was in the hospital with a symptom related to her pregnancy, thus in violation of public charge laws.[49]

Pryk's doctor certified that she was "able to travel without danger to life," which allowed her deportation proceedings to move forward.[50] But travel to where exactly, and for how long? Did the doctor mean there was no threat to her life if she traveled from Philadelphia to Ellis Island? Or was he guaranteeing a safe trip across the Atlantic to Bremen, Germany, and then by train and carriage to Rzeszow her hometown in Galicia? There were international agreements about safe deportation between the United States and various countries in Europe, but the laws were rarely enforced.[51]

That Karolina Pryk was using a public hospital made her deportable under U.S. law, as "likely to become a public charge." A warrant was made for her deportation, but the Commissioner of Immigration was the ultimate authority. Pryk assured the inspectors that she was gainfully employed and could support the child on her own in the United States; however, immigration inspectors believed that as an unmarried mother, she would become a public charge. Their prediction had little to do with the reality of her situation: she told them that in the United States she "works less and gets paid more" than when she lived in Rzeszow, and thus could support her child much more easily.[52] The commissioner was not persuaded. She then presented three letters from her fiancé Wladislaw promising he would marry her and live with her once he arrived in the United

States. Pryk also offered her cousin's husband's pledge to take responsibility for her until she became self-sufficient. After reviewing the new documents, the Commissioner of Immigration reversed his orders. Karolina Pryk had found a way to stay in the country; but to do so, she had to give legal power to her male relatives. Wladislaw's promise was one of the main reasons she could stay in the country. Her relation to both Wladislaw and her male cousin changed the way her "condition" was understood and judged: her pregnancy was permissible because men promised to financially support her and ensure she stayed within the confines of heteronormativity. Karolina Pryk's only course of resistance to state patriarchal control of her mobility was to submit to familial and sexual patriarchal control. It is worth noting that the officers were not concerned with Wladislaw or her cousin's husband's employability—what mattered was their gendered and racial categories.

The reversal of Karolina Pryk's deportation orders made clear that women's deportability laid almost exclusively in the hands of the men in their lives. Married women were rarely deported, particularly if their husbands were gain-fully employed. Men who impregnated women never shared the "condition" of pregnancy. When Katrina Teyzar received care at Tewksbury Hospital in Massachusetts in 1900, seven months after her arrival to the United States from Syria, she, and not her husband Selim, came under the state's scrutiny. The surgeon medical director followed the rules set out by the Bureau of Immigration and Naturalization. Following his examination of her, he concluded she had been one month pregnant when boarding the ship to the United States and informed the Commissioner of Immigration of her status.[53] After an investigation, the commissioner decided that she could stay in the country. "The woman does not wish to return to Syria," he reasoned, "and it would hardly seem best to separate her from her husband."[54] That Teyzar would be deported by herself, and not with her husband, speaks to the ways women were ultimately categorized and policed by their sexual behavior. Like Wladislaw, Selim was both part of the reason she was deportable and also the reason for her redemption.

"Who Will Pay?" wrote an immigrant inspector in bold, above the series of investigations that included Anna Metan, Karolina Pryk, and Katrina Teyzar.[55] The women came under scrutiny because they could not pay for their hospital bills, thus exposing themselves to the state and medical profession's judgments about their pregnancies. Officers harnessed public charge law to defend normative values regarding women and families. But even those who could pay were not immune to the use of law as a tactic to police their bodies. In Detroit, migrant pregnant women who did not rely on public funds were nevertheless targeted by immigration enforcement and deported retroactively for breaking a law. Again, immigration law became a useful tool for controlling societal norms, and mobile pregnant women were especially vulnerable to this policing.

Passing the Time in Detroit

Lela May Smith was nineteen when she decided to leave her home in Oxford County, Canada. Her parents thought she was going to Detroit to look for a job in a factory, but in fact Smith was pregnant and planned to conceal it from them. She left their house and met William Chambers, the man who impregnated her, at the train station in Detroit. He took her to a hospital in the city, where they then arranged her stay at the private maternity home of Mrs. Elizabeth Marr in the Brush Park neighborhood, just north of the downtown.[56] Marr promised that "ladies [were] taken care of before and after confinement; children placed in a good home."[57] Marr had only recently opened her home, and already, seven other Canadian women had sought refuge there to wait out their pregnancy in seclusion and have their baby adopted.[58] Smith planned to stay there through her delivery and arrange the baby's adoption through Marr. Chambers was paying for her stay, and the two did not seem to have the intention of marrying each other.

Many unmarried pregnant women sought refuge far from home as they waited out their labor. Elizabeth Conway traveled from Windsor, Canada, by ferry to Marr's, and like Lela May Smith, she used the pretense of work to travel.[59] Tilly Nicholson changed her name to Mary Downing when she arrived in Detroit, looking for a place to have her child away from her family.[60] And many women arriving at Ellis Island did so as well, although most emigrated permanently.[61] The social pressures of the white working class and aspiring middle class were immense; women who strayed outside the realm of "respectability" risked not only their reputation but also that of their family.[62] Maternity homes offered both distance and seclusion for women while pregnant, and the promise that the child would be given to a "good family" afterward. These homes also perpetuated the narrative that women could offer their child for adoption and "forget about the whole ordeal."[63] As Mrs. Burr, another midwife, assured her potential client Winnie Marlette, "I will adopt your child [out] which will admit your going from here free with no care as to the future of the little one." Ann Fessler has shown this myth was largely untrue: many women were haunted for years by the memories of their baby, and they kept their plight silent to avoid stigma.[64] Nevertheless, for many young women with some means, maternity homes were their best option. Anglo Canadian women, living in a patriarchal society that that shamed women's sexuality, could use maternity homes as an escape from community judgment.

Smith found the address for Marr's maternity home in the medical and personal advertisement section of a Detroit newspaper. The city had been a site of private lying-in homes for decades, and white female reformers called Detroit a "baby farm," referring to the number of babies born in Detroit to Canadian women and left up for adoption.[65] Detroit newspapers circulated around the

MEDICAL.

A.—DRS. KENNEDY & KERGAN, specialists in chronic, blood, skin and private diseases. 148 Shelby st., Detroit. Mich.

Cook'sCotton Root Compound

The Great Uterine Tonic and the only safe, effectual monthly regulator on which women can depend. Sold in three degrees of strength: No. 1, $1; No. 2, 10 degrees stronger, $3, and No. 3, for special cases, $5 per box. Sold by all druggists or at Gray & Worcester's or Grunow & Patterson's drug stores, Detroit. Insist on having Cook's Cotton Root Compound.

CONFIDENTIAL treatment in male and female troubles, irregularities, etc.; quick relief guaranteed. DR. ROBBINS, specialist. Wetherbee bldg., 130 Farmer st.

DR. ELIZA LANDAU, expert in female troubles, irregularities, etc.; thirty years' New York City practice; reliable; long experience makes my practice easy. 42 Bagley ave, Detroit.

DR. ALICE LONSDALE cures female troubles by electricity; reliable and skillful treatment. 142 East Elizabeth.

LADIES—Dr. La Franco's compound, safe, speedy regulator, 25c; druggists or mail; booklet free. DR. LA FRANCO, Philadelphia.

LADIES' AILMENTS, etc., treated; maternity care complete in physician's home; discreet, confidential. DOCTOR, 430 Va. st., Buffalo.

PRIVATE LYING-IN HOME for ladies before and during confinement; strictest secrecy; also babies for adoption. L. MARR, matron, 413 Lafayette ave. Phone W. 985.

STRICTLY private home; everything complete for ladies before and during confinement. Call or correspond; be convinced; few may work for board; infants adopted; reasonable; born in or out of home. Mrs. Murrer, 709 Grand River. Grand 245-J.

Figure 4.2. Example of medical ads in the *Detroit Free Press*, advertising both lying-in homes and "monthly regulators." *Detroit Free Press*, June 22, 1906.

Great Lakes regions in Canada and the United States, containing dozens of advertisements for various homes in the city. Some of the homes were described euphemistically, advertising to "any poor girl in trouble needing advice, friendship, or help." Other ads were more direct, such as Mrs. John, who advertised a "ladies' private home before and during confinement; communication strictly confidential; charges moderate."[66] Lela May Smith needed a place that also adopted out children. In Canada, a child could not be adopted until age two; for women like Smith who did not want her community to find out she had a child; such a long wait was not an option.[67] Homes that offered adoption could still be dangerous for the child, as not all were created equal. One midwife in Detroit was so notorious that word circulated that "babies at her place died like flies."[58] Another "doctor" was a barber with made-up degrees.[69] Lacking verifiable information and public oversight, women were at their most vulnerable with strangers who may have cared little about them or their babies.

Detroit was the closest large U.S. city to Ontario, and its rapid industrialization offered an anonymity women could not find in smaller communities in Canada.[70] In the early twentieth century, around 200,000 people traveled between Detroit and Canada each month, with many commuting daily for work or leisure.[71] Traffic at the official crossing point was high, but immigration control was markedly less rigid than it was at other entry sites. As Detroit Immigration Inspector Oliver Frick explained, "the class of immigrant is highly desired. The largest percentage are English, Canadian, and people of Celtic extraction. Naturally, those are the kinds of folks Uncle Sam stands ready to receive." Moreover, Frick explained that "most newcomers are traveling westward with the intention of settling the far west."[72] Migrants' whiteness and participation in settler colonialism produced a particular kind of border policing in Detroit. Farther west, both Canadian and U.S. immigration officials heavily policed the mostly Asian laborers who crossed the U.S.-Canadian border for work. The local immigration officials could make their own rules for entry, "so as not to unnecessarily delay, impede, or annoy passengers," but agreements between the U.S. and Canadian governments in the early twentieth century authorized special inspection of Asian migrants wishing to cross the border.[73] In this way, race was built into the laws that governed border inspection and surveillance, and for women like Lela May Smith, Elizabeth Conway, and Tilly Nicholson, their whiteness shielded their bodies from surveillance at the border, even as they entered Detroit visibly pregnant and sometimes alone or with another female friend.

What Frick failed to tell the public in his interview was that two years earlier in 1907, John H. Clark, an immigration inspector stationed in Seattle, had visited Detroit and "in consultation with other officers," found women traveling across the border for "purposes of confinement."[74] Clark blamed the newspapers that circulated ads in both Detroit and Ontario, and launched an investigation into the lying-in homes in Detroit. He commissioned Earl Coe to investigate both the homes and the citizenship status of the women who used them. While the women themselves were not permanent migrants—most had the intention of going back to Canada after giving birth—their babies would be born in the United States and thus gain birthright citizenship. The officers favored the homes that offered uplift and reform for young women but were leery of those that only offered care.[75] By using immigration law, the government was able to gain access to the maternity homes and police young women's sexuality and autonomy in an otherwise private space, developing the "social control" that deportation could ensure in an otherwise transnational city.

Coe visited over a dozen homes, and while most refused to show him records, he surmised that at least half the women who used them were Canadian. His investigation revealed some of the real problems of the lying-in home industry in Detroit: some were run by frauds, like Wesley Robbins, who was actually a barber. Some had arrest records, like Mrs. Allen, who disposed of a baby in a dumpster in Rochester, New York. Instead of focusing on the doctors and midwives, however, Coe wrote to his superiors about the Canadian "girls" who were using the facilities.[76] Two of those "girls" were Lela May Smith and Elizabeth Conway.

Conway and Smith were both Canadian and eight and a half months pregnant, staying at the home of Marr when they were given a warrant for deportation.[77] They required a medical certificate to ensure that their transport across the border and into Canada would not endanger their lives. Commissioner Frick did not seek advice from Marr, who had been caring for the two women for months, but rather from a doctor working for the government. The doctor believed the two could travel but recommended a companion travel with them. The commissioner was in a hurry to deport them before the babies were born, so that they could not gain U.S. citizenship—thus he asked for all correspondence between Detroit, Washington, DC, and Canada to be done by telegraph.[78] The state's use of law and technology worked against the women as the rush for their deportation competed with the countdown to their delivery.

The women were cited in violation of the law because they entered the country without inspection. However, in their interview, each woman said that she had never been approached to be inspected, and if she had, inspectors only asked to look at her bags.[79] The compulsory inspections had been made into law only that year and had been applied nominally because most of the passengers were white and officers were told not to "unnecessarily annoy" them. Inspection was lax.[80] The Canadian women also were not using public funds like many women who were deported from the East Coast. Staying in a private maternity home was not against the law, but the state could harness its immigration laws to effectively criminalize the women based on their pregnancies.

Rachel Gordon was given a warrant for her deportation shortly after Coe's investigation. After looking into her case, the commissioner decided to let her stay in the city. She had worked in Detroit as a domestic servant for nine years, since 1898, and in that time had gone on only short visits to Canada. Her story seemed to move the immigration agent. Like the others, Rachel Gordon was asked about the father of the expected child. She told the inspectors that she had met and gotten engaged to a man named "Samuel Bondy, chef in the Oriental Hotel. But he is not in the city just now."[81] The Oriental Hotel was a "gentleman's bathhouse" in the city, offering Turkish and Russian electric baths, "marvels of luxury," and "Oriental life and splendor."[82] Once she revealed Samuel Bondy's career, the inspectors' questioning shifted toward Bondy and his status. They asked if he was American; she said she believed so. Oliver Frick, who conducted the interview, asked if "he seduced her under the promise of marriage." She said yes and told the inspectors that she had even bought a wedding dress in anticipation, but "trouble came up between" them.[83] The revelation that Bondy worked at the Oriental Hotel had perhaps appealed to Frick's xenophobia and desire to protect white women's virtue.

Upon reviewing the case, Commissioner John H. Clark recommended that Rachel Gordon be allowed to remain in the country. He reasoned that she had been in the country for over eight years and "is the victim of seduction by some resident of Detroit, who is alleged to be an American citizen." He concluded that "it does not seem that this girl should be subjected to the humiliation of deportation, notwithstanding her unfortunate plight." Clark had shown no such compassion to the other women, although they too were pregnant and unmarried. Gordon's time as a worker in Detroit surely helped her case, but her description of her "seducer" seemed to play a larger part in eliciting his sympathies. Clark was suspicious of his citizenship, and Bondy's work at the Oriental Hotel made him fit well into the contemporary "white slavery" narrative, in which young white women were supposedly at risk of being seduced by immigrant men in public spaces and coerced into sex work or abandoned.[84] In this way, Samuel Bondy's sexuality and suspected immigrant background changed Gordon from a criminal into a victim. Clark and Frick's racializing of the baby's father had changed their view of the mother. Rachel Gordon may have known that. She may have practiced her story before her interrogation with Frick, making sure to emphasize being led on by Bondy, and his job at the Oriental Hotel. The records leave no indication of her intent, but, knowing she faced deportation, Gordon may have played into a narrative that would serve her to stay in the city she had called home for eight years.

Unlike Rachel Gordon, Elizabeth Conway and Lela May Smith were deported. Both had planned for their babies to be adopted out by Marr, but immigration inspectors insisted that the children be born in Canada, as that was the country within which they should "properly look for maintenance."[85] At eight and a half months pregnant in the frigid January weather, Elizabeth Conway and Lela May Smith were boarded on a ferry to sort out their deliveries and the adoption of their babies. The father of Smith's baby had moved out west, and she did not want anyone to "see her in this condition," so her options were limited.[86] William Chambers, the father of Lela May Smith's unborn child, lived in Detroit, and they were in communication. In similar positions but different circumstances, the women set sail on the short ferry ride to Canada.

Both women traveled to the residence of Francis MacLean in Waterville, Canada, on the night of their deportation, January 23.[87] It is unclear what happened to Elizabeth Conway that night, or the baby she would deliver. She eventually married a man in 1916 named Garnet Harshaw and had a child she named Eleanore with him the next year.[88] He died a few years later, and she raised Eleanore alone, but with the respectable label of "widow" instead of "unmarried."[89] Perhaps she never told anyone about her other child.

Lela May Smith also got married. On January 24, 1908, the day after she was deported, William Chambers met her at Francis MacLean's house.[90] That afternoon, they were married by a reverend, and then they hired a taxi straight back to Marr's maternity home.[91] Two weeks later Smith gave birth.[92]

Immigration inspector Oliver Frick caught wind of Smith's return to the United States. He was indignant and determined to deport her again and arrest Marr and Chambers. Although Smith came into the country as a married woman, Frick again cited that she was not investigated correctly and needed to go through the proper channels to enter.[93] Without asking Marr, who had cared for Smith and attended her birth, Frick called on an assistant surgeon who worked for immigration to determine when Smith could travel. The surgeon was confident that she just needed a week to recover. On March 3, after trying to appeal the decision, Smith and her baby were deported to Windsor to start the process over.[94] Although she appealed to the heteronormative standards of immigration by getting married, her strategy so vexed Frick that he criminalized her again, even though there would be no fear that she or her baby would become "public charges."

Some of the most intimate moments of Lela May Smith's life—her pregnancy, the birth of her child, her marriage—hinged on the way legal and medical mechanisms interpreted her body. Her womb and its potentialities were seen only through its service to the state, robbing her of her body and its many possible futures.[95] In 1912, Lela May Smith and William Chambers divorced, citing cruelty; they remarried ten years later.[96] For her and so many other women, it was viscerally clear how the legal system intertwined with their own bodies to render them acceptable or not for the future of the state, with no consideration of their own futures. Each woman faced a cruel dilemma: the more her reproductive capabilities were judged and policed, the more she needed to travel; however, the more she traveled, the more at risk she was of legal repercussions. For women like Anna Metan and Lela May Smith, mobility was the best way to navigate their limited control over their bodies and futures, but exercising mobility made them more visible to the state and its control.

In the early twentieth century, migrants' bodies took on new meaning as U.S. lawmakers extended the time migrants could be considered deportable based on when and where authorities believed migrant bodies developed a "condition."

In turn, migrants' bodies became a critical site to enforce cultural and social norms interpreted as disease within the United States. Pregnant unmarried women in motion were a threat to all forms of patriarchal control: family, marriage, and nation. Perhaps most threatening of all was that women were doing fine without these controls: each woman not only traveled without a husband or father but also proved she did not need one. In this way, violent policing was used to ensure patriarchy's necessity.

Immigration authorities in collaboration with medical professionals reasserted their power through controlling place and time, thus reinforcing patriarchal authority over women's bodies. Through new technologies in science and law, pregnancy could be linked to a specific time and place, suturing the child and mother to a nation and marital status. For each woman discussed in this chapter, the meaning of her pregnancy was dictated by ideas of citizenship and respectability codified into law and practice—a meaning she had little say in creating.

One of Earl Coe's biggest complaints throughout his investigation was the state of recordkeeping at the homes he visited. He lamented that "in the end, he found it quite impossible to obtain authentic information. In fact, all information was refused."[97] At the home of Burr, he found that the "books at her place were totally valueless . . . the address in each case is lacking and what names that appear might be regarded as fictitious." Most of the midwives investigated kept no records, perhaps knowing how easily they could be weaponized by the state and medical officials who collaborated with them. Coe did find a letter sent from Burr to a young woman named Winnie Marlette. Marlette had tried to enter the United States to stay with Burr but had been turned away at the border for being single and pregnant. Burr wrote to her again, inviting her to "stay as long as you desire . . . I will endeavor to make your visit as pleasant as I can. I am your friend." Today, as women's lives are put at risk by laws attempting to control their reproductive choices, perhaps we can look toward Burr, who, even for just a few months, helped women reclaim their own sense of time and place.

Notes

1. Warrant: Arrest of Alien, Department of Commerce and Labor, September 27, 1907, RG 85, file 51736/113, National Archives Record Administration (NARA), Washington, DC.

2. It was not until the turn of the twentieth century that women began to go to hospitals to give birth. Even then, most women gave birth at their homes within their communities. Salim Al-Gailani and Angela Davis, "Introduction to 'Transforming Pregnancy since 1900,'" *Studies in History and Philosophy of Biological and Biomedical Sciences* 47 Pt. B (September 2014): 229–32, https://doi.org/10.1016/j.shpsc.2014.07.001.

3. "Worst Hospital in State Says Commissioner," *Buffalo Inquirer,* May 7, 1910.

4. Dana L. Saylor, "A Timeline of Immigration in Buffalo," *Buffalo Spree*, November 30, 2020.

5. Elizabeth Licata, "A Timeline of Polish Americans in New York," *Buffalo Spree*, November 17, 2020.

6. Letter from Robert Hall to John H. Clark, 13 September 1907, Albany, NY, RG 85, file 51736/113, NARA.

7. Act of March 3, 1903, Pub. L. No. 57–162, 32 Stat. 1213 (1903).

8. Joanne Hayle, "Galicia and Lodomeria: Forgotten in History," *Owlcation*, September 24, 2023.

9. Eithne Luibhéid, *Entry Denied: Controlling Sexuality at the Border* (Minneapolis: University of Minnesota Press, 2015), 9.

10. Warrant: Arrest of Alien, Department of Commerce and Labor, September 27, 1907, Washington, RG 85, file 51736/113, NARA.

11. See Dorothy Roberts, *Killing the Black Body: Race, Reproduction, and the Meaning of Liberty* (New York: Vintage, 1998); Laura Briggs, *How All Politics Became Reproductive Politics: From Welfare Reform to Foreclosure to Trump* (Berkeley: University of California Press, 2018). For more on the concept of organized abandonment, see Ruth Wilson Gilmore, *Golden Gulag: Prisons, Surplus, Crisis, and Opposition in Globalizing California* (Berkeley: University of California Press, 2007).

12. Torrie Hester, *Deportation: The Origins of U.S. Policy* (Philadelphia: University of Pennsylvania Press, 2017) 2.

13. Daniel Kanstroom, "Deportation, Social Control, and Punishment: Some Thoughts about Why Hard Laws Make Bad Cases," *Harvard Law Review* 113, no. 8 (2000): 1890–1935, 1896.

14. Among other restrictions, the Page Act of 1875 expressly forbade the "importation of women for the purposes of prostitution." In practice, the law allowed migration agents to criminalize and police poor and Asian women, categorizing them as "prostitutes" and prohibiting their entry to the country. Through this law, immigration agents stopped Asian women from entering the United States. See Erika Lee. "The Chinese Exclusion Example: Race, Immigration, and American Gatekeeping, 1882–1924," *Journal of American Ethnic History* 21, no. 3 (2002): 36–62, http://www.jstor.org/stable/27502847.

15. Luibhéid, *Entry Denied*, 35.

16. For more on the white racial violence that led to the Chinese Exclusion Act, see Beth Lew-Williams, *The Chinese Must Go: Violence, Exclusion, and the Making of the Alien in America* (Cambridge, MA: Harvard University Press, 2018).

17. Erika Lee, *At America's Gates: Chinese Immigration during the Exclusion Era, 1882–1943* (Chapel Hill: University of North Carolina Press, 2003).

18. Hester, *Deportation*, 28.

19. Genevieve Carpio, *Collisions at the Crossroads: How Place and Mobility Make Race* (Oakland: University of California Press, 2019), 24.

20. Act of March 1891, Pub. L. No. 51–551, 26 Stat. 1084a (1891).

21. See Torsten Feys's chapter in this volume.

22. Act of February 1907, Pub. L. No 59–96, 34 Stat. 898 (1907).

23. The Mann Act, which prohibited traffic of women across state lines, also served to police interracial couples, particularly Black men and white women. Black and brown

men would specifically be targeted for traveling with their white female partners. See Grace Peña Delgado, "Border Control and Sexual Policing: White Slavery and Prostitution along the U.S.-Mexico Borderlands, 1903–1910," *Western Historical Quarterly* 43, no. 2 (2012): 157–78.

24. Hester, *Deportation,*145.

25. United States, *Immigration Laws and Regulations of July 1, 1907* (Washington, DC: Government Printing Office, 1907), 34–35.

26. United States, *Immigration Laws and Regulations of July 1, 1907*, 37.

27. Warrant: Arrest of Alien, Department of Commerce and Labor, September 26, 1910, RG 85, file 53088/6, NARA.

28. Committee Opinion, "Methods for Estimating Due Date," Committee on Obstetric Practice, American College for Obstetrics and Gynecology, Society for Maternal-Fetus Care, May 2017.

29. Lauren Mitchell, "Alienating Aesthetics: Performance Art and the Medical Imagination" (PhD diss., Vanderbilt University, 2019), 73–75.

30. Deirdre Cooper Owens, *Medical Bondage: Race, Gender, and the Origins of American Gynecology*, illustrated edition (Athens: University of Georgia Press, 2017), 15.

31. Al-Gailani and Davis, "Introduction to 'Transforming Pregnancy since 1900,'" 229–32.

32. Sara DiCaglio, "Staging Embryos: Pregnancy, Temporality and the History of the Carnegie Stages of Embryo Development," *Body and Society* 23, no. 2 (2017): 3–24, 8.

33. Jennifer J. Hill, *Birthing the West: Mothers and Midwives in the Rockies and Plains* (Lincoln, NE: Bison Books, 2022), 158.

34. Mariana Valverde, *The Age of Light, Soap, and Water: Moral Reform in English Canada, 1885–1925* (Toronto: University of Toronto Press, 2008), 19.

35. Elizabeth Freeman, *Time Binds: Queer Temporalities, Queer Histories* (Durham, NC: Duke University Press, 2010), 6.

36. Elizabeth F. Cohen, *The Political Value of Time: Citizenship, Duration, and Democratic Justice* (Cambridge, UK: Cambridge University Press, 2018), 12.

37. Megan Burke, "Gender as Lived Time: Reading *The Second Sex* for a Gendered Phenomenology of Temporality," *Hypatia: A Journal of Feminist Philosophy* 33, no. 1 (January 2020).

38. Luibhéid, *Entry Denied*, 17.

39. Ledger for the Immigration Service, Black Rock Station, May 2, 1908, RG 85, file 51736/113, NARA.

40. Martha Gardner, *The Qualities of a Citizen: Women, Immigration, and Citizenship, 1870–1955* (Princeton, NJ: Princeton University Press, 2009).

41. Amy L. Fairchild, *Science at the Borders: Immigrant Medical Inspection and the Shaping of the Modern Industrial Labor Force* (Baltimore: Johns Hopkins University Press, 2003).

42. Annual Report of the Commissioner General of Immigration to the Secretary of Commerce and Labor (Washington, DC: Government Printing Office, 1905).

43. "Interview with Karolina Pryk conducted by J.S. Rodgers," April 10, 1908, RG 85, 51790/12, NARA.

44. Inspectors spent very little time with each migrant during health inspection on Ellis Island, but they firmly believed they could diagnose illness at a glance quickly. Samuel Grubbs, a health inspector at Ellis Island, wrote that he and other inspectors held a "magical intuition . . . which suspected at a glance a handicap that might require a week to prove." S. B. Grubbs, *By Order of the Surgeon General* (Greenfield, IN: Wm. Mitchell Printing Company, 1943), https://catalog.hathitrust.org/Record/001558796.

45. Fairchild, *Science at the Borders*, 40.

46. For more on Angel Island, see Erika Lee and Judy Yung, *Angel Island: Immigrant Gateway to America* (Oxford: Oxford University Press, 2010). For more on the U.S.-Mexico Border, see Julian Lim, *Porous Borders: Multiracial Migrations and the Law in the U.S.-Mexico Borderlands* (Chapel Hill: University of North Carolina Press, 2017).

47. Scholars of the U.S.-Mexico border generally agree that before the Mexican Revolution and World War I, border control was generally lax, and Mexicans were rarely targeted. In the first years of the twentieth century, immigration officials were more worried about Chinese, Japanese, eastern European and Syrian migration across the border. Scholars generally agree that immigration law enforcement shifted its focus to Mexican migrants after World War I and especially after the criminalization of undocumented entry in 1929. See David Dorado Romo, *Ringside Seat to a Revolution: An Underground Cultural History of El Paso and Juarez, 1893–1923* (El Paso, TX: Cinco Puntos Press, 2005); Kelly Lytle Hernández, *Migra!: A History of the U.S. Border Patrol* (Berkeley: University of California Press, 2010).

48. "Interview with Karolina Pryk conducted by J.S. Rodgers," NARA.

49. "Application for Warrant of Arrest: Karolina Pryk," April 2, 1908, Philadelphia, RG 85, 51970/14, NARA.

50. "Memorandum Regarding Warrant Proceedings: Karolina Pryk," April 4, 1908, Philadelphia, RG 85, 51970/14, NARA.

51. Hester, *Deportation*, 136.

52. "Interview with Karolina Pryk conducted by J.S. Rodgers," NARA.

53. "Certificate by Surgeon General of Massachusetts" February 2, 1901, RG 85, 25597, NARA.

54. Letter from the Massachusetts Commissioner of Immigration to the General Commissioner, February 6, 1901, RG 85, 25597, NARA.

55. US Subject Index to Correspondence and Case Files of the Immigration and Naturalization Bureau, RG 85, 53549/87, NARA.

56. Interview with Lela May Smith, undated, RG 85, 51647/15, NARA.

57. Medical Ads, *Detroit Free Press*, December 2, 1907.

58. Letter from Earl Coe to O. Frick, December 8, 1907, RG 85, 51777/013, NARA.

59. Letter to F.P. Sargent, January 18, 1908, RG 85, 51847/14, NARA.

60. Letter to F.P. Sargent.

61. Gardner, *The Qualities of a Citizen*, Chapter 1.

62. Ann Fessler, *The Girls Who Went Away: The Hidden History of Women Who Surrendered Their Children for Adoption in the Decades Before Roe v. Wade* (New York: Penguin Books, 2006), 101.

63. Fessler, *The Girls Who Went Away*, 175.

64. Fessler, *The Girls Who Went Away,* 17.

65. "Investigation into Lying in Hospitals," December 8, 1907, 1, RG 85, 51777/013, NARA.

66. *Toronto Mail and Empire,* December 2, 1907, RG 85, 51777/013, NARA.

67. "Report of the Hearing in the Case of Lela May Smith," undated, RG 85, 51647/16, NARA.

68. "Report of the Hearing in the Case of Lela May Smith," 6.

69. "Report of the Hearing in the Case of Lela May Smith," 7.

70. Ashley Johnson Bavery, *Bootlegged Aliens: Immigration Politics on America's Northern Border* (Philadelphia: University of Pennsylvania Press, 2020), 5.

71. Letter from John H. Clark to F. Sargent," December 21, 1907, RG 85, 51647/16, NARA.

72. 'Immigration Tide Hits High Mark," *Detroit Free Press,* October 21, 1909.

73. Act of February 1907, Pub. L. No 59–96, 34 Stat. 898 (1907).

74. Letter to F.P. Sargent from John H. Clark, December 12, 1907, RG 85, 177/013, NARA.

75. Valverde, *The Age of Light, Soap, and Water,* 13.

76. "Investigation into Lying in Hospitals," NARA.

77. "Investigation into Lying in Hospitals," NARA, 12–15.

78. Letter to F.P. Sargent from J. Clark, January 8, 1908, RG 85, 51647/15, NARA.

79. Interview with Elizabeth Conway, January 10, 1908, RG 85, 51847/14, NARA; Interview with Lela May Smith.

80. The Immigration Act of 1907 states that Canadian ports could have discretion in implementing immigration inspection. Act of February 1907, Pub. L. No 59–96, 34 Stat. 898 (1907).

81. Interview with Rachel Gordon, January 15, 1908, 51847/15, NARA.

82. Dan Austin, "Oriental Hotel," HistoricDetroit.com, https://historicdetroit.org/buildings/oriental-hotel; "Oriental Hotel's Unique Café," *Detroit Free Press,* July 14, 1901.

83. Interview with Rachel Gordon.

84. For more on fears of "white slavery," see Brian Donovan, *White Slave Crusades: Race, Gender, and Anti-Vice Activism, 1887–1917* (Urbana: University of Illinois Press, 2006).

85. Letter from J. Clark to J. Sargent, January 18, 1908, RG 85, 51647/15, NARA.

86. Interview with Elizabeth Conway.

87. Letter to F. Sargent from J. Clark, February 6, 1908, RG 85, 51847/16, NARA.

88. Archives of Ontario, *Registrations of Marriages, 1869–1928*; Reel: 380, Toronto, Ontario.

89. Archives of Ontario, Collection: MS935; Reel: 264; The National Archives at Washington, DC, Series Title: *Card Manifests (Alphabetical) of Individuals Entering through the Port of Detroit, Michigan, 1906–1954.*

90. Testimony of Francis MacLean, February 28, 1908, RG 85, 51847/16. NARA.

91. Testimony of Georges Stephens, February 28, 1908, RG 85, 51847/16, NARA.

92. Letter to F.P. Sargent from Emmitt Wallace, January 25, 1908, 51847/16, NARA.

93. Letter to F.P. Sargent from J. Clark, February 5, 1908, RG 85, 51847/16, NARA.

94. Letter from Immigration Commissioner in Montreal, Canada, to O. Frick, March 6, 1908, RG 85, 51847/16, NARA.

95. Nada Elia, "Roe V Wade: Don't Despair, Radicalize," *The New Arab*, July 14, 2022.

96. Michigan Department of Community Health, Division of Vital Records and Health Statistics, *Michigan, Marriage Records, 1867–1952*, Lansing, MI, Film: *179*, Film Description: *1924 Wayne.*

97. "Investigation into Lying in Hospitals," NARA.

5   Between Arabic, English, and Spanish

Syrian Muslim Migrations from Mexico to the Midwest in the Early Twentieth Century

ASHLEY JOHNSON BAVERY

In the first two decades of the twentieth century, thousands of Muslim immigrants left the Ottoman state of Greater Syria for Mexico, building a Mahjar (Syrian-Lebanese diaspora) that soon stretched into the American Midwest. The United States officially categorized Syrians as white Europeans in 1909, allowing them legal entrance into the United States, but along U.S. ports of entry, immigration officials used discretionary laws and border practices to exclude Muslim Syrians.[1] As a result, Syrians hoping to reach the United States relied on a vast smuggling network that facilitated their journeys through Mexico and their unauthorized crossing over the U.S. southern border. Mexico, however, became much more than a transit nation for Syrians. Because Porfirio Díaz's administration categorized Syrians as white Europeans and encouraged them to settle, many migrants stayed in Mexico for weeks, months, or years, where they learned Spanish, married Mexican women, built Mexican businesses, and even naturalized as Mexican citizens. When war in Mexico and the pull of industrial jobs prompted members of the Mexican Mahjar to cross the border into the United States, they brought Mexican wives and children, lived alongside Mexican families, and on lunch breaks in Iowa's meatpacking plants and Gary's steel mills, they spoke Spanish with Mexican coworkers. It was never a one-way route. Syrians returned to Mexico and in the next generation, their children traveled north to live with family in the Muslim communities of Iowa, Indiana, Michigan, and Ohio. This article examines the unauthorized and authorized routes Syrians took from the Mediterranean, a group of migrants not traditionally categorized as Europeans, but who shifted in and out of categories of whiteness and Europeanness on their journeys through Mexico and into the American Midwest. Ultimately, it demonstrates that throughout the twentieth century, Syrian migration challenged U.S. immigration practices by creating invisible kinship networks that defied racial categories and allowed Syrians to conduct trade and travel across the border in either direction, depending on the political, economic, and racial climates of the United States or Mexico.

The Syrians who first forged these networks were young men, equally eager to make their fortunes in the mines of Mexico or the railroads of America's industrial heartland. For instance, in the spring of 1912, Muhammad Khaleed, a young Muslim living in the town of Qatana, Syria, received news from his cousin in Grand Rapids, Michigan, that the Pere Marquette Railroad was hiring workers at the rate of $2 a day. This was more than eight times what Khaleed could expect to make in a day of plowing local fields, so he convinced his friends Hassan Hammoody, Abdulkarim Khateep, and Ahmad Kawayda to accompany him to Grand Rapids, where they hoped to make enough money to marry and start families, while perhaps also avoiding the Ottoman draft. The men, all of whom were in their early twenties, boarded a ship from Beirut to Marseille, and once in France they decided to travel to Veracruz, Mexico. News that Ellis Island officials routinely excluded men with Muslim names most likely influenced their decision to travel through Mexico, but the young men also had friends in Mexico City, whom they hoped to visit before deciding whether to proceed on to the United States. Once in North America, the men spent several weeks in Mexico City with Hussein Elcourday, a friend from their village, who decided to join their party's journey into the United States. At the Nuevo Laredo border, however, U.S. immigration officials rejected all five men. Two of the men received a diagnosis for the eye infection trachoma, and the remaining three faced rejection under the "likely to become a public charge" clause of the 1891 Immigration Act, a catchall exclusion used by inspectors who wanted to keep particular migrants out of the United States.

News of the men's exclusion reverberated through the Syrian community of Grand Rapids, where the city's 200 Muslim migrants worried that their own cousins, brothers, and wives might be excluded at the border. When Khaleed's cousin took up a collection among the local community, Mahjaris opened their pocketbooks and enlisted local grocer Said Zehra, a Syrian with Mexican contacts, to travel south and help the five men cross into the United States. With funding from the Grand Rapids Muslim community in hand, Zehra headed to the border and contacted a local network of Syrian smugglers for help. Thus, despite beginning their journey with a handful of contacts in the United States, by the time the five migrants reached the U.S.-Mexico border, they had tapped into a transnational network of Syrians and Mexicans in two nations committed to help them cross the border.

This migration network facilitated Khaleed and his friends' unauthorized entry into the United States, but the contacts they made along the route drew some of the men back to Mexico. Said Zehra tried to pull strings in Nuevo Laredo's Syrian community, but at the border, U.S. inspectors remembered the five men and turned them away a second time. Undaunted, Zehra suggested that the party take a break and head back to Mexico City, where they all lived with Syrian friends and peddled dry goods for several weeks, getting to know the local community of Arabic-speaking Maronites, Muslims, and Mexicans. Finally, Zehra heard from contacts in Arizona that border crossing was easier there, and he steered the men toward Nogales, urging them to give Christian names and different hometowns to cross the border into Arizona. The deception worked, and the men crossed the border surreptitiously and boarded a train bound for Grand Rapids. Once in the city, Khaleed's cousin helped the unauthorized Syrians find work on the Pere Marquette Railroad, where they lived and labored alongside Mexican immigrants for several months before immigration officials picked them up for questioning and deported them back across the southern border. Four of the deported men relied on the friendships they had made in Mexico, found jobs, and settled into Mexico City's Muslim community. Muhammad Khaleed alone decided to return north to the United States, this time using the help of smugglers in Nuevo Laredo to help him across. Khaleed settled in the United States and became a citizen after enlisting in World War I, but his time in Mexico proved helpful throughout his life in the Midwest: it left him with a good grasp of Spanish and connections across the southern border on which he could rely for trade, marriage, or migration.[2]

Examining the unauthorized migrations of Muhammad Khaleed and the thousands of other Syrians whose racial categories shifted as they traveled back and forth between Mexico and the United States over the course of their lifetimes helps reposition mainstream scholarship on unauthorized border crossing and migration. A robust literature on immigration policy examines the ways European, Chinese, and Mexican migrants navigated restrictive U.S. policing and border policies to reach the United States. In these works, which necessarily focus on the coercive power of the American state, Mexico emerges as a place migrants hope to leave, a nation to exit or traverse on their difficult journeys to destinations in the United States.[3] Scholars of Arab American history have positioned Middle Eastern migrants within this history, presenting Mexico as a "back door," an alternate route taken by those who could not pass health exams at Ellis Island.[4] Recent literature in borderlands, ethnic, and American studies has emphasized the fluidity of exchange among migrants of multiple ethnic and racial backgrounds as they forged identities across several nation-states and established interracial communities in American cities.[5] Sarah Gualtieri in particular has charted the routes Syrian migrants took on their way to borderland regions in Texas and California, terming the identity many Middle Easterners forged with Mexican culture *Arab Latinidad*.[6] This chapter builds on Gualtieri's work and extends the history of Syrian transnational exchange beyond the borderlands of Mexico and the U.S. West and Southwest. It argues that networks forged across North America became particularly crucial for Muslim Syrians, who faced racialization because of their religion.[7] Julian Lim has demonstrated how Muslims faced particular exclusions at the border because their religion set them apart from the nation's Christian majority.[8] This article traces how this process of racialization extended beyond the border, finding that once in midwestern industrial centers, Muslims found themselves more isolated than Christian Orthodox or Maronite Mahjaris. Members of the surviving midwestern Mahjar carry the memories of family in Mexico. Seated in the Islamic Center of Michigan City in 2021, seventy-three-year-old Maria Dabagia recounted the history of her great-grandmother, who traveled to Mexico with her husband and crossed the border to Indiana, only to have her husband return south across the border the following year. "That's how my grandmother found out she had a half-brother in Mexico!" She exclaimed excitedly. "I think my great-grandfather was here for a while and then he went back to Mexico. He had a whole new family down there."[9] Drawing on the cross-border lives of men like Dabagia's great-grandfather, this chapter demonstrates that over the course of the twentieth century, Syrians crossed and recrossed the U.S.-Mexico border both with and without permission from two North American states, linking the industrial power of the American Midwest to trade networks in Mexico for decades.

The American Midwest matters to the history of the Muslim Mahjar because Muslims settled the region in large numbers and built America's first mosques across the heartland. The majority of the U.S. Mahjar was Christian, but by the turn of the twentieth century, Muslim Syrians established settlements in New York, Iowa, Indiana, and Michigan.[10] Syrians tend to position their migration as a flight from Ottoman persecution and conscription in the Ottoman Army, but in reality, the region's booming silk trade put cash into the pockets of men who otherwise would have been confined to lives as peasants in a feudal system.[11] The class shake-up produced migration within Greater Syria, as men left villages for work in urban centers like Damascus and Beirut, and when the price of silk began to fall in the 1890s, these entrepreneurs sought affluence and opportunity abroad.[12]

The growing railroad industry provided these early Muslim migrants their first jobs in the United States, bringing thousands of young men to the Midwest. Along the shores of Lake Michigan, Mahjaris built freight train cars for Haskell and Barker Company before it merged with Pullman Standard and laid tracks for the Pere Marquette Railroad in Grand Rapids, Michigan.[13] The invention of the refrigerated railway car turned Sioux City, Iowa, into a meatpacking boom town, and many young migrants set aside Islamic doctrine for highly paid jobs in

Iowa's grisly hog slaughterhouses.[14] Within a few years, most of these Syrians left the stockyards and established dry-goods businesses in Sioux City, Fort Dodge, and Cedar Rapids, Iowa, encouraging kin to join them and peddle their goods across the vast prairies.[15] In 1913, when Ford Motor Company offered men five dollars a day, some Syrians headed to the Detroit region, where they settled first in Highland Park and then in Dearborn, Michigan, building greater Detroit into the heart of America's Muslim community.[16] In the absence of federal welfare programs, early Muslims established mutual benefit societies, and by the 1930s, they built some of America's first mosques in Highland Park (1921), Michigan City (1924), and Cedar Rapids (1934), signaling Muslims' commitment to life in the American Midwest.[17]

To reach Muslim communities in the Midwest, however, Syrians first had to navigate U.S. immigration laws designed to exclude them. At Ellis Island in particular, Muslims faced high rates of exclusion under the 1891 Immigration Law, which barred polygamists from entrance into the United States.[18] In the early 1900s, inspectors conflated Islam with polygamy, and many immigration officials justified rejecting thousands of Muslim immigrants on the grounds that their religion permitted the practice. The Asiatic Exclusion League, a nativist organization founded in San Francisco, championed this harsh interpretation of the polygamy law so as to keep "Mohammedan natives of India who are all admittedly polygamist" out of the United States.[19] Indeed, inspectors routinely barred South Asians, Turks, and Syrians who could not prove their Christianity at Ellis Island, a practice that only eased in 1913, when the Ottoman Embassy objected to the exclusion of several high-profile dignitaries and demanded that the United States revise its policies. In response, the Bureau of Immigration clarified that the 1891 law applied only to *practicing* polygamists and issued a circular with questions meant to help inspectors parse whether an immigrant believed in polygamy in theory or hoped to take up the practice in the United States.[20] Such delicate distinctions were often lost in the chaos of questioning through interpreters at ports of entry or on individual inspectors who used polygamy exclusions to cast Muslim immigrants as perpetual foreigners and incompatible with American values. When Mufti Mohammed Sadiq, a Muslim scholar and missionary for the Ahmadiyya movement, traveled to the United States in 1921, authorities detained him for seven weeks while he argued that there was a clear distinction between the behaviors *required* of Muslims, such as prayer, and those *permitted*, like polygamy.[21]

Health inspections presented another way for immigration inspectors to exclude Syrians at ports of entry. The 1891 Immigration Law barred any immigrant deemed medically unfit to enter the United States, and migrants from the Ottoman Empire faced higher levels of exclusion than other white immigrants for trachoma, an eye infection that could cause blindness if left untreated.[22] In reality, less than 2 percent of those categorized as Syrian were medically excluded at Ellis Island.[23] The perception that Syrian migrants carried the disease, however, meant that immigration inspectors began excluding any Arab from the Mediterranean with the slightest sign of an eye problem, causing even healthy immigrants to seek alternate routes for entering the United States.[24]

Soon, Syrians rejected at Ellis Island began traveling to the U.S. southern border, giving Mexico a reputation as a back door for immigrants carrying contagious disease. Scholarship on Syrian immigrants to the United States tends to emphasize this narrative, asserting that these migrants began traveling through Mexico to avoid health inspections, or that they were even routed south by smugglers or inspectors at Marseille.[25] Some immigrants did fit this pattern, but like the actual numbers of Syrians infected with trachoma, these numbers were exaggerated by panicked immigration inspectors and the press. In 1906, the *El Paso Times* warned that a "question of infinitely more importance than that of Chinese immigration" was the "invasion of diseased Syrians" into El Paso and cities across the United States.[26] By 1910, U.S. immigration inspectors at El Paso and Eagle Pass noted with alarm that "two to three hundred Syrians a month" had begun to cross the border, and they suspected them of "harboring contagion."[27] Panicked reports linking Syrians to trachoma gave immigration authorities and the American public the impression that the only possible reason these migrants had for crossing through Mexico was to violate American immigration policy.

In reality, thousands left Greater Syria for Mexico with the express intention of living, working, or visiting kin there before some hoped to continue north. Mexico had a large Middle Eastern population, with thousands of Maronite, Orthodox, and Muslim Syrians and Turks who had no intention of crossing the border into the United States.[28] These men and women migrated to Mexico for the same reasons they traveled to the United States, and as Camila Pastor has noted, many Syrians viewed all of the Americas as a "vast and undifferentiated land of opportunity" where they could make money and return to their villages in Greater Syria.[29] In fact, within many families, brothers and cousins chose to migrate to the United States and Mexico at the same time, testing the opportunities in both places and exchanging news about living and economic conditions.[30] Between 1900 and 1910, 5,756 Middle Eastern foreigners, most of whom came from Eastern Mediterranean Arab provinces of the Ottoman Empire, traveled to Mexico and settled along the railroad lines that had been built by the Porforio Díaz administration (1875–1910) to stimulate commerce and trade.[31] In particular, Syrians settled in Mexico City, Veracruz, Monterrey, Chihuahua, Torreón, and on the Yucatan peninsula, and engaged in trade and commerce. As in the United States, the majority of the Mexican Mahjar was Christian, but communities of Sunni and Shi'a Muslims formed in Tampíco and

Torreón, respectively, where migrants established themselves as textile traders and merchants.[32] During his tenure as president, Porforio Díaz encouraged European immigration to Mexico with economic incentives, and to fit this description, Syrians emphasized their whiteness, casting themselves as European settlers who promised to stimulate the nation's economy.[33]

News that Mexico was hospitable to Muslims encouraged Syrians battling legal acceptance in the Midwest to consider traveling south. This was particularly true in the first decade of the twentieth century, when courts routinely denied citizenship to Syrians on the grounds that they were not "free white persons" as required by the 1790 Naturalization Act.[34] In 1909, Michigan City's LaPorte County Superior Court began turning away all Syrians and Turks who petitioned for citizenship on the grounds that "the United States does not grant Asiatics the privilege of becoming naturalized citizens."[35] The Syrian Christian community responded by launching a legal crusade that set out to prove Syrians' whiteness as Mediterranean peoples, and in 1914, after a series of state-level court cases, a U.S. circuit court ruled in *Dow v. United States* that "Syrians" were indeed white and descendants of Europeans. Claims to citizenship, however, hinged on Syrians' Christianity, and Muslim migrants continued to face barriers to legal acceptance that drove many to seek refuge in Mexico.[36] For instance, when a young Shi'a Muslim's final citizenship petition was rejected by a local court in 1914, he left his pregnant wife on the shores of Lake Michigan and set out for Torreón, Mexico, where he hoped to find work and friendship in the local Shi'a Muslim community and take advantage of Porforio Díaz's favorable policies toward foreigners.[37] Indeed, he was not alone, and in the first two decades of the twentieth century, Syrians regularly moved from the Midwest to cities in Mexico, joining friends and family in both North American nations.[38]

The outbreak of the Mexican Revolution in 1910 ended these favorable policies toward foreigners, and the threat of violence caused many Syrians to flee north. The Mexican nationalists who ousted Díaz resented foreign immigrants, who they felt dominated trade and industry that should be in the hands of native Mexicans. By 1911, violence against foreigners, particularly Chinese immigrants, became commonplace in northern Mexico. Torreón's location as a key railroad hub linking central and southern Mexico to the northern region of the country had attracted hundreds of Syrians, Turks, Chinese, and eastern Europeans, turning it into an international hub of transportation and trade. On May 15, 1911, when followers of revolutionary leader Francisco Madero claimed Torreón, they slaughtered 303 Chinese and five Japanese people in a bloody massacre that signaled to foreigners in the city that the revolutionaries were not on their side.[39] Syrians, particularly Muslims, were not exempt from the violence. In Torreón and further north across Chihuahua, revolutionaries pillaged Syrian businesses and killed foreigners including the young Muslim brothers who left widows and small children in Michigan City, Indiana.[40] Amid xenophobic violence and economic instability, hundreds of Syrians fled north across the border.[41] For instance, when revolutionary troops occupied the Baja California mining town of Santa Rosalía, dozens of Muslim Syrians who had operated shops for miners and railroad workers in the town left their businesses and headed north.[42] Even Syrians who chose to stay in Mexico often sent their families to the United States. Julian Drube, a Syrian merchant living in Juarez, brought his wife and daughter to El Paso in 1914, citing "anti-foreign violence" in the revolution as his reason for sending them north.[43] Thus, instead of using Mexico as a transit nation or stopping point on their way to the United States, most Syrians in Mexico had settled there intending to live in the nation's robust Arab community and only headed north to flee the violence, upheaval, and uncertainty caused by the Mexican Revolution.

Like the polygamy law, immigration inspectors used the "likely to become a public charge" (LPC) clause to further exclude Syrians based on their supposed religious difference. While states and municipalities had long used "poor laws" to expel or bar immigrants, the 1891 Immigration Act passed America's first federal LPC law.[44] Under the act's provisions, inspectors made subjective decisions based on an immigrant's appearance and the amount of money carried to determine whether the person might seek public assistance in the future.[45] Historians have analyzed the gendered and racialized use of the LPC clause, which came to be used as a "catchall" tool inspectors used when they could not find or prove another reason for exclusion.[46] While these works have deftly demonstrated how the LPC clause policed Mexican border crossing in the 1920s, examining border crossing files for the prior decade reveals that Syrians of all religions were regularly excluded as LPC by inspectors who doubted their reasons for crossing via Mexico.[47] In interrogations, inspectors peppered these migrants with questions about polygamy and "Mohammedanism," revealing that they continued to fear the religious threat they thought Syrians posed to the United States.[48] Tellingly, an inspector at Eagle Pass, Texas, sent out a circular to the entire Immigration Service that warned: "even if a Syrian calls himself Joseph or Moses, he is probably hiding a Mohammedan name and should be kept out."[49] Thus, in addition to using the LPC laws for gendered and racialized exclusion, inspectors turned religion (or perceived religion) into a major factor in determining whom to allow into the United States.

Even Muslim migrants with sufficient money faced exclusion under the LPC clause, causing many to change their names when crossing the border. In the wake of the Chinese massacre in Torreón, Mexico, Youssef Khalil Al Maso decided to shut down the textile shop he had run for six years in the city, and he traveled to the U.S. border with $380 cash and the address for his cousin Hamed in Chicago. Despite his significant funds and the name of a family member ready to help, an Immigration Service inspector at Eagle Pass excluded him as LPC. It is impossible to know the exact circumstances of Al Maso's exclusion, but because inspectors routinely turned Muslims away at the border, it may be that his name, Khalil, a common Islamic men's name, flagged the suspicions of inspectors who associated Muslims with polygamy and un-American values.[50] The fact that many Muslims adopted Christian names to cross the border suggests that migrants understood inspectors' anti-Muslim exclusionary practices and endeavored to get around them.[51] By 1917, Antonio Kazen, a Syrian merchant in Laredo, confirmed to U.S. inspectors that "all Syrians, whether Christians or Mohammedans, give Christian names at the port of entry."[52] This method allowed Muslim Syrians to hide their religion from immigration inspectors, but as state officials learned of the practice, migrants sought new ways to evade restrictive immigration practices.

By the 1910s, a smuggling industry began to specialize in guiding Syrians of all religions across the southern border into the United States. Smuggling rings developed on the U.S.-Mexico border in the wake of Chinese exclusion laws, and early smugglers brought Chinese across the border by the hundreds. As smuggling rings grew, their operations soon expanded to cater to southern and eastern Europeans and migrants from across the Ottoman Empire who had been excluded as LPC, diseased, or illiterate in the 1910s.[53] Soon, smugglers such as Khalil Koury, a Christian Syrian in El Paso, began to specialize exclusively in helping Syrians from all backgrounds cross the border. Koury, a slender, middle-aged Muslim from Beirut, whose dark hair was tinged with grey, donned a dark suit and each day waited patiently at the border line in Juaréz, Mexico, searching for migrants rejected under trachoma or LPC restrictions. He made small talk with passersby and police in perfect Spanish, but when he spied a likely candidate, he reassured the migrant in Arabic and guided the person to his boardinghouse, where he charged 25 cents a day for room and board and had a doctor on call who claimed to treat trachoma for $10. Once fed and treated, Koury charged his boarders an extra $70 to $80 to guide them into the United States through a network of paid border guards and interpreters. Immigration inspectors disparaged the "small fortune" Koury amassed by "grafting upon his countrymen," but for many migrants, Koury represented the only hope they had of reaching friends and relatives' in the United States.[54]

Muslim mutual benefit societies began collecting money to fund relatives and friends' journeys through Mexico, connecting Mexico to the American Midwest with a network of wire transfers, bribes, and agreements made in Arabic, Spanish, and English. In 1912, the Muslim community in Sioux City received a telegram from Marseille that eleven Syrians, most of them relatives of their community in Iowa, were stranded in Marseille without funding to continue their journeys to the United States.[55] By this time, Sioux City had a population of nearly 500 Muslim Syrians, most of whom worked in the bloody killing floors of local slaughterhouses.[56] Unlike the Poles, Czechs, and Christian Syrians living in the city, Muslims found themselves racialized on account of their religion. Ten years prior, when their population numbered around eighty, the *Sioux City Journal* profiled the "Mohammedans of the colony," who "clung tenaciously to their faith," with practices antithetical to American values, the paper claimed.[57] In the face of nativism, Muslim migrants banded together to form a mutual aid society that helped local community members in times of sickness and unemployment, paid for funerals, and funded immigration expenses, legal and unauthorized, for relatives to come to the United States. When news circulated that relatives and friends from their homelands needed help, the community took up a collection and commissioned local grocery firm Beshara and Hassen to wire funds to the migrants. When news of the international money transfer reached the border at Laredo, inspectors excluded the men and accused them of heading to Sioux City as "contract laborers," where the grocery firm intended to employ them as peddlers for low wages. But the eleven men's testimony, which remained consistent throughout their Board of Special Inquiry hearing, reveals that the men relied on the benevolence of cousins, brothers, and strangers to pay for transportation costs along with unforeseen "payments" to border agents, interpreters, doctors, lawyers, and boardinghouse workers along their journey. Revealing concerns about Islam, U.S. inspectors asked each man about polygamist beliefs and questioned skeptically about the debts they would owe to Sioux City Muslims. When an inspector asked Hassan El Ghani a third time how he planned to repay his debt to his brother, he replied, "money between my brother and I has no difference. When I need money he gives me and if he needs money and I have it I give him." Indeed, migrants relied on family connections and community ties across multiple nations to fund immigration routes that served to connect communities in Greater Syria with those in Mexico and in the American Midwest.[58] The "Sioux City Mohammedan Society" funded the passage of dozens of migrants through Mexico, as did similar mutual aid societies in Michigan City, Indiana, and Grand Rapids and Highland Park, Michigan.[59] And while the U.S. government investigated these cases as nefarious smuggling operations, they represented Muslim migrants' efforts to help kin navigate migration routes from cities in Mexico and the Middle East.

Once in the U.S. Midwest, Syrian Muslims retained their ties to Mexico. While some migrants had spent only a few days in Mexico, the vast majority had lived in Veracruz, Mexico City, or Nuevo Laredo for weeks, months, or years and had learned Spanish and taken Spanish names, drawing them to workplaces and neighborhoods where Mexicans lived.[60] In Sioux City, Mexicans and Syrians worked together in meatpacking plants, where they probably shared breaks from the killing floors to have a bite to eat and reminisce about warmer weather and the slower pace of life south of the border.[61] In Grand Rapids, Muslim Syrians and Mexicans both worked on the Grand Central Railroad and lived as neighbors. While segregated northern neighborhoods may have pushed both ethnic groups into the same working-class streets, Syrians and Mexicans also shared experiences that drew them to the same spaces. For instance, when Muslim Syrians Mike Maloley, Jusmi Farhat, and Mostafa Eglaway settled their families on Grand Rapids's Wealthy Street alongside dozens of Mexican migrants, they may have felt comfortable with Mexican families because of past migrations. Indeed, Maloley and his wife Sophia named their daughter Maria, indicating possible time spent in a Spanish-speaking country.[62] Similar patterns formed in Michigan City and Detroit, where Muslim Syrians worked alongside Mexicans in railway car and automobile factories, sharing city streets and boardinghouses with Mexican workers. And in some cases, they even told U.S. Census workers they were Mexicans, indicating the extent to which many of these Muslims identified with Latinx culture.[63] For instance, after Ali Sobh had lived in Torreón, Mexico, for several years, he journeyed north to visit his uncle Sam, who ran a boardinghouse for steelworkers in Gary, Indiana. Sobh found work at the steel mill, and because he spoke little English, associated exclusively with Mexican steelworkers in Spanish, even bringing men home to share traditional dinners of kibbeh and fattoush with his uncle's family.[64] Thus, instead of just remembering their passages through Mexico, Syrian migrants retained active ties to Mexico and forged friendships and alliances with Mexican communities once they reached industrial centers in the Midwest.

Marriages between Syrians and Mexicans further solidified the bond between these two immigrant communities in the Midwest. In her landmark study of Arab Americans, Alixa Naff noted that Muslim men faced a shortage of marriageable Muslim women in the United States, and therefore tended to marry outside their ethnicity, finding Irish, Polish, and other European wives once they reached the United States.[65] Overlooked, however, is the fact that many Syrian men married Mexican women on their journeys through Mexico, bringing children born and partially raised in Mexico to midwestern cities like Dearborn and Michigan City.[66]

During World War I, Syrians unable to file for draft exemptions became frustrated with life in the United States and looked to friends and family in Mexico. When the United States entered into the war, U.S. authorities presumed Muslim Syrians were in league with the Ottomans and viewed them with suspicion. In an effort to prove their loyalty and earn a faster route to citizenship, thousands of these immigrants and their sons volunteered to fight for the United States.[67] On the other hand, many Syrians did not want to risk their lives fighting against an empire where they had family and many wished to return.[68] Technically, those who retained Ottoman subjecthood qualified for an exception from the draft as "neutral allies," but claiming an exemption was a messy, frustrating process and the government drafted many men who hoped to avoid fighting in Europe. Without further recourse, some Syrians crossed the border into Mexico, where they disappeared into Syrian communities and could not be found by U.S. authorities.[69]

To help midwestern Muslims evade the draft, local Syrians with longstanding connections to Mexico developed smuggling networks to guide countrymen across the southern border. In Detroit, Amen Mobarak, a Syrian who had lived in Mexico for several years, organized a draft-dodging enterprise with countrymen Mohamed Salem, Mohamed Abess, Said Hashem, Charles Berry, Mohamed Ali Hassain, and George Eamy that guided dozens of Detroit Muslims to Mexico.[70] In October of 1917, four of these men piled into an old Hudson automobile and drove to Battle Creek, Michigan, where Mustafa Salem was in training at Camp Custer. The men met Salem on one of his breaks, switched his military uniform for a three-piece civilian suit, and sent him on a train to Chicago, where he met Amen Mobarak and several other Syrian draft dodgers. Mobarak worked at Henry Ford's River Rouge plant and had ties to Dearborn's Muslim community, but he was also married to a Mexican woman and maintained the contacts he had made when he lived in Mexico. Tapping into this network, Mobarak arranged for Salem's transport to El Paso, where Mexican officials who had been warned to be on alert for draft dodgers took a bribe to look the other way.[71] And Mobarak did not hold a monopoly on midwestern smuggling. By late 1918, the U.S. Bureau of Investigation reported similar operations out of St. Louis, Missouri, and Des Moines, Iowa, all of which helped Syrians evade draft laws, from which many of them may have been exempt in the first place.[72] Thus, World War I sparked a reverse migration from the United States to Mexico, as many who had crossed the border in the decade prior returned in the opposite direction.

In the wake of World War I, Syrians negotiated a new global power structure in ways that allowed them opportunities for migration. With the Allied defeat of the Ottoman Empire, the 1920 Treaty of San Remo granted Great Britain and France power over the Middle East with mandate governments in Palestine and Greater Syria, respectively.[73] People living in these regions were eligible for French and British passports, while those living abroad could apply for citizenship at local consulates.[74] The collapse of the Ottoman Empire meant an end to Ottoman bans on immigration, and thousands of migrants planned an exit from the Arabic-speaking regions of the Mediterranean. The United States had enacted immigration quotas in 1921 and 1924, leaving Mexico as an attractive option for Syrians hoping to reach North America, and soon Mexico received an influx of Syrian migrants.[75]

Syrians living in Mexico took advantage of their European papers to cross the border into the United States. The end of the Mexican Revolution coincided with the end of the First World War, bringing the promise of peace and prosperity to Muslim communities in Mexico. Most European merchants had fled during the revolutionary upheaval, leaving trade opportunities open to the Syrians who remained in the country. Migrants tapped into the Mahjari communities that had long spanned the border with the United States to create vast trading networks. Moreover, French identity papers gave these migrants an edge over Mexican traders, who faced racialized harassment from Immigration Service and new Border Patrol officers.[76] For instance, in 1923, Ahmed Chameel, a Muslim trader living in Torreón, applied for entrance into the United States at Eagle Pass, Texas, for twenty days to trade in the United States. On his manifest, Immigration Service inspectors first assigned his nationality as Syrian before crossing this out and writing "French subject," a designation that made him appear more desirable to inspectors who had begun to police all Mexican crossers with the LPC clause.[77]

Other Syrians claimed European status to attempt crossing the border into the United States. In 1921, Mansour Hanna left his wife and five of his seven children in Jerusalem and set out for Mexico, where a friend told him wages had reached ten dollars a day. Once in Veracruz, however, Hanna and his two eldest sons had trouble finding stable work and decided to cross the border for Liberal, Kansas, where Hanna had lived from 1903 to 1904 and had even begun the process of applying for U.S. citizenship. When immigration authorities barred Hanna and his sons at El Paso, he paid a smuggler to take them across, and when caught, he emphasized his British subjecthood, not his time spent in the United States, to legitimize his entry. When an inspector recorded his nationality as Syrian, Hanna corrected him, "No, I am British. Write down that I am British."[78] Hanna's assertion that his Britishness should allow him special consideration at the border convinced several immigration inspectors, who sent his file to Commissioner of Immigration W. W. Husband. Although Husband rejected Hanna's plea, calling him a "typical back-door smuggled alien," the fact that Hanna's case made it so high reveals that in some cases, claiming British or French nationality helped Syrians navigate tightening border laws.

In the decades that followed, members of the midwestern Mahjar maintained relationships with Mexicans in their neighborhoods and workplaces. During the Great Depression, Syrians who could not find work in the United States returned across the southern border, where they hoped the new Mexican economy might provide opportunities. When the United States increased wartime production and industrial jobs surged, Syrians living in Mexico joined family members in Chicago, Gary, and Detroit for jobs in electric, steel, and automotive plants.[79] And while some of these migrants settled in the United States, others returned south to the North American nation they considered their home. Ali Sobh had left his wife and five children in Torreón for several seasons to join his uncle

Sam Hamod in Gary, where he easily found work in the steel mills on the shores of Lake Michigan. In 1959, Hamod sponsored the family's immigration and brought Ali Sobh, his Syrian Christian wife Mehive, and their Mexican children Adel, Monir, Yamil, Ale, and Nadia to the United States. Despite the high wages Sobh earned in the steel plants, he and Mehive preferred their life in Torreón and eventually returned to Mexico, where he said the pace was slower, the air clearer, and the people friendlier. Once back in Mexico, Sobh drew on his memories of the Shi'a mosque in Michigan City to advocate for a mosque in Torreón, and in 1989, the city's Shi'a community opened the Suraya Mosque, offering local Muslims a place of worship and concrete evidence of the Muslim Mahjar's long history in Mexico.[80]

Family ties continued to reinforce the connection between the Muslim Mahjar in Mexico and the United States. Neffew Sam Jezzeny, a founding member of the Michigan City community, had a brother who had chosen to settle in Mexico at the same time he found a job working for Pullman Standard. While Neffew's brother had no intention of leaving Mexico, his son, José González, migrated north to live with his uncle. Known affectionately to the Michigan City Islamic Center community as Uncle José, González attended Friday Jumma prayer at the mosque, married a local Mexican woman, and settled in Elkhart, Indiana.[81] In Toledo, Ohio, where a large Syrian population had settled in the 1950s, young members of the community struggled to find suitable Muslim marriage partners. While many in the community sought out Muslim spouses in Dearborn, Michigan City, and Cedar Rapids, or married non-Muslims, others turned to family connections in Latin America. In 1962, Hussein Boraby and his friend Ollie Rahal headed to Tampíco, Mexico, to stay with Boraby's uncle Luis, who had married a Mexican woman and ran a successful business in the textile trade. On their trip, both young men became besotted with Luis's half-Mexican daughters Sara and Sofía and proposed marriage to the sisters. Thus, in 1965, Hussein married his cousin Sara, while Ollie married Sofía, and they went to Toledo, where the Spanish-speaking sisters could communicate only in the limited Arabic they had learned from their father.[82] Indeed, connections established by blood and marriage maintained relationships across the Syrian diaspora as family members crossed between the United States and Mexico for visits and marriage well into the latter half of the twentieth century.

Examining Muslim migration between Greater Syria, Mexico, and the United States resituates the history of unauthorized immigration from the Mediterranean to the Americas. Following the lives of individual migrants instead of state reports, this chapter reveals that Syrians viewed Mexico as much more than a land mass than stood between them and destinations in the United States. In fact, many Syrians wanted to visit kin in Mexico, stayed there, and returned when they confronted struggles in the United States. When Syrian American

Mary Shamey learned that the sister she thought had died long ago in Mexico was alive, she visited her long-lost sister in 1947 and hosted her in Dearborn in 1979. With a laugh she remembered that they could barely understand each other. "One spoke Arabic mixed with English and the other Arabic mixed with Spanish."[83] Syrians who settled in the Midwest maintained ties to Mexico, which they used for business, marriage, and kinship, meaning that Muslim communities in America's heartland would maintain relationships across the southern border for generations.

Notes

1. Most of the migrants in this study come from modern-day Lebanon and today would consider themselves Lebanese. This article adopts the term Syrian to encompass migrants from the Arabic-speaking region of the Ottoman Empire because it is how the migrants identified themselves throughout the late nineteenth and early twentieth centuries.

2. Immigration and Naturalization Service Records, "Grand Rapids Smuggling Investigation," January 7, 1914, File 53620/303, RG 85, U.S. National Archives, Washington, DC (henceforth INS).

3. For a sampling of this important literature, see: Libby Garland, *After They Closed the Gates: Jewish Illegal Immigration to the United States, 1921–1965* (Chicago: University of Chicago Press, 2014); Kelly Lytle Hernández, *Migra!: A History of the U.S. Border Patrol* (Berkeley: University of California Press, 2010); Erika Lee, *At America's Gates: Chinese Immigration during the Exclusion Era, 1882–1943* (Chapel Hill: University of North Carolina Press, 2003); Miguel Antonio Levario, *Militarizing the Border: When Mexicans Became the Enemy* (College Station: Texas A&M Press, 2012); S. Deborah Kang, *The INS on the Line: Making Immigration Law on the US-Mexico Border, 1917–1954* (New York: Oxford University Press, 2017); Rachel St. John, *Line in the Sand: A History of the Western U.S.-Mexico Border* (Princeton, NJ: Princeton University Press, 2012). My own book on European unauthorized immigration across the U.S.-Canada border takes this approach, positioning Canada as a nation through which Italians and Eastern Europeans passed on their way to automobile jobs in Detroit. Ashley Johnson Bavery, *Bootlegged Aliens: Immigration Politics on America's Northern Border* (Philadelphia: University of Pennsylvania Press, 2020).

4. Theresa Alfaro-Velcamp, *So Far from Allah, So Close to Mexico: Middle Eastern Immigrants in Modern Mexico* (Austin: University of Texas Press, 2007), 37; Deirdre M. Moloney, *National Insecurities: Immigrants and U.S. Deportation Policy since 1882* (Chapel Hill: University of North Carolina Press, 2012), 117–19; Alixa Naff, *Becoming American: The Early Arab Immigrant Experience* (Carbondale: Southern Illinois University Press, 1985), 93, 102–3. Recently, migration historians have begun to complicate this literature by interrogating the gendered dynamics of border crossing within the Syrian diaspora. Devi Mays, *Forging Ties, Forging Passports: Migration and the Modern Sephardi Diaspora* (Stanford, CA: Stanford University Press, 2020); Randa Tawil, "A 'Flying Carpet to Doom': Retracing Gender and Orientalism through the Transnational Journeys of a Syrian Migrant Woman, 1912–1949," *Frontiers* 43, no. 1 (2022): 120–44.

5. On migrants' fluid identities, see: Julian Lim, *Porous Borders: Multiracial Migrations and the Law in the U.S.-Mexico Borderlands* (Chapel Hill: University of North Carolina Press, 2017); Natalia Molina, *How Race Is Made in America: Immigration, Citizenship, and the Historical Power of Racial Scripts* (Berkeley: University of California Press, 2019); Camila Pastor, *The Mexican Mahjar: Transnational Maronites, Jews, and Arabs Under the French Mandate* (Austin: University of Texas Press, 2017); Elliot Young, *Alien Nation: Chinese Migration in the Americas from the Coolie Era through World War II* (Chapel Hill: University of North Carolina Press, 2014). For examples of how South Asian migrants established interracial communities with Mexicans and African Americans, see: Vivek Bald, *Bengali Harlem and the Lost Histories of South Asian America* (Cambridge, MA: Harvard University Press, 2015); and Karen Isaksen Leonard, *Making Ethnic Choices: California's Punjabi Mexican Americans* (Philadelphia: Temple University Press, 1992).

6. Sarah Gualtieri, *Arab Routes: Pathways to Syrian California* (Stanford, CA: Stanford University Press, 2020), 5.

7. Scholars of race, particularly anthropologists and sociologists such as Louise Cainkar, Jeffrey Guhin, and Moustafa Bayoumi, have begun to theorize Islam as a racialized category. Moustafa Bayoumi, *This Muslim American Life: Dispatches from the War on Terror* (New York: New York University Press, 2015); Louise A. Cainkar, *Homeland Insecurity: The Arab American and Muslim American Experience After 9/11* (New York: Russell Sage Foundation, 2009); Jeffrey Guhin, "Colorblind Islam: The Racial Hinges of Immigrant Muslims in the United States," *Social Inclusion* 6, no. 2 (2018): 87–97. While their studies have focused on the late twentieth century, Khaled Beydoun has charted the long history of American Islamophobia, arguing that Muslims have experienced racialization because of their religion since the early twentieth century. Khaled A. Beydoun, "The Arc of American Islamophobia: From Early History through Present," in Kathleen Belew and Ramón A. Gutíerrez, eds., *A Field Guide to White Supremacy* (Berkeley: University of California Press, 2021).

8. Julian Lim, "Mormons and Mohammedans: Race, Religion, and the Anti-Polygamy Bar in US Immigration Law," *Journal of American Ethnic History* 41, no. 1 (2021): 8.

9. Interview with Phil and Maria Dabagia, May 13, 2021, Michigan City, IN. For similar histories of families who passed through Mexico, see: Phone interview with Bill Aossey, March 29, 2021; Phone interview with Mohammed Igram, March 19, 2021.

10. Alixa Naff posited that 5 percent to 10 percent of Syrian immigrants to the United States were Sunni and Shi'a Muslims. Naff, *Becoming American*, 2. Recent studies using Ottoman sources have suggested that between 15 percent and 20 percent of Syrians were actually Muslim and that anti-Turkish, anti-Muslim sentiments at the time discouraged migrants from identifying as Muslim. Sally Howell, *Old Islam in Detroit: Rediscovering the Muslim American Past* (New York: Oxford University Press, 2014), 300.

11. Abraham Fouad Khater, *Inventing Home: Emigration, Gender, and the Middle Class in Lebanon, 1870–1920* (Berkeley: University of California Press, 2003).

12. Pastor, *Mexican Mahjar*, 25–27.

13. Gladys Bull Nicewarner, *Michigan City, Indiana: The Life of a Town* (Michigan City, IN: Nicewarner, 1980), 212–13; Islamic Center of Michigan City, "Islam in Michigan City: Past and Present," 1980, Courtesy of Phil Dabagia.

14. "500 Syrians in Sioux City," *Sioux City Journal*, June 29, 1913.

15. Naff, *Becoming American*, 155; Yahya Aossey, *Fifty Years of Islam in Iowa: 1925–1975* (Cedar Rapids, IA: Unity Publishing Company, 1975).

16. Interview with Phil and Maria Dabagia, May 13, 2021, Michigan City, IN; Howell, *Old Islam*, 33–34.

17. Alixa Naff claims that Muslim migrants were men and did not bring children, but immigration records demonstrate that by the 1910s, hundreds of women were attempting to cross into the United States. Naff, *Becoming American*, 90; Ancestry.com Operations, Inc., *U.S., Border Crossings from Mexico to U.S., 1895–1964* (database on-line), Provo, UT, 2006. Syrians in Highland Park, Michigan, established America's first known mosque in 1921, but the organization fell apart by the Depression. Howell, *Old Islam*, 50. In Michigan City, Mahjaris established the Bader Elmoneer Society before incorporating an official mosque in 1924. "Islam in Michigan City: Past and Present," 1980; "Certificate of Incorporation," May 10, 1924, Courtesy of Phil Dabagia. In Iowa, young migrants created the Rose of Fraternity Lodge before building an official mosque in 1934; Aossey, *Fifty Years of Islam*, 1–2. Muslim Mahjaris also established mutual benefit societies in Sioux City and Grand Rapids, though the communities never established official mosques in these cities. INS, "Grand Rapids Smuggling Investigation," January 7, 1914, File 53620/303; INS, "Sioux City Smuggling Investigation," May 3, 1913, File 53387/35–43.

18. For an excellent overview of this law's impact first on Mormons, then on Muslims, see Julian Lim, "Mormons and Mohammedans."

19. INS, "Asiatic Exclusion League to the Commissioner of Immigration," July 13, 1910, File 52961/12.

20. INS, "Immigration Circular to All Districts," June 16, 1913, File 52737/499.

21. Howell, *Old Islam*, 49.

22. Moloney, *National Insecurities*, 115.

23. Sarah Gualtieri, *Between Arab and White: Race and Ethnicity in the Early Syrian American Diaspora* (Berkeley: University of California Press, 2009), 55.

24. Moloney, *National Insecurities*, 115.

25. Gualtieri, *Between Arab and White*, 55; Moloney, *National Insecurities*, 115; Naff, *Becoming American*, 102–3.

26. "Have Bad Eye Disease," *El Paso Times*, April 17, 1906.

27. Fastor, *Mexican Mahjar*, 29.

28. For more on the robust history of Syrians in Mexico, see: Angelina Alonso Palacios, *Los libeneses y la industria textil en Puebla* (Mexico City: Secretaría de Educación Pública, Cultura, 1983); Marcos Arana Cervantes, *Ramas del mismo cedro: vox viva de la comunidad libenesa de Guadalajara* (Mexico City: Centro Libanés de Guadalajara, 2006); Martha Díaz de Kuri and Lourdes Macluf, *De Líbano a México: crónica de un pueblo emigrante* (Mexico: Gráfica, 1995); Lourdes Macluf and Martha Díaz de Kuri, *De Líbano a México: la vida alrededor de la mesa* (Mexico City, 2002); Zisane Zeraoui, *El Islam en América Latina* (Mexico City, Instituto Tecnológico y de Estudios Superiores de Monterrey, 2012).

29. Fastor, *Mexican Mahjar*, 4.

30. Interview with Brahim Hakim, Michigan City, IN, May 13, 2021; Phone interview with Sam Hamod, March 10, 2021.

31. Pastor, *Mexican Mahjar*, 36.

32. Alfaro-Velcamp, *So Far from Allah*, 66; Pastor, *Mexican Mahjar*, 36.

33. Alfaro-Velcamp, *So Far from Allah*, 15; Pastor, *Mexican Mahjar*, 84.

34. Gualtieri, *Between Arab and White*, 61–62.

35. "Turks and Syrians Barred from Citizenship," *Rushville Republican*, October 9, 1909.

36. Gualtieri, *Between Arab and White*, 58–59.

37. Interview between Janice Terry and Don Unis, July 29, 1996, Dearborn, MI, Box 1, Janice Terry Papers, Bentley Historical Library. In 1886, the Díaz government passed the Foreignness and Naturalization Law, which allowed foreigners who had resided in Mexico for two years to petition for citizenship and required migrants who came to work for the Mexican government to be treated as Mexican citizens. Pastor, *Mexican Mahjar*, 84.

38. For further examples, see Ancestry.com Operations Inc., "Joseph and Hebib Nickolas Entries," *1920 United States Federal Census*, Provo, UT, 2002. "Mustafa Ali File" and "Mohammed Hassan File," International Institute Records, Calumet Regional Archives, Gary, IN.

39. Grace Pena Delgado, *Making the Chinese Mexican: Global Migration, Localism, and Exclusion in the U.S.-Mexico Borderlands* (Stanford, CA: Stanford University Press, 2012), 101–3.

40. Alfaro-Velcamp, *So Far from Allah*, 78–79; Interview with Don Unis.

41. An analysis of border crossing files on the U.S.-Mexico border for 1912 alone reveals that of the 1,029 immigrants classified as Syrian crossing from Mexico to the United States, at least 309 had lived in Mexico for over a year, suggesting that they had hoped to stay in Mexico before the revolution. Ancestry.com Operations, Inc., *U.S., Border Crossings from Mexico to U.S., 1895–1964*, Provo, UT, 2006.

42. On the takeover of Santa Rosalía, see: Kenneth J. Grieb, "Pascual Orozco, Jr.," in *Encyclopedia of Latin American History and Culture*, vol. 4 (New York: Charles Scribner's Sons, 1996), 241; and Hector Agradano, "Rails to Revolution: Railroads, Railroad Workers and the Geographies of the Mexican Revolution" (PhD diss, the Graduate Center, City University of New York, 2019), 107–9. For evidence of Syrian Muslims leaving Santa Rosalía, see files of Maram Hammy, Mohamed Hamdy, Fatima Hamdy, Shaleen Henainy, Salim Mustafa, Saleem Saseen, Saleem Saum, Haim Shakey, Anton Trad, Khaleel Trad, and Syra Trad, in *Manifests of Statistical Alien Arrivals at El Paso, Texas, May 1909–October 1924*, NAI: 2843448; INS, Record Group Title: *Records of the Immigration and Naturalization Service, 1787–2004*.

43. "Julian Drube Application for Entrance to the United States," April 8, 1918, "Investigative Case Files of the Bureau of Investigation 1908–1922," database with images Fold3.

44. Hidetaka Hirota, *Expelling the Poor: Atlantic Seaboard States and the Nineteenth-Century Origins of American Immigration Policy* (New York: Oxford University Press, 2017), 203.

45. Charles Gordon, Stanley Mailman, and Stephen Yale-Loehr, *Immigration Law and Procedure*, vol. 5 (Newark, NJ: Matthew Bender & Company, 2008), 281.

46. ˹ane Perry Clark, *Deportation of Aliens from the United States to Europe* (New York: Columbia University Press, 1931), 104. On the gendered use of the LPC clause, see Margot Canaday, *The Straight State: Sexuality and Citizenship in Twentieth-Century America* (Princeton, NJ: Princeton University Press, 2009); and Martha Gardner, *The Qualities of a Citizen: Women, Immigration, and Citizenship in Twentieth-Century America* (Princeton, NJ: Princeton University Press, 2009). On the use of the LPC clause to exclude Mexicans, see Roger Daniels, *Guarding the Golden Door: American Immigration Policy and Immigrants since 1882* (New York: Hill and Wang, 2004), 60–61.

47. Despite the Mexican Revolution and migrants' long periods spent in Mexico, inspectors continued to view Syrians on the southern border with suspicion because they were entering through Mexico, not New York. For examples, see: INS, George Tannous File, September 12, 1911, File 53303/16; Merchid Tannous File, September 14, 1933, File 53303/7; "Supervising Inspector at Laredo to Commissioner General of Immigration," September 6, 1912, File 53387/35.

48. INS, "File on Eleven Syrians Routed Through Mexico to Sioux City, Iowa," January 11, 1911, File 53387/35.

49. INS, "File on Eleven Syrians Routed Through Mexico to Sioux City, Iowa."

50. Ancestry.com Operations, Inc., Youssef Khalil Al Maso File, 1912, *U.S., Border Crossings from Mexico to U.S., 1895–1964*, Provo, UT, 2006. From 1882 to 1924, shipping companies that were responsible for immigrants' return if rejected at the border often required immigrants to carry $50, turning this amount into the benchmark for determining whether an immigrant was "likely to become a public charge." For a detailed history of the LPC provision, see: U.S. Citizenship and Immigration Services, "Historical Origins of the Likely to Become a Public Charge (LPC) Exclusion," Public Charge Provisions of Immigration Law: A Brief Historical Background, August 18, 2019, https://www.fairus .org/sites/default/files/2019-07/lpc-hist-bckgrnd-final-long-92018.pdf.

51. As an example, Muhammad Khaleed and his friends, the group profiled at the beginning of this chapter, changed their names to gain passage into Nogales, Arizona, and continue on to Grand Rapids, Michigan. INS, File 53620/303.

52. "Report on *Al Jawater*," June 29, 1917, "Investigative Case Files of the Bureau of Investigation 1908–1922," database with images Fold3.

53. On Chinese smuggled across the border, see Lee, *At America's Gates*. For an examination of smuggling rings specializing in Europeans, particularly Jewish migrants, see Garland, *After They Closed the Gates*.

54. INS, Khalil Koury File, April 21, 1907, File 51615/108.

55. INS, "Sioux City Investigation," May 28, 1912, File 53387/35.

56. "500 Syrians in Sioux City," *Sioux City Journal*, June 29, 1913.

57. "Christians Versus Mohammedans," *Sioux City Journal*, July 8, 1902.

58. INS, "Sioux City Investigation."

59. INS, "Sioux City Smuggling Investigation," May 3, 1913, File 53387/35–43; INS, "Grand Rapids Smuggling Investigation," January 7, 1914, File 53620/303; Interview with Phil and Maria Dabagia, May 13, 2021, Michigan City, IN.

60. Hundreds of Syrians entering the United States through Mexico listed Spanish first names such as Jose, Francisco, and Miguel. Ancestry.com Operations, Inc., *U.S., Border Crossings from Mexico to U.S., 1895–1964*, Provo, UT, 2006.

61. In the 1930 Census, both Syrians and Mexicans listed their place of employment as "Union Stock Yards," so they worked in the same spaces. Ancestry.com Operations, Inc., *1930 United States Federal Census*, Provo, UT, 2002.

62. Ancestry.com Operations, Inc., *The 1930 Census Reveals That Syrians Shared Buildings, Streets and Neighborhoods with Mexicans in Four Regions of Grand Rapids, 1930 United States Federal Census*, Provo, UT, 2002.

63. Dozens of Mahjaris with Muslim names lived on the same streets and in the same buildings as Mexican immigrants. For examples of Mahjaris citing Mexican nationality, see the files of Mustafa and Rofiala Zorah, Ancestry.com Operations, Inc., *1920 United States Federal Census*, Provo, UT, 2002.

64. Phone Interview with Sam Hamod, March 10, 2021.

65. Naff, *Becoming American*, 242, 245.

66. For examples in Dearborn, see census entries for John and Mary Rice, Mustafa and Rosa Hamood, and Mohamed and Maria Hassen, Ancestry.com Operations, Inc., *1930 United States Federal Census*, Provo, UT, 2002. For examples of intermarriage between Syrian Muslim men and Mexican women in Michigan City, see Mustafa and Rosalia Zorah, *1920 Census*; and Samuel and Teresa Allie, and James and Julia Autum; *1930 Census*.

67. On the large number of Syrians who fought in WWI for the United States, see Howell, *Old Islam*, 35. In 1918, Congress drafted a law that waived the five-year residency requirement for immigrant volunteers in the armed forces, encouraging many Syrians and Lebanese to sign up. Stacy Farenthold, *Between the Ottomans and Entente: The First World War in the Syrian and Lebanese Diaspora, 1908–1925* (New York: Oxford University Press, 2019), 71.

68. Howell, *Old Islam*, 310.

69. Farenthold, *Between the Ottomans*, 74–76.

70. Report Re: Charles Berry, October 10, 1917, Espionage Folders, Box 29, W.J. Cameron Subject Files, Accession 44, Benson Ford Research Center, Dearborn, MI.

71. "Reports on Draft Dodgers to Mexico," January 4–12, 1918, "Investigative Case Files of the Bureau of Investigation 1908–1922," database with images Fold3.

72. *"Bureau of Investigation File on Syrians in Mexico,"* January 25, 1918, and *"Bureau Report on Draft Evaders in Mexico,"* September 29, 1918, "Investigative Case Files of the Bureau of Investigation 1908–1922," database with images Fold3.

73. For more on the British mandate in Palestine, see Roza I. M. El-Eini, *Mandated Landscape: British Imperial Rule in Palestine, 1929–1948* (London: Routledge, 2006); on the French mandate in Syria and Mount Lebanon, see Farenthold, *Between the Ottomans*, 87, 110.

74. Chris Gratien and Emily K. Pope-Obeda, "Ottoman Migrants, U.S. Deportation Law, and Statelessness During the Interwar Era," *Mashriq & Mahjar: Journal of Middle East Migration Studies* 5, no. 2 (2018): 13.

75. Pastor, *Mexican Mahjar*, 90.

76. Alfaro-Velcamp, *So Far from Allah*, 80; Pastor, *Mexican Mahjar*, 86.

77. Ancestry.com Operations, Inc., "Ahmed Chameel Manifest," October 19, 1923, Eagle Pass Border Crossing Files, *U.S., Border Crossings from Mexico to U.S., 1895–1964*, Provo, UT, 2006.

78. INS, Mansour Hanna File, 1921, File 55063/488.

79. In an interview, Sam Hamod mentioned that his uncle Ali Sobh traveled to Gary from Mexico regularly (presumably without papers) in the 1940s and 1950s to work in the city's steel mills. Sobh's brother-in-law Alexander Darwich also migrated to the United States several times from Torreón, Mexico, where he found work in steel mills, packing houses, and eventually at Western Electric in Cicero, Illinois. "Sam Hamod File," International Institute Records, Calumet Regional Archives, Gary, IN; Phone interview with Sam Hamod, March 10, 2021.

80. "Sam Hamod File," International Institute Records; Phone interview with Sam Hamod, March 10, 2021; "El Islam en La Laguna, Una Tradicional Minoría Religiosa," *El Siglo de Torreón*, August 10, 2008.

81. Interview with Brahim Hakim, Michigan City, IN, May 13, 2021.

82. Phone interview with Manira Sallock, March 19, 2021; Archivo General del Registro del Estado (Civil Registry State Archives), Tamaulipas, México; Ohio Department of Health, State Vital Statistics Unit, "Omar Hussein Boraby Entry," Index to Annual Births, 1968–1998, Columbus; "Ollie Rahal Obituary," *Toledo Blade*, April 15, 2015.

83. "Mary Shamey Interview with Alixa Naff," May 3, 1988, Dearborn, MI, Naff Papers, National Museum of American History, Washington, DC.

6   Don't Ask, Don't Tell

Polish Undocumented Home Care Workers in Late Twentieth-Century Chicago

MARY PATRICE ERDMANS
AND POLINA ERMOSHKINA

In Polish community, it means better job. . . . Of course, not for
somebody who has a legal paper. But for the people who are here
illegal for two to three years to make money, it is kind of good job.
—Marek, home care worker

Marek and Anna came to Chicago in September 1988; he was a doctor of internal medicine and she had just finished six years of medical school at Jagiellonian University in Krakow, Poland. They owned an apartment in Krakow that they bought with savings from Anna's six-month stint working in Chicago in 1985. This time they both went abroad, leaving their nine-month-old daughter behind with her grandparents. Marek and Anna arrived on B-2 tourist visas valid for six months, intending to work for a year and return, even though they had no legal authorization to work in the United States. Within a year of departure, Poland non-violently transformed from a communist political economy into a capitalist democracy. Given the volcanic changes in the economy, the government, and every major institution—the health care industry was in terrible disarray—Marek and Anna postponed their return and continued to work in the United States and save money, all the while watching the value of their savings erode as the introduction of market principles and the relaxation of government controls led to extreme inflation in Poland.

As live-in care providers, both had what were considered "good" positions. Marek took care of wealthy, stroke-paralyzed, eighty-two-year-old Joe, whose children hired Marek so that Joe could age in place in his two-story home in the northwest corner of Chicago. The children did not ask about Marek's legal status when they interviewed him, they did not ask to see any identification, and they were not concerned about his poor English skills, as Joe could hardly speak. They did ask about Marek's medical experience and were impressed that he was a doctor. Marek started in December of 1988 at $225 a week, working seven nights and six days (he was off from 10 a.m. to 6 p.m. on Sundays). For those twelve hours off, the family paid an agency $200 for a "professional" who had six weeks of home care training.[1] By the second year, he made $350 week (and was off from 8 a.m. to 8 p.m. on Sunday).

Some good aspects of the job were that the family did not interfere too much with Joe's care, and Marek had control over household routines. Compared to his first job, working for a cleaning service at a hotel chain, this live-in job was not physically exhausting, and in his free time (during Joe's naps and the evenings), he could study English. Also, Marek paid no room or board, so he was able to save most of his wages. At the time that Mary Erdmans conducted the interview in 1992, he had been with Joe for thirty months. He said: "I don't like this job very much, but I see that the job provides me with money, and a time to study, and a nice home in a nice neighborhood." This last factor was important, as many of his undocumented peers were living in considerably poorer conditions in *Jackowo*, the Polish ghetto on the northwest side of Chicago.

Another positive aspect of the job, from Marek's perspective, was that his wife, Anna, could stay with him on weekends. Anna worked as a caretaker for a wealthy ninety-one-year-old woman living in a retirement community, and it was also a good work situation because no proxy was bothering her, she had her own sleeping area, and she had some free time during the day. She started in 1988 at $250 a week, and moved up to $350, working six days and six nights. In this retirement community with 250 units, she was in a network of other Polish eldercare and domestic workers with whom she socialized during the week, sharing Polish food, information, and jobs.

After being gone for two years, Anna returned to Poland for her daughter, who was almost three years old, and brought her back to the United States because, as Marek said: "we noticed that we could become doctors here." He had learned English well enough to pass the medical entrance exam. He applied to twenty-four hospitals, had twelve interviews, and was entering a residency program in Chicago in the fall of 1992. He converted his expired B-2 tourist visa to a J-1 exchange visitor visa. Marek found his own replacement, just as Joe's previous Polish caretaker found Marek. They put an advertisement in the Polish-language newspaper, the *Dziennik Zwiazkowy*, and within three hours, he received nine calls.

Anna's client sponsored her on an H-1B work visa.[2] It took one year and $5,000 of Anna's funds for a lawyer, but with the H-1B visa, she could live and work in the United States legally and negotiate a better wage. With her daughter now in the country, Anna worked only one day a week for the same woman ($160 for ten hours) and found another Polish live-in to replace her for the other six days.

Marek and Anna represent one type of undocumented Polish worker in Chicago in the early 1990s in one specific labor niche, providing elder home care. They were men and women in their late twenties and early thirties, professionals with medical education and training in Poland who had a two-pronged migration plan—they would try to pass a medical exam in the United States and work toward legal status, or they would work for a few years and return home with savings to advance their medical careers in Poland.

Not all Polish undocumented migrants working in the home care (HC) sector look like Anna and Marek. Among a group of thirty-five Polish HC workers in Chicago in 1992, we identified four migration projects that coalesced and diverged around motives for migration and intentions for return. Anna and Marek represent what we call the *medical migrants* project. A second migration project we termed *older temporary migrants*: women in their late forties and fifties without spouses (including women who were divorced or widowed) who came to earn money for remittances and retirement and expected to return to Poland. A third project was the *younger temporary migrants*: university-educated men and women in their twenties intending to stay for a short time who were motivated as much for adventure as money. A fourth migration project was composed of *permanent residents*: mostly women (some men) who were in the country as lawful permanent residents at the time of the interview. Their stories are useful for understanding how legal status shapes job choice and intentions to return.

In this essay, we first explain why Polish undocumented workers were in the HC industry in Chicago and describe the sample. We then define the characteristics of the four migration projects and examine how motivations and intentions shape the experiences of undocumented migrants.

Undocumented Polish Migrants

Social scientists estimate that 2 million undocumented migrants were living in the United States in 1980, and between 1 million and 5 million in 1990.[3] While Mexicans were the largest group of undocumented migrants, Poles were the largest group of undocumented migrants from Europe.[4] Mexicans and Poles also constituted the two largest groups of undocumented workers in Chicago,[5] and they had the largest immigrant populations in 1990, with 270,000 documented Mexicans and 81,500 Poles.[6]

Poles were emigrating because of poor economic, political, and social conditions in their homeland, which in the late twentieth century took the form of a crumbling one-party state, inefficient state-controlled markets exploited by the USSR, and repressive social controls. The official collapse of communism in 1989 and introduction of "shock therapy" capitalism created instability in labor markets during the period of transition.[7] In 1992, when the interviews in this essay were collected, Poland was mired in the institutional disarray of early capitalism, with high rates of inflation and unemployment.[8]

The number of Polish immigrants to the United States rose exponentially in the first half of the 1990s—almost as many Poles were admitted in three years between 1990 and 1992 (65,240) as in the previous decade (see Table 6.1). Chicago saw a similar sharp increase in the early 1990s, with 1,000 to 2,000 Polish migrants arriving annually between 1972 and 1989, climbing to 10,000 annually in the 1990s.[9] While this increase was certainly related to changes in Poland—the aforementioned transitional turbulence as well as the opening of Poland's formerly closed borders[10]—it also represents changes in immigration policy in the United States. The 1990 Immigration Act increased the total ceiling for immigrant admissions (from 270,000 to 700,000) and created special programs like the Diversity Visa program that admitted over 50,000 Polish immigrants.[11]

Polish migrants were pulled to Chicago through the tradition of migration. Centuries of migration between Poland and the United States created thick migration networks that shaped imaginations, created conduits for temporary and permanent visa invitations, and provided a physical community of homes, shops, and places to work. Nine million people claimed some ancestral attachment to Poland on the 1990 U.S. Census, and roughly 10 percent of them lived in the Chicago metropolitan area. This old and large community had well-developed formal and informal ethnic labor networks.[12]

The Polish community in Chicago included immigrants as well as what the United States government calls "nonimmigrants," who were in the United States

Table 6.1. Polish Immigrants and Nonimmigrants Admitted into the United States, 1960–1992

Year	Total number Polish immigrants admitted	Total number Polish nonimmigrants admitted	Total number (and percent) of Polish nonimmigrants admitted as "visitors for pleasure"
1960–1969	77,650	166,815	121,390 (73%)
1970–1979	42,378	352,269	239,619 (68%)
1980–1989	81,578	449,235	356,266 (79%)
1990–1992	65,240	207,432	147,973 (71%)
1960–1992	266,846	1,175,751	865,248 (74%)

Annual Report of the Immigration and Naturalization Service, 1960–1976; *Statistical Yearbook of the Immigration and Naturalization Service*, 1977–1992. Tables: Immigrants admitted by class of admission and region and selected country of birth; Nonimmigrants admitted by class of admission and region and selected country of citizenship. Washington, DC: GPO.

on temporary visas for purposes such as work (H-1), study (F-1), and pleasure (B-2), the largest category. A half a million Poles were admitted on B-2 tourist visas as "temporary visitors for pleasure" between 1980 and 1992 (see Table 6.1). These visitors for pleasure, known in the community as *wakacjusze* (vacationers) and *turysci* (tourists), often worked without authorization (see Joanna Wojdon's essay in this volume for the negative portrayal of the *wakacjusze* in Polish media). Most intended to stay a few months or years and then return to Poland,[13] but many overstayed their visas. In the early 1990s, Poles had the highest estimated "overstays" for tourists arriving by air (37 percent).[14] Entry by air with a valid visa set Poles apart from many undocumented workers from Mexico and Central America, who were more likely to have arrived by land and without documentation.[15]

The language of immigrant and nonimmigrant reinforces traditional theories that conceptualize migration as movement and resettlement from place x to place y. In contrast, a transnational paradigm sees migration as a fluid relationship between place x and place y.[16] In a transnational paradigm, return migration is always in the mix. In recent years, scholars of Polish migration have drawn attention to this fluidity, referencing Zygmunt Bauman's concept of "liquid modernity" to emphasize how Poles "tend to settle within mobility, staying mobile as long as they can in order to improve or maintain a particular quality of life."[17] These scholars focus on Polish migration in the post-2004 period after accession to the European Union.[18] Their language captures this fluidity, referring to "pendulum," "circular," and "shuttle" migration as well as "transnational commuting."[19] Others note that circular migration was not new in the post-2004 era[20] but was already noticeable after the opening of Poland's western border in 1989,[21] which is when most of the Poles in our study migrated. In our analysis, we explore the fluidity of their migration projects.

Undocumented Polish Workers as Elder HC Providers

Home care is the provision of services (medical, housekeeping, personal) to clients in their own home. HC workers are "the backbone" and "frontline hands-on" of long-term home services to older adults.[22] For emotional, social, and financial reasons, most Americans prefer to age in their own residences rather than nursing homes or other institutional settings.[23] By 1992, more than 1 million people in the United States were receiving home care.[24]

An increased need for HC workers in the latter part of the twentieth century came from a confluence of demographic changes and neoliberal cost-containment policies. Demographic changes included people living longer and traditional caregivers (i.e., daughters) living farther away. The age group sixty-five and older doubled between 1950 and 1984 as a result of large pre-1921 birth cohorts and increased longevity.[25] Moreover, an increasing number of women began working outside the home in the 1970s, by choice and by necessity as wages flatlined.[26] The total percent of women participating in the paid labor force more than doubled (25 percent to 56 percent) from 1940 to 1988.[27] Adult children were also increasingly living farther away, and families were less likely to be living in multi-generational dwellings.[28] These changes increased the need for formal HC workers for the elderly.

In the 1970s, the health care industry, along with other institutions in the United States, adopted neoliberal practices to contain costs and increase profits.[29] Long-term institutionalized care was not only socially and emotionally undesirable but also expensive, and costs were pushed onto patients. Both private and public health care payers introduced capitation mechanisms, prospective payment plans, and diagnosis-related groups, all of which placed ceilings on reimbursements. Deregulation and the privatization of health care also left people discharged from hospitals and care units "quicker and sicker," with insurance companies paying less, and subsequently more caregiving provided in the home.[30] While some third-party payers covered some costs, most did not cover long-term, twenty-four-hour home care.[31] The aging population and decline in traditional informal (unpaid) caregivers created a need for formal caregivers that the for-profit health care system would not meet.

Historically, African American and migrant women have provided the social reproductive labor needed to care for the young, the old, and the infirm.[32] African American women were more often working in the South and on the East Coast, the Irish in New England, Mexicans in Los Angeles, Central Americans in Washington, DC, and the Japanese on the West coast.[33] African American women began leaving domestic services when gains from the civil rights movement created new job opportunities. Between 1930 and 1980, the number of African American women working in the elder HC industry dropped almost by half,[34] and the number of migrant workers increased. By 1990, the elder HC workforce was composed primarily of African American people and migrants from the economic periphery in the Global South.[35]

Live-in elder HC jobs are not desirable jobs in part because of their secondary labor market characteristics: low pay (usually minimum wage), few benefits (no paid vacations, health insurance, or retirement or pension programs), and high instability (in this case, clients dying or moving to institutionalized care).[36] Poor job conditions contribute to high job turnover rates, ranging from 30 percent to 90 percent annually in the 1980s.[37] In addition, the live-in aspect of the job creates a unique set of conditions. First, the time-consuming 24–7 nature of the work makes the job undesirable for people who want a social life outside of work. Live-in care is also emotionally difficult because of the close, extended interpersonal relations that exist within constrained space.[38] Because workers "share their lives with the care recipients," the expectation is that they will become closer and more "strongly committed to their care recipients, who are also their employers."[39]

In sum, the need for HC workers increased as traditional unpaid, informal caregivers became less available, and the job conditions did not attract a stable workforce. This created a niche for undocumented migrant workers.

Description of the Study

In 1992, Mary Erdmans interviewed thirty-five Polish immigrants working in the HC market in the greater Chicago metropolitan area.[40] The one- to three-hour interviews (transcribed and translated when necessary) included demographic information and work histories as well as open-ended questions about the process of finding jobs, tasks performed at their jobs, satisfaction with jobs, and plans for returning to Poland.[41]

The workers ranged in age from twenty-five to fifty-nine, and twenty-seven were women. Overall, the sample was highly educated; all but three had some postsecondary education, and three-quarters had been attending university or working in professional occupations before emigrating. Over half had some medical education, including: five doctors, four medical school graduates, three registered nurses, three medical technicians, a midwife, a physical therapist, and a chemist.

Most (74 percent) arrived between 1988 and 1992 as "nonimmigrants" (twenty-nine arrived on B-2 tourist visas, three with student F-1 visas); but three entered with permanent residency.[42] On arrival, almost all (94 percent) of the nonimmigrants had visas valid for three to six months; at the time of the interview, twenty-one had expired visas, four had valid tourist visas but no authorization to work, and the others had permanent legal resident status. Most planned to return to Poland, both at the time of arrival (86 percent) and at the time of the interview (69 percent). We take this intention as an indication of fluidity. And yet, we acknowledge that intention is different from action. When they arrived, two-thirds intended to stay less than two years, but at the time of the interview, two-thirds had stayed longer than intended. The desire to stay or return did not map exactly onto legal status: four migrants with expired temporary visas did not intend to return, and four with permanent residency did.

The thirty-five migrants had a total of 151 jobs in the United States, and of these, 110 were HC positions (75 percent live-in positions).[43] Roughly one-third of the jobs ended within the first month, another quarter lasted over a year, and seven women had worked in positions for longer than three years (the longest was six years). Two-thirds of the 110 clients were women and all were white. Almost all the clients were comfortably middle-class people who could afford to pay for private HC out of pocket and who often used domestic cleaning and lawn care services.[44]

Workers earned on average $50–$60 per day for live-in positions (the range was $26 to $100) and $5–$7 per hour for come-and-go positions. Salaries were higher ($70 per day) for those who had better English proficiency, medical training, previous HC experience with older adults, or a driver's license.[45] Migrants with skills and experience could be more selective. For example, Anna went to six different job interviews before she agreed to a job (where she stayed for three years).

In Chicago, clients and workers found each other through employment agencies, newspapers, and word of mouth. Three-quarters of all the jobs were found through employment agencies that, as one agent described, operated as a "kind of a brokerage. You are standing between this who wants to buy and this who wants to sell." These agencies were brokering both undocumented and documented workers in several sectors, including elder HC, childcare, domestic work, landscaping, cleaning services, construction, and light factory work. Others found jobs through friends and relatives, as well as by placing their own advertisement in the newspaper, being recommended for jobs by a hospice worker, and "buying" a job from someone returning to Poland. "Buying" a job cost the same as the agency charged—one week's salary.[46]

The Polish undocumented migrants in this study had two characteristics that set them apart from many other undocumented migrants: they often had post-secondary educations, and they were racialized as white. Both their education (especially medical skills) and whiteness were valued by their white clients. One employment agency worker said it was not uncommon for clients or proxies calling to ask: "Are your workers white?"[47] Both higher levels of education and whiteness worked to their advantage as they maneuvered being undocumented. Their experiences stand in contrast to those of Mexican undocumented migrants.[48] In general, undocumented Polish workers could work in this labor sector with little concern that they would be caught and deported.

When interviewed for the job, the most common questions were about previous experience and medical skills. The client or family also tried to determine how long the worker would stay in the United States. The migrants said "at least six months"—whether they were intending this or not—because it helped secure the job. In almost all cases, neither the agency nor the client asked the worker about their work permit or visa status. Anna said, "you are telling your name and that is it. They don't even ask about any ID." Out of the 110 HC jobs in this study, the interviewees reported only four families who asked them if they had "a green card." In three cases, the worker did, and in the fourth, he lied and said he did. In none of the four cases did they have to show documentation.

While the Immigration Reform and Control Act (IRCA) of 1986 included harsh penalties for undocumented workers who were caught—and called for employers of undocumented workers to be financially penalized—the perceived risk of getting caught by immigration officials in the home care sector was low.[49] The employment agencies brokering these jobs were not checking documents and were not worried about the Immigration and Naturalization Service (INS). One employment agency worker said: "I think maybe they [the INS] check it out when you have a factory job. But on domestic jobs, I don't even know if Immigration is looking for people who are working domestic jobs." Another agent said legality was not an issue. "Most times they have no papers, they say, 'My papers are at home,' and they simply tell you that they are legal. But for babysitters and elderly care and domestics we don't need the papers because most Americans don't want to show this income." The nature of the work—in private homes—made it inefficient for a watchdog agency (underfunded from the beginning) to crack down on individual families hiring undocumented workers unless they came to national attention, as they did for Zoe Baird and Kimba Wood in "Nannygate" in 1993.[50] In our interviews, the workers did not mention deportation, or fear of deportation, although a "don't ask, don't tell" strategy was present. During the interviews, Erdmans never asked them directly: "Do you have authorization to work?" instead, she asked what their visa was on arrival, how long it was valid for, and whether they had ever updated or changed it.

Migration Projects

We identify four migration projects—medical migrants, older temporary migrants, younger temporary migrants, and permanent residents—organized around motivations for migration and intentions for returning or staying. We look at how these projects influenced their experience as undocumented workers in the elder HC industry.

Medical Migrants

Medical migrants were in their late twenties and early thirties, with medical degrees and an intention and pragmatic plan to stay in the United States as permanent residents working in the medical field. This group included four men and five women. They were either studying for a medical exam, had already taken an exam, or were planning to take an exam but first needed to learn English. Medical training was a necessary but not sufficient condition for this project; it was the intention to resettle in the United States as doctors and nurses that made them medical migrants.

Medical migrants needed work that gave them time to study and that did not physically exhaust them.[51] Marek said, "it was important that I don't do physical work, which tires me out. This work lets me study, sometimes 5, 6, 7 hours a day." Medical migrants reported some of the highest salaries of the four groups and better living and working conditions, that is, the nonmonetary aspects of the job that included control over household schedules and meals, private living space, and time off during the day for exercise.[52]

In four of the cases, the migration interrupted a short career as practicing doctors and nurses in Poland. The others migrated at the end of their university education. Their decisions to migrate were related to the social-economic disarray in Poland in general and the health care industry more specifically (they arrived between 1988 and 1991). They had no intention to remain in the United States permanently working in a secondary labor market position with a significant drop in social status. Staying abroad for a few years and returning, they could reclaim their medical trajectories in Poland, but the migration project held out the possibility of moving into a primary labor market position in a core country.[53]

Older Temporary Migrants

In this project, the migrants came when they were older, they did not interrupt careers or disrupt family relations, their main motivation was to earn money for remittances and retirement, and they planned to return when they retired. Eleven migrants had this project, and all of them were women.[54] All but one had expired B-2 visas. Their age ranged from forty-six to fifty-nine, and any children they had were adults. Nine had no spouses (widowed, divorced, or separated) and the other two were with their spouses in Chicago—as such, marriages did not complicate their migration projects, as can be the case with married women migrants.[55] In general, the lowest wage earners were in this group. Over half made less than $60 a day, but those with experience and higher education had some of the highest wages.

They all stated an intention to return to Poland (seven had children living there), but they were in no hurry as they were earning dollars and had no careers or jobs to return to in Poland.

They had been working without documentation for an average of three years, and several had been working for five years or longer. Their expired visas kept them in the United States as they could not engage in more circular migration. They planned to return near retirement age, which for women in Poland was sixty.[56]

The older temporary migrants had varied education and work histories in Poland. Five had university degrees and twenty-five-plus-year tenures in professional occupations (such as engineer, statistician, and teacher). Three others had worked in technical, skilled labor, and clerical positions in large state industries in communist Poland, which were transitioning to private ownership in the early 1990s. The final three had checkered work histories (such as multiple manual and clerical jobs in Poland). Despite these differences, none of them expected to return to their careers or jobs. In general, the new capitalist labor market was not that welcoming to older women.[57]

Some women with this project appeared motivated by what Małek has called *migrantki eskapistki*, that is, women motivated to emigrate because they were escaping difficult family relations.[58] Two women spoke of "bad marriages," and four others were divorced. Maria, who was fifty-one when we interviewed her and had been in the United States for four years, said: "My best friend came here, and she know that I have trouble with ex-husband. She wanted to take me from him. I had a good job [in Poland], so [it] was not because of money."

Basia, a fifty-five-year-old divorcee who had been in the United States since 1986, was a former engineer and had worked twenty-five years in a municipal construction office. She summed up her motives for coming to the United States, her intentions for returning, and the role of her family in her migration project:

> I came to America to earn some money. You know, in Poland was a communist government and nation was very poor. I wanted to buy condominiums for my sons, it was impossible to buy [with] Polish currency. If you had dollars, it was much, much easier and faster. My sons finished studies and they have no place to live with their families. You are waiting over 20 years in Krakow for government apartment. So I came here to America to help my family. I am helping everybody. I am sending money to Poland all the time. They were communist for 50 years. Right now is new democracy, but is very hard economic situation. My son is a surgeon and is earning $150 per month.

As an undocumented worker, Basia was saving money for her retirement and sending money back to Poland. She stayed in her first HC position for four and a half years until her client died. In her current job, she is caring for a ninety-two-year-old client she refers to as "Mama," living in a large, comfortable house in a wealthy suburb.

It was only among these older temporary workers that we found kinship patterns of caring in their descriptions of their clients. They referred to clients as their "mother" or "mama" and talked about feeling like "a part of the family." A gripping example was Marysia, who had been caring for Betsy for four years, her first and only HC job. When Marysia was hired, Betsy was in a nursing home, her body curled into a fetal position and her nails dug into the palms of her hands. The son did not expect his mother to live long and hired Marysia so that Betsy could spend the remaining time in her small, 1,000-square foot house in a Southwest suburb. Marysia was forty-eight at the time and spoke very little English. She had left a bad marriage and a twenty-five-year-old daughter in Poland. She had a vocational secondary education and had worked for twenty-five years as an electrician. She moved in with Betsy, worked seven days and nights, starting at $240 a week, and after four years earned $300. She had a few hours off on Sunday if the son visited. Marysia was gentle and affectionate with Betsy, kissing her face, touching her hair, and criticizing the son for not visiting his mother more. Betsy not only regained her ability to speak but now speaks some Polish. Marysia does not plan to return to Poland until after Betsy dies, and her reason for returning is "because of my daughter." These and other stories of deep intimacy and tender caregiving were found only among these older temporary migrants.

Younger Temporary Migrants

Similar to the older temporary migrants, the younger temporary migrants did not interrupt careers or family relations: they migrated before they began careers in Poland, and they were unmarried and childless. This group of five men and women was the smallest. They were the most recent arrivals and they all had postsecondary degrees (four in the medical field). In contrast to the medical migrants, they were younger, and none intended to stay in the United States working in the medical profession as lawful permanent residents. They differed from the older temporary migrants in that they had been in the United States for a shorter period of time, but similar in that they intended to return. Moreover, while the goal was to return to Poland with dollars, unlike the older women who were sending money back to their children in Poland, these younger migrants had no economic obligations to family, that is, they were not helping extended family members or parents. Any money they saved would be for themselves.

Witek arrived in Chicago in 1991 and in the course of one year, he worked at eight HC positions, lasting between two days and four months (three clients died, four clients moved, and he quit one job after two days). He received an MA in psychology in 1989 and continued for another year studying philosophy before deciding to travel, earn some money, and then return to Poland to decide what to do as a career. While he talked kindly of his past clients, he said he was not attached to them because he did not stay in a position for very long. He never rented an apartment in Chicago. When one HC job ended, he called the Polish employment agency and they sent him to another job, sometimes that same day. He did not interview for jobs, and several times he was hired for short-term work. He never used the phrase "treats me like family" or any such language to signal fictive kin or affectionate feelings. Several of his clients were so infirm and near death that he could not carry on a conversation with them. He had an instrumental rather than emotional relationship with his clients.

Twenty-five-year-old Jakub had three clients in six months. His uncle was living in Chicago, and a few weeks after university graduation he came to visit, travel, and earn some money with the intention of returning to Poland within a year to start his engineering career. These younger temporary migrants' choices were similar to what is known today as "taking a gap year" (taking time off after completing undergraduate studies, before moving on to career or professional education). This migration project was not directed at career building or accruing savings (though they hoped to return with some savings); instead, experience and travel were primary motivations, and they intended to return. Younger and educated workers were well positioned to take advantage of the changes in Poland, but in the early 1990s, with the instability in the nascent market economy, it was rational to spend a year or so abroad earning hard currency, learning another language, experiencing a new culture, and then returning to Poland to start a career.

Permanent Residents

Ten migrants in the study had lawful permanent resident status in 1992 at the time of the interview. Four of them arrived with permanent immigration visas ("green cards") that gave them authorization to live and work in the United States. Six others received lawful permanent resident status after being in the United States without an immigrant visa for several years (they initially arrived with non-immigrant B-2 tourist visas that they overstayed). Three received lawful permanent status through the Diversity Visa lottery, two through marriage, and one through IRCA. This group ranged in age from twenty-four to fifty-seven; two were men (the predominance of women reflects the HC market). This group included the earliest arrivals (1972 and 1976) and one of the latest arrivals in 1992. Their education ranged from high school to master's degrees. Some intended to return to Poland, others were staying, and some did not know.

They were a group because they shared the same documentation status in 1992. They were permanent legal residents with authorization to work in the United States. This group is important, as we argue that the undocumented status kept them in their HC positions. As the epigraph states, "for people who are here illegal . . . it is kind of good job." So what about those who arrived as legal residents or became legal? How did that influence their motivations, intentions, and experiences in the HC field?

First, the legal status allowed for spouses and children to be together as a family unit. All but one of the permanent residents had their families living with them in Chicago—either in a separate residence, or in two cases, in the client's home.

Second, legal status made it easier to take come-and-go positions (such as working an eight-hour shift rather than being a live-in caregiver), with higher wages, through a state-registered HC provider agency. After receiving legal status, five migrants moved from live-in to come-and-go positions, making similar wages but working significantly less time. Four others continued to work as live-in caregivers. Two of them were recent arrivals and assumed they would move out of the HC industry when their language skills improved. The third was an older woman with her own family in Chicago who preferred the live-in position because she found it more peaceful and spacious in the client's home than her family's crowded apartment. The fourth was Dorota, who had been in the United States since 1976 and was fifty-six at the time of the interview. She had been an undocumented HC worker for ten years and received legal status with IRCA. She explored other work options (nursing homes and hospitals), but she saw live-in HC as the best chance for building her savings, and she said it was easier caring for one person than "14, 16, sometimes 20 patients" in a nursing home.[59] She was the highest-paid worker in our study, earning $500 a week, and she did not pay room and board or taxes. She intended to return to Poland, so the free room and board were attractive features of the live-in position, as they allowed her to save more money.

Third, permanent status made the migrant projects more fluid. For some, it made circular migration possible. Kasia, whose husband lived in Poland, planned to keep her come-and-go HC work but would return periodically to Poland. The built-in instability of the job (clients dying or moving to institutional care) made it possible for her to leave and return to the HC industry. Other older permanent residents talked about returning to Poland to retire, and in this way, they acted like temporary older workers. Dorota said, "[When] I retire, I go back in Poland, I not stay in United States. Because I have beautiful home, I have everything. I buy in Poland for me nice furniture. Now I am ready coming back."

Younger permanent residents expressed no intention of returning to Poland, nor did they plan to stay in the HC positions. Ewa started working in HC when she first arrived (soon after completing a three-year degree in accounting). She quickly moved out of elder HC work into childcare, and then moved into clerical work that was more in line with her training. A recent arrival at the time of the interview, Michał had just started a $420/week HC job that he did not like, but he said it was better than the $240 he was previously earning in a nursing home. His family was in Chicago, but the apartment they were renting was small. He planned to leave HC work as soon as possible—his first strategy was to improve his English.

While the younger permanent residents either left or intended to leave HC positions, the older permanent residents stayed in HC work, and the permanent status helped them negotiate better working conditions (including moving to come-and-go positions and better pay). The older ones had been in the United States for longer, and they had experience in HC and better English skills. Even as lawful permanent residents, they found private HC work more satisfying and better paying than institutional caregiving work.

Fluid and Permanent Migrations

A transnational paradigm understands migration as a fluid process that includes returning to the home country. Polish migration scholars have drawn attention to the fluidity of migration after Poland's accession to the European Union in 2004.[60] In our case study, we also find fluidity in Polish migration projects in Chicago at the end of the twentieth century. This fluidity suggests that the post-2004 period should be understood as a continuation of old patterns adapted to new situations.

We saw both fluidity and stability in this community of undocumented HC workers. The intention of both the older and younger temporary workers was to return. The older temporary workers would stay as long as they could (because of their undocumented status, nothing was for certain), and then retire in Poland; the younger temporary migrants intended to return in a year to start their careers in Poland. Intentions shaped employment strategies: those with temporary projects expressed no desire to leave the HC market, because the live-in position, compared to other positions open to undocumented workers in Chicago, paid sufficiently well and included room and board. Moreover, there was low risk of being caught by the INS when working in private homes. Older workers also seemed to have more emotional attachment to their clients and stayed with them for years, whereas younger workers had more instrumental and shorter relations.

In contrast to the temporary migrants, those who were medical migrants or lawful permanent residents had different employment strategies. They tried to secure better-paying and higher-status jobs (even careers). Moving from un-documented status to lawful permanent resident status changed their relation to the market—they had more opportunities to look for work related to their education, they could resume educational or career tracks in the United States, and they could settle by bringing their children and spouses to Chicago. Not all the medical migrants had secured permanent visas, but they all held that as a possibility (even if far-fetched) and so created strategies to achieve that (by studying English and taking medical exams, for example). Not all permanent residents intended to stay. Several older migrants had strategies similar to the older temporary migrants—they would return to Poland when they retired, but in the present, they would earn and save as much as possible. They were the ones who stayed in the HC positions, some moving into the more desirable come-and-go positions, and all others commanding higher salaries.

Returning to Poland attenuates both the instrumental and social value of the HC jobs. Wages, the instrumental value of work, increased substantially for Poles temporarily working abroad, because the wages were spent in Poland. While HC workers in the United States often reported low wages as a primary source of job dissatisfaction, the Polish HC workers in our sample were usually satisfied with their salaries.[61] When asked, "What's the best part of this job?" many answered, "the pay." This is because they were primarily saving and not spending their dollars in the United States, which is why the live-in positions worked for them.

While the instrumental value of work almost always increases for labor migrants, the social value (status) does not. For some, the drop in social status can be significant, typified by educated Polish professionals scrubbing toilets and cleaning bedpans.[62] But just as returnees spend their savings in the home country, so too is social status located at home for those who return. Michael Piore argues in *Birds of Passage* that because the social identity of temporary migrant workers is located in the home country, the work abroad is "asocial," as migrants "come from the outside and remain apart from the social structure in which the jobs are located."[63]

The social status of the HC work and the wages' value changed when migrants became permanent residents, because their wages were now primarily spent in the United States, and the most important social structure was located in the United States (or in the Polish community in the United States). As stated, HC positions were considered "not so bad" compared to other job opportunities for undocumented workers. Even permanent residents who were older continued to work in HC. But for younger migrants and those with advanced education and professional careers in Poland, staying in the United States in a HC position would represent downward social mobility—even a failed migration project. For the older temporary migrants who were at the end of their work histories in Poland and with their social status more established in Poland, staying abroad longer increased their material wealth without a corresponding drop in social status.

Some workers talked about status decline, especially those who had been doctors in Poland. Anna said: "we are high educated people, and there is some degradation for us . . . they are treating us like we are lower class." But others maintained a psychological distance between what they were doing temporarily and who they were professionally. Marek countered Anna by saying, "No, in Polish community it means better job. Better than cleaning, working on roof, working in a factory. Of course, not for somebody who has a legal paper. But for the people who are here illegal for two to three years to make money, it is kind of good job." The status of the job was not compared to Poland but to the range of jobs available to undocumented workers. If their reference group shifted to the United States, the status of the job dropped considerably. Jakub, who had a master's degree, said about his HC position: "For American citizens, nobody will be work like that who have education. My problem is language." And if his undocumented status changes, his opportunities will change as well.

Educated migrants who pursue undocumented labor options are generally limited in the job choices available to them. Most Poles interviewed in this study were willing to work in undesirable jobs because they understood their situation to be a short-term strategy employed for longer-term gains. It was their ultimate goal to return to Poland, where the wages earned abroad increased in value, and that made their choices more palatable. Among the jobs available to undocumented workers, home care work was perceived to be one of the better options. Relatively high-quality living conditions, free room and board, and employment that was less visible to state authorities all made home health care jobs attractive to undocumented Poles—even the most educated among them. The job is a job, not a career. As Jakub correctly noted, the typical HC worker in this secondary labor market position did not have a university degree.[64]

Conclusion

The undocumented migrants in this study varied in their motivations for migration and intentions for return, and in this variation, we can begin to unpack the term "undocumented." Some undocumented migrants hoped to stay in the United States and move out of HC work (medical migrants and younger permanent residents), and others intended to return to Poland (temporary migrants and older permanent residents). Working without authorization as live-in caregivers for the elderly served different purposes: as stepping stones for medical migrants, as retirement supplements and remittances for older temporary workers, and as savings and experience for younger temporary workers.

These undocumented European migrants had a different experience in the United States than those from Mexico or Central America.[65] They were not crossing a land border without documentation but instead were arriving by air with a six-month visa. They were preferred by clients because they were white, a preference that many wealthy white clients have expressed.[66] They had higher levels of education and found work conditions that were not as strenuous as other physical labor. And they were not the "face" of an undocumented migrant or "illegal alien," that is, a brown face, someone to fear, someone from south of the border.[67] As such, they had a lower risk of being apprehended and deported. The employment agencies' open operation at that time, and the workers' own statements, suggest little fear that the agencies, the workers, or the clients were on the INS officials' radar. There were no reports of workplace raids of these domestic residents or other forms of state policing because of these jobs' private nature.

The poor conditions in the elder HC labor market led to high turnover rates, and the presence of undocumented workers in this market did not change these conditions. Instead, they reduced pressure on the industry to make changes beneficial to workers, most of whom were women of color and migrants from peripheral regions, many of whom, to this day, continue to experience the racism present in this system.[68]

Notes

1. Marek's pay at $350 was equivalent to roughly $700 in 2022; the median rent in Chicago in 1992 was $474 a month.

2. The Immigration Act of 1990 created the H-1B skilled worker visa program. These visas for temporary skilled workers were part of the category "nonimmigrants" and required a sponsor.

3. Jeffrey Passel and Karen Woodrow, "Geographic Distribution of Undocumented Immigrants: Estimates of Undocumented Aliens Counted in the 1980 Census by State," *International Migration Review* 18, no. 3 (1984): 642–71; Karen Woodrow-Lafield, "Estimating Authorized Immigration," in *Migration between Mexico and the United States, Binational Study, Volume 2: Research Reports and Background Materials* (Washington, DC: U.S. Commission on Immigration Reform, 1998).

4. Among the 1986 Immigration Reform and Control Act applications, 1,229,016 Mexicans and 17,014 Poles applied for legalization in the United States. Illinois had the third-highest number of applicants for legalization, behind California and Texas. *Statistical Yearbook of the Immigration and Naturalization Service* (Washington, DC: Government Publishing Office, 1990), 91.

5. Mary Patrice Erdmans, "Poland," in *The New Americans: A Guide to Immigration since 1965*, eds. Mary C. Waters and Reed Ueda (Cambridge, MA: Harvard University Press, 2007), 570–79.

6. Rob Paral, *Hope and Dreams: A Statistical Profile of the Non-Citizen Population of Metropolitan Chicago* (Chicago: Latino Institute, 1994).

7. Tadeusz Kowalik, *From Solidarity to Sellout: The Restoration of Capitalism in Poland* (New York: Monthly Review Press, 2011); Peter Stalker, *Workers without Frontiers: The Impact of Globalization on International Migration* (Geneva: International Labour Organization, 2000).

8. Magdalena Rek-Woźniak and Wojciech Woźniak, "From the Cradle of Solidarity to Land of Cheap Labour and the Home of Precarious. Strategic Discourse on Labour Arrangements in Post-Socialist Poland," *Social Policy & Administrations* 51, no. 2 (2017): 348–66; Krystyna Iglicka, "Mechanisms of Migration from Poland before and after the Transition Period," *Journal of Ethnic and Migration Studies* 26, no. 1 (2000): 61–73.

9. Mary Patrice Erdmans, "New Chicago Polonia: Urban and Suburban," in *The New Chicago: A Social and Cultural Analysis*, eds. John Koval, Larry Bennet, Michael Bennet, Roberta Garner, Fassil Demissie, and Kiljoong Kim (Philadelphia: Temple University Press, 2006), 117.

10. Dariusz Stola, "Opening a Non-Exit State: The Passport Policy of Communist Poland, 1949–1980," *East European Politics and Societies* 29, no. 1 (2015): 96–119.

11. P.L. 101–649, the Immigration Act of 1990, included slots for 55,000 "diversity immigrants," designed for people from countries adversely affected by the 1965 Immigration Act. For a thorough discussion of this program, see Carly Goodman's essay in this volume. Before this act, an average of 7,000 Poles were admitted annually; once this act took effect, those numbers were cut in half. Between 1992 and 1997, roughly 53,000 Poles were admitted as diversity immigrants. Erdmans, "Poland," 572–73.

12. Mary Patrice Erdmans, *Opposite Poles: Immigrants and Ethnics in Polish Chicago, 1976–1990* (University Park: Pennsylvania State University Press, 1998).

13. Erdmans, *Opposite Poles*, 76–78.

14. *Illegal Immigration: INS Overstay Estimation Methods Need Improvement* (Washington, DC: Government Accounting Office, 1995), 8.

15. Among the 1.7 million IRCA legalization applicants (83 percent were from Mexico and Central America), only 18 percent said they overstayed their visas, and the vast majority (87 percent) entered "without inspection" (*Statistical Yearbook* 1990: 91).

16. Janine Dahinden, "Transnationalism Reloaded: The Historical Trajectory of a Concept," *Ethnic and Racial Studies* 40, no. 9 (2017): 1474–85; Mary Patrice Erdmans, "Transnational Activities and Identities: The Relations between Solidarity Refugees and Those Left Behind," in *Diaspora Polska w Ameryce Polnocnej* [*Polish Diaspora in North America*], eds. Rafal Raczynski and Katarzyna Morawska (Gdynia, Poland: Museum of Emigration, 2018), 355–73; Peggy Levitt and B. Nadya Jaworsky, "Transnational Migration Studies: Past Developments and Future Trends," *Annual Review of Sociology* 33 (2007): 129–56; Ewa Morawska, "The Impact of Past and Present Immigrants' Transnational Engagements on Their Home Country Localities: Exploring an Underinvestigated Aspect of the Transnationalism-Migration Relationship," *Studia Migracynjne—Przeglad Polonijny* 1, no. 147 (2013): 7–31.

17. Elżbieta Goździak, "Polish Migration after the Fall of the Iron Curtain," *International Migration* 52, no. 1 (2014): 1.

18. See, for example, Izabela Czerniejewska and Elżbieta M. Goździak, "Aiding Defeated Migrants: Institutional Strategies to Assist Polish Returned Migrants," *International Migration* 52, no. 1 (2014): 87–99; Agnieszka Fihel and Izabela Grabowska-Lusinska, "Labour Market Behaviours of Back-and-Forth Migrants from Poland," *International Migration* 52, no. 1 (2014): 22–35; Jakub Isański, Agata Mleczko, and Renata Seredyńska-Abou Eid, "Polish Contemporary Migration: From Co-Migrants to Project ME," *International Migration* 52, no. 1 (2014): 4–21; Ewa Morawska, "National Identities of Polish (Im)migrants in Berlin: Four Varieties, Their Correlates and Implications," in *Europeanization, National Identities and Migration*, eds. W. Spohn, and A. Triandafyllidou (London: Routledge, 2003), 171–91.

19. Fihel and Grabowska-Lusinska, "Labour Market Behaviours"; Elżbieta Goździak, "Biała Emigracja: Variegated Mobility of Polish Care Workers," *Social Identities* 22, no. 1 (2016): 26–43.

20. Barbara Cieślińska, "The Experience of Labour Emigration in the Life of Married Women: The Case of Podlasie, Poland," *International Migration* 52, no. 1 (2014): 56–73.

21. Krystyna Iglicka, "Mechanisms of Migration from Poland before and after the Transition Period," *Journal of Ethnic and Migration Studies* 26, no. 1 (2000): 61–73; Marek Okólski, "Incomplete Migration: A New Form of Mobility in Central and Eastern Europe. The Case of Poles and Ukrainian Migrants," in *Patterns of Migration in Central Europe*, eds. Claire Wallace and Dariusz Stola (London: Palgrave, 2001), 105–28.

22. Esther Iecovich, "What Makes Migrant Live-In Home Care Workers in Elder Care Be Satisfied with Their Job?" *The Gerontologist* 51, no. 5 (2011): 617.

23. James Callahan, *Aging in Place* (Amityville, NY: Baywood, 1993); Timothy Diamond, *Making Gray Gold: Narratives of Nursing Home Care* (Chicago: University of Chicago Press, 1992).

24. Genevieve Strahan, "An Overview of Home Health and Hospice Care Patients: Preliminary Data from the 1992 National Home and Hospice Care Survey," *Advanced Data* 256 (1993): 1–11.

25. Jacob Siegel and Cynthia Taeuber, "Demographic Perspectives on the Long-Lived Society," *Daedalus* 115 (1986): 77–117.

26. Linda George and Lisa Gwyther, "Caregiver Well-Being: A Multidimensional Examination of Family Caregivers of Demented Adults," *The Gerontologist* 26, no. 3 (1986) 253–59; Deborah Klein, "Women in the Labor Force: The Middle Years," *Monthly Labor Review* 98, no. 11 (1975): 10–16.

27. *Handbook of Labor Statistics,* 1989.

28. Charles H. Mindel, "Multigenerational Family Households: Recent Trends and Implications for the Future," *The Gerontologist* 19, no. 5 (1979): 456–63.

29. David Harvey, *A Brief History of Neoliberalism* (New York: Oxford University Press, 2007).

30. Linda A. Bergthold, Carroll L. Estes, and Augusta Villanueva, "Public Light and Private Dark: The Privatization of Home Health Services for the Elderly in the U.S.," *Home Health Care Services Quarterly* 11, no. 3/4 (1990): 7–33; Joanne Schwartzberg, "The Changing Face of Home Care: A Physician's View," *Caring* 7, no. 7 (1988): 4–11.

31. Schwartzberg, "The Changing Face of Home Care"; Nancy M. Kane, "The Home Care Crisis of the Nineties," *The Gerontologist* 29 (1989): 24–31.

32. Grace Chang, *Disposable Domestics: Immigrant Women Workers in the Global Economy,* 2nd ed. (Chicago: Haymarket Books, 2016); Evelyn Glenn, "From Servitude to Service Work: Historical Continuities in the Racial Division of Paid Reproductive Labor," *Signs: Journal of Women, and Culture and Society* 18, no. 1 (1992): 1–43.

33. Francine Blau, "Women in the Labor Force: An Overview," in *Women: A Feminist Perspective,* 3rd ed., ed. Jo Freeman (Palo Alto, CA: Mayfield Publishing Company, 1984), 297–315; Evelyn Glenn, *Issei, Nisei, War Bride: Three Generations of Japanese American Women in Domestic Service* (Philadelphia: Temple University Press, 1986); Pierrett Hondagneu-Sotelo, *Gendered Transitions: Mexican Experiences of Immigration* (Berkeley: University of California Press, 1994); Terry Repak, "Labor Recruitment and the Lure of the Capital: Central American Migrants in Washington, DC," *Gender and Society* 8, no. 4 (1994): 507–34; Mary Romero, *Maid in the U.S.A.* (New York: Routledge, 1992).

34. Lynn Burbridge, "The Labor Market for Home Care Workers: Demand, Supply, and Institutional Barriers," *The Gerontologist* (1993): 41–46.

35. Cynthia J. Cranford, *Home Care Fault Lines: Understanding Tensions and Creating Alliances* (Ithaca, NY: Cornell University Press, 2020); Diamond, *Making Gray Gold*; Rebecca Donovan, "We Care for the Most Important People in Your Life: Home Care Workers in New York City," *Women's Studies Quarterly* 1, no. 2 (1987): 56–65; Rebecca Donovan, "Work Stress and Job Satisfaction: A Study of Home Care Workers in New York City," *Home Health Care Services Quarterly* 10, no. 1/2 (1989): 97–114; Penny Hollander Feldman, "Work Life Improvements for Home Care Workers: Impact and Feasibility," *The Gerontologist* 33 (1993): 46–54.

36. Donovan, "Work Stress and Job Satisfaction"; Kane, "The Home Care Crisis of the Nineties."

37. Feldman, "Work Life Improvements for Home Care Workers."

38. Abigail B. Bakan and Daiva K. Stasiulis, "Making the Match: Domestic Placement Agencies and the Racialization of Women's Household Work," *Signs: Journal of Women in Culture and Society* 20, no. 2 (1995): 303–35; Cati Coe, *The New American Servitude: Political Belonging among African Immigrant Home Care Workers* (New York: New York University Press, 2019); Virpi Timonen and Martha Doyle, "Migrant Care Workers' Relationships with Care Recipients, Colleagues and Employers," *European Journal of Women's Studies* 17, no. 1 (2010): 25–41.

39. Iecovich, "What Makes Migrant Live-In Home Care Workers in Elder Care Be Satisfied with their Job?" 619.

40. Erdmans had been doing fieldwork in the Polish community in Chicago since 1986 and recruited participants using snowball sampling. To preserve confidentiality, Erdmans destroyed the contact information and anonymized the respondents. "Illegal Home Care Workers: Polish Immigrants Caring for American Elderly," *Current Research on Occupations and Professions* Volume 9, eds. Helena Lopata and Anne Figert (Greenwich, CT: JAI, 1996), 267–92.

41. Five interviews were conducted in Polish, two with a translator and three without.

42. Two arrived in the 1970s (1972, 1974), and seven arrived between 1985 and 1987.

43. Most (73 percent) had more than one HC position, and half (n=18) had three or more positions (one outlier had eleven jobs, the next highest was eight). There were sixteen jobs that lasted less than a week (in nine, the worker quit, and in seven, the client died).

44. We have ancestry data on sixty-two clients: twenty were Jewish, seven Polish, one Mexican American, and the others of European descent or defined as "American." The majority (58 percent) of the clients were over eighty years old, and workers were hired for long-term care; another third (38 percent) were between sixty and seventy-nine years old, and most had a debilitating illness such as cancer. Five younger clients hired workers temporarily after an operation. Almost two-thirds of the clients lived alone—without children or spouse—and most had disabilities that required help with daily living tasks (dressing, cleaning, and eating).

45. In her study of Polish eldercare workers in Europe, Goździak writes that public and private employers were looking for workers with "compassion and a good heart," enough strength to lift patients, and language skills sufficient enough for "chit chat." Goździak, "Biała Emigracja," 28.

46. The agency, however, collected a fee from both the client and worker. The fee was good for one month, and if the client died or was institutionalized or the worker left, the agency would provide another job or worker. Mary Erdmans interviewed three workers at agencies, and none of them mentioned any state oversight or policing of these agencies. This perceived absence of oversight could indicate the state's tacit acceptance of undocumented migrants in these markets.

47. For a similar "white" request, see Bakan and Stasiulus, "Making the Match," 1995, whose study of domestic workers in Canada found that clients explicitly requested "European" workers rather than Caribbean workers, because they wanted a worker "with

a culture and standard of living similar to their own" (p. 310). For a more current study of white racial preference, see Coe, *The New American Servitude*, 2019, who studied home care workers from Africa in New Jersey. While all the clients were wealthy and white, all the live-in HC workers were African, even though clients often specifically requested white workers, or as the title of Chapter 1 reads: "Anyone Who Is Not African." Coe found that the hiring agencies valued the African immigrants as workers (dependable, responsible, and hard workers), and had to overcome client biases to place these workers in homes. Often, "patients asked for an 'American,' which the agencies took as a euphemism for 'white'" (p. 67).

48. See Consuelo Arbona, Norma Olvera, Nestor Rodriguez, Jacqueline Hagan, Adriana Linares, and Margit Wiesner, "Acculturative Stress among Documented and Undocumented Latino Immigrants in the United States," *Hispanic Journal of Behavioral Sciences* 32, no. 3 (2010): 362–84; Sandra Dozier, "Emotional Concerns of Undocumented and Out-of-Status Foreign Students, *Community Review* 13 (1993): 33–38.

49. In Pub. L. No. 99–603 (Act of November 6, 1986), Immigration Reform and Control Act of 1986, Sec. 274 makes it "unlawful for a person or other entity to hire, or to recruit, or to refer for a fee, for employment in the United States" an "unauthorized alien with respect to such employment." Steven M. Kaplan, "The Employer Sanctions Provision of IRCA: Deterrence or Discrimination," *Georgetown Immigration Law Journal* 6, no. 3 (1992): 545–65.

50. Nancy Zarate Byrd, "The Dirty Side of Domestic Work: An Underground Economy and the Exploitation of Undocumented Workers," *DePaul Journal for Social Justice* 3, no. 2 (2010): 245–76.

51. Compared to construction or janitorial work, HC it is not as physically tiring, though it can be an exhausting job, because, as Ela said: "you can't leave." Joanna described her job "like a prison for mind." Marek said: "It is much easier physically, but mentally very difficult to stay alone with old man." Karolina gave an example of a "bad" job: "I was locked up with an old lady and she was hard to stay with. I could not call anyone. I could not watch TV. That lady was even upset when I was reading a book." For a more contemporary version, see Coe, *The New American Servitude*, 2019, who describes the difficult experiences of being a live-in worker.

52. Mary Patrice Erdmans, "Nielegalni Imigranci I Domowa Opieka Pielegniarska: Pozarynkowe Warunki Osiagania Zadowolenia z Pracy, ["Illegal Immigrant Home Care Workers: Non-Market Conditions of Job Satisfaction"]. *Studia Migracynjne—Przeglad Polonijny* 22, no. 2 (1996): 53–69.

53. These medical migrants differ from the Polish nurses and doctors working on contracts in Arab countries in the 1980s, who returned at the end of their contracts and made no efforts to stay on permanently. Goździak, "Polish Migration after the Fall of the Iron Curtain," 34.

54. In the global division of reproductive labor, when women from peripheral regions migrate to core regions to care for the young or the elderly, it can create problems of caregiving for their own children and parents left behind, Chang, *Disposable Domestics*, 2016. In our study, this was less of an issue because the younger temporary migrants did

not have children, the children of the older migrants were adults, and the permanent residents were able to bring their family to Chicago. It is only the medical migrants who, for a few years, left their children in Poland in the care of grandparents.

55. Cieślińska, "The Experience of Labour Emigration in the Life of Married Women," 2014.

56. During the economic transitions of the late 1980s and early 1990s, early retirement was given to workers whose companies had closed. A. Chłoń-Domińczak, "Impact of Retirement Age Changes on the Old-Age Pension Take Up in Poland after 1990," *Ubezpieczenia Społeczne. Teoria I Praktyka* 3 (2019): 46.

57. Cieślińska, "The Experience of Labour Emigration in the Life of Married Women." These migrants were not "problematic" temporary migrants who "abandon" their jobs in Poland to work abroad temporarily and become unemployed when they return. See Fihel and Grabowska-Lusinska, "Labour Market Behaviours," 2014.

58. Agnieszka Małek, *Migrantki-opiekunki: Doświadczenia Migracyjne Polek Pracujacych w Rzymie* [Migrant Nannies: The Migration Experience of Polish Women Working in Rome] (Krakow: Wydawnicto Uniwersytetu Jagiellońskiego, 2011).

59. In a more recent study, Cranford also found that live-in caregivers in her study had previously worked in long-term residential facilities and preferred home care because "people were treated like in a factory" in the facilities. Cranford, *Home Care Fault Lines,* 34.

60. See, for example, Czerniejewska and Goździak, "Aiding Defeated Migrants"; Fihel and Grabowska-Lusinska, "Labour Market Behaviours"; Isański et al., "Polish Contemporary Migration"; Morawska, "National Identities of Polish (Im)migrants in Berlin."

61. Donovan, "Work Stress and Job Satisfaction."

62. Urszula Chowaniec, *Melancholic Migrating Bodies in Contemporary Polish Women's Writing* (Newcastle upon Tyne, UK: Cambridge Scholars Publishing, 2015).

63. Michael Piore, *Birds of Passage: Migrant Labor and Industrial Society* (New York: Cambridge University Press, 1979), 34.

64. Diamond, *Making Gray Gold*; Donovan, "We Care for the Most Important People in Your Life, 1987; Donovan, "Work Stress and Job Satisfaction," 1989; Feldman, "Work Life Improvements for Home Care Workers"; Kane, "The Home Care Crisis of the Nineties."

65. David Gutierrez, *Walls and Mirrors: Mexican Americans, Mexican Immigrants, and the Politics of Ethnicity* (Berkeley: University of California Press, 1995); Douglas S. Massey and K. Gentsch, "Undocumented Migration to the United States and the Wages of Mexican Immigrants," *International Migration Review* 48, no. 2 (2014): 482–99.

66. Bakan and Stasiulis, "Making the Match"; Coe, *The New American Servitude*; Cranford, *Home Care Fault Lines.*

67. Leo R. Chavez, *Covering Immigration: Population Images and the Politics of the Nation* (Berkeley: University of California Press, 2001).

68. Coe, *The New American Servitude*; Cranford, *Home Care Fault Lines*; Abigail S. Rosenfeld, "Consider the Caregivers: Reimagining Labor and Immigration Law to Benefit Home Care Workers and Their Clients," *Boston College Law Review* 62, no. 1 (2021): 315–56.

References

Arbona, Consuelo, Norma Olvera, Nestor Rodriguez, Jacqueline Hagan, Adriana Linares, and Margit Wiesner. "Acculturative Stress among Documented and Undocumented Latino Immigrants in the United States." *Hispanic Journal of Behavioral Sciences* 32, no. 3 (2010): 362–84.

Bakan, Abigail B., and Daiva K. Stasiulis. "Making the Match: Domestic Placement Agencies and the Racialization of Women's Household Work." *Signs: Journal of Women in Culture and Society* 20, no. 2 (1995): 303–35.

Bergthold, Linda A., Carroll L. Estes, and Augusta Villanueva. 1990. "Public Light and Private Dark: The Privatization of Home Health Services for the Elderly in the U.S." *Home Health Care Services Quarterly* 11, no. 3/4 (1990): 7–33.

Blau, Francine. "Women in the Labor Force: An Overview." In *Women: A Feminist Perspective,* 3rd ed., edited by Jo Freeman, 297–315. Palo Alto, CA: Mayfield Publishing Company, 1984.

Burbridge, Lynn. "The Labor Market for Home Care Workers: Demand, Supply, and Institutional Barriers." *The Gerontologist* 33 (1993): 41–46.

Byrd, Nancy Zarate. "The Dirty Side of Domestic Work: An Underground Economy and the Exploitation of Undocumented Workers." *DePaul Journal for Social Justice* 3, no 2 (2010): 245–76.

Callahan, James. *Aging in Place.* Amityville, NY: Baywood, 1993.

Chang, Grace. *Disposable Domestics: Immigrant Women Workers in the Global Economy,* 2nd edition. Chicago: Haymarket Books, 2016.

Chavez Leo. R. *Covering Immigration: Population Images and the Politics of the Nation.* Berkeley: University of California Press, 2001.

Chłoń-Domińczak, A. "Impact of Retirement Age Changes on the Old-Age Pension Take Up in Poland after 1990." *Ubezpieczenia Społeczne. Teoria I Praktyka* 3 (2019): 41–65.

Chowaniec, Urszula. *Melancholic Migrating Bodies in Contemporary Polish Women's Writing.* Newcastle upon Tyne, UK: Cambridge Scholars Publishing, 2015.

Cieślińska, Barbara. "The Experience of Labour Emigration in the Life of Married Women: The Case of Podlasie, Poland." *International Migration* 52, no. 1 (2014): 56–73.

Coe, Cati. *The New American Servitude: Political Belonging among African Immigrant Home Care Workers.* New York: New York University Press, 2019.

Cranford, Cynthia J. *Home Care Fault Lines: Understanding Tensions and Creating Alliances* Ithaca, NY: Cornell University Press, 2020.

Czerniejewska, Izabela, and Elżbieta M. Goździak. "Aiding Defeated Migrants: Institutiona_ Strategies to Assist Polish Returned Migrants." *International Migration* 52 no. 1 (2014): 87–99.

Dahinden, Janine. "Transnationalism Reloaded: The Historical Trajectory of a Concept." *Ethnic and Racial Studies* 40, no. 9 (2017): 1474–85.

Diamord, Timothy. *Making Gray Gold: Narratives of Nursing Home Care.* Chicago: University of Chicago Press, 1992.

Donovan, Rebecca. "We Care for the Most Important People in Your Life: Home Care Workers in New York City." *Women's Studies Quarterly* 1, no. 2 (1987): 56–65.

Donovan, Rebecca. "Work Stress and Job Satisfaction: A Study of Home Care Workers in New York City." *Home Health Care Services Quarterly* 10, no. 1/2 (1989): 97–114.

Dozier, Sandra. "Emotional Concerns of Undocumented and Out-of-Status Foreign Students. *Community Review* 13 (1993): 33–38.

Erdmans, Mary Patrice. "Nielegalni Imigranci I Domowa Opieka Pielegniarska: Poza-rynkowe Warunki Osiagania Zadowolenia z Pracy" ["Illegal Immigrant Home Care Workers: Non-Market Conditions of Job Satisfaction"]. *Studia Migracynjne—Przeglad Polonijny* 22, no. 2 (1996a): 53–69.

Erdmans, Mary Patrice. "Illegal Home Care Workers: Polish Immigrants Caring for American Elderly." In *Current Research on Occupations and Professions*, Volume 9, edited by Helena Lopata and Anne Figert, 267–92. Greenwich, CT: JAI, 1996b.

Erdmans, Mary Patrice. *Opposite Poles: Immigrants and Ethnics in Polish Chicago, 1976–1990*. University Park: Pennsylvania State University Press, 1998.

Erdmans, Mary Patrice. "New Chicago Polonia: Urban and Suburban." In *The New Chicago: A Social and Cultural Analysis*, edited by John Koval, Larry Bennet, Michael Bennet, Roberta Garner, Fassil Demissie, and Kiljoong Kim, 115–27. Philadelphia: Temple University Press, 2006.

Erdmans, Mary Patrice. "Poland." In *The New Americans: A Guide to Immigration since 1965*, edited by Mary C. Waters and Reed Ueda, 570–79. Cambridge, MA: Harvard University Press, 2007.

Erdmans, Mary Patrice. "Educational and Occupational Trends of Polish Immigrants in the United States, 1960–2000." In *The Polish Diaspora in America and the Wider World*, edited by Adam Walaszek, Agnieszka Stasiewicz-Bienkowska, and Janusz Pezda, 161–72. Krakow, Poland: Polska Akademia Umiejetnosci, 2012.

Erdmans, Mary Patrice. "Transnational Activities and Identities: The Relations between Solidarity Refugees and Those Left Behind." In *Diaspora Polska w Ameryce Polnocnej* [*Polish Diaspora in North America*], edited by Rafal Raczynski and Katarzyna Mo-rawska, 355–73. Gdynia, Poland: Museum of Emigration, 2018.

Feldman, Penny Hollander. "Work Life Improvements for Home Care Workers: Impact and Feasibility." *The Gerontologist* 33 (1993): 46–54.

Fihel, Agnieszka, and Izabela Grabowska-Lusinska. "Labour Market Behaviours of Back-and-Forth Migrants from Poland." *International Migration* 52, no. 1 (2014): 22–35.

George, Linda, and Lisa Gwyther. "Caregiver Well-Being: A Multidimensional Examina-tion of Family Caregivers of Demented Adults." *The Gerontologist* 26, no. 3 (1986): 253–59.

Glenn, Evelyn. *Issei, Nisei, War Bride: Three Generations of Japanese American Women in Domestic Service*. Philadelphia: Temple University Press, 1986.

Glenn, Evelyn. "From Servitude to Service Work: Historical Continuities in the Racial Division of Paid Reproductive Labor." *Signs: Journal of Women, and Culture and Society* 18, no. 1 (1992): 1–43.

Goździak, Elżbieta. "Polish Migration after the Fall of the Iron Curtain." *International Migration* 52, no. 1 (2014): 1–3.

Goździak, Elżbieta. "Biała Emigracja: Variegated Mobility of Polish Care Workers." *Social Identities* 22, no. 1 (2016): 26–43.

Gutierrez, David. *Walls and Mirrors: Mexican Americans, Mexican Immigrants, and the Politics of Ethnicity*. Berkeley: University of California Press, 1995.

Handbook of Labor Statistics. *U.S. Department of Labor, Bureau of Labor Statistics Bul-letin*. Washington, DC: Government Publishing Office, 1989.

Harvey, David. *A Brief History of Neoliberalism.* New York: Oxford University Press, 2007.

Hondagneu-Sotelo, Pierrette. *Gendered Transitions: Mexican Experiences of Immigration.* Berkeley: University of California Press, 1994.

Iecovich, Esther. "What Makes Migrant Live-In Home Care Workers in Elder Care Be Satisfied with Their Job?" *The Gerontologist* 51, no. 5 (2011): 617–29.

Iglicka Krystyna. "Mechanisms of Migration from Poland before and after the Transition Period." *Journal of Ethnic and Migration Studies* 26, no. 1 (2000): 61–73.

Illegal Immigration: INS Overstay Estimation Methods Need Improvement. Washington, DC: Government Accountability Office, 1995.

Isański, Jakub, Agata Mleczko, and Renata Seredyńska-Abou Eid. "Polish Contemporary Migration: From Co-Migrants to Project ME." *International Migration* 52, no. 1 (2014): 4–21.

Kane, Nancy M. "The Home Care Crisis of the Nineties." *The Gerontologist* 29 (1989): 24–31.

Kaplan, Steven. M. "The Employer Sanctions Provision of IRCA: Deterrence or Discrimination." *Georgetown Immigration Law Journal* 6, no. 3 (1992): 545–65.

Klein, Deborah. "Women in the Labor Force: The Middle Years." *Monthly Labor Review* 98, no. 11 (1975): 10–16.

Kowalik, Tadeusz. *From Solidarity to Sellout: The Restoration of Capitalism in Poland.* New York: Monthly Review Press, 2011.

Levitt, Peggy, and B. Nadya Jaworsky. "Transnational Migration Studies: Past Developments and Future Trends." *Annual Review of Sociology* 33 (2007): 129–56.

Małek, Agnieszka. *Migrantki-opiekunki: Doświadczenia Migracyjne Polek Pracujacych w Rzymie* [Migrant Nannies: The Migration Experience of Polish Women Working in Rome]. Krakow: Wydawnicto Uniwersytetu Jagiellońskiego, 2011.

Massey, Douglas S., and K. Gentsch. "Undocumented Migration to the United States and the Wages of Mexican Immigrants." *International Migration Review* 48, no. 2 (2014): 482–99.

Mindel, Charles H. "Multigenerational Family Households: Recent Trends and Implications for the Future." *The Gerontologist* 19, no. 5 (1979): 456–63.

Morawska, Ewa. "National Identities of Polish (Im)migrants in Berlin: Four Varieties, Their Correlates and Implications. In *Europeanization, National Identities and Migration*, edited by W. Spohn and A. Triandafyllidou, 171–91. London: Routledge, 2003.

Morawska, Ewa. "The Impact of Past and Present Immigrants' Transnational Engagements on Their Home Country Localities: Exploring an Underinvestigated Aspect of the Transnationalism-Migration Relationship." *Studia Migracynjne—Przeglad Polonijny* 1, no. 147 (2013): 7–31.

Okólski, Marek. "Incomplete Migration: A New Form of Mobility in Central and Eastern Europe. The Case of Poles and Ukrainian Migrants." In *Patterns of Migration in Central Europe*, edited by Claire Wallace and Dariusz Stola, 105–28. London: Palgrave, 2001.

Paral, Rob. *Hope and Dreams: A Statistical Profile of the Non-Citizen Population of Metropolitan Chicago.* Chicago: Latino Institute, 1994.

Passel, Jeffrey, and Karen Woodrow. "Geographic Distribution of Undocumented Immigrants: Estimates of Undocumented Aliens Counted in the 1980 Census by State." *International Migration Review* 18, no. 3 (1984): 642–71.

Piore, Michael. *Birds of Passage: Migrant Labor and Industrial Society.* New York: Cambridge University Press, 1979.

Rek-Woźniak, Magdalena, and Wojciech Woźniak. "From the Cradle of Solidarity to Land of Cheap Labour and the Home of Precarious. Strategic Discourse on Labour Arrangements in Post-Socialist Poland." *Social Policy & Administration* 51, no. 2 (2017): 348–66.

Repak, Terry. "Labor Recruitment and the Lure of the Capital: Central American Migrants in Washington, DC" *Gender and Society* 8, no. 4 (1994): 507–34.

Romero, Mary. *Maid in the U.S.A.* New York: Routledge, 1992.

Rosenfeld, Abigail S. "Consider the Caregivers: Reimagining Labor and Immigration Law to Benefit Home Care Workers and Their Clients." *Boston College Law Review* 62, no. 1 (2021): 315–56.

Schwartzberg, Joanne. "The Changing Face of Home Care: A Physician's View." *Caring* 7, no. 7 (1988): 4–11.

Siegel, Jacob, and Cynthia Taeuber. "Demographic Perspectives on the Long-Lived Society." *Daedalus* 115 (1986): 77–117.

Stalker, Peter. *Workers without Frontiers: The Impact of Globalization on International Migration.* Geneva: International Labour Organization, 2000.

Statistical Yearbook of the Immigration and Naturalization Service. Washington, DC: Government Publishing Office, 1990.

Stola, Dariusz. "Opening a Non-Exit State: The Passport Policy of Communist Poland, 1949–1980." *East European Politics and Societies* 29, no. 1 (2015): 96–119.

Strahan, Genevieve. "An Overview of Home Health and Hospice Care Patients: Preliminary Data from the 1992 National Home and Hospice Care Survey." *Advanced Data* 256 (1993): 1–11.

Timonen, Virpi, and Martha Doyle. "Migrant Care Workers' Relationships with Care Recipients, Colleagues and Employers." *European Journal of Women's Studies* 17, no. 1 (2010): 25–41.

Woodrow-Lafield, Karen. "Estimating Authorized Immigration." In *Migration between Mexico and the United States, Binational Study, Volume 2: Research Reports and Background Materials.* Washington, DC: U.S. Commission on Immigration Reform, 1998.

PART III

Global Productions of Illegality

7 The Maritime Origins of the Deportation Nation

Viapolitics of Unauthorized European Migration to the United States, 1819–1914

TORSTEN FEYS

Interviewed by the *New York Times* on the "evils of immigration" in 1911, New York Commissioner of Immigration William Williams held only one actor accountable for problems with the nation's immigration system. His greatest concern was the arrival of "undesirables," meaning anyone who could not become a "productive and valuable" citizen. With nearly 900,000 people passing through Ellis Island the year before, the commissioner tightened inspections. He illustrated undesirables with concrete examples, highlighting problems with their capacity to earn a living that were linked to their health, gender, age, social status, and race. Williams concluded each example by asking: *why should a shipping company bring in a case like that?* He did not blame migrants, European authorities, or other actors for their arrival. Williams only accused shipping companies of being careless in enforcing U.S. immigration laws before leaving Europe. When asked if European governments could help keep out undesirables, Williams replied, "the simplest way would be for shipping companies to absolutely refuse passage to those who are likely to be shut out on this side. That could be done without undue difficulty."[1]

As a key figure within the immigration administration, Williams's testimony illustrates how shipping companies were viewed both as cause and solution for undesirable migration. Transferring the liability for unauthorized migration to transport companies placed them at the heart of migration governance, where they continue to stand today, albeit still as largely overlooked actors. As a notable exception, William Walters drew attention to the importance of transport networks in contemporary migration studies by coining the concept of "viapolitics" as a way "*to theorize the place of journeys and transport systems within the studies of the governance of migration and mobility.*" He contends that transport vehicles, companies, and hubs greatly affect power relations governing human mobility and are pivotal in enforcing them. Migration becomes viapolitical when the policing of routes and vehicles constitutes a central strategic undertaking in the governance of migration.[2]

This article uncovers how transatlantic shipping companies became an integrated part of federal U.S. migration policies and were used to stem unauthorized European immigration before World War I. It highlights the introduction of carrier sanctions, penalties designed to impose immigration controls on transport companies, as a key means to transfer the responsibility of enforcing federal migration laws onto shipping lines.

Today, carrier sanctions are mainly associated with the responsibility of transport companies to control the identity of their passengers by preventing people

Figure 7.1. Commissioner of Immigration for the Port of New York William Williams (holding documents) next to President Taft (waving) at Ellis Island. Taft appointed Williams to run the most important immigrant inspection station with a firm hand for a second term in 1909. Williams did so by increasing the shipping companies' responsibilities to enforce migration laws in both Europe and the United States. The commissioner blamed the shipping lines for the influx of undesirable migrants and, as a deterrent, increased the financial penalties on shipping companies for doing so. Courtesy of Prints and Photographs Division, Library of Congress, LC-B2-2089-13.

without proper documents from traveling and by preventing stowaways from boarding vessels. Companies generally have to cover the cost of detention and return of passengers in violation of those rules and also risk significant fines for violations (for example, a minimum of 3,000 Euros set by European Union directive). Data on penalty enforcement indicate that these vary from country to country and are waived in the case of justifiable asylum claims. Authorities generally seek arrangements of compliance and cooperation, rather than deterrence, to consolidate good relations with carriers; hence, both parties seek to avoid sanctions.[3] Yet there is a recent trend to impose fines more strictly, and they are rarely reversed when appealed in courts.[4] Carrier sanctions have increasingly pushed transport companies to invest in security controls and train personnel to screen irregular migrants. Scholars observed that since the 1980s, western state authorities retooled carrier sanctions in combination with visa requirements mainly to bypass the non-refoulment provision of the Geneva Convention and reduce refugee flows from particular countries. The main purpose has been to discourage unauthorized migrants before departure or in transit, but also to decrease the number of asylum seekers at the borders. Thus, those regulations reshape carriers into remote control instruments par excellence, diverting rejected passengers into perilous clandestine routes.[5]

Some contemporary scholars only vaguely point to nineteenth century shipping as a predecessor. Going back to a period that has often been referred to as the era of free mass migration, when identity papers were not compulsory to travel, this case study shows that carriers' role went far beyond administrative controls. Its focus on U.S. federal legislation directs attention mainly on the period after 1882. Yet, as other scholars have highlighted, the influence of transatlantic shipping companies on U.S. migration governance dates back long before, to when individual states still managed immigration. They showed how shipping interests successfully undermined restrictions on entry by questioning their constitutionality in court. For state laws that were upheld, shipping lines played out the keen rivalry among Atlantic ports to attract the lucrative transatlantic passenger trade and threatened to move their business if authorities enforced measures strictly.[6] The federal authorities could not decide on who was allowed to enter, but only on how they traveled, which was deemed a commerce issue. Transport conditions were regulated via so-called passenger acts, first enacted in 1819, to protect passengers from being exploited at sea. Yet, as scholars observed, certain clauses could also affect immigrants' entry. For instance, by setting minimum space requirements per traveler, such acts could potentially influence the prices of the crossing. A significant increase of space allotment would normally be followed by a sharp rise in ship ticket prices and would inhibit the poorest from leaving Europe. The 1879 Fifteen Passenger Bill, which President Rutherford Hayes vetoed, explicitly limited the number of Chinese migrants per ship, highlighting Congress's awareness of using such acts for gatekeeping. In theory, those regulations pioneered practices Aristide Zolberg coined as "remote controls"—migration policies that move the screening process as close as possible to the place of departure, to ultimately prevent undesirables from leaving. (The screening can be carried out by state officials, but the responsibility often is outsourced to private companies.) In practice, however, space allotment was only one of many factors influencing the total cost of moving. Moreover, on the federal level, the shipping lobby questioned the legality of passenger acts, and they obstructed the acts' enactment and enforcement.[7]

Yet transatlantic shipping lines began to lose some of their leverage when New York dominated traffic around 1850. Their position decreased further in 1876, when the U.S. Supreme Court transferred the responsibility over immigrants' admission from states to the U.S. federal government. Based on the Constitution, the Court expanded its interpretation of immigration as a commerce issue. Before that, a popular strategy of shipping lines was to question aspects of federal passenger acts for overstepping their jurisdiction and touching on immigration issues that belonged to state authorities, or vice versa. With federal jurisdiction regulating both immigration and passenger acts, this strategy was no longer an option. Ironically, but not surprisingly, the shippers had initiated the case that led to the 1876 Supreme Court decision. Up to this point, shipping interests had started every Supreme Court challenge on this subject, highlighting their pivotal role in shaping the legal framework governing migration.[8] Yet the strategies the transatlantic shipping companies reverted to after the 1870s remains overlooked and is the main focus here.

The remote control paradigm encouraged scholars to further explore how federal laws passed after 1876 induced state officials and shipping lines to inspect passengers' eligibility away from American borders and on European soil at ports of embarkation, major transit hubs, and land borders. Transferring medical inspections and identity controls beyond the borders turned consular offices and shipping infrastructure into front lines for immigration enforcement. Passenger liners constructed and managed major lodging and inspection facilities at these points across Europe to increase their grip on transit migration. This infrastructure represents an apex of what Dorothee Schneider coined the commercialization of border controls during this era.[9] However, Janet Gilboy argues that commercialization and privatization are misleading concepts because carriers are not the primary authors, nor the beneficiaries of the misconduct they police, nor do they draw benefits from the cooperation with the government.[10] Indeed the term "third-party liability system" more accurately describes this relationship. These practices became less important during the 1920s, when American consular agents took up the responsibility to prevent the departure of unauthorized migrants by issuing visas according to the quota acts. Zolberg marks this transition as the triumph of remote control, and it has been considered a crucial step into states' efforts to monopolize the legitimate means of movement and to degrade carriers to mere "sheriff's deputies."[11]

This narrative externalized the role of shipping lines outside of U.S. boundaries, without uncovering how they were institutionalized as key domestic actors as well. This paper does so from the perspective of transatlantic transport companies. Sharing this perspective, Drew Keeling claimed that shipping companies were the most critical component of state enforcement mechanisms simply because they possessed much more expert knowledge and resources than immigration authorities. Passenger lines collaborated on implementing immigrant controls only when they did not severely diminish their passenger numbers.[12] Yet this collaboration eventually set the foundation to impose harsh restrictions with the quota acts, which the shipping companies also helped enforce. This chapter argues that federal laws and regulations induced shipping companies to put their expert knowledge at the disposal of the inexperienced Bureau of Immigration, which used shipping lines to close its backlog on resources and expertise. To fully grasp the integration of shipping lines in immigration enforcement and get further insights on the power relation between carriers and state authorities, this analysis first uncovers how federal immigration laws co-opted transport companies on paper. The analysis starts in 1819 with the first Passenger Act but centers on how shipping lines were also integrated into post-1882 immigration acts. Second, using shipping company archives, immigration records, and newspaper accounts, this chapter details how federal regulations were translated in practice after 1882. Next, the analysis zooms in on shipping companies' role in closing loopholes and stemming unauthorized entries, directly via maritime ports and indirectly via land borders. The analysis exposes the strengths and weaknesses of migration control based on carrier sanctions, and how they affect the transfer of power between shippers and government. Shipping company archives allow the role and business logic of transport companies to be uncovered in much more depth than previous studies have done.

The Legal Framework: Integrating Carriers into Migration Governance

Passenger acts served in the first place to set minimum requirements of space, health, and hygiene, and they protected passengers from exploitation. Commercial motives drove this humanitarian concern to prevent migrants from becoming public charges on arrival, thereby ensuring their immediate contribution to local labor markets. To this end, passenger acts could also be used to give competitive advantages to national ships over foreign vessels to gain dominance over this key commodity on the transatlantic trade route. This extra commercial dimension linked migration to, and often made it subordinate to, maritime interests. By protecting British shipowners against foreign competition, the British 1803 Passenger Vessels Act served as a reference for many countries in the Atlantic World.[13] Various European countries adopted similar legislation to direct the transatlantic migrant flow to national ports and shipping companies. However, the United States did not use the passenger acts or subsequent migration policies to give advantages to its merchant marine, except for once. In 1847, Congress approved an amendment to the Passenger Act that increased the capacity of American sailing packets in particular and spurred their dominance on the market. This was short lived, as American shipowners, in part due to the Civil War, completely missed the transition from sail to steamships. European companies took over the market, and various attempts to redress this situation, including one by JP Morgan, failed.[14]

Congress never gave in to the continuous lobbying of American shipowners to amend laws and give them an edge on foreign competitors. Why it never did still awaits a conclusive answer. However, this policy consolidated the disentanglement of maritime interests and migration and facilitated congressional decisions to exclude immigrants when it obtained the authority to do so. Enforcing restrictions on shipping companies that lacked congressional support to bring in immigrants was easier when companies were foreign.[15] As Sophie Scholten observes, the imposition of carrier sanctions depends on the relationship of each company with state authorities, which show more reluctance to penalize national companies.[16] Unburdened of having to consider the interests of the U.S. merchant marine, Congress could more freely pass legislation integrating shipping companies into immigration enforcement.

This strategy was already clear in the first federal law regulating migration. The Passenger Act of 1819 stipulated multiple sanctions, such as fines against shipowners in the amount of $150 for each passenger carried exceeding established limits. Ships could even be forfeited for severe violations. The act also included fines for neglecting to deliver passenger manifests with each person's name, age, gender, occupation, country of origin, and intention of becoming an inhabitant of the United States.[17] A subsequent amendment lowered excess fines to $50 but made ship captains liable for prosecution for a misdemeanor, with prison sentences of up to one year for overloading.[18] Fines were also added for violations of new health and hygiene requirements.[19] In sum, by 1847, carrier sanctions included not only significant administrative fines, but also prison sentences and the forfeiting of ships that could completely disrupt commercial operations.[20] The law clearly intended to deter vessels from violating the transport conditions but also incorporated them into immigration inspection procedures well before the federal government began to assume those duties at ports of entry. Passenger manifests became a cornerstone in establishing immigrants' eligibility on arrival, and shipping companies retained the responsibility to compose these.[21] The 1819 act set the tone for subsequent federal immigration laws that regulated the general conditions of entry for aliens, except Chinese people, for whom separate laws existed. The Chinese restriction and exclusion laws, passed from 1882 onward, were crucial in the emergence of federal immigration policy and made it an attribute of national sovereignty.[22] Yet, because they are part of a separate legal and enforcement regime, they are not considered here.[23] This analysis centers on federal laws passed after 1882 (and referred to here as immigration acts) that were implicitly limited to transatlantic migration until the 1900s laws, when they sporadically became entangled with transpacific migrations that had been governed by the Chinese exclusion acts.[24]

Post-1882 immigration acts relied on a legal framework established by Atlantic seaboard states, which were largely responsible for governing immigrant entry up to the 1870s. Legislation passed by Eastern seaboard states in the early nineteenth century called on shipping companies to act as enforcement agents when they were charged with collecting passenger fees to finance state immigration inspection costs.[25] The first Immigration Act (1882) copied this principle by imposing a 50 cent head tax on all noncitizen passengers arriving from a foreign port. Again, shipping companies were charged with collecting those fees and transferring them into the Immigrant Fund, used to now cover the national government's growing enforcement apparatus.[26] Subsequent reforms steadily doubled head taxes; from $1 (1891), to $2 (1903), $4 (1907), and $8 (1917).[27] Shipping companies not only collected funds for immigration enforcement; they also paid for crucial and expensive aspects of migration governance. U.S. immigration laws transferred all costs for the return of passengers not permitted to land in the country directly onto the shipping companies themselves.[28] The 1882 law opened the door to deport undesirables after landing, a practice that 1891 reforms generalized by extending the period and reasons for deportability. Along with being charged with the cost of shipping unlawful post-entry passengers back, shipping companies were also responsible for the maintenance of any unlawful passengers held in detention on land after 1891.[29] In 1903, half of all the post-entry expellees' inland transportation costs to the port of deportation were tacked on as well.[30] If excluded aliens needed assistance due to their ill health or because of their status as a minor, shipping companies were also obligated to pay for the accompanying person.[31] Failing to return such passengers resulted in a minimum fine of $300, and as long as that was unsettled, the ship could be refused clearance at any American port.[32] In sum, shipping lines collected the funds to finance immigration inspections while bearing an important part of the logistical and financial burdens surrounding enforcement. Unlike with undocumented passengers today, shipping lines covered the cost of all unauthorized migrants and not just those who entered illegally due to their own neglect.

The weaknesses of federal immigration law enforcement in the late nineteenth century led to reforms. The 1891 Immigration Act addressed perceived gaps in existing legislation by placing federal authorities in charge of inspection, and in the founding of the Bureau of Immigration in Washington, DC, to coordinate and systematize the process. Yet despite their newfound authority, federal immigration officials continued to be highly reliant on shippers to determine passengers' admissibility. The amount of information collected on passenger manifests had vastly expanded and was used not only to establish alien eligibility before embarkation, but also to verify the identity of passengers upon arrival and to monitor and police migrant behavior after their entry as well. Shipping companies also had to conduct a personal and physical examination of all passengers registered in the manifests, which were verified by American consuls in foreign ports. Manifests sorted passengers into maximum groups of thirty people who were processed jointly on arrival. To ensure the manifests' accuracy, the law imposed a $10 fine per flagrant omission or mistake.[33] Passports were not yet compulsory, but most people traveled with some kind of identity document. Hence shipping companies were held responsible for organizing the information of a great variety of papers in various languages and recording those who traveled without sufficient documentation. To monitor the growing transatlantic mobility, ships also had to compose lists of aliens leaving the United States.[34]

American authorities increased pressure on shipping companies to keep out two excludable classes of people around the turn of the century. First, the 1891 Immigration Act excluded persons carrying "contagious and loathsome" diseases. A 1903 amendment added a $100 fine for shipping companies that transported passengers with severe medical cases that should have been detected before embarkation.[35] Second, to deter smugglers, "aiding the entry of an alien not lawfully entitled to enter the U.S." was defined as a misdemeanor, carrying maximum penalties of $1,000 and a year in prison, extended to two years by 1903.[36] Shipping personnel, especially, were feared as potential smugglers. Lawmakers therefore increased the responsibilities of shipping companies in the landing process, and in transferring passengers from their ships to immigrant inspection stations. Failing to do so (and thereby facilitating illegal landing) made them liable to misdemeanor charges. This liability had to ensure that shipping companies took due precautions to ensure that their passengers passed immigration inspection.[37]

Other clauses made shipping companies responsible for making sure that all migrant agents representing them carry a translation of the most recent U.S. immigration laws and make those terms available to potential clients.[38] In an effort to stem the tide of immigration, shipping lines were also banned from advertising overseas migration through any means other than publishing sailing schedules, facility information, and transport conditions, both in Europe and the United States.[39] The jurisdiction to enforce these two sections abroad was highly questionable, yet shipping lines did not challenge them in court, and by complying, they helped to normalize remote control policies. The numerous sections of the immigration laws pertaining to shipping lines stress their centrality in the legal framework. U.S. immigration laws therefore highlight how much the state equated immigration with direct overseas arrivals via maritime ports. No references were made about immigrants entering via land borders until 1891, when two clauses applied another regime discussed below. Using the phrase "illegal landing" to refer to unauthorized migrants further highlights how much maritime routes impregnated the legal framework.

Yet laws on paper leave many facets of the story untold. Some aspects were not stated explicitly, such as the bias of treating third-class passengers as immigrants and cabin passengers as travelers. A clear class distinction existed based on travel accommodation, as most of the clauses applied only to lower classes. Wealthier travelers enjoyed privileges, such as bypassing immigration inspection stations altogether. However, no reference of this appears in the laws, which contain many more ambiguities. The immigration acts' vagueness was mostly purposeful, to grant those responsible for their implementation a lot of leeway to establish rules to carry out the provisions, explicitly allowing them to impose further measures on shipping companies.[40] Moreover, scholars have highlighted the gap between the intent and the practical outcome of legislation, partly due to difficulties of enforcement.[41] To fully understand how carrier sanctions helped integrate shipping companies into migration governance, this analysis looks at the enforcement of passenger and immigration acts on American soil.

Shipping Companies and the Enforcement of Immigration Policies

In the past two decades, scholars including Erika Lee have shifted the focus from the laws and congressional debates to their enforcement, using court cases, newspapers, archives of key figures, and pro- or anti-immigration associations—as well as the huge paper trail left by immigration officials.[42] The archives produced by the Bureau of Immigration detail the practices of screening immigrants' eligibility and getting rid of the so-called undesirables before and after landing. They highlight the discrepancy between laws in the books and their enforcement. For instance, as much as immigration acts fail to distinguish between class, they also make no explicit distinction between gender, yet these acts applied in totally different ways between women and men.[43] Also, while not containing any racial or nationality bias (except in the case of Chinese migrants), and designed implicitly to regulate transatlantic flows, they applied more strictly to migrants from eastern and southern Europe.[44] Bureau of Immigration records reveal the actual agency of different state actors, but they also draw attention to the role of non-state actors. Scholars have focused on interest groups that openly advocated or opposed immigration restrictions, such as labor unions, anti-immigration associations or philanthropic organizations, ethnic associations, and religious institutions.[45]

Nonetheless, some actors have remained under the radar, not least of which include shipping companies, despite their omnipresence in the law, newspapers, court cases, and the states' immigration records. Steamship companies were not only essential to global movement of people, but they also shaped modern-day migration governance systems. Company records of passenger liners constitute the missing link in this analysis of the law's implementation. Unfortunately, almost no archival records of shipping lines operating during this formative period have been preserved, except for the Holland America Line (HAL) running a service between Rotterdam and New York. The HAL records include correspondence between the New York head agent and the board of directors, lobbyists, and immigration inspectors, among others, and they provide unique insights on how these carriers influenced the enactment, enforcement, and evasion of immigration laws.

HAL formed part of a North Atlantic passenger shipping cartel that mitigated the competition between passenger lines via price agreements, route-setting, and distributing market shares. The cartel enhanced the cohesion between the companies and the efficiency of their lobbying efforts against immigration restrictions. The more these restrictions became a central theme in Congress, the more they threatened the market stability of shipping cartels.[46] They drew half of their revenue from third-class passengers, 20 percent from cabin class, and the rest from mail and freight, which highlights their dependency on migrant transport.[47]

The HAL archives have already been used to show that shipping companies were not a passive actor in the development of federal migration policies. They led a pro-immigration lobby against radical restrictive reforms. They were a leading actor in a loose coalition of advocacy groups that successfully postponed the adoption of a literacy test until 1917.[48] Yet this achievement must be balanced with concessions shipping lines were forced to make with the passage of each new law. While not significantly restricting immigration, the reforms slowly undermined the shipping lines' dominant position in migration governance. Carriers did not necessarily oppose the new responsibilities. For instance, the logistic burden and costs of controlling passengers in Europe were minor compared to the risks of exposing themselves to arbitrary strict enforcement if conducted by government officials. Carrier companies' precarious position was highlighted following the cholera scare of 1892, when American health inspectors were dispatched to European ports to oversee new pre-embarkation controls, disinfections, and quarantine measures. Each official imposed different regimes, causing serious competitive disadvantages from one port to the other. Fierce protests questioning their jurisdiction forced American authorities to call back their health inspectors while shipping lines took over these responsibilities.[49]

Shipping companies questioned the jurisdiction of American regulatory legislation not only on European soil, but also on European ships in American ports. Soon after the law's passage, a Dutch vessel entered New York in violation of the 1882 Passenger Act. The Royal Netherlands Steamship Company refused to comply, arguing that it followed its domestic laws regarding space requirements and contesting American authority over foreign ships. But following the legal advice of the Dutch envoy in Washington, the company dropped the lawsuit to avoid a lengthy trial that had slim chances of success and that would harm its reputation. Around that time, diplomats had come to acknowledge immigration as a matter of national sovereignty, and their interventions on behalf of shipping interests reduced markedly. Shipping lines no longer contested the authority of American passenger acts on foreign ships.[50] According to certain scholars, they did not need to, as shippers could rely on a highly sympathetic Bureau of Navigation that supervised the laws' implementation but rarely prosecuted or collected fines for violations. This led to the assumption that passenger laws failed to influence transport conditions, mainly because of the highly organized shipping lobby's effectiveness.[51]

Yet a closer look at enforcement of the 1882 Passenger Act indicates that the Bureau of Navigation did actively enforce new minimum space requirements. Authorities not only imposed fines of $50 per passenger in excess but also arrested captains and head agents of repeat offending companies, such as the Royal Netherlands Steamship Company. Even if they were quickly released on bail, arrests and imprisonments severely disturbed the operations of passenger lines, and repeated violations could even jeopardize their access to American ports. Arrests and prosecution for excess passengers continued during the 1880s. For instance, the HAL posted a $2,500 bond for the release of a ship captain arriving with fifty-eight excess passengers in 1887. It hired lawyers to defend the company before the courts and the Treasury Department, which assessed a fine of $2,900. The New York head agent reassured his directors that prison sentences were never carried out and that the fine would be reduced significantly or dropped by entering into agreements with the district attorney.[52] Nonetheless, the cases illustrate that American federal authorities lost any reluctance to regulate migration issues unilaterally and used carrier sanctions to force their adherence. Even if the sanctions were not carried out in full, officials thoroughly checked incoming ships and pursued violations, putting a heavy burden on the New York shipping agencies. It drew negative attention in the press, harming the company's reputation. Finally, it also affected the relations with inspectors, who formed prejudices against the line. For all these reasons, the HAL New York head agent urged the Rotterdam office to avoid further excesses at the port of embarkation. These mainly occurred during peak season, not on purpose but due to the carelessness of the Rotterdam boarding supervisors. The issue disappeared by the 1890s, as most passenger lines improved their service, using second-class cabin accommodation with closed berths instead of dormitories as a new standard. However, ships leaving from Mediterranean ports failed to follow suit until a 1907 reform of the Passenger Act compelled all companies to upgrade their standards.

A perennial lack of funds also led to assumptions that the Bureau of Immigration was not able to properly enforce immigration laws. Indeed, the bureau itself frequently repeated this claim.[53] Yet what scholars overlooked is that the bureau compensated for its lack of resources by engaging carriers ever more in the work of immigration law enforcement, while in the meantime gradually increasing their revenues. Funding was especially scarce when courts withdrew the authority over migration from states and, concomitantly, the revenues necessary for enforcement. The 1882 Immigration Act created a source of revenue for a new national bureaucracy by imposing a head tax of 50 cents on incoming foreign passengers. The 1891 law doubled the tax to finance the newly founded federal Bureau of Immigration, responsible for upholding the immigration laws.[54] The bureau successfully pushed to double the head tax, as its main source of revenue, during each major reform of the immigration laws, in 1903, 1907, and 1917. Shipping companies duly collected the tax, which was used to tighten inspections on them and their passengers. The shipping lobby opposed each increase but without success. Initially adding a surcharge of about 2.5 percent on the shipping ticket, the tax surpassed the 10 percent mark by 1907. The head tax does not appear to have been prohibitively expensive for most migrants, as the influx continued to increase.[55] This allowed the Bureau of Immigration to grow rapidly. Starting with only five staff members, it employed 2,400 people by the 1920s.[56] Moreover, the increases turned the bureau into a revenue producer for the state. For instance, in 1911, 913,880 taxable entrants contributed to more than 1 million dollars of revenue after deducting all enforcement costs.[57] Funding clearly was no longer a major issue for enforcement, allowing the bureau to homogenize, professionalize, and expand inspections from ports of entry to land borders, the interior, and abroad.

The main reason, however, for this positive balance was that shipping lines covered many costs, not least those of deportation. Keeling argued that expellees hardly affected the shipping lines' finances, as ships rarely left New York at full capacity, so they never took up the space of a paying customer. Also, deportation rates remained low, balancing between 0.23 percent to 2 percent from 1892 to 1914. When considering diseased immigrants liable to fines, the average rate fell to one for every 400 accepted European passengers. The average fare of $34 collected from third-class passengers largely offset the costs of returning the unlucky few who were rejected.[58] Indeed, the estimated cost of $8 to transport these passengers was not significant for carriers.[59] Moreover, the fine was actually enforced on only a small minority of diseased immigrants. For instance, in 1911, although the commissioner general of immigration labeled the fine one of the most useful provisions of the law, he enforced it only on 237 of the 3,154 potential cases, a mere seven percent. The fines only generated an additional $23,700 of revenue from all shipping lines, yet the provision was praised especially for its deterrent effect on embarking passengers in poor health in particular and suppressing shipping lines in general. This reference year illustrates that fines were only imposed exceptionally before World War I, because shipping lines had greatly improved screenings before embarkation.[60]

Fines and the cost of transporting expellees remained only a fraction of the total costs of immigration enforcement that shipping lines covered. However, scholars have pointed to the costs of controlling passengers in Europe and lost revenue associated with rejecting immigrants before embarkation as adding to the total cost of enforcing U.S. immigration laws for shippers.[61] Although scholars acknowledged these strict financial costs, they overlooked the cost of hiring, training, and retaining qualified doctors and experts to the shipping lines another measure that allowed the U.S. government to save on those costs. Regulatory expenses were thus shifted onto the private sector, and onto migrants themselves when companies passed those expenses onto the consumers. Such a model afforded the U.S. government maximum cost-saving measures.[62] For instance, in 1911, 22,349 foreigners were rejected at American ports and another 2,788 (mostly Europeans) were removed from the interior.[63] Had the Bureau of Immigration paid for their shipping costs directly, rather than transferring the costs onto shipping companies, it would have incurred the commercial cost of an average third-class passenger fare of $35 for every expellee, totaling $879,795 for that year alone. Not only did that figure represent a quarter of the administration's annual revenue, but, very importantly, the policy prevented deportation from becoming a source of income for shipping companies. That alternative structure certainly would have removed any incentives for the companies to screen for migrant eligibility in Europe in the first place.

Always seeking ways to cut their costs, shipping companies managed to get deportation costs struck from the 1882 passenger acts.[64] Yet those efforts proved in vain, as the costs were adopted in the 1882 Immigration Act immediately after. Shipping records do not indicate that the clause's legality was challenged in courts, yet court records still await systematic research to fully assess shipping companies' legal challenges in general and more specifically regarding deportation costs. HAL archives show that companies tried to neutralize the effects of adverse legislation by passing on deportation costs to third parties. For example, on so-called prepaid tickets, sold in American immigrant communities and sent to family or friends in Europe, the HAL added a clause that held the buyer responsible for the costs of return if the passenger was denied entry. However, transferring such costs was successfully challenged in U.S. courts for contravening the deportation clause of the 1882 Immigration Act. As another strategy, the HAL contemplated forcing high-risk passengers to buy a return ticket before embarkation that would be reimbursed if they landed successfully, but this entailed too many practical impediments. Shipping companies also explored the possibility of transferring the responsibility to the migrant agents selling tickets, but a lack of consensus buried the initiative.[65] Even if the deportation rates and costs remained relatively low, transferring the cost and responsibility over enforcement set a trend that proved impossible to reverse.

Not that shipping lines stopped trying. When the cost of maintaining detained passengers was added, the HAL refused to cover these expenses by claiming that the law ascribed those costs to the Immigration Fund. HAL officials were convinced that U.S. immigration inspectors purposely expanded the time they took to examine HAL passengers in retribution for their challenge. Faced with government harassment and a lack of support from other shipping companies, the HAL ultimately conceded its legal challenge. Even so, the HAL tried to recoup the costs of detention by passing them on to passengers, family, and friends of migrants, yet with limited success. These costs were especially significant for detained passengers who required medical care. For instance, when passengers affected with trachoma were suddenly sent to New York City hospitals that charged double the rates that the state hospitals charged before, the HAL saw its bill for fourteen passengers receiving treatment surge to $540—only $100 of which could be billed to third parties. The Bureau of Immigration refused the HAL's requests to deport such passengers immediately to avoid astronomical bills. The whole point of increasing hospital bills was to sanction carriers for bringing diseased passengers and encourage further outsourcing of the state's gatekeeping apparatus to shipping lines. Thereafter, the HAL hired an ophthalmologist and a dermatologist in Rotterdam to track trachoma and favus, the most common diseases among rejected immigrants, before departure. To improve its relationship with immigration and health inspectors, the HAL also employed American doctors aboard its ships.[66]

By the turn of the century, shipping cartels representing most transatlantic lines established the "Ellis Island Committee," staffed with representatives of different companies to coordinate joint strategies against unfavorable enforcement of immigration laws. Mediation with key U.S. administrators was a first step, yet they would not refrain from taking legal action if necessary. Shipping companies' legal challenges frequently called into question immigration officials' interpretation or enforcement of laws rather than challenge the laws themselves. Companies in the cartel agreed to share legal expenses associated with test cases. Noteworthy test cases brought about by shipping lines challenged the deportability of children of naturalized citizens, the costs for attendants accompanying expellees who required assistance, the cost of maintaining detained migrants who did not face exclusion, and the costs of deportees violating sex trafficking laws. Litigation often served to pressure the opposing parties to reach a compromise long before the courts established a verdict, but some cases went all the way to the Supreme Court.[67]

As lawsuits were costly, time consuming and not always successful, shipping companies preferred other modes of action. Sources tend to highlight conflict over cooperation and depict the working relationship between the Bureau of Immigration and shipping companies as contentious. Quite often the opposite was true. They were in fact codependent in conducting their core business: shipping companies relied on immigration inspectors' approval for landing migrants, while inspectors relied on shipping lines to carry out examinations. The awareness of this reality contributed to a functioning working relationship between both parties, as evidenced by the low rejection rates and the rare imposition of fines. The latter were generally dismissed and only sustained for flagrant violation or to mark a regime change within the administration. This regime change often occurred after presidential elections, as key positions in the immigration bureaucracy were filled by political appointees who sought to impose their various interpretations of the law. On the whole, however, enforcement strategies were characterized by gradual changes rather than major reversals.[68]

Shipping Companies and Loopholes in Immigration Policies

U.S. policies to restrict transpacific and transatlantic migration led to different border regimes and strategies to get around those restrictions by using loopholes in the law. Shipping companies adapted and played a paradoxical role of both obstructing and facilitating unauthorized migration.[69] Shipping companies induced loopholes for three main reasons. First, each rejected migrant had a deterrent effect on the decisions of other potential candidates to migrate. Making sure that passengers fulfilled their intention to move prevented them from returning home and discouraging others. Loopholes served to channel people who were less likely to pass standard inspections or had been rejected already. Second, some loopholes functioned as a business opportunity for shipping companies to expand certain services and make more money. Third, undesirable migrants who bypassed inspections exposed the weaknesses of the U.S. immigration authorities. This helped shipping lines redress the power balance over migration control, which legal reforms were shifting in favor of immigration authorities.

The biggest loophole in transatlantic migration consisted of traveling in second-class accommodations, because only a superficial on-board screening process was applied to those passengers. This led to rejection rates that were ten times lower than those among third-class passengers. Shipping companies actively promoted second-class transportation as a means to bypass migration inspection, to the great frustration of immigration inspectors. Shipping agents also encouraged passengers with a higher probability of rejection to bypass New York, which was known for stricter enforcement, and enter via cities with lower rejection rates, such as Boston, Baltimore, and Philadelphia instead. Such strategies were technically legal. Shipping lines were generally more guarded against more legally dubious strategies including accepting fraudulent American citizenship papers, evidence of questionable marriages, and sanctioning fraudulent crewmen or stowaways so as not to anger or undermine U.S. officials.[70]

Scholars have documented how migrants sometimes became seamen with the express intention to hitch a free ride to the United States.[71] The use of this practice to dodge immigrant inspection has not received enough scholarly attention. Opportunities to jump ship became more common with the transition from sail to steamships. Labor-intensive passenger liners could employ over a thousand crew members who need not have any sailing-related knowledge or skills.[72] To facilitate sea trade, the hiring of seamen had been regulated by international treaties, and it depended on contracts with shipmasters. If seamen broke their contracts by leaving a port of call, they forfeited their pay and faced possible charges. In theory, this served as a deterrent to desertion. In practice, a significant number of crewmen jumped ship, especially in New York City, where they were in high demand and were offered favorable wages by competing shipping companies that did not inquire about their legal standing. That the Hamburg America Line, the biggest shipping and passenger company at the time, registered 1,093 deserted seamen in New York City in 1909 indicates the magnitude of this phenomenon.

Immigration authorities believed that these figures included migrants who entered the country without inspections. Those accusations implied that shipping companies, or at least crews, were "selling" employment as a strategy to help migrants evade restriction. To curb the practice, the Bureau of Immigration started prosecuting shipping companies for illegally landing deserting seamen under the immigration laws. The Cunard Line was the first to be convicted of that charge and was fined $500, a figure that implied a judgment of negligence rather than criminal intent. A cohort of shipping companies backed Cunard's appeal to prevent the establishment of a potentially detrimental precedent that would make it more difficult for them to hire and maintain a full crew. The Supreme Court eventually overruled the decision on the grounds that the government had not proved intent. The verdict released Cunard of its indemnity and set free the sailors detained on suspicion of jumping ship. However, the verdict only encouraged the Bureau of Immigration to redouble its efforts. It appointed inspectors to collect evidence overseas. Following their trip, inspectors reported a web of agents in Russian and various Mediterranean ports offering seamen's positions to rejected migrants. Yet issues with jurisdiction and collection of evidence stymied real action.[73]

The U.S. government's most ambitious attempt to curb the practice is highlighted by the case it built against the Hellenic Line in 1911. Suspecting the existence of a smuggling ring within the company, Brooklyn district attorney and federal immigration inspectors raided the *Athinai* when it landed in February. The raid led to the arrest of twenty-seven men, mostly crew members, and the New York–based head agent of the company. The arrests followed a month-long investigation led by A. Seraphic, a field officer of the Bureau of Immigration who collected evidence in an investigation that spanned Europe and the activities aboard various ships. The investigation showed that every ship of the Hellenic Line systematically landed passengers as crew members over the course of the past year. Inspectors managed to detain a number of passengers who were willing to testify that they had paid large sums of money to crew members to bypass immigrant inspection. The lawyer for the liner denounced the raid as a political stunt and an attempt to leverage power over crews. He stated that the defendants had taken strict measures to prevent such landings. The liner's lawyer obtained release on bail of the New York head agent of the company, the ship captain, key officers, and engineers so that it could keep sailing. The trial was set to start when the *Athinai* returned to New York again six weeks later. To the authorities' surprise, the released defendants skipped bail and the ship arrived with another captain and crew. After twenty people were held under arrest since February and another forty detained as witnesses, the trial went ahead without some of the defendants. It led to the conviction of fifteen people, including the company's head agent, who served a year in prison, and the collection of the impressive sum of $41,290 in fines and bail forfeitures. A similar case against the Austrian American Line followed another government investigation of illegal smuggling from the port city of Fiume. These cases demonstrate a pattern of evasion on the part of some shipping lines, ticketing agents, crewmen, and others who helped migrants bypass U.S. immigration laws. They also highlight the difficulties to close loopholes; while the Bureau of Immigration tried to tackle illegal entries in 1911, only 150 people were returned to Europe for entering without inspections that year.[74]

We don't know the full extent of these practices. Not only was it difficult for U.S. government agencies to obtain evidence overseas at the time, but even less evidence of the clandestine practices survives in records relied upon by historians. Even when evidence was collected and charges were brought, crew members' mobility made it difficult to prosecute individuals. Moreover, European agents complicit in the sale of crewmen positions remained entirely out of state authorities' reach. At the same time, the *Athinai* case demonstrates the lengths to which the government was willing to go in an attempt to crack down on the practice. That the Hellenic Line was not an established member of the shipping cartel may in part explain its greater inclination to take such a risk. Cartel lines were less likely to violate these laws systematically as it went against their interests. There were difficulties and costs contracting replacement seamen in New York, so shipping lines shared an interest in preventing desertion. Moreover, most liners wanted to avoid giving the U.S. government reasons to increase its oversight of their operations. Indeed, immigration inspectors used the *Athinai* case to demand legal reforms and acquire more power over crews of foreign ships. Otherwise, inspectors remained dependent on the shipmasters' goodwill to report deserters, who proved hard to trace. Unlike passengers, they were not registered on arrival. As reforms lingered, Williams ordered immigration inspectors to collect head taxes from the shipping companies for deserters as a penalty, until the court decided migration inspectors did not have the authority to do so. The immigration law of 1917, finally, gave the immigration bureau the right to supervise the landing of all seamen, so long as it didn't interfere with their liberty to bargain for employment with shipmasters and brokers.[75]

The regulation of seamen illustrates that immigration inspectors could only stretch the laws and responsibilities of shipping lines to a certain extent. Imposing head taxes or fines for illegal landings of deserted seamen onto shipping lines, to pressure them to close this loophole, was deemed illegal by courts. Carrier sanctions were not always the winning answer to the limitations the U.S. government faced in enforcing its immigration laws. It fueled the desire within the Bureau of Immigration to depend less on shipping companies and increase its resources and power to close loopholes by itself.

Land Borders as the Weakest Link of Carrier Sanctions?

Research indicates that countries where most of the passengers come in via ships and planes rely much more heavily on carriers for immigration control than countries where people enter via land borders.[76] In the United States, carrier involvement to control transatlantic migration proved efficient as long as passengers continued to arrive at American port cities. However, as restrictions against immigration increased, more European migrants sought to bypass controls using indirect routes to the country via Canada, Cuba, and Mexico. In doing so, they traced well-trodden paths established by Asian migrants who sought to circumvent an even tighter regulation regime.[77]

The 1891 Immigration Act reflects this rising issue, as previous acts applied exclusively to people entering via port cities but this act now expanded to *"foreigners coming in by vessels or otherwise,"* meaning by land. Subsequently, immigrant inspectors were appointed at principal land border points to prevent unauthorized crossings. Yet these controls could not *"impede, obstruct, unnecessarily delay or annoy passengers in ordinary travel between neighboring countries."*[78] The Immigration Act of 1903 stipulated that the Bureau of Immigration was allowed to sign contracts with foreign transport lines to monitor entries.[79] Yet the Bureau of Immigration never managed to impose the same level of cooperation from railroads as from shipping lines, where migrants constituted the bulk of the passengers. Sifting out the minority of unauthorized migrants was clearly subordinate to guaranteeing a fluid transport of cross-border passengers by land for any other reason.[80] Traffic was significant on the northern border, as illustrated by the daily passage of 125 international passenger trains from twenty-six different companies passing through Buffalo alone.[81] Although the laws seemed to open opportunities to incorporate railroads in immigration control via carrier sanctions, these did not materialize. The massive logistics to impose such screenings to capture only a fraction of passengers seemed to have outweighed the benefits of integrating international railroads into border control mechanisms, like shipping companies. Further research is needed to uncover whether railroads acted as agents of enforcement for the U.S. government in ways that mirrored shipping lines. Either way, railroads would not have prevented illegal entries on foot, small boats, ferries, automobiles, or other means of transport across the land border.

American authorities relied on remote border controls and border diplomacy. The Bureau of Immigration negotiated the right to conduct inspections in Canadian ports of all passengers with final destinations in the United States. Still, mala fide passengers could easily bypass controls by keeping their intentions silent. Canadian immigration laws were more liberal for European migrants and imposed far less regulation on shipping lines. Some companies therefore saw a business opportunity in opening connections to Canada, hoping to profit from migrants going to the United States via indirect routes. The most efficient way to close this back door was border diplomacy—pressuring Canadian authorities to emulate American immigration policies. Yet Canada's first major immigration reforms remained much more liberal than U.S. gatekeepers hoped.[82] Canadian laws mirrored American policies in the case of most excludable classes, illegal landings, deportation procedures, and bureaucratic structure. But there were differences. For instance, Canada imposed no head tax on migrants but introduced post-entry grounds for deportations earlier than the United States. Shipping companies also were much less involved in immigration enforcement and were less exposed to carrier sanctions in Canada. Shipping lines traveling to Canadian ports risked only minor fines for errors in passenger manifests, carrying excess passengers, or knowingly assisting illegal landings. Moreover, shipping agents, captains, and crews didn't face jail time for major violations. The only costs deferred to transport companies were those of providing inspection facilities, returning excluded and deported aliens, and the hospital bills of aliens arriving with diseases caused by the companies' own improper vigilance. If medical inspectors judged otherwise, the bill was first passed on to the immigrant and then to the Minister of Interior. In practice, this meant that the Canadian Parliament defrayed most costs of enforcement. For instance, the costs to ship post-entry deportees back to Europe also could not be transferred to shipping companies. However, unlike the United States, Canada treated land entries much more similarly to maritime entries, imposing similar requirements and carrier sanctions on railroads and on shipping lines.[83]

Further research on the enforcement of Canadian laws may uncover whether and why the reliance on carriers decreased when arrivals occurred via land borders. Considering the gap between the laws on paper and their enforcement in practice, such study is also necessary to establish how Canadian authorities relied on transport companies and how Canada's migration policies diverged from those of the United States. On the latter, scholars have already pointed to the limits of border diplomacy, which was further accentuated with the introduction of a literacy test and quotas in the United States, while Canadian authorities continued to encourage European migration.[84] Discrepancies in gatekeeping were even larger at the southern border, where remote border controls and border diplomacy with Mexico were far less fruitful by comparison. Mexican authorities hoped to increase their share of international trade by accommodating shipping companies. Those policies designed to stimulate trade and increase passenger flows imposed hardly any controls of entry and opened Mexico as a prime back door for unauthorized overseas migration to the United States. These indirect routes via neighboring countries turned overseas migration from a maritime to a terrestrial border issue, reducing the possibilities to manage such flows via carrier sanctions on shipping lines. This evolution is marked by the rapid increase of the number of immigration inspection stations opened at the southern border after 1900 and the establishment of the U.S. Border Patrol in 1924. These stations initially targeted unauthorized transpacific and transatlantic migrants more than Mexicans.[85]

Immigrant officials tightened enforcement at land borders but also in the interior by creating a "Deportation and Transportation Division" in 1919, which took charge of coordinating expulsions from the interior. The division formalized and systemized a network of deportation trains to minimize costs associated with deportations that became more difficult to pass on to transport carriers.

The division retained flexibility to contract new modes of transportation if they were more cost effective, though. Immigrant authorities gradually reduced their dependency on carriers as enforcers, seemingly until the arrival of airlines.[86] A historical overview of U.S. penalties on airlines presents one interesting perspective to connect this pioneering period with the current use of carrier sanctions. Transporting significant numbers of international passengers per carrier, on fixed routes and through specialized hubs, are infrastructural characteristics that international airplanes share with passenger shipping companies. As transport networks greatly affect the power relations between migrants and states, a comparison will broaden our understanding of carrier sanctions in the *longue durée*.

Conclusion

State authorities have exploited carriers' powerful position to prevent unwanted passengers from boarding for centuries. American passenger and immigration acts mandated that shipping companies explicitly take part in enforcing the country's immigration policies. Carrier sanctions served to solidify that relationship. Immigration authorities did not hesitate to stretch the enforcement of those laws as far as possible to transfer the costs and responsibilities of migration control. Carriers' involvement was not limited to countries of origin and transit but remained crucial on arrival and afterward, as periods of immigrants' deportability extended. Shipping companies were held responsible for preventing undesirables from boarding, for those who arrived at the gates and who managed to enter undetected. However, shipping lines were not passive actors. They frequently constrained and contested the limits of immigration enforcement in courts of law. They also indirectly undermined American enforcement practices by exploiting loopholes to evade immigration restrictions. As American authorities attempted to close those loopholes, unauthorized migrants turned to the strategy of entering the United States via neighboring countries where carrier regulations were looser and penalties were lighter. Those strategies undermined a monitoring system that was based on carrier sanctions. To what extent this shifted the liability for unauthorized entries onto the individual migrant and spurred the development of "crimmigration" is a subject for further research.[87] Also, how different modes of transport compare and connect in the past, such as shipping lines with railroad companies and airlines, is still awaiting further research. This analysis therefore highlights the (dis)continuities of how authorities outsource mobility controls to carriers, and it refines our knowledge of how transport infrastructure affects migration governance. This discussion also examines the idea that unauthorized migration develops around transport networks and shows that carriers play a paradoxical role: helping state authorities to push back unauthorized migrants while also providing loopholes for unauthorized migrants to enter anyway.

Notes

The author thanks Danielle Battisi and S. Deborah Kang for their very generous efforts in setting up the conference at the Karsh Institute of Democracy and editing this collected volume that resulted from it. Also, thanks to the participants and reviewers for their valuable input.

1. "Commissioner Williams Analyzes Immigration Evils," *New York Times* (NYT) January 15, 1911.

2. William Walters, "Aviation As Deportation Infrastructure: Airports, Planes, and Expulsion," *Journal of Ethnic and Migration Studies* 44, no. 16 (2018): 2796–817; William Walters, "On the Road with Michel Foucault: Migration, Deportation and Viapolitics," in *Foucault and the History of Our Present*, eds. Sophie Fuggle, Yari Lanci and Martina Tazzioli (Basingstoke, UK: Palgrave Macmillan, 2015), 94–110.

3. Sophie Scholten, *The Privatisation of Immigration Control through Carrier Sanctions* (Leiden, the Netherlands: Brill, 2015), 5, 194.

4. Theodore Baird, "Carrier Sanctions in Europe: A Comparison of Trends in 10 Countries," *European Journal of Migration and Law* 19, no. 3 (2017): 307–34.

5. Matthew Gibney and Randall Hansen, "Asylum Policy in the West: Past Trends, Future Possibilities," in *Poverty, International Migration and Asylum. Studies in Development Economics and Policy*, eds. George Borjas and Jeff Crisp (London, UK: Palgrave Macmillan, 2005), 71–96; Erika Feller, "Carrier Sanctions and International Law," *International Journal of Refugee Law* 1, no. 1 (1989): 48–66; Pauline Maillet, *Nowhere Countries: Exclusion of Non-Citizens from Rights through Extra-Territoriality at Home* (Leiden, the Netherlands: Brill, 2020), 182–200; Scholten, *The Privatisation of Immigration Control.*

6. Katherine Carper, "The Migration Business and the Shift from State to Federal Immigration Policy," *Journal of the Civil War Era* 11, no. 3 (2021): 340–60; Hidetaka Hirota, *Expelling the Poor: Atlantic Seaboard States and the 19th-Century Origins of American Immigration Policies* (Oxford, UK: Oxford University Press, 2017); Kevin Kenny, *The Problem of Immigration in a Slaveholding Republic: Policing Mobility in the Nineteenth-Century United States* (Oxford, UK: Oxford University Press, 2023); Benjamin Klebaner, "State and the Local Immigration Regulation in the United States before 1882," *International Review of Social History* 3, no. 2 (1958): 269–95; Elliott Young, "Beyond Borders: Remote Control and the Continuing Legacy of Racism in Immigration Legislation," in *A Nation of Immigrants Reconsidered: US Society in an Age of Restriction, 1924–1965*, eds. Maddalena Marinari, Madeline Y. Hsu, and Maria Cristina Garcia (Urbana: University of Illinois Press, 2019), 26; Aristide Zolberg, "The Archaeology of Remote Control," in *Migration Control in the North Atlantic World*, eds. Andreas Fahrmeir, Olivier Faron and Patrick Weil (New York: Berghahn Books, 2003), 195–221.

7. Torsten Feys, *The Battle for the Migrants: The Introduction of Steam-Shipping on the North-Atlantic and Its Impact on the European Exodus 1840–1914* (St. John's, Nfld: International Maritime Economic History Association, 2013), 11–61; Maldwyn Jones, "Aspects

of North Atlantic Migration: Steerage Conditions and American Law, 1819–1909," in *Maritime Aspects of Migration*, ed. Klaus Friedland (Cologne, Germany: Bohlau Verlag, 1989), 321–31; Drew Keeling, *The Business of Transatlantic Migration between Europe and the United States, 1900–1914* (Zurich, Switzerland: Chronos Verlag, 2012), 175; Beth Lew-Williams, "Before Restriction Became Exclusion: America's Experiment in Diplomatic Immigration Control," *Pacific Historical Review* 83, no. 1 (2014): 29; Aristide Zolberg, *A Nation by Design: Immigration Policy in the Fashioning of America* (New York: Russell Sage Foundation with Harvard University Press, 2006), 185–93.

8. Carper, "The Migration Business," 340–41; Klebaner, "State and the Local Immigration Regulation," 269–95.

9. Tobias Brinkmann, ed., *Points of Passage: Jewish Migrants from Eastern Europe in Scandinavia, Germany, and Britain 1880–1914* (New York: Berghahn Books, 2013); Amy Fairchild, *Science at the Borders: Immigrant Medical Inspection and the Shaping of the Modern Industrial Labor Force* (Baltimore: Johns Hopkins University Press, 2003); Allison Schmidt, "The Long March through Leipzig: Train Terminal Chaos and the Transmigrant Registration Station, 1904–1914," *Journal of Migration History* 2, no. 2 (2016): 307–29; Dorothee Schneider, *Crossing Borders: Migration and Citizenship in the Twentieth-Century United States* (Cambridge, MA: Harvard University Press, 2011), 11; Katja Wüstenbecker, "Hamburg and the Transit of East Europeans," in *Migration Control in the North Atlantic World*, eds. Andreas Fahrmeir et al. (New York: Berghahn Books, 2003), 223–36; Young, "Beyond Borders," 26–33.

10. Janet Gilboy, "Compelled Third-Party Participation in the Regulatory Process: Legal Duties, Culture and Non-Compliance," *Law and Policy* 20, no. 2 (1998): 135–55.

11. John Torpey, "On the Coming and Going: On the State Monopolization of the Legitimate 'Means of Movement,'" *Sociological Theory* 16, no. 3, (1998): 239–59; Zolberg, *A Nation by Design*, 244, 264–67.

12. Keeling, *The Business of Transatlantic Migration*, 143–46, 167.

13. Rolf Engelsing, *Bremen als Auswandererhafen, 1683–1880* (Bremen, Germany: C. Schünemann, 1961), 49–76; Marianne Wokeck, *Trade in Strangers: The Beginnings of Mass Migration to North America* (University Park: Pennsylvania State University Press, 1998), 59–73; Zolberg, *A Nation by Design*, 44–45.

14. Carper, "The Migration Business," 345–47; Feys, *The Battle for the Migrants*, 38–39, 163–210; Jones, "Aspects of North Atlantic Migration," 324–26; Keeling, *The Business of Transatlantic Migration*, 61–142; Zolberg, *A Nation by Design*, 131.

15. Feys, *The Battle for the Migrants*, 211–62.

16. Scholten, *The Privatisation of Immigration Control*, 190–92.

17. U.S. Congress, An Act Regulating Passenger Ships, 55th Cong., 2nd sess., March 2, 1819, 498–99, sec. 1–3.

18. $150 in 1819 and $50 in 1847 have a relative inflated worth of $3,320 and $1,710, respectively. Measuring Worth, https://www.measuringworth.com/dollarvaluetoday, accessed October 1, 2021; U.S. Congress, An Act to Regulate the Carriage of Passengers in Merchant Vessels, 29th Cong., 2nd sess., February 22, 1847, 147–48, sec. 1–5.

19. U.S. Congress, An Act to Regulate the Carriage of Passengers in Steamships or Other Vessels, 33rd Cong., 2nd sess., March 3, 1855, 715–21, sec. 1–12; U.S. Congress, An

Act to Regulate the Carriage of Passengers by Sea, 47th Cong., 1st sess., August 2, 1882, 184–91, sec. 1–14.

20. Passenger Act 1847, sec. 1–5.

21. Passenger Act 1819, sec. 2.

22. Lew-Williams, "Before Restriction Became Exclusion," 49–54.

23. As Kevin Kenny argued, to complete the picture of the antebellum federal origins of immigration policy, the analysis needs to encompass the mobility restrictions, criminalization, and exclusion of Native Americans and especially of African Americans. This assessment should be extended to how these policies influenced practices of policing transatlantic mobility after the Civil War, but, like the transpacific exclusion of Asians, this falls out of the scope here. Kevin Kenny, "Mobility and Sovereignty: The Nineteenth Century Origins of U.S. Immigration Policy," *Journal of American History* 109, no. 2 (2022): 284–97; Kenny, *The Problem of Immigration in a Slaveholding Republic*.

24. Immigration acts initially stated explicitly that they did not apply to Chinese laborers.

25. Hidetaka Hirota, "The Moment of Transition: State Officials, the Federal Government and the Formation of American Immigration Policy," *The Journal of American History* 99, no. 4 (2013): 1092–108; Hirota, *Expelling the Poor*; Carper, "The Migration Business," 351–54.

26. U.S. Congress, An Act to Regulate Immigration, 29th Cong., 1st sess., August 3, 1882, 214–15, sec. 1–5, 1.

27. U.S. Congress, An Act in Amendment to the Various Acts Relative to Immigration, 51st Cong., 2nd sess., March 3, 1891, 1084–86, sec. 1–13, 1; U.S. Congress, An Act to Regulate the Immigration of Aliens into the U.S., 57th Cong., 2nd sess., March 3, 1903, 1213–22, sec. 1–39, 1; U.S. Congress, An Act to Regulate the Immigration of Aliens into the US, 59th Cong., 2nd sess., February 20, 1907, 898–911, sec. 1–44, 2; U.S. Congress, An Act to Regulate Immigration of Aliens, 64th Cong., 2nd sess., February 3, 1917, 874–98, sec. 1–38, 2.

28. Immigration Act 1882, sec. 5.

29. Immigration Act 1882, sec. 4; Immigration Act 1891, sec. 11. This is the best example of how federal policies are rooted in preceding Atlantic seaboard state polices. See Carper, "The Migration Business"; Hirota, *Expelling the Poor*; Kenny, *The Problem of Immigration in a Slaveholding Republic*.

30. Immigration Act 1891, sec. 10; Immigration Act 1903, sec. 20–21.

31. Immigration Act 1903, sec. 11.

32. Immigration Act 1903, sec. 19.

33. Immigration Act 1891, sec. 7–8; U.S. Congress, An Act to Facilitate the Enforcement of the Immigration and Contract-Labor Laws of the United States, 52nd Cong., 2nd sess., March 3, 1893, 569–71, sec. 1–10.

34. Immigration Act 1907, sec. 12.

35. Immigration Act 1891, sec. 1; Immigration Act 1903, sec. 9.

36. Immigration Act 1891, sec. 6; Immigration Act 1903, sec. 8.

37. Immigration Act 1882, sec. 2; Immigration Act 1891, sec. 8.

38. Immigration Act 1893, sec. 8.

39. Immigration Act 1891, sec. 4.

40. Immigration Act 1882, sec. 3–4.

41. Kitty Calavita, "US Immigration Policymaking: Contradictions, Myths and Backlash," in *Regulation of Migration: International Experiences*, eds. Anita Bocker et al. (Amsterdam: Het Spinhuis, 1998), 147.

42. Erika Lee, "A Nation of Immigrants and a Gatekeeping Nation: American Immigration Law and Policy," in *A Companion to American Immigration*, ed. Reed Ueda (Oxford, UK: Wiley-Blackwell, 2006), 7–12.

43. Deirdre Moloney, *National Insecurities: Immigrants and U.S. Deportation Policy since 1882* (Chapel Hill: University of North Carolina Press, 2012).

44. Vincent Cannato, *American Passage: The History of Ellis Island* (New York: Harper Perennial, 2010); Feys, *The Battle for the Migrants*, 228–311.

45. See, for instance, Cannato, *American Passage*; Torrie Hester, *Deportation: The Origins of U.S. Policy* (Philadelphia: University of Pennsylvania Press, 2017); Moloney, *National Insecurities*; Daniel Tichenor, *Dividing Lines: The Politics of Immigration Control in America* (Princeton, NJ: Princeton University Press, 2002).

46. Feys, *The Battle for the Migrants*.

47. Keeling, *The Business of Transatlantic Migration*, 1–13, 44, 63.

48. Torsten Feys, "Between the Public and the State: The Shipping Lobby's Strategies against US Immigration Restrictions 1882–1917," *International Immigration Review* 51, no. 2 (2017): 344–74.

49. Howard Markel, *Quarantine! East European Jewish Immigrants and the New York City Epidemics of 1892* (Baltimore: John Hopkins University Press, 1999); Alan Kraut, *Silent Travelers: Germs, Genes and the "Immigrant Menace"* (Baltimore: Johns Hopkins University Press, 1994); Feys, *The Battle for the Migrants*, 236–38.

50. Feys, *The Battle for the Migrants*, 217–19.

51. Jones, "Aspects of North Atlantic Migration," 326–31.

52. Feys, *The Battle for the Migrants*, 241.

53. Cannato, *American Passage*, 228–29; Keeling, *The Business of Transatlantic Migration*, 186.

54. Hirota, "The Moment of Transition," 1092–108; Zolberg, *A Nation by Design*, 189–93.

55. Feys, *The Battle for the Migrants*, 278–99.

56. Schneider, *Crossing Borders*, 74.

57. Daniel O'Keefe, *Annual Report of the Commissioner of Immigration 1911* (Washington, DC: Government Printing Office, 1912), 11.

58. Keeling, *The Business of Transatlantic Migration*, 170–71.

59. Feys, *The Battle for the Migrants*, 125.

60. O'Keefe, *Annual Report*, 9, 123–24.

61. Brinkmann, *Points of Passage*, 2, 11–16; Keeling, *The Business of Transatlantic Migration*, 171.

62. Many administrators other than Williams advocated this policy, including: Joseph Senner, "The Immigration Question," *Annals of the American Academy of Political and Social Science* 10, no. 1 (1897): 7.

63. O'Keefe, *Annual Report*, 7.

64. Jones, "Aspects of North Atlantic Migration," 329; Zolberg, *A Nation by Design*, 192–93.

65. Feys, *The Battle for the Migrants*, 265–68.

66. Feys, *The Battle for the Migrants*, 235.

67. See Feys, *The Battle for the Migrants*, 273, 304–9; "To Test the Law Deporting Aliens" NYT, September 10, 1910. The latter discussed Red Star Line's refusal to cover the deportation of Annie Rafilowich, arriving in 1905.

68. Cannato, *American Passage*; Feys, *The Battle for the Migrants*, 211–314.

69. For shipping companies' role in the transpacific, see Klaus Barde, *Immigration at the Golden Gate: Passenger Ships, Exclusion and Angel Island* (New York: Bloomsbury Academic, 2008). For a comparison between Atlantic and Pacific border regimes, see: Torsten Feys, "The Smuggling of Contraband Chinese and 'European' Chinese: Comparing Transpacific with Transatlantic Illegal Migration to the US 1875–1917," in *Tribute, Trade and Smuggling*, ed. Angela Schottenhammer (Wiesbaden, Germany: Otto Harrassowitz Verlag, 2014), 291–319; Torsten Feys, "Bounding Mass Migration across the Atlantic: European Shipping Companies between Border Building and Evasion 1860–1920s," *Journal of Modern European History* 14, no. 1 (2016): 78–100.

70. For evolutions in second-class passenger service, see: Keeling, *The Business of Transatlantic Migration*, 52–53, 228–30, 286–87. For a discussion of shipping lines and loopholes, see: Feys "The Smuggling of Contraband Chinese and 'European' Chinese," 291–319; Feys, "Bounding Mass Migration across the Atlantic," 78–100.

71. David C. Mauk, *The Colony That Rose from the Sea: Norwegian Maritime Migration and Community in Brooklyn, 1850–1930* (Urbana: University of Illinois Press, 1997); Lewis Fischer, "The Sea As a Highway: Maritime Service As a Means of International Migration 1863–1913," in *Maritime Aspects of Migration*, ed. Klaus Friedland (Cologne, Germany: Bohlau Verlag, 1989), 290–309.

72. Kristof Loockx, *From Sail to Steam: Two Generations of Seafarers and the Maritime Labour Market in Antwerp 1850–1900* (PhD diss., Antwerp University, 2020).

73. Feys, *The Battle for the Migrants*, 304–6; Feys, "The Smuggling of Contraband Chinese and 'European' Chinese," 297–98; National Archives, Washington, DC, Records of Immigration & Naturalization Service, 53033/31, Deserted Seamen Braun Report 1908; 53033/31A, Desertion from German Ships 1912; "Immigration Law Relaxed," NYT, September 8, 1907.

74. "May Discipline the Greek Line," NYT, December 22, 1910; "Unearth Plot to Smuggle in Aliens," NYT, January 6; "Raid Greek Liner," NYT, February 26; "Indicted Officers Quit Their Ship," NYT, April 18; "Turned Away 14,500 Aliens This Year," NYT, November 13, 1911; O'Keefe, *Annual Report*, 149.

75. Feys, "The Smuggling of Contraband Chinese and 'European' Chinese," 298; Feys, *The Battle for the Migrants*, 304.

76. Scholten, *The Privatisation of Immigration Control*, 71.

77. See for instance Ashley Johnson Bavery, *Bootlegged Aliens: Immigration Politics on America's Northern Border* (Philadelphia: University of Pennsylvania Press, 2020); Kornel Chang, *Pacific Connections: The Making of the U.S. Canadian Borderlands* (Berkeley: University of California Press, 2012); Patrick Ettinger, *Imaginary Lines: Border Enforcement*

and the Origins of Undocumented Immigration, 1882–1930 (Austin: University of Texas Press, 2009); Joseph Nevins, *Operation Gatekeeper: The Rise of the "Illegal Alien" and the Making of the U.S.-Mexico Boundary* (New York: Routledge, 2002); Bruno Ramirez, *Crossing the 49th Parallel: Migration from Canada to the United States, 1900–1930* (Ithaca, NY: Cornell University Press, 2001); Roberto Romero, *The Chinese in Mexico, 1882–1940* (Tucson: University of Arizona Press, 2010).

78. Immigration Act 1891, sec. 8

79. Immigration Act 1903, sec. 32.

80. U.S. Congress, An Act in Amendment to the Various Acts Relative to Immigration, 51st Congress, 2nd session, March 3, 1891, 1084–86, section 1–13; U.S. Congress, An Act to Regulate the Immigration of Aliens into the US, 57th Congress, 2nd session, March 3, 1903, 1213–22.

81. William Siener, "Through the Back Door: Evading the Chinese Exclusion Act along the Niagara Frontier 1900 to 1924," *Journal of American Ethnic History* 27, no. 4 (2008): 50–51.

82. Ninette Kelley and Michael Trebilcock, *The Making of the Mosaic: A History of Canadian Immigration Policy* (Toronto: University of Toronto Press, 2010), 115–22; Feys, "The Smuggling of Contraband Chinese and 'European' Chinese," 311; Ramirez, *Crossing the 49th Parallel*, 41–45.

83. Statutes of Canada, An Act Respecting Immigration and Immigrants, Ottawa, 6, Ch. 19, July 13 1906, sec. 1–73; Statutes of Canada, An Act Respecting Immigration, Ottawa, 9–10, Ch. 27, May 9, 1910, sec. 1–82, https://pier21.ca/research/immigration-history/canadian-immigration-acts-and-legislation, accessed October 3, 2021; Barbara Roberts, *Whence They Came: Deportation from Canada, 1900–1935* (Ottawa: University of Ottawa Press 1988), 11–19, 54–55.

84. Kelley and Trebilcock, *The Making of the Mosaic*, 138–41, 154–55.

85. Ettinger, *Imaginary Lines*, 60–159; Feys, "The Smuggling of Contraband Chinese and 'European' Chinese," 312–18; Kelly Lytle Hernández, *Migra! A History of the U.S. Border Patrol* (Berkeley: University of California Press, 2010); Nevins, *Operation Gatekeeper*, 29–31, 152; Romero, *The Chinese in Mexico*, 3–57.

86. Adam Goodman, *The Deportation Machine: America's Long History of Expelling Immigrants* (Princeton, NJ: Princeton University Press, 2020), 77–106; Ethan Blue, *The Deportation Express: A History of America Through Forced Removal* (Oakland: University of California Press, 2021).

87. Juliet Stumpf, "The Crimmigration Crisis: Immigrants, Crime and Sovereign Power," *American University Law Review* 56, no. 2, (2006): 367–419.

8 Finding the "Most Desirable" Refugee

Russian Refugees in Constantinople and American Humanitarian Migration Networks, 1920–1923

E. KYLE ROMERO

At a special meeting of the League of Nations in 1922, League of Nations High Commissioner on Refugees Fridtjof Nansen made an impassioned plea to league representatives. The league formed Nansen's office only a year earlier, giving him the task of dealing with refugees fleeing the Russian Civil War. With limited funds, the high commissioner had been focusing on dealing with refugee populations in major city centers, chief among them being Constantinople, where 130,000 Russian soldiers had fled across the Black Sea from the encroaching Red Army. Constantinople existed in a strange geopolitical limbo, occupied and administered by the Allied powers even as Mustafa Kemal solidified a new Turkish state in eastern Anatolia.[1] Historian Davide Rodogno terms spaces like Constantinople "sovereignty deficits," places where imperial fallout generated opportunities for state and non-state organizations to coerce migration, manage people's daily lives, and facilitate grander ambitions of national reconstruction.[2] In Constantinople, Nansen's new office had greater leeway and leverage to try to manage the lived experiences of refugees. Even with such a narrow geographical focus, Nansen needed more funds for transportation. With tens of thousands of lives at risk, Nansen pleaded for the league to free up more funds so that he could work on the refugee problem. The league representative of the British government, Lord Arthur Balfour, believed that the stakes were even higher than tens of thousands of lives.[3]

While the plight of the Russian refugees in Constantinople struck Balfour as a worthy cause to donate to, he argued that there would be a greater loss if the League of Nations did not act. He began his response with a nod to humanitarian geopolitics: "Now America, unfortunately as I think, is not a member of the League of Nations but it is quite clear that there are large sections, and most important and valuable sections of American opinion who are deeply concerned with the state of Europe on humanitarian as well as on political and economic grounds . . . and have been prepared to assist in any efforts. . . . " For Balfour, the league needed to offer some kind of sum for this project, or else they would risk alienating the good favor of Americans, particularly American humanitarian organizations. How would American institutions react, Balfour wondered, if the league could not "even to go the length of finding the 20,000 pounds . . . "[4] Balfour's address to the league had a measure of success—they voted to supply Nansen with additional funds, but Nansen would need to connect with American aid institutions to complete his work. Even though Nansen, the League of Nations, and former Allied powers all worked to provide leadership on the issue of Russian refugees, the financial power of American aid institutions could not be ignored.[5]

Although refugees have been an ever-present facet of history, this period in the 1920s witnessed a new approach to the disciplining and management of refugee flows by various state and non-state actors. Scholars Peter Gatrell, Katarzyna Nowak, and Lauren Banko have termed this transition "refugeedom": the beginning of a movement by humanitarian actors, nation-states, and supranational organizations to categorize refugees as figures of concern that could be defined, understood, and managed by technocratic means.[6] In Constantinople in 1922, hundreds of thousands of Russian refugees would be categorized, analyzed, and managed by humanitarian workers and league officials in an attempt to control their movement and "solve" the refugee crisis through strategic relocation. Over the following year, tens of thousands of the Russian refugees in Constantinople would move out of the city, either voluntarily or through coercion. Thousands would be forced out by being stricken from feeding rolls and denied food by humanitarian organizations so the refugees would vacate Constantinople. Tens of thousands more would be funneled to nearby countries willing to accept laborers. And, extraordinarily, roughly 2,000 Russian refugees would also make it to the United States in a time when American policymakers were passing the most restrictive, nativist laws in the nation's history.

This piece follows how a variety of organizations, from the League of Nations to the U.S.-based humanitarian group the American Relief Administration, implemented a series of aggressive resettlement projects to move Russian refugees out of Constantinople. First, this chapter traces Nansen's plans to resettle tens of thousands of Russian refugees in neighboring countries, hinging on collaboration with the newly established International Labor Office (ILO). Working with the ILO, Nansen sought to identify and categorize refugees based on skills and training. Functioning as an international labor broker, Nansen believed that he could move refugees around the globe to nations willing to take in eager workers. This plan ran into the realities of global migration restriction regimes.[7] Many nations remained skeptical, if not outright hostile to Russian refugees due to a fear of Bolshevism, despite the fact that the Russian refugees in Constantinople had actually fled from the Bolsheviks in the first place. Running low on funds and with decreasing political clout, Nansen turned to the powerful U.S.-based humanitarian group the American Relief Administration (ARA) to help resettle refugees from Constantinople in neighboring countries.

Founded by Herbert Hoover in 1919, before his stint as president of the United States, the American Relief Administration distributed over 1 billion dollars' worth of food in Europe and the Middle East in the years after World War I.[8] The ARA used a vast network of food and transportation infrastructure throughout Europe, managed by hundreds of American bureaucrats and statisticians. Based on principles from Hoover's past as an engineer, the ARA prized what it termed "scientific humanitarianism," an approach to aid rooted in nutrition and calculated relief, rather than what it deemed as inferior charity. Hoover had resigned from leading the ARA to take the post of Secretary of Commerce in the United States, but he remained quietly involved in directing the ARA from Washington. An avowed anti-Bolshevik, Hoover urged the ARA to help the Russian refugees in Constantinople, mostly as a way to stymie Soviet interests. Throughout its existence from 1919 to 1923, the ARA always claimed to be apolitical, but its humanitarian projects often sought to accomplish geopolitical goals.[9] Following the directions of Hoover, the American Relief Administration sent Arthur Ringland to Constantinople. A mid-level bureaucrat within the ARA, Ringland leveraged the clout of the United States' largest humanitarian organization to try to disperse the remaining Russian refugees as quickly as possible, with little attention paid to specific circumstances. Ringland embodied many of the ARA's principles, a rigid dedication to statistics and bureaucracy, and a scientized approach to relief distanced from concepts of emotion and charity. Symbolizing this approach, the process of resettling the refugees out of Constantinople became ominously known as "liquidation." Ringland and his ARA supervisors visualized the refugees not as people, but instead as a liquid held in the city of Constantinople, dehumanizing them in their imaginaries. The ARA sought to funnel that liquid away before, in their minds, the city would flood. Leveraging the ARA's political and economic clout, Ringland secured bilateral agreements with neighboring nations to create dispersal plans for thousands of refugees throughout eastern Europe.

In another ambitious resettlement plan, Ringland set up a committee of Americans in Constantinople to vet the "most desirable" Russian refugees for resettlement in America. Concepts of desirability stemmed entirely from Ringland, mostly based on his particular conception of "what would make a good American," founded in vague concepts like economic productivity.[10] Ringland's criteria for productivity echoed many of the beliefs shared among other humanitarian civilizing missions in the 1920s. Historian Julia Irwin, writing about the American Red Cross in the same period, notes that "through their aid, they believed, they could nurture a solid commitment to democratic governance and engineer more advanced, enlightened postwar societies."[11] Rooted in this progressive-era mindset about "civilization," Ringland and his committee melded notions of masculinity, Americanism, and perceived civilizational enlightenment into their vetting process.

Despite the U.S. Congress passing a series of progressively restrictive immigration quota laws, Ringland maneuvered nearly 2,000 refugees through the United States's increasingly byzantine and restrictive immigration system.[12] In contrast to Nansen, who had failed to get Russian refugees to the United States, Ringland leveraged both political favors and ideological factors to secure visas for vetted refugees. The ARA called in favors from the State Department and used Ringland's vetting process as a means to work around America's stringent quota system. With the support and explicit approval of the ARA and Ringland's committee, nearly 2,000 Russian refugees received priority admittance under the harsh new restrictive quota system in the United States, taking up nearly all the available spots for Russian immigrants under the country's new laws. The plan's success relied on a network of sympathetic sponsors in the United States, who guaranteed payment for Russians to travel to the United States and other settlement costs. The arrangement presaged the more formalized system of refugee resettlement, built in cooperation with non-state organizations, that would emerge after World War II.[13]

After a few months of vetting, Ringland's committee fell into infighting as members clashed over differing visions over who "deserved" to be resettled in America. The fallout of Ringland's system also revealed conflicting visions of the various goals of humanitarian work, a conflict that held deeply gendered dimensions. The male ARA committee members approved refugees who conformed to an ill-defined set of American ideals, emphasizing ideals like productivity and flexibility to new ideas, and those the committee thought could contribute to American economic growth. They identified these economic characteristics as essentially masculine, mirroring many of the same logics that motivated the immigration policy debates occurring within the United States at the time.[14] However, Anna Mitchell and Alma Ruggles, humanitarian workers for the Phelps-Stokes private relief fund, sought to resettle Russian refugees who needed the most help, particularly the ill and disabled. When confronting the private relief fund workers, Ringland and his subordinates castigated their decisions as childish, naïve, and fundamentally unaware of what made a "good American."

Long associated with the gendered labor of women and religious charity, humanitarian work underwent a series of dramatic shifts over the twentieth century as men came to dominate the field of philanthropic relief. Recent works in the history of humanitarianism have traced the ways that men sought to "scientize" and masculinize humanitarian work in the early twentieth century, moving away from sentimentality as the driving force for charity.[15] The conflict between Ringland and Mitchell reveals that this process did not occur easily or quickly, but instead in a messy transition as aid workers clashed over relief and resettlement strategies. These two visions collided, and the refugee-vetting panel collapsed, but that collapse revealed the contrasting humanitarian imaginations of its members and the gendered conflict at the core of their disagreements.

At a time when American policymakers were sharply restricting the movement of foreign nationals to the United States, the migration process facilitated by the American Relief Administration reveals the complex and irregular nature of immigration policing regimes. Few histories have explored refugee resettlement plans to the United States in the interwar years.[16] Although the ARA's "liquidation" plan transported only 2,000 refugees to the United States, the organization's manipulation of the quota system reveals the fissures and filters within the American immigration regime. Historian Paul Kramer writes that "modern state boundaries are best imagined not as walls but as filters, usually seeking less to block human movement entirely than to select, channel, and discipline it."[17] As an outside organization, albeit one with extensive ties to the government, the ARA's ability to vet "desirable" refugees and have them pass through the quota system demonstrated its understanding of the state's definition of desirable immigrants. The committee's early successes demonstrated that, despite its vagueness, the ARA committee members' conception of masculine "American-ness" resonated with immigration officials in the United States and with the general public. The origins of American refugee policy can be traced to these transnational non-state actors who sought to prioritize refugee resettlement rooted in gendered notions of labor and refugee deservedness. Ultimately, the ARA's vision of refugee resettlement would prove more influential in the long term, creating a system that would be adopted by the U.S. government when creating its first formalized refugee resettlement policies in the wake of World War II. Even as regular forms of immigration to the United States were being harshly policed, the ARA's clout afforded an irregular pathway for Russian refugees deemed desirable by the organization and the U.S. state.

The Russian Question in Constantinople

Following the disruptions of World War I, the Bolshevik revolution, and the Russian Civil War, flows of Russian refugees had become a distressingly common phenomenon in Europe. The first refugees came from Russia in a trickle. Made up largely of aristocrats, landowners, and the other wealthy elite of the Tsarist state—either ousted by Bolsheviks or fleeing from the possibility in the revolution's early days—these first refugees found easy settlement across the noble houses of Europe. The torrent would come soon afterward. As the Russian Civil War intensified in the wake of World War I, Russian peasants, farmers, and fleeing soldiers abandoned their homeland and sought refuge anywhere possible. From 1917 to 1919, hundreds of thousands of refugees trekked west on land into Europe or by sea through Constantinople. These first refugees were often poor and ultimately transient. The fleeing Russians quickly boarded ships from the Black Sea to the Aegean.[18]

In the fall of 1920, however, another wave of Russian refugees overwhelmed the fragile equilibrium in the Allied-occupied city of Constantinople. The White Army, composed of Tsarist military forces and other opponents of the Bolsheviks, with the support of European allies, suffered successive losses throughout the war. General Pjotr Wrangel, the latest in a long line of commanders facing the Red Army, saw his forces pushed back through the Crimea all the way to the Black Sea. Recognizing defeat, in November 1920, Wrangel ordered the complete and final evacuation of Russia in the face of the encroaching Bolshevik army. At this point, Wrangel's army consisted of not only military men but also their families and other army followers, roughly 130,000 people. Using the remnants of the White fleet stationed in the Black Sea, Wrangel ushered his army, now refugees from their homeland, onto ships destined for Constantinople.

Russian refugees in Constantinople presented a unique challenge for humanitarian relief. Wrangel had ordered his men and their families to stay in the city. Some of Wrangel's advisors urged him to disband the army, allowing the refugees to move out of Constantinople and pursue resettlement in other cities or countries. However, Wrangel sought to create a Russian government-in-exile and refused requests from his soldiers to leave the overcrowded city and find refuge elsewhere.

The governments of the Allied powers framed the need to deal with the refugees not in terms of charity, but instead almost exclusively in terms of international security. According to Michael Barnett, "At issue was not the compassionate desire to relieve the suffering of displaced peoples, but a fear that the mass movements of people was undermining peace and security."[19] European nations feared the stateless Russian refugees would, at best, impede economic recovery after World War I and, at worst, spread the seeds of Bolshevism west. One American aid worker visiting Constantinople wrote, "The situation in Constantinople is critical, owing to the possibility of local disorders and the threat of ideological spread . . . threats of mob violence must surely stimulate evacuation."[20] Even if Wrangel allowed the refugees to leave the city, chances that other nations would accept them willingly were slim. A League of Nations observer wrote, "No country, in European post-war conditions, was willing to admit unidentified and destitute aliens, and least of all Russians, who might prove to be secret emissaries of the Third International."[21] Even though Wrangel's soldiers had fought against the Red Army, fears of Bolshevism stymied resettlement efforts for any Russian nationals. Fears of this type of a security risk spurred the Allied powers to devise a more formal process to solve the "Russian refugee question." They turned to the League of Nations to begin a process of resettling the Russian refugees by whatever means possible.

In February 1921, only a few months after Wrangel's refugees landed in Constantinople, the League of Nations created a new position in its growing bureaucracy: the High Commissioner for Refugees. The league named Fridtjof Nansen, a famous Norwegian explorer and diplomat, to the post. His first task was managing the massive Russian refugee crisis. The Russian Revolution and the ensuing civil war had created roughly 2 million stateless people who held no internationally recognized legal status, and held no right to international travel beyond special dispensations offered by various national governments. Nansen first sought to address the Russian refugee crisis by repatriating willing Russians who had taken refuge in Europe and the eastern Mediterranean. Many European observers assumed that after the Russian Civil War ended, refugees would be allowed to return home. A League of Nations official commented that the league had "organised its whole relief and particularly its educative work on the assumption that the economic restoration of Russia would eventually call for a large number of workers, both manual and intellectual, and that the 'active forces' for this task would be found among the refugees."[22] This view was common among refugees as well, even if they feared political persecution when returning to Russia, due to their opposition to the Bolshevik regime.

According to historian Peter Gattrell, the refugees expected to return to their *soslovie*, or estate, after the civil war ended. Gattrell explains, "No one thought that an individual would remain a refugee for the rest of her or his life."[23] The newly established Soviet Union, however, viewed the refugees as ideological opponents of the new regime, at best, and secret counter-revolutionaries sent by European governments to destabilize the nation, at worst.[24] In 1921, the Soviet Union revoked the citizenship of the Russian refugees who had fled. In a global environment increasingly focused on defining borders, identifying citizens, and categorizing others, there was no formal system in place to recognize the refugees as members of a nation. One League of Nations official worried about the creation of a people who "cannot travel, marry, be born, or die without creating legal problems to which there is no solution."[25] By revoking the refugees' citizenship status, the Soviet government effectively ended any chance of their large-scale repatriation, in Constantinople or elsewhere.

With little enthusiasm for repatriation from the Soviet Union and the refugees themselves, Nansen turned toward more manageable projects to relieve the refugee crisis. As the league provided only a small budget for staffing and little to no money for direct aid, Nansen decided to tackle the Russian refugee problem by first targeting cities with the largest numbers of refugees. Constantinople became his first zone of operation. Nansen established a league office in the Allied-held city and began to assess the scope of the refugee problem there. However, according to the league, the high commissioner would *not* aid or relieve these refugees but rather "make the refugees self-supporting by dispersing them throughout countries." Essentially, the league tasked Nansen to become a labor manager, coordinating flows of refugee workers to where they could best find work and provide for the international economy.[26] Historian Laura Robson terms this process the creation of "human capital," using refugees as easily coerced labor in the emerging system of global industrial capitalism.[27] This "dispersal" process would become the chief means by which the league and, eventually, the American Relief Administration, would seek to address the Russian refugee population in Constantinople. This process rested on an ill-defined concept of refugees becoming "incorporated into local economies" at some point after their dispersal. Incorporation into local economies, a term they never defined, signaled for Nansen and league observers that their work in responding to the crisis had ended. They assumed that this process of incorporation would occur naturally once refugees were dispersed out of the city.[28] Under this definition, the league could solve the Russian refugee question in Constantinople by merely moving the refugees out. This narrower, idealistic view allowed Nansen and the league to focus entirely on transportation rather than the refugees' long-term success under their care.

With repatriation impossible and the Allied powers unwilling to assist or let the refugees remain in the city without a plan for evacuation, Nansen began a three-pronged process to move refugees out of the city. Nansen's plan proceeded from the league's command for Nansen to function as an international labor organizer. First, Nansen convinced Wrangel to allow the remnants of his army to leave the city. Through a series of backdoor negotiations, and a forceful entreaty from the Allied powers, Wrangel gave up on his plans to create a government-in-exile.[29] Next, Nansen initiated a large-scale bureaucratic operation to identify, register, and categorize the refugees living in the city. The league's process of categorization revolved around labor. The league directed the International Labor Organization (ILO) to begin a census of the displaced Russian refugees. The ILO sought to create a "makeable society," where the organization maneuvered unrestricted flows of labor to the places that needed them most.[30] This ambitious goal frequently ran up against the increasingly xenophobic and restrictive migration laws passed in the wake of World War I.[31] Working with Nansen, the ILO interviewed tens of thousands of Russian refugees in the city, giving each of them a lengthy questionnaire focused on their occupational skills. From that data, the ILO produced fact sheets on the refugees and compiled databases on their skillsets. Nansen believed this information could convince governments that were skeptical toward the refugees that they could benefit from their resettlement.[32] Next, the Nansen office sought to categorize and classify the refugees through creating a novel legal status paired with a new form of legal document: the Nansen Passport. This certificate authorized the bearer as a "refugee," which, after being accepted by a joint committee of sixteen governments in July 1922, became a certifiable category and legal status with the authority and the ability to move between countries. For the first time in history, the term "refugee" had an internationally agreed upon definition: a Russian fleeing the Bolsheviks. The Nansen Passport could be used in the same way as a natural passport, but it did not allow for a return visa.[33] Nansen and the ILO's major achievement in creating the Nansen Passport was to render the refugees legible to states seeking an eager labor force.

This ambitious plan immediately ran into several roadblocks. First, and most important, the Office of the High Commissioner for Refugees had little funding and limited staff. While the ILO had a large network in Switzerland, its surveys did not assess all the refugees in Constantinople.[34] The league would distribute hundreds of thousands of Nansen Passports, but many refugees were unaware, were unable to receive them, or were not able to qualify for their protections due to a lack of identifying documents.[35] Geopolitics posed a major problem as well. Even with labor data, few nations subscribed to Nansen's optimistic view of an unrestricted labor force migrating freely throughout Europe and the eastern Mediterranean. The few countries that initially expressed any willingness to resettle Russian refugees, neighboring countries like Bulgaria and Serbia as well as eastern European communities with Russian-speaking populations like Czechoslovakia, required the league to pay for transportation, food, bedding, and even months of wages for any refugees dispersed to their countries, in some cases.[36] In response, Nansen approached the league for more funds. Lord Balfour's remonstrations encouraged the league to donate a small sum. However, the British representative's conclusion that the league needed to appeal to the "valuable sections of American opinion who are deeply concerned with the state of Europe on humanitarian as well as on political and economic grounds" prompted Nansen to look outside of the league to facilitate a more rapid refugee dispersal. Nansen therefore turned to American humanitarian aid institutions already embedded in the landscape of postwar Europe and the eastern Mediterranean for relief funding, food, and transport in Constantinople.[37] In the fall of 1922, nearly two years after Wrangel's fleet had arrived in Constantinople, Nansen convened representatives from the major American aid organizations in Constantinople at the league offices in the city to try to address the series of refugee crises engulfing the city. An unlikely organization, the American Relief Administration, would take over Nansen's dispersal plans. For roughly a year, the organization would engage in a series of large-scale diplomatic interventions to try to rapidly evacuate the refugees from Constantinople.

The ARA's Selective Immigration Plan

Before the process of humanitarian professionalization that occurred in the late nineteenth and early twentieth century, relief work had traditionally been associated with women and the female realm. Historian Julia Irwin argues that the work of the American Red Cross in World War I played a huge role in "legitimizing humanitarian work as a career choice for American men."[38] As one of the premier U.S. aid organizations, the American Red Cross (ARC)'s adoption of professionalized structures and its aggressive recruiting campaign for medical and social welfare professionals codified new gender norms into humanitarian practice. These changes highlight the gendered aspects of what Keith Watenpaugh terms "modern humanitarianism," or the "replacement of independent missionary-based charity with secular, professional, and bureaucratized intergovernmental forms of aid and development."[39] Women, of course, still played a huge role in administering relief, but the professionalization of aid work brought new, gendered conceptions of humanitarianism, identifying data-driven and scientific approaches as more masculine.

Founded in 1919 by Herbert Hoover, the American Relief Administration (ARA) embraced this new, scientized approach to aid. From 1919 to 1923, the ARA operated an enormous organization that spanned all of Europe and into the Middle East, providing food and humanitarian aid to millions.[40] The ARA consisted of two large branches: technocrats who managed food aid and young men who distributed it. Hundreds of young men, mostly demobilized Army and Navy veterans, received the food and distributed it to the needy in dozens of cities across Europe and the Middle East. Building on models like the ARC, the ARA went one step further: they employed men only as distributors of aid. The ARA maintained a small outpost in Constantinople to facilitate travel for a massive Russian famine relief campaign begun in 1921. The ARA donated food for Russian refugees, but it claimed impartiality in any larger plans for resettlement. Nansen, however, wanted to recruit the ARA's assistance for his resettlement scheme. Since the ARA had to keep a treaty with the Soviet Union to enter the country for famine relief, Nansen hoped that the ARA's involvement in refugee resettlement would not lead to recrimination from the Bolsheviks.

Implementing a refugee resettlement plan in Constantinople sparked disagreement in the ARA's upper echelons. One director, Edwin Sherman, wrote in correspondence that he believed, "so far as the ARA is concerned, we should confine our activities solely to feeding that we may not become involved in any of the political phases connected with this situation."[41] The ARA repeated this mantra of apolitical aid throughout its work, but the organization's immense funding and authority granted it enormous leeway in shaping the political fate of its charges. Hoover, however, believed that the ARA was in the position to effect change, writing to his former subordinates that the ARA should "do what they can to fix the situation."[42] Hoover's involvement stemmed from his deeply held anti-Bolshevik beliefs. In a letter to President Wilson written in 1919, well before the ARA came to Constantinople, Hoover spared no criticism against Bolshevism: "The propaganda of Bolshevism, however, in my view will stir other populations only in ratio to their proportions of the suffering and ignorant and criminal. I feel myself, therefore, that the political danger of spread of Bolshevism by propaganda is a direct factor of the social and political development of the population which they attempt to impregnate."[43] Much like Wilson and other statesmen at the time, Hoover believed that socialism did not stem from politics but rather social illness. The only solution to the "radical swings of the pendulum" that characterized Bolshevism and other tyrannies, for Hoover, resided in alleviating the "root causes": famine, starvation, and disenfranchisement.[44] By aggressively resolving the Russian refugee crisis in Constantinople, in Hoover's mind, the ARA could offer counter-evidence to Bolshevism's perceived socioeconomic failures.

The ARA directors deferred to their former chief. To assuage the fears of ARA managers, Hoover sought another source of capital. The ARA had been funded largely by the American government at its inception, but the organization relied mostly on private donations for its relief work by 1922. Uneasy about using donated money to manage the "political phases connected with this situation," Hoover contacted the Rockefeller Foundation in the United States and requested a one-time donation of funds to respond to the Russian refugee situation in Constantinople. The Rockefeller Foundation, which provided grants for education, development, sanitation, and medical projects, offered the ARA a special dispensation of $100,000 to "disperse the refugees in the vicinity of Constantinople."[45] Although it had never offered support for the ARA before, the Rockefeller Foundation encouraged an approach to charity, which it termed "scientific philanthropy," that paralleled the ARA's technical focus.[46]

To administer the fund, the ARA sent one of its long-serving veterans, Arthur Ringland, to Constantinople to assess the refugee situation. After serving as an officer in the U.S. Army during World War I, Ringland ended up in the orbit of Herbert Hoover during his tenure as Chief Allied Relief Officer. Hoover tapped Ringland for a leadership position in the American Relief Administration's work in Europe. Unlike many veterans who signed up for postwar relief work, Ringland did not serve as a food distributor. Instead, he worked directly under Hoover in London, coordinating transportation and distribution from the home office. By the fall of 1922, it seems that Ringland had had enough of working in London, as one of his close friends in the administration wrote that he was "dying to get to Russia." At that time, the ARA had just started a massive campaign to relieve the Russian famine of 1921. Thousands of ARA employees had flocked to Russia, coordinating the transport of millions of pounds of food to villages along the Volga River. Ambitious ARA workers saw Russia as the best location to effect change and, perhaps more important, earn recognition and promotion. Located just across the Black Sea from the main ARA staging point in Russia, Constantinople offered Ringland a potential stepping stone to his desired promotion to work in the Russian relief campaign.[47]

Under Ringland's guidance, the ARA began to look for solutions to the Russian refugee crisis in the city. Ringland first turned to the Soviet Union. Using contacts in the Bolshevik state that he gained from his compatriots in the field in Russia, Ringland concurred with the league's conclusion that repatriation to the new Soviet Union would only end in death or forced labor for the former members of the White Army, and maybe even their families.[48] With repatriation out of the question, Ringland turned to another standby of ARA policy: the bilateral treaty. Nansen's office in Constantinople had been engaged in long negotiations with Serbia and Bulgaria to accept Russian refugees. Both nations tentatively accepted league resettlement plans, but they laid out strict procedures for migration, chief of these being that the refugees needed to be provided with food and basic supplies for six months in their new nations.[49] Ringland threw the ARA's political clout behind the negotiations. He promised funding and food from the ARA to both nations if they each promised to take 5,000 refugees from Constantinople. Bulgaria and Serbia agreed to a plan that put the League of Nations in charge of the camps in each nation, and each nation agreed to provide half of the financial aid to transport and house the refugees in those camps as long as "the ARA [would] provide the food for the 5,000 refugees which it is expected will be sent to the Camp at Cattaro [in Serbia]."[50] Ringland repeated this process, in smaller numbers, with Slovenia and Croatia.[51] Thanks to the contacts forged by Hoover and other ARA directors around Europe, Ringland managed to begin moving refugees out of Constantinople by the spring of 1923.[52] This process of shifting refugees out of Constantinople soon took on the portentous sounding title of "liquidation." The term "liquidation" highlighted the ARA's scientized, engineering-based approach. Although not an engineer himself, Ringland embodied many of Hoover's bureaucratic, statistics-based principles, seeing the refugees in Constantinople as numbers on a spreadsheet that needed to be funneled out of the city by any means necessary.

Using the rolls created by Nansen and the ILO, Ringland regularly wrote to his superiors with specific numbers of refugees "liquidated."[53] Ringland's campaign to evacuate and resettle refugees built on many of the precedents established by the league, particularly the league's rigid focus on labor as the key criterion for resettlement. In one instance of aggressive liquidation measures, several thousand Russian refugees refused to be resettled in Bulgaria. They feared that Bulgaria would be taken over by the USSR. Ringland dismissed this concern out of hard, writing, "and then we had to reckon with the psychology of the Russian refugee—and this is beyond comprehension."[54] Ringland disregarded these refugees' fears, instead striking their names off the ARA relief provisions list to try to force them out of the city. Either by evacuation or starvation, Ringland removed the refugees from his rolls. With this type of brutal efficiency, in six months, the ARA had facilitated the liquidation of 15,000 refugees across the Balkans and the eastern Mediterranean. Without food aid, thousands of Russian refugees were forced out of Constantinople to find aid, housing, and support. Their ultimate fate is not recorded in ARA records—Ringland does not account for their fates after being stricken from the rolls. By erasing the names of even those recalcitrant refugees who stayed in the city, Ringland also lowered the total refugee count in Constantinople, at least on paper. This process received the support of Nansen and the bureaucratic machinery of the League of Nations, both eager to lower the statistics of refugees in the city.

By the summer of 1922, Ringland had lowered the number of refugees on the ARA and the League of Nations rolls to around 8,000 people. Reaching out to his supervisor in Europe, Ringland had a new proposal: send the refugees to the United States. Writing to the ARA European director Walter Lyman Brown, second in command of the ARA, Ringland admitted, "our refugees are of the class most difficult to absorb in America. These will have a hard experience wherever they go." Despite this, Ringland believed that some of the refugees could become productive in the United States. Ringland devised a plan "to evacuate an equal number of able-bodied to America . . . provided the League contributes the average cost of European evacuations and the Amcross throws in its share. Both the League and Amcross [*sic*] agree in principle to this proposal of ours."[55] With support from the league and the American Red Cross, Ringland sought to send those he identified as the best, most productive of the remaining refugees to the United States.

Ringland's plans to send refugees to the United States ran up against not only the realities of transportation but also the increasingly nativist and restrictive immigration policies being passed in the United States in the 1920s. In the wake of World War I, economic decline and rising xenophobia in the United States led to the federal government passing a series of stringent anti-immigration laws that used a rigid quota system, severely restricting immigration to America. The Emergency Quota Act of 1921 established quotas based on "national origins" rather than residency or citizenship, restricting the number of immigrants admitted to the United States annually to 3 percent of the number of residents from that country living in the United States as of the 1910 census. This policy would later be the basis of the 1924 Johnson-Reed Act, which would govern immigration law in the United States for nearly forty years.[56] For the Russian refugees in Constantinople, the Emergency Quota Act applied to all people born within the boundaries of the Soviet Union, excepting those of Asian descent, who were outright banned from the United States. The Russian quota totaled roughly 2,000 immigrants per year.

While the new U.S. laws drastically reduced total immigration numbers, the policy still had skilled worker exceptions, as well as yearly renewed quotas for each nation.[57] Using ARA contacts in the U.S. government, transnational networks of humanitarian support, and a selection process that championed notions of masculine Americanness, Ringland believed that he could maneuver Russian refugees through the byzantine system of immigration in the United States by carving out as many skilled worker exceptions as possible and, for the rest, prioritizing his chosen refugees in the small quota numbers available to Russian nationals.[58] Although some humanitarian organizations in Europe and the Middle East had sought to facilitate emigration for refugees to America before, such plans were normally implemented ad hoc and in small, personal cases. Ringland imagined a much bigger, more organized procedure. Ringland formed, essentially, an immigration vetting organization to try to send "a hand-picked lot" to the United States, either exempt from or gaining priority in the immigration quotas.[59] Ringland selected this panel based on the humanitarian networks already present in Constantinople. Large organizations like the U.S. Navy, the American Red Cross, and Near East Relief secured seats on the panel. However, Ringland also solicited membership from smaller, private relief funds, in particular the Phelps-Stokes Fund, a charity created by wealthy philanthropist Anson Phelps-Stokes and managed by Phelps's sister-in-law Anna Mitchell.[60] In her role as director of the fund, Mitchell commanded a great deal of authority among the humanitarian community in Constantinople, warranting her two seats on the panel, hers and another for her employee Alma Ruggles. With the committee in place, Ringland began to structure the process by which the panel would interview, assess, and eventually recommend selected immigrants to resettle in the United States.

Ringland's vision of what made a qualified refugee revolved around conceptions of productivity and an openness to a vague concept of Americanness defined around individualism and economic productivity. To select those fit for this conception of citizenship, Ringland "made a very thorough examination of all refugees, indexed, tabulated, and divided them into groups." Unlike the ILO's questionnaire, which focused on work history and skills, Ringland's examination included more nebulous questions. In interviews and exams, Ringland's panel asked refugees not only to state their work history but also to explain how they made their work especially productive. They asked one carpenter if he would partake in more training to learn how to build cabinets. An academic who studied Russian literature was questioned about his opinions on American authors and his willingness to learn the American literary canon. The panel pressed a shepherd on whether he would use mechanized agricultural tools. In most cases, the panel pressed the refugees on questions of additional work training and willingness to start projects on an individual basis.[61] These questions about productivity and individualism suggest that Ringland viewed refugees' "deservedness" to come to the United States not on their needs, but on how they could strengthen the American economy.

This vetting process emphasized not only the refugees' economic potential but also their perceived willingness to assimilate and conform to American values. Ringland also instituted a caveat for resettlement that echoed Hoover's management of the ARA. Once the refugees were vetted and approved, the panel forced each refugee to sign a pledge swearing that they would repay any money expended on their behalf within one year. In Ringland's mind, this policy encouraged the refugees to work harder and more productively, eschewing welfare or charity.[62]

The panel did not operate in consensus throughout this process. In particular, Mitchell and Ruggles criticized Ringland's myopic focus on economic productivity. Mitchell and Ruggles sought to expand the vetting process to include Russian refugees in dire need of medical care, but Ringland vetoed their proposals. In many ways, Mitchell and Ruggles's conception of humanitarianism relied on older tropes of missionary-based relief work.[63] Their reports on the Russian refugees highlighted individual suffering—rather than the ARA's broader, statistics-driven accounts—and Christian morality and charity as the root of humanitarianism. Keith Watenpaugh describes the professionalized, science-focused vision of humanitarianism as "modern humanitarianism," which stands in contrast to pre-modern humanitarianism, more focused on sensationalism and emotions. In a letter to Helen Bristol, one of Mitchell's allies in the city, Mitchell vented her frustration with Ringland's vetting process: "You know what our troubles over the refugees in the past have been: the struggle to find them work or to get them to a country where they had a chance; to connect them with their family or friends; to prevent them dying in the street when ill."[64] Despite Mitchell's entreaties, Ringland remained focused solely on sending "productive" refugees to the United States, those who could help serve America the most, in his mind.

Mitchell viewed this type of resettlement plan as misguided, at best, and based on disingenuous data. Ringland had brutally cut down on refugee numbers in the city by striking any refugee who refused a dispersal plan off the list. To Mitchell, the Ringland vetting methods punished any Russian refugee who rightly feared persecution in the Soviet Union. She described one "former Wrangelite officer who refused evacuation to Bulgaria on fear of Soviet influence," whom Ringland then struck from the ARA provision rolls. When the officer applied for the panel's resettlement plan, Ringland and the ARA members denied his application. Mitchell argued that this ruthless efficiency downplayed the extent of the problem that she and her coworkers saw every day: "Now, we have been told in the papers—and the people told in America—that the problems here have been solved, 'the situation liquidated,' that all the Russians have been cared for and evacuated by the League, the ARA, and the ARC. Wonderful, heartening words—if only there were not these 8000 who are left! Perhaps they are too few to interest America; it is different with those of us who see them." In panel meetings and in her personal letters, Mitchell emphasized the continuity of the Russian refugees, even as Ringland's liquidation methods had struck them from official rolls.[65]

As the leader of the panel, however, Ringland vetoed Mitchell's objections. After two weeks of examinations and questioning, the panel selected 1,100 refugees "as suitable to come to [the United States]."[66] This group consisted largely of academics, students, and workers with professional or artisanal skills, almost entirely workers who fit Ringland's vision of productivity and individualism. Each of these refugees, at some point during the examination process, expressed an eagerness to engage in individual work and learn new, productive habits. In addition to winnowing down the refugees, Ringland also used the new data to help refugees build their economic networks in the United States. Ringland's committee worked closely with the Russian Refugee Relief Society, a mutual aid society founded by Russian immigrants in the United States, which operated as something like an informal resettlement agency for Russian refugees. Ringland sent the society the complete set of data that his panel collected, including personal data, skills, and former professions, to help the refugees find work in America. The Russian Refugee Relief Society (RRRS) offered guarantees to ARA contacts in the Department of Commerce and Labor—where the Bureau of Immigration had been relocated to in 1903—that any refugees sent to the United States through Ringland's plan would be assisted with finding a job immediately on arrival.[67]

With these assurances in place, the Bureau of Immigration agreed to give priority in the quotas to Russian refugees from Constantinople. With only about 2,000 quota slots open for Russian immigrants under the new immigration regime, Ringland's selected refugees would take nearly all the available slots. Further, the bureau agreed to grant any Russian refugee vetted by Ringland's panel with a Nansen Passport special exemption as a "skilled worker." With the support of aid networks in both Constantinople and the United States, Ringland's plan faced only one final hurdle: visas. The few hundred Russian refugees who had qualified for Nansen Passports could move out of Constantinople with relative ease, but for the others, Ringland needed special visas.[68] Using his contacts within the State Department, Ringland's supervisor, Walter Lyman Brown, secured immigration visas for Ringland's refugees to travel to the United States, with the State Department supplying as many as the ARA needed for those its committee approved.

After securing the additional visas, Ringland's panel in Constantinople used League of Nations funds to transport the refugees to the United States, where they were allowed entry with only a cursory check by immigration enforcement officers. In Ringland's mind, acceptance by U.S. customs officials justified the panel's ideological vetting process. In June of 1923, the first 1,100 Russian refugees arrived in the United States. With visas supplied by the State Department for travel, assurances from the Bureau of Immigration for quick inspections, and guarantees for work in the United States, the refugees gained entry to the United States and filled more than half of the quota for Russian immigrants. Ringland's prioritization of "productive" labor skills and individualistic ambition seemed to resonate with immigration officials in the United States, who allowed the refugees access after only a cursory examination. Political leverage also smoothed the immigration process. Christian Herter, one of Ringland's subordinates in Constantinople, explained, "The immigration authorities, because the ARA was interested in this work, were extremely lenient in the interpretation of their laws. In addition, great pressure was brought to bear upon them by members of the Russian Refugee Relief Committee in New York."[69] Herter references here the Russian Refugee Relief Society (RRRS), a group of donors and Russian expatriates in the United States who sought to ease the process for refugees fleeing from Bolshevik Russia. The ARA's authority eased the migration process on both sides of the Atlantic. Ringland and his panel in Constantinople believed that their vetting guaranteed the refugees a productive life in the United States. Herter continued, "The committee had no trouble in getting positions for them and they have become useful and good prospective citizens."[70] After landing in New York City, the Russian Refugee Relief Society, in tandem with ARA home office worker Frank Page, helped the refugees look for jobs in their fields of work.[71]

This arrangement between the vetting panel in Constantinople and a domestic relief committee in the United States became a blueprint for the process of refugee resettlement during the early Cold War, which required potential refugees to have a "sponsor" in the United States willing to help them find work and housing.[72] As a nongovernmental organization working in tandem with the State Department and the Bureau of Immigration to funnel "desirable" refugees to the United States, the ARA established precedents that would guide American refugee policy for decades. Despite America's harsh, restrictive immigration laws, the ARA had managed to negotiate a flow, small but still significant, of Russian refugees to the United States. The ARA had worked within the filter of the U.S. immigration system, channeling immigrants to the United States through the Constantinople committee's vetting process.

Ringland had set up the committee in Constantinople as more or less of a permanent structure, with hopes that his vetting process could be expanded to other sites of refugee flows. The panel in Constantinople continued to vet Russian refugee applicants throughout June 1923, as the first group went through. Ringland imagined that this process would quickly deal with the 7,000 or so remaining refugees in the city. He saw so much promise in the committee vetting process that he even published an article to spread among his fellow relief professionals in the United States.[73] Writing to his supervisor, Ringland crowed, "So much interest has been roused in the Committee's effort to intelligently select immigrants for America that it is planned to publish a full report of the work in pamphlet form." For Ringland, this type of "intelligent" vetting could be used by other humanitarian agencies to facilitate more resettlement plans in the United States. "We hope by the circulation of this report among public society and public spirited individuals at home to stimulate interest in our immigration problem."[74] Ringland even imagined that his committee in Constantinople could resettle other groups of refugees as well—if the vetting panel had a clear vision of American values. However, Ringland would not realize these aspirations. In July, shortly after the first convoy of refugees arrived in the United States, Ringland received the promotion that he had been searching for. His superiors offered him the chance to take on managerial work in Russia.[75] In his absence, an alternate vision of assisting refugees would emerge, eventually bringing down Ringland's "intelligent" process that had maneuvered around America's immigration policies.

Alternate Visions of Humanitarianism

With Ringland in Russia, the panel he had established soon fell to bitter infighting. Conflicts within Ringland's refugee vetting system soon revealed the committee members' gendered assumptions. When female members of the vetting panel challenged Ringland's vision of resettlement and sought to send refugees who were the most in need of modern public welfare services to the United States, the supporters of Ringland's plan responded with antagonistic, gendered criticism. These separate visions over refugee deservedness illuminate the ways that gendered thinking pervaded intra-humanitarian conflict in the years after World War I.

After Ringland's departure for Russia, Anna Mitchell and her allies were able to sway the panel's work, resulting in acrimonious fights between Mitchell and Ringland's subordinates who remained on the committee. Ringland had turned control over the vetting panel to Major Davis of the American Red Cross, an aging relief worker who had arrived in the city not long before Ringland. Mitchell and Ruggles found Davis far more amenable to changing Ringland's criteria that the vetting panel used for screening the Russian refugees, to emphasize need rather than economic productivity. Working with Davis, Mitchell added several hundred new refugees onto the committee's rolls, including disabled veterans, older men and women, and children. Since the U.S. State Department had guaranteed as many visas as the committee requested, the panel received un-vetted visas for these several hundred new refugees on the second convoy destined for America. The rest of the panel, largely made up of Ringland's allies and supporters, had no knowledge of these additions until after the convoy had left for the United States. Christian Herter, Ringland's chief subordinate in Constantinople, complained, "In just about a week things were in a state of absolute chaos."[76] Herter considered Mitchell and Ruggles's approach to refugee resettlement naïve and childish. Herter exclaimed, "Miss M is the intensely sentimental type and has allowed herself to be worked on by the plausible Russians who are shabby and dirty and apparently suffering—but who are really nothing but bums and loafers."[77] Herter's emphasis on "bums and loafers" highlights his dedication to Ringland's desire for the refugees to be economically productive. Mitchell's gullibility, Herter concluded, had no place in the statistics-driven, technocratic work of the ARA. To Herter, Mitchell's "sentimental" approach to humanitarianism made her unfit for the more professional, masculine work of modern humanitarian organizations. Herter also castigated Major Davis of the American Red Cross, accusing him of losing his wits in his old age and becoming susceptible to the wiles of Mitchell and Ruggles. Herter continued, "You know Major Davis is constitutionally incapable of saying 'no' especially to a lady. This is a trait which has been growing on him of late to an alarming extent. So when Miss Mitchell discovered that there were a lot of poor dears here whose money was all gone or who were out of work, he allowed her to juggle with the lists."[78] Herter did not dispute that the refugees Mitchell and Ruggles included in the lists needed relief, but he articulated a different vision of who deserved refuge in America and who, in his mind, would become the best kind of American citizen. Herter writes of Mitchell, "She looks at this thing not from the point of which types will make good future US citizens, and become good active, useful workers, but from the view of which ones are in a hopeless condition and ought to be helped to a more comfortable place."[79] This contrast between the two visions of deservedness demonstrated that the core of Ringland's first selection process revolved around concepts of masculinity as much as economic productivity.

Despite Herter's vitriol, the second convoy of refugees made it to the United States. At the border, Mitchell's vision for a system of resettlement where need trumped the ARA's masculine ideals of Americanness collided against the realities of America's increasingly restrictive immigration system. When the second convoy of refugees arrived, the Russian Refugee Relief Society reached out to the committee, saying that the second convoy of refugees "were very inferior." In a cable from ARA headquarters in New York, ARA secretary Frank Page hurriedly wrote to Ringland's allies in Constantinople that the Bureau of Immigration had refused access for several dozen of the refugees: "Thirteen deported about twentyfive [*sic*] admitted not capable self support. . . . Immigration authorities giving us all cooperation possible, but if inferior refugees not self supporting or desirable as citizens, the authorities are fully justified deporting them."[80] Even the refugees who made it through customs inspections found difficulties.

The RRRS was surprised this batch of refugees did not arrive with the occupational data that Ringland had collected, making it more difficult to connect the refugees with job opportunities. The Russian Refugee Relief Society informed Herter that " . . . the Russians who have come over in charge of the convoys, who were men originally picked by Ringland, are perfectly frank in their statements that the original lists have been discarded and now to get on the immigration list at Constantinople, bribery, lying, and appealing to sentimentality of certain members of the committee are all that is necessary." Neither the RRRS nor Herter provided evidence for this bribery, but it highlights the internecine conflicts among the refugees themselves, some of whom seemed to take satisfaction in being vetted by Ringland's panel.

The clear delineation between refugees chosen by the ARA and those chosen by Mitchell and Ruggles led to increased scrutiny by American officials. The first convoy of Russian refugees had received speedy approval in the United States, passing briskly through the Department of Immigration's screening processes. The second convoy set off alarms among immigration officials, who deemed the newest convoy of refugees to be "unfit, especially in comparison to the first batch."[81] From his contacts at the Bureau of Immigration, Herter heard that the latest convoy of refugees "was a very inferior lot of people and in addition to the aged and infirm were included a number of distinctly undesireables." In stark contrast to the first convoy of refugees, this second convoy included those deemed most in need by Mitchell and Ruggles: widows and soldiers crippled by war. The Department of Immigration and the ARA saw these refugees as undesirable, unable to work in the United States, and therefore undeserving of residency. However, despite this increased scrutiny, the extant infrastructure of the resettlement project still maneuvered the refugees through the established irregular channel. The visas supplied by the State Department and the presence of the RRRS prompted immigration officials to follow the same procedures they had previously: the refugees were allowed in.

Ringland's work in Russia ended only a few weeks after his arrival in June, when it was reported that the Soviet Union had started exporting grain in violation of the treaty the nation had signed with the ARA. After weeks of travel, Ringland returned to Constantinople to find his committee in the throes of a civil war. Herter and Ringland's supporters accused Mitchell, Ruggles, and Davis of naiveté, shortsightedness, and worst in their minds, putting the needs of the Russian refugees above the needs of the United States. In a letter explaining the conflict to his supervisor, Herter concluded that the goal of resettlement should be about strengthening the United States. In an indignant conclusion, Herter commented, "There is not a question that the committee in Constantinople has forgotten about America and is just looking at the condition in Constantinople."[82] By the time that Ringland had ascertained the extent to which the committee vetting process had broken down, according to Herter, "It was in ruins and he was too late to set it right."[83] Seeing the responses of the State Department and the RRRS, Ringland pulled ARA support from the vetting panel. Without the support of the ARA and its network in the United States, the committee's work quickly fell apart.

A "Solved Problem"

From the moment that tens of thousands of Russian refugees entered Constantinople, humanitarian aid organizations in Constantinople saw those refugees who had fled civil war first and foremost as a problem to be solved, a vessel for enacting differing visions of humanitarianism. Seeking to satisfy the demands of his office, Fridjtof Nansen approached the Russian refugee crisis as a labor broker, trying to arrange contracts and deals with nations to facilitate migration. Along with the ILO, Nansen imagined a world where free, unrestricted labor could be managed by a centralized body. This imaginary clashed with the realities of states that, in the wake of war, saw migration as a security threat. Arthur Ringland of the American Relief Administration sought to quickly "liquidate" the Russians in Constantinople through a series of aggressive projects, from leveraging the ARA's financial clout to a vetting panel that would navigate America's restrictive immigration system.

The ARA, the U.S. State Department, and the Bureau of Immigration clearly had similar conceptions of what type of refugee would make a successful American. Ringland articulated a consistent vision for the refugees he vetted on his commission: they needed to be driven and individualistic, and have skills that could benefit the United States and lead to long-term productivity. This reflected long patterns in the history of U.S. immigration policy, and it evidently resonated with American officials, who questioned the refugees' potential productivity only when Mitchell and Ruggles used a different vetting process. However, Ringland's efforts did not always have the results he imagined.

The voices of the Russian refugees who underwent the ARA's resettlement plan are rare in the ARA's records. In a rare letter in the archives from one of the Russian refugees, one of the resettled refugees, Valentin Glazoff, wrote a letter to Herbert Hoover himself in 1924. Glazoff had been one of the unofficial leaders of the Russian refugees in Constantinople, and he mentions in his letter that he had been keeping tabs on many of his fellows after their resettlement in the United States. Glazoff's letter begins in the most grateful tones, praising Hoover's organization for "affording [us] the benefit of immigration into the U.S.A., thus escaping from the gloomy and wretched Constantinople existence." Access to higher learning in the United States particularly enchanted Glazoff, who continued, "Some of us, already knowing the language, got the chance to study in Universities whereby our ultimate goal to follow again the path of culture and civilization was achieved." Glazoff concluded his letter to Hoover on a more somber note, noting "the great majority of us [the Russian refugees] are still forced to earn our living by physical labor."[84] Glazoff then included a request for additional aid for those members of the refugee community who struggled to even find physical labor jobs. Glazoff's alternating praise and anxiety highlights the complexities and the reality of life in the refugee resettlement process.

The letter demonstrates how Ringland's ideological standards of American-ness did not result in guaranteed success, but rather, it highlights the intended audience for such vetting: the American state. In a time of unprecedented immigration restriction, Ringland's vetting offered the State Department and the Department of Immigration a means to create an irregular channel for "desir-able" immigrants. Although it formed the crux of the disagreement between Ringland and Mitchell that tore apart the vetting committee, Ringland's ideo-logical standards did not result in the unmitigated success he had imagined. Glazoff's letter reveals that Ringland's concepts of deservedness and economic productivity as markers of becoming a successful American did not always bear a relationship to reality. This letter only offers insight into the refugees who made it to the United States, as the ARA did not keep any records for the tens of thousands of other Russian refugees coerced out of Constantinople. Without adequate networks of support after migration, Russian refugees often struggled. Ringland's single-minded dedication to merely liquidate refugees ignored the larger goal of long-term resettlement, to the expense of the tens of thousands of refugees under his organization's care. By manipulating its network of po-litical contacts in the U.S. government and setting up the infrastructure for an informal, private resettlement agency in America, the ARA had figured out a process to maneuver through the restrictive U.S. immigration laws by gaming the quota system and securing exceptions. This process would leave a lasting legacy. Decades later, the U.S. government would use this same process to iden-tify and resettle those displaced by World War II and build the first formalized system of refugee resettlement in the United States.

Notes

1. While under occupation, the Allied powers, as well as the various humanitarian organizations operating in the city, referred to the city as Constantinople, in the tradition of the Ottoman Empire, rather than the Turkish name for the city, Istanbul. When the Allied powers withdrew on October 4, 1923, the Turkish state under Mustafa Kemal renamed the city Istanbul. In an attempt to be sensitive to the temporal complexities of linguistics, this paper refers to the city while under occupation as Constantinople, before its official renaming.

2. Davide Rodogno, "Non-State Actors' Humanitarian Operations in the Aftermath of the First World War: The Case of Near East Relief," in Fabian Klose, ed., *The Emergence of Humanitarian Intervention: Ideas and Practice from the Nineteenth Century to the Present* (Cambridge, UK: Cambridge University Press, 2016), 190.

3. This was the same Lord Balfour of the famous Balfour Declaration of 1917. Then serving as foreign secretary, Balfour penned a letter to Baron Walter Rothschild stating the British government's approval for the creation "of a national home for the Jewish people" in Palestine after the end of World War I. Later scholars have aptly traced how Balfour, as well as other British and French politicians, used promises of a Palestinian homeland for Jews to co-opt allies during the war. For more on Balfour and his statement's legacy, see Jonathan Schneer, *The Balfour Declaration: The Origins of the Arab-Israeli Conflict* (New York: Random House, 2012); David Fromkin, *A Peace to End All Peace: The Fall of the Ottoman Empire and the Creation of the Modern Middle East* (New York: Holt, 1989).

4. "Report by Nansen on Constantinople Russian Refugees, 1922," Folder—Geneva Office: Correspondence Sent—Russian Refugees, Box: Chronological Letters and Telegrams Sent from Geneva, Commission Files of the Refugees Mixed Archival Group (Nansen Fonds). League of Nations Secretariat Archives.

5. This type of interaction between supranational organizations and nongovernmental organizations (NGOs) has long been a standard practice for relocating and resettling displaced people. For a series of case studies on this process, see Marlou Schrover, Teuntje Vosters, and Irial Glynn, eds., "NGOs and West European Migration Governance (1860s until Present) Introduction to a Special Issue," *Journal of Migration History* 5, no 2 (September, 2019): 189–217.

6. Peter Gatrell, Katarzyna Nowak, and Lauren Banko, "What Is Refugee History, Now?' *Journal of Global History* 17, no. 1 (2022): 1–19.

7. For more on the shifting global restrictions on migration in the interwar years, see Marilyn Lake and Henry Reynolds, *Drawing a Global Colour Line: White Men's Countries and the International Challenge of Racial Equality* (Cambridge, UK: Cambridge University Press, 2008).

8. Bertrand M. Patenaude, *The Big Show in Bololand: The American Relief Expedition to Soviet Russia in the Famine of 1921* (Stanford, CA: Stanford University Press, 2002), 20.

9. For the most complete account of the ARA's work, see Patenaude, *The Big Show in Bololand*. For more on Hoover and his claims of impartiality in humanitarian work, see Elisabeth Piller, "American War Relief, Cultural Mobilization, and the Myth of Impartial Humanitarianism, 1914–1917," *Journal of the Gilded Age and Progressive Era* 17 (2018).

10. Correspondence from Ringland to Walter Lyman Brown, June 4, 1923. Box 440, Folder 1, Reel 514, ARA Russian Operational Records.

11. Julia Irwin, *Making the World Safe: The American Red Cross and a Nation's Humanitarian Awakening* (Oxford, UK: Oxford University Press, 2013), 158.

12. For foundational histories on the passage of restrictive immigration laws, see John Higham, *Strangers in the Land: Patterns of American Nativism, 1860–1925* (New Brunswick, NJ: Rutgers University Press, 2002); Mae M. Ngai, *Impossible Subjects: Illegal Aliens and the Making of Modern America* (Princeton, NJ: Princeton University Press, 2004).

13. The 1948 Displaced Persons Act (DP act) transformed American policy on refugee resettlement. Before the act's passage, refugees could come to the United States only through the immigration quota system—or in cases like the Russian refugees from Constantinople, through exceptions in the process. The DP act created a separate channel for refugees with its own quotas unrelated to national origins, although it did restrict migration to those who were granted DP status by the United Nations in the wake of the war. The DP act created a governmental commission, much like Ringland's, that vetted refugees and connected them to private sponsors in the United States. Carl J. Bon Tempo, *Americans at the Gate: The United States and Refugees during the Cold War* (Princeton, NJ: Princeton University Press, 2008), 34–85.

14. For more on the debates surrounding immigration restriction and the dynamics of race and gender, see Ngai, *Impossible Subjects*; Matthew Frye Jacobson, *Barbarian Virtues: The United States Encounters Foreign Peoples at Home and Abroad, 1876–1917* (New York: Macmillan, 2001).

15. See Irwin, *Making the World Safe*, 7–9; and David Keith Watenpaugh, *Bread from Stones* (Berkeley: University of California Press, 2015), 18–24.

16. Most scholarly works on American refugee history in the interwar years focus on the U.S. response to Jews fleeing Nazi Germany. For more on this, see: See Richard Breitman and Allan J. Lichtman, *FDR and the Jews* (Cambridge, MA: Harvard University Press, 2013); Richard Breitman and Alan M. Kraut, *American Refugee Policy and European Jewry, 1933–1945* (Bloomington: Indiana University Press, 1988); David S. Wyman, *Paper Walls: America and the Refugee Crisis, 1938–1941* (Amherst: University of Massachusetts Press, 1968); Alan M. Kraut, Richard Breitman, and Thomas W. Imhoof, "The State Department, the Labor Department, and German Jewish Immigration, 1930–1940," *Journal of American Ethnic History* 3, no. 2 (1984): 5–38; Saul S. Friedman, *No Haven for the Oppressed: United States Policy toward Jewish Refugees, 1938–1945* (Detroit: Wayne State University Press, 1973); Shlomo Shafir, "American Diplomats in Berlin, 1933–1939, and Their Attitude to the Nazi Persecution of the Jews," *Yad Vashem Studies on the European Jewish Catastrophe and Resistance*, no. 9 (1973): 71–104; Henry L. Feingold, *The Politics of Rescue: The Roosevelt Administration and the Holocaust, 1938–1945* (New Brunswick, NJ: Rutgers University Press, 1970).

17. Paul Kramer, "The Geopolitics of Mobility: Immigration Policy and American Global Power in the Long Twentieth Century," *The American Historical Review* 123, no. 2 (April 2018): 399.

18. Account of Mrs. Bristol's Relief Work in Constantinople November 1920–August 1923. Box 74, Folder—Russian Refugees. Mark Lambert Bristol Papers.

19. Michael Barnett, "Refugees and Humanitarianism," in *The Oxford Book of Refugee and Forced Migration Studies,* eds. Elena Fiddian-Qasmiyeh, Gil Loescher, Katy Long, and Nando Sigona (Oxford, UK: Oxford University Press, 2014), 245.

20. Correspondence from J. W. Krueger to Ross Hill, September 30, 1922. Box 438, Folder 1, ARA Russian Operational Records.

21. Carlile Aylmer Macartney, *Refugees: The Work of the League* (London: League of Nations Union Press, 1931), 15.

22. Macartney, *Refugees,* 14.

23. Peter Gatrell, *A Whole Empire Walking: Refugees in Russia During World War I* (Bloomington: Indiana University Press, 2005), 197.

24. Macartney, *Refugees,* 16.

25. Gatrell, *A Whole Empire Walking,* 194.

26. Macartney, *Refugees,* 22.

27. Laura Robson, *Human Capital: A History of Putting Refugees to Work* (New York: Penguin Books, 2023).

28. This concept of being "incorporated into the economy" dominated thinking about refugees in this period. This terminology dominated debates over the long-term process of resettling Greek refugees who had fled the violence of the Greco-Turkish war, as well as those newly created "Greeks" made by the Lausanne Treaty. In an attempt to ameliorate the worst effects of Lausanne, the league helped facilitate a resettlement commission for Greek refugees, named the Refugee Settlement Commission, chaired by former U.S. ambassador Henry Morgenthau Sr. In its year-long debates over how to resettle the Greek refugees, the commission offered contrasting versions of economic incorporation. Some believed that whenever a refugee got a job, they had become incorporated. Others pointed to long-term success, including maintaining housing, job productivity, and a healthy family life. The nebulousness of this term reflects some humanitarian aid groups' eagerness to "solve" a crisis quickly. For more on the Refugee Settlement Commission, see the Commission Reports of the RSC, Box 31, Folder—Refugee Settlement Commission. Henry Morgenthau Sr. Papers.

29. Macartney, *Refugees,* 15

30. For more on this, see Jasmien VanDaele, "Engineering Social Peace: Networks, Ideas, and the Founding of the International Labor Organization," *International Review of Social History* 50 (2005): 435–66.

31. VanDaele, "Engineering Social Peace," 442.

32. Macartney, *Refugees,* 22.

33. The Nansen Passport would be extended to Armenians on May 31, 1924, but for these two years, the only type of "legal refugee" was Russian. Michael R. Marrus, *The Unwanted: European Refugees in the Twentieth Century* (New York: Oxford University Press, 1985); Claudena Skran, *Refugees in Inter-War Europe: The Emergence of a Regime* (Oxford, UK: Oxford University Press, 1995).

34. Macartney, *Refugees,* 16.

35. The league distributed around 450,000 Nansen Passports, and nearly 2 million refugees were displaced from Russia by the conflicts there. Otto Hieronymi, "The Nansen Passport: A Tool of Freedom of Movement and of Protection," *Refugee Survey Quarterly* 22, no.1 (April 2003): 36–47.

36. Correspondence from Krueger to Ross Hill, September 21, 1922. Box 438, Folder 1, ARA Russian Operational Records.

37. Nansen would follow this same plan with a subsequent refugee crisis in 1923, when the Treaty of Lausanne formally ended the Greco-Turkish War and empowered the nations of Greece and Turkey to denaturalize and expel over one and a half million residents of their nations in what would later become known as the Greco-Turkish population exchange. Authorized by Nansen and the league, American organizations like Near East Relief and the American Red Cross oversaw and funded much of the actual resettlement process of the exchange, easing the pathway for consolidating ethno-states in the eastern Mediterranean. E. Kyle Romero, "Nations on the Move: U.S. Humanitarians and Refugee Management in the Eastern Mediterranean, 1918–1923," *Diplomatic History* 73 (October 2022).

38. Irwin, *Making the World Safe*, 8.

39. Watenpaugh, *Bread from Stones*, 2.

40. For the most complete and thorough history of the American Relief Administration's work in Europe and in Russia, see Patenaude, *The Big Show in Bololand*.

41. Correspondence from Edwin Sherman to W.B. Poland, July 1, 1922. Box 438, Folder 1, ARA Russian Operational Records.

42. Letter from Herbert Hoover to Woodrow Wilson, April 25, 1919. Box 22, Folder 4, Reel 32. Pg. 1, ARA Russian Operational Records.

43. Hoover to Wilson, April 25, 1919.

44. Hoover to Wilson, April 25, 1919.

45. Annual Report of Executive Committee, 1922. Papers Box 2, Folder—American Relief Administration, Lewis Strauss Papers. The Rockefeller fund would take on a more explicitly political role in U.S. foreign policy in the early Cold War. See David Ekbladh, *The Great American Mission: Modernization and the Construction of an American World Order* (Princeton, NJ: Princeton University Press, 2011); Nicholas Cullather, *The Hungry World: America's Cold War Battle against Poverty in Asia* (Cambridge, MA: Harvard University Press, 2013).

46. Watenpaugh, *Bread from Stones*, 75.

47. Correspondence from Christian Herter to Lyman Brown, September 17, 1923. Box 440, Folder 1, Reel 514, ARA Russian Operational Records.

48. Correspondence from Edwin Sherman of the ARA to WB Poland, July 1, 1922. Box 438, Folder 1, Reel 512, ARA Russian Operational Records.

49. Correspondence from Krueger to Bicknell, November 18, 1922. Box 438, Folder 1, Reel 512, ARA Russian Operational Records.

50. Krueger to Bicknell, November 18, 1922.

51. Krueger to Bicknell, November 18, 1922.

52. Correspondence from Ernest Bicknell to J.W. Krueger, December 7, 1922. Box 438, Folder 1, ARA Russian Operational Records.

53. Correspondence from Arthur Ringland to Walter Lyman Brown, June 4, 1923. Box 440, Folder 1, Reel 514, ARA Russian Operational Records.

54. Correspondence from Ringland to Walter Lyman Brown, March 4, 1923. Box 439, Folder 4, Reel 513, ARA Russian Operational Records.

55. Ringland to Walter Lyman Brown, March 4, 1923.

56. These laws represented only the latest in a long line of restrictive immigration policies enforced federally and in U.S. states. For more on this policy history, see: Hidetaka Hirota, *Expelling the Poor: Atlantic Seaboard States and the Nineteenth-Century Origins of American Immigration Policy* (Oxford, UK: Oxford University Press, 2017); Ngai, *Impossible Subjects*; Matthew Frye Jacobson, *Barbarian Virtues*; Lucy E. Salyer, *Laws Harsh as Tigers: Chinese Immigrants and the Shaping of Modern Immigration Law* (Chapel Hill: University of North Carolina Press, 1995); Daniel J. Tichenor, *Dividing Lines: The Politics of Immigration Control in America* (Princeton, NJ: Princeton University Press, 2002); Higham, *Strangers in the Land*; and Roger Daniels, *Guarding the Golden Door: American Immigration Policy and Immigrants since 1882* (New York: Hill and Wang, 2004)

57. See Paul Kramer, "Imperial Openings: Civilization, Exemption, and the Geopolitics of Mobility in the History of Chinese Exclusion, 1868–1910," *The Journal of the Gilded Age and Progressive Era* 14, no (July 2015): 317–47.

58. Correspondence from Ringland to Walter Lyman Brown, March 4, 1923. Box 439, Folder 4, Reel 513, ARA Russian Operational Records.

59. Correspondence from Christian Herter to Walter Lyman Brown, October 2, 1923. Box 440, Folder 1, Reel 514, ARA Russian Operational Records.

60. Anson Phelps-Stokes made his fortune from a variety of business ventures, but he received his start in business from working at his grandfather's exporting and mining business, the Phelps Dodge Company. Stokes's grandfather had started the company along with William Earl Dodge and Daniel James Dodge. Cleveland Dodge, the son of William Earl, would go on to become president of the company, and one of the primary financiers of Near East Relief.

61. Correspondence from Ringland to Walter Lyman Brown, June 4, 1923. Box 440, Folder 1, ARA Russian Operational Records.

62. Ringland to Walter Lyman Brown, June 4, 1923.

63. Watenpaugh, *Bread from Stones*, 12–18.

64. Correspondence from Anna Mitchell to Helen Bristol, December 24, 1923. Box 440, Folder 1, ARA Russian Operational Records.

65. Ringland to Walter Lyman Brown, June 4, 1923.

66. Correspondence from Chris Herter to Walter Lyman Brown, October 2, 1923. Box 440, Folder 1, Reel 514, ARA Russian Operational Records.

67. The extent to which Hoover, then serving as the Secretary of the Department of Commerce and Labor, knew about Ringland's U.S. resettlement plan is unclear. Ringland directed most of his requests for refugee access and visas to his direct superior, Walter Lyman Brown, the director of the ARA in Europe. Brown undoubtedly had a direct line of contact to Hoover, but his papers do not show any explicit requests for aid from Hoover.

68. Correspondence from Ringland to Walter Lyman Brown, June 4, 1923. Box 440, Folder 1, Reel 514, ARA Russian Operational Records.

69. Correspondence from Arthur T. Dailey to Edgar Rickard, August 2, 1923. Box 440, Folder 1, ARA Russian Operational Records.

70. Herter to Walter Lyman Brown, October 2, 1923. Later in his life, Herter became a successful career politician, serving as a House member and then governor of Massachusetts. In 1957 Dwight D. Eisenhower appointed Herter Under Secretary of State, serving under John Foster Dulles. When Dulles became ill in 1959, Herter gained the appointment as Secretary of State. Herter served as secretary during the famous U-2 spy incident and the early stages of America's effort to stymie Fidel Castro's revolution in Cuba.

71. Dailey to Rickard, August 2, 1923.

72. Bon Tempo, *Americans at the Gate*, 34–59.

73. Correspondence from Arthur Ringland to Walter Lyman Brown, June 4, 1923. Box 440, Folder 1, ARA Russian Operational Records.

74. Ringland to Walter Lyman Brown, June 4, 1923.

75. Correspondence from Christian Herter to Lyman Brown, September 17, 1923. Box 440, Folder 1, Reel 514, ARA Russian Operational Records.

76. Herter to Lyman Brown, September 17, 1923.

77. Herter to Lyman Brown, September 17, 1923.

78. Herter to Lyman Brown, September 17, 1923.

79. Herter to Lyman Brown, September 17, 1923.

80. Cable from Frank Page to American Relief Administration in Constantinople, August 24, 1923. Box 440, Folder 1, Reel 514, ARA Russian Operational Records.

81. Correspondence from Christian Herter to Unknown, September 17, 1923. Box 440, Folder 1, ARA Russian Operational Records. This correspondence from Herter is unaddressed but seems to carry his most sincere thoughts on the matter. He begins the letter with the claim that he has to "let off a little steam" about the controversy, and that if he "were a free agent," he would bring this controversy to Washington and have Mitchell and the Phelps-Stokes Fund rebuked. The recipient seems not to be a member of the ARA, since Herter deemed it necessary to explain the ARA's role in Constantinople, but someone who is familiar with Arthur Ringland, whom he refers to only as "Ring."

82. Correspondence from Christian Herter to Walter Lyman Brown, October 2, 1923. Box 440, Folder 1, Reel 514, ARA Russian Operational Records.

83. Herter to Walter Lyman Brown, October 2, 1923.

84. Correspondence from Valentin Glazoff to Herbert Hoover, April 8, 1924. Box 440, Folder 1, Reel 514, ARA Russian Operational Records.

9 Polish *Vacationers'* American Dream and Nightmare

JOANNA WOJDON

In the 1970s and 1980s several hundred thousand Poles a year were coming to the United States as tourists, even though the average monthly salary in Poland oscillated between $20 and $30, and a passport was often regarded as a privilege bestowed on well-behaving citizens by the communist authorities. "Vacationers," as they were called both in Polish American communities and the Polish press, were seeing few tourist attractions, though. Instead, they quickly joined American labor markets in areas where employers did not inquire about their immigration status. In doing so, they often overstayed their tourist visas and settled in the United States more or less permanently. This chapter examines this specific immigration cohort within the context of other twentieth century Polish migration waves, and it also considers political changes in Poland under communist rule. The analytical framework is based on the self-image of the "vacationers" as presented in two Polish-language novels published in the United States in the 1980s, and the content of the official press published in Poland under communist censorship control. Although they represent opposing political sides, they carry a similar message of temptations and hardships in immigrants' lives, with the apparent goal to question the myth of America that prevailed in Polish society at the time.

Immigration from Poland

Intensive emigration at the turn of the nineteenth and twentieth centuries brought between 1 million and 2 million Poles to the United States. In the interwar period, the U.S. immigration quota system set the yearly limit of around 6,000 immigration visas for Polish citizens, thus impeding further growth of the Polish American population.[1] After World War II, the Displaced Persons Act of

1948 facilitated the entry of over 110,000 Polish nationals to the United States.[2] Its passage coincided with the almost complete closure of Poland's borders by the Soviet-backed communist leadership in Warsaw. Due to the ongoing Cold War and the Stalinist policy of isolating the Soviet bloc behind what Winston Churchill called the "Iron Curtain," getting a passport to leave Poland became virtually impossible. According to the findings of Dariusz Stola, "in 1954, in a country of 27 million people, only 52 individuals obtained passports for private trips to the West and some 50 got emigration permits."[3] Statistically, in Stalinist Poland it was easier to obtain a government position than a passport.

The system became slightly more liberal after the death of Stalin in 1953 and subsequent relaxation of Soviet control. The resulting "thaw" in internal policy in Poland that peaked in 1956 brought more freedom in many areas, from the economy (for example, the end of the kolkhoz system in agriculture), to religious practices (Primate Wyszynski was released from detention, religious instruction was allowed at schools, and chaplains were permitted to visit hospitals and prisons), to human mobility. Unlike many other elements of "liberalization" that were gradually cancelled, the number of trips to capitalist countries kept increasing: from 50,000 to 60,000 a year in the early 1960s to about 100,000 annually in the second part of the decade.[4] Yet only after 1970, as the new First Secretary of the Communist Party, Edward Gierek, came into power, did the number of successful passport applications surpass that of the rejections.

Gierek, who spent his youth as a labor migrant in Belgium and France, proposed a program of modernization for Poland that included an opening of the border, to fulfill both his political and economic goals.[5] Poles wanted to travel abroad and to keep in touch with "the West." Therefore, Gierek calculated that a liberal passport policy would shore up popular support for his regime. Although it was never publicly mentioned in Poland, such openness could also bring an infusion of money into the national economy by way of individual earnings of those who traveled, and through acquiring foreign loans that depended at least to some extent on the political freedom in the country, which the authorities allowed to be monitored internationally by signing the Helsinki accords in 1975. Subsequently, the number of visits to the West increased steadily in the 1970s, and by 1980, around 700,000 Poles yearly were permitted to travel abroad.[6]

The growth was possible not only because the passport policies were relaxed in Warsaw, but also because of the energy, will, and determination of Poles who actively responded to those changes.[7] They chose the United States as one of the most popular destinations for their visits. They made use of the social networks that survived the war and early postwar years, including existing contacts with family members and with former residents of their home villages or regions.[8]

The passport, however, was still regarded as a privilege, not a civil right. The decisions of the passport bureau depended on the officers' goodwill and on the applicant's "correct" political behavior,[9] but at times the individual decisions were hard to predict.[10]

Moreover, passport fees were prohibitively expensive. A regular passport for just one trip overseas could cost the equivalent of a four-month salary for the average Polish citizen (though there was a complicated system of special rates and discounts).[11] Most Polish visitors therefore took jobs immediately upon arrival to the United States, although they were not authorized to do so with a tourist visa.[12] Since an average monthly salary in Poland at the time fluctuated between $20 and $30, one could earn the equivalent of a two-month Polish salary in just one day in America.[13]

Even the state somehow recognized the clandestine migration strategies that citizens deployed once they received a passport. When the heating system in Poland's consulate in Chicago broke down one day, a Polish plumber was called to fix it: a man who traveled to the United States while on unpaid leave in Poland, took a job—most likely illegally—with a company that was dealing with heating and air conditioning, and after hours, partially using his employer's equipment, provided the service at the consulate for free.[14]

Vacationers Come on Scene

In an officially distributed Polish movie of 1977, *Kochaj albo rzuć* (Love or Leave), directed by Sylwester Chęciński, Ania, the young Polish visitor to her Polish American relatives in Chicago, takes a job as a window cleaner in one of the skyscrapers. At the end of the movie, Ania returns to Poland as initially planned. In reality, many Poles did not. They realized that even the low wages an undocumented worker could earn in the United States let them enjoy the quality of life that by far surpassed the one behind the Iron Curtain.

Poles who fled the country had been frustrated by the limited availability of consumer goods back in Poland, black market exchanges, food shortages, and queues that made daily routines tiresome and time-consuming. Many sought high-quality medical care, daily exchanges without bribes, and of course, civil rights and political freedoms. The correspondence of Polish intellectuals visiting the "free world" for research or lecturing, such as Stefan Kisielewski and Władysław Bartoszewski, reflected Poles' unwillingness to return home and struggle with realities of life under communism.[15]

Under those circumstances, it is unsurprising that many Poles either traveled abroad with the intention to flee their homeland or decided to overstay their tourist visas once in the United States, though it meant violating immigration laws with all the consequences of illegal immigration status. They could try to ask for political asylum in the United States, but that would bring them to the attention of the immigration authorities, whom they were trying to avoid as much as possible. Unlike in the past few decades, most of the migrants could not claim to suffer political persecution in Poland, as the system was less oppressive than it was in the Stalinist times. If they were denied asylum, they would be deported to Poland. Therefore, many preferred not to even try. On the other hand, if they decided to return to Poland on their own will at a certain point, they would not be able to reenter the United States in the foreseeable future. First, Polish passports were usually issued for one trip only, and obtaining a new one would be extremely difficult because they had already abused one. Moreover, their data in the records of American immigration authorities would not permit them to obtain the U.S. visitor's visa again. They could, therefore, either keep living illegally in the United States or go to Poland and never return.

The so-called "vacationers" (*wakacjusze*) chose the former option. They were the people who officially came to the United States on tourist visas (on vacation) but ultimately violated their nonimmigrant status numerous ways at various stages of their stay.

Officially, the vacationers did not register as emigrants in Poland nor as immigrants in the United States. Many did not even sell their property in Poland, and their apartments simply remained unoccupied as they pretended to be going for only a short visit. Some emigrated with just one suitcase so as not to raise the suspicion of border control officers in Poland or immigration authorities at their destination, just as a recognized ceramic designer Lubomir Tomaszewski did in 1966: "He was leaving as if he were going on holiday on the *Batory* [steamship]. [With] two suitcases and the allowed six dollars in his pocket."[16] Nor was it uncommon for vacationers to keep their intention to migrate secret, even from their closest relatives and friends. Others might initially have intended to return but decided otherwise once they saw the opportunity for advancement in the United States. It was not difficult for them to join one of the thriving Polish American communities (which provided jobs, housing, and all other services) and disappear from the radar of the Immigration and Naturalization Service (INS).

The motives of emigration varied, and they often combined "push" and "pull," as well as economic and political, personal, and system-related factors, distinguished by sociologists of migration. Tomaszewski saw little opportunity to develop his artistic career within the framework of the centrally planned socialist economy, which hindered his opportunities for personal development, international contacts, and contracts and profits from the international exchange. But emigration also let him escape from personal problems related to his failing marriage. Last but not least, he had relatives in America who provided him with a formal invitation and some minimal support on arrival.[17]

Vacationers and Polish American Communities in the 1970s

The exact number of "vacationers" was never easy to determine. The Polish Passport Bureau estimated in its internal (unpublished) reports that in 1977, more than 20,000 Poles overextended their stays abroad (in the United States and elsewhere in the West). By 1980, the annual number of overstayers grew to 68,000.[18] Regardless of the cohort's exact size, vacationers had significant cultural resonance. A popular Polish American joke by the mid-1970s asserted that to establish the number of the Poles in Detroit, one needed to count the number of basement windows and multiply it by ten—testifying to the poor living conditions of this cohort, analyzed in more detail in the following sections of this chapter.[19]

Discretion was their strategy of survival. The less visible they remained to both American and Polish authorities, the safer they felt. Unlike the political migrants of the 1940s and early 1950s, or later the Solidarity activists of the 1980s, they voiced no claims and had no big expectations or ambitions to play a political role, even within the Polish American ethnic community, as such an approach could direct other people's (including the media's) unwanted attention on them. They never asked for political advocacy but instead concentrated on earning a living and accumulating funds to save or send back to Poland.

The newcomers made use of the social networks within the Polish ethnic community, which helped them organize their new lives regardless of their legal status or their proficiency in English. At a closer look, though, it turned out that the worlds of vacationers and Polish American ethnics crossed only occasionally and quite superficially. The vacationers enlivened the ethnic life as consumers of ethnic food, readers of the ethnic press, audiences of Polish radio and TV broadcasts, and Polish Mass attendees, but they did not engage in Polish American organizational activities. On a daily basis, the barriers of life experiences, social status, and even language separated them from the established ethnic community. However, neither group perceived this separation as a problem, at least until the end of the decade.

Anna Sosnowska-Jordanovska claims, for example, that even as late as the 1990s the leading Manhattan-based Polish language daily, *Polish Daily News* (*Nowy Dziennik*) did not cover the events happening in the rapidly expanding Polish community of Greenpoint, Brooklyn, where the immigrants from the Peoples Republic of Poland had been arriving and settling down en masse. Instead, *Polish Daily News* concentrated on Polish ethnic life in Manhattan, dominated by the "old" Polonia and the displaced persons wave of the 1940s and 1950s.[20]

The Polish & Slavic Federal Credit Union (PSFCU), established in 1976, was a notable exception, as its main clientele were vacationers who had problems opening a bank account in mainstream American banks due to irregularities in their immigration status. The PSFCU offers included cash deposits, money transfers to Poland, and even loans.[21] Its headquarters were in the heart of Polish Greenpoint, and its first logo was designed in 1979 by Andrzej Pitynski, at that time himself a vacationer taking various menial jobs on his path to establish himself in the United States. Only in the decades that followed did he become a famous sculptor whose works can be found both in the United States—including the statue in Jersey City commemorating the Katyn massacre—and in Poland.[22] The PSFCU was largely ignored by the established Polish American community, however. In the 1980s and 1990s it experienced difficulties, including accusations of mismanagement and fraud.[23] Eventually, its strategies proved effective, however, for today it is one of the largest and still growing Polish American financial institutions that sponsors many cultural and educational activities, including well-established endeavors of the Polish ethnic group in the United States.[24]

In the 1970s, the vacationers were at times objects of interest but not active subjects within the Polish American umbrella organization in the United States, the Polish American Congress (PAC). Already in 1970, the Illinois state division of the PAC, located in Chicago, reported advising the newcomers on various issues, in person and by phone, as well as organizing English language courses for them. Delaware and Michigan state divisions provided similar services.[25] The problems of illegal Polish workers and their encounters with the American legal system were also discussed. These people experienced difficulties in communication due to the language barrier and lack of familiarity with the legal procedures, and some were even abused by their lawyers, sometimes of Polish origin. The PAC-Illinois thus appealed to the Polish Advocates Society to make sure that its members treat their Polish clients fairly. The PAC also decided to cooperate more closely with the Chicago branch of the Polish Immigration Committee, which specialized in supporting the Polish refugees, and to refer the immigrants there for legal assistance.[26]

The vacationers also appeared in the PAC documents in the context of protests against the American immigration officers' repressive practices toward the Polish nationals.[27] One of the most publicized cases involved forty-one Polish women who worked as cleaning ladies at offices in the Sears Tower in Chicago. In 1975, they became subject to INS control and subsequent arrest. Moreover, the immigration officers used brutal methods and derogatory remarks about Poles in general. The PAC leaders voiced their profound dissatisfaction at meetings with immigration authorities, while some Polish Americans even took to the streets of Chicago.[28]

House cleaning was one of the most popular jobs that Polish female vacationers took, not only in Chicago but also in other major American cities. According to Sosnowska-Jordanovska's findings, cleaning jobs at Manhattan offices were regarded as proof of the Polish group's high status in inter-ethnic competition, due to the job's relatively high salaries, security, and sustainability. It took years before Polish women were able to enter this section of the job market. Once they broke in, they took care to keep it in Polish hands, just as Polish men sought dominance in contracting.[29]

The Polish American Congress accused the INS of prejudice against Polish nationals, which they argued was not only on display at the Sears Tower raid but also exercised on a regular basis at the Chicago O'Hare airport, where, they claimed, Polish arrivals were a priori regarded as violators of immigration law. For example, all the adults were asked if they were going to work during their stay in the United States. Already in 1974, PAC President Aloysius Mazewski, a lawyer by profession, had filed a complaint with the INS asserting mistreatment of Polish nationals. The PAC argued that entry procedures for Poles were handled in an unfriendly and unprofessional manner, without regard to official regulations, and subject to the whims of individual inspection agents. Furthermore, the PAC complained that Polish visitors were not given information on their rights (for example, that they did not have to answer any questions in the absence of their lawyer) but were instead threatened with deportation. In one of the 1976 issues of the PAC Illinois State Division's bulletin, a special instruction for the newcomers was published in Polish that the readers were encouraged to share with their prospective guests from Poland.

Some of the Poles were arrested and deported, and others kept changing jobs and apartments to avoid the police.[30] The Connecticut and Pennsylvania PAC state divisions also filed protests against the mistreatment of Poles by immigration officers in Hartford and Philadelphia, respectively.[31]

It was only after a series of meetings and exchange of correspondence with Mazewski, involving the U.S. congressmen from Chicago and both ethnic and mainstream media, that the situation at the O'Hare airport slightly improved, according to Mazewski's reports. However, during a meeting with the director of the Chicago office of INS on July 15, 1981, Mazewski still complained that the officers were often rude and sometimes even aggressive toward the Poles.[32]

Along with these interventions, the Polish American Congress kept lobbying against stricter immigration regulations whenever these matters were discussed publicly. Mazewski had asked for a more open U.S. immigration policy during his first meeting with President Nixon in 1968.[33] In 1970 Charles Burke, director of the Washington, DC, office of the PAC, reported on contacts with the Italian American, Greek American, Lithuanian American, and Irish American organizations regarding proposed changes in the immigration regulations.[34] In 1978 and 1979 the PAC promoted Polish candidates for the Federal Advisory

Committee on Immigration and Naturalization, but they were unsuccessful.[35] All those efforts were to be multiplied in the following decade due to developments in Poland.

The Solidarity Movement in Poland

The unprecedented liberalization of the regime related to the "Solidarity" movement that formed in August 1980 also meant more liberal passport policy in Poland. In 1981 the number of Poles who traveled to Western countries rose to almost 1,250,000. Many were asking for political asylum, arguing that the political system in Poland was to blame for all their miseries.

The American immigration authorities, however, were even more reluctant than ever before to grant asylum to Polish nationals. The relaxation of the regime that opened the Polish borders meant to the INS that political oppression in Poland had stopped. The INS demanded detailed information on the applicants' activities that could potentially make them the object of political persecution. Some immigrants claimed they could not reveal such information, as it could cause harm to their relatives or associates in Poland, in case the application were rejected and they were deported to Poland—as well as harm to themselves.

Others lacked this kind of political background but were simply fed up with living under communism. Those who were able to legalize their immigration status on arrival are not part of this research. But they also experienced certain difficulties in their relations with Polish American communities and with mainstream American society.[36] Those who chose to follow the patterns established by the earlier waves of vacationers, and simply joined the Polish communities without regularizing their immigration status, are included.

The Warsaw regime's liberal policies proved to be short-lived. Martial law was introduced on December 13, 1981, as a means to counteract the Solidarity movement's increasing political role. It meant, among other things, complete closure of the Polish borders. Poles were prohibited from leaving the country, and returning to Poland was also impossible in the first phase of martial law. On the positive side, the Poles who happened to be visiting the United States legally when martial law was introduced could now benefit from special immigration regulations. According to the provisions of "Extended Voluntary Departure," they were not supposed to be deported until the situation in Poland improved, even if they had been previously denied political asylum. Obtaining political asylum became easier.[37]

Extended Voluntary Departure was extended in six-month intervals until 1987. The PAC lobbied for the extensions, and then for finding a permanent solution. At the same time, it engaged in debates on the new immigration law. Restrictions of the Immigration Reform and Control Act of 1986 were to be accompanied with the abolition of penalties for the prior violators of the immigration law. During the debates, PAC President Mazewski successfully lobbied for January 1, 1982, as the deadline for the violations to be covered by the abolition. The date of 1982 made it possible to encompass both the vacationers of the 1970s and the large wave of Polish immigrants from the Solidarity years of 1980 and 1981. By the mid-1980s, when the issue was discussed, PAC leaders argued that regardless of their initial motives to immigrate, those people had proved their loyalty to the United States, kept raising their American children, and were hardworking taxpayers and never public charges.[38] Once the bill was adopted in 1986, they all could legalize their status.

The 1986 law did not entirely solve the issue of irregular Polish immigrants. Starting in 1983, the provisions of martial law were gradually relaxed in Poland, and Poles' mobility began to grow again. It surpassed half a million trips per year in 1984 and approached 1 million in 1986.[39] This new wave of vacationers was hoping to make their American dream come true.

On the one hand, they were similar to their predecessors: arriving on tourist visas, often without clear plans for the future, but with some contacts in the Polish American community, or at least with expectations thereof. On the other hand, the times had been changing and the generosity of the Polish American community was diminishing. At least since 1980, Polish Americans had been busy aiding the Poles in need in Poland and in the refugee camps in Western Europe.[40] However, as a rule, they refused to pay particular attention to the needs of newcomers in the United States. The American economy, they claimed, was already offering multiple opportunities to those who wanted to work. Thus, they expected the new immigrants not only to earn a living by taking whatever jobs were available (even below their qualifications), but also to actively contribute to the Polish American efforts.[41]

But the newcomers were also tired. The atmosphere of apathy prevailed in post–martial-law Poland. Disillusioned with the collapse of the Solidarity movement, the Poles were reluctant to engage in social activities. Their interests did not extend beyond securing a decent life for themselves and their closest family. Emigration was often their way to retire from, not to get involved in, social or political engagement. It turned out, however, that on many occasions America did not meet their expectations, either, or that their feelings of disillusionment and pessimism were given the most publicity.[42]

Transnational Representations of Vacationers

Two Books in America

Difficult, even traumatic experiences were not uncommon for the newly arrived Polish immigrants of various immigration cohorts. For example, Stanislaus Blejwas analyzed the conflicts within the Polish community ignited by the post-WWII immigration wave, while Mary Erdmans focused on the young immigrants of the 1960s who were challenging the Polish ethnic leadership in Chicago at the turn of the 1970s and 1980s.[43]

Two books were pivotal for critical reflections on the vacationers.[44] Both were published in the mid-1980s in the United States, beyond the reach of the Warsaw regime's censorship office. It gave the authors the freedom to express their genuine thoughts, apparently addressed to the Polish, not American, readership, since both were written and published in the Polish language.

The very titles are telling: *Wakacjuszka* (A female vacationer), by Zofia Mierzyńska, gave name to this whole immigration cohort, while *Dolorado,* by Edward Redliński, emphasizes newcomers' preoccupation with dollars. Both were based on firsthand observations and include autobiographical elements. Unlike many other ego-documents, however, instead of defending the stances of one's own cohort, they paint extremely critical pictures of the vacationers.

The main issue discussed in *Dolorado* is an internal conflict of a newly arrived visitor from Poland who is not sure whether his fascination with America overshadows his longing for his home village, or perhaps his homesickness dominates over all the opportunities offered by the United States. This, indeed, is a common dilemma of first-generation immigrants, as the studies on nostalgia reveal.[45]

From the historian's point of view, the arguments that Redliński provides in his internal monologue are even more interesting, for they shed light on the realities of vacationers' lives and perceptions. *Dolorado* had a follow-up short story *Dwa Michały* [Two Michaels], describing how the author was cheated in the process of writing and disseminating *Dolorado* by his fellow countryman in dire need of U.S. dollars. Money is, thus, the leading motivation and ultimate goal of the vacationers. They pay little attention to anything else, including their own health, safety, and well-being, not to mention personal relations or moral values. Cheating, blackmailing, or abusing one's position are their survival strategies. They take menial jobs and live in terrible conditions among their own kin, which gives them little incentive to learn English or interact with mainstream society. Meanwhile the Polish community has much less to offer in terms of personal development, cultural life, or even pure entertainment, if compared to the mainstream American society—but also to the Polish society back in Poland. Their lives are indeed miserable, but the idea of returning to Poland and daily struggles with overall inefficiency in all spheres of life looms even worse.

Mierzyńska's book raises the same issues, but her emphasis is on the moral standing of her female protagonist, Anielcia. She uses her sex appeal whenever it may help improve her situation through, for example, a better paid job, nicer lodgings, or, ultimately, an opportunity to obtain a permanent resident permit: "the green card." At the same time, she keeps supporting her husband and children in Poland and attending religious ceremonies at a Polish church. She frequently excuses her morally dubious behavior by emphasizing her family's well-being back home. Mierzyńska describes in detail Anielcia's appalling living conditions, such as shared beds in filthy basements. She provides numerous examples of hard physical work performed by unskilled and highly educated immigrants alike, stressing how doctors, teachers, and engineers often lagged behind those who had been used to hard physical work in Poland. Like Redliński, Mierzyńska shows little sympathy for the Polish migrants. The Poles—and Polish Americans—are presented as ruthless, selfish, and insincere individuals who try to use their position whenever they can and exploit the ignorance and naivete of the most recent newcomers. Like Redliński, Mierzyńska sees the opportunities offered by mainstream society, but they remain beyond Anielcia's reach, due to both language barriers and the peasant mentality that she keeps, regardless of the time she spent in Chicago. As the time passes, Anielcia becomes a richer but definitely not better person. Like Redliński, Mierzyńska discusses the issue of nostalgia, but in her portrayal, the vacationers' ultimate motivation is individual liberty and emancipation from community traditions, social obligations, and family ties in Poland.

Both books offer a gloomy portrayal of the vacationers' lives in America. Striving for freedom and opportunities that were denied to them under communist rule, they end up in a Polish neighborhood of an American city beyond anybody's control or oppression, where it is certainly easier to secure one's basic needs. However, in doing so, the immigrants not only limit their aspirations but also betray their most basic human values. Their life becomes a caricature of their "American dream" even though they try to keep up appearances.

These reflections shed light on the vacationers' dilemmas and traumas, on the split between nostalgia and disgust with Poland, and between fascination and disgust with America, especially in its Polish ethnic version. Encapsulated in catchy stories, written with irony and humor, these books could motivate the vacationers' own reflections and perhaps new, more ambitious or honest choices. They could also serve as the authors' autotherapy and certainly brought them recognition (or notoriety, especially in Mierzyńska's case). Their echoes could be found in the Polish press published in Warsaw, under control of the regime and addressed to those who had not emigrated (yet).

The Press in the People's Poland

Mainstream journalists in Poland had long covered Polish American life, though it remained on the margins of their publications, dominated by the political dynamics of the Cold War. For example, "Trybuna Ludu," the official organ of the Polish United Workers' Party (the ruling Communist Party in Poland), had a permanent correspondent in Washington, DC, who mainly focused on propagandist interpretations of the U.S. political activities. But these journalists also shed some light on American social issues. Among them were topics such as unemployment and racial discrimination, which evoked a kind of schadenfreude as they never appeared in the Cold War Poland. From time to time, Polish Americans were also presented in the media.[46]

From the beginning of the post-Stalinist "Thaw" of 1956, two contradictory trends could be observed in those publications. They correspond with the socialist-nationalist dichotomy observed in other spheres of communist propaganda.[47] On the one hand, the journalists expressed their genuine interest and even pride in the Polish presence in and impact on America, "the America"—the world superpower, with its developed economy and political position. On the other hand, they tried to debunk the "milk and honey" myth of capitalist America, where anyone's dreams could come true, and the people of Polish descent enjoyed their lives in comfort and happiness.[48]

In the 1970s, with Gierek's populist policies promoting openness to the West on the one hand and prioritizing nationalism over socialism on the other, the number of publications related to Polish Americans grew significantly. Their tone changed as well. They now tended to present a warmer picture of prominent individuals who were proud of their Polish heritage or struggling with anti-Polish stereotypes. This new tone corresponded with the atmosphere depicted in the *Kochaj albo rzuć* movie, with its slightly paternalistic attitude, but generally appreciative of Polish Americans' attachment to the land of their ancestors. For example, an article in a popular Kraków-based weekly, *Przekrój*, presented the history of the Gromada family, who emigrated from the Subcarpathian Podhale region before World War II but cultivated Polish highlanders' culture in the United States and raised their children, Janina and Tadeusz, so that they spoke Polish but also became prominent activists of the Polish Institute of Arts and Sciences of America.[49] Edward Piszek, a Polish American millionaire from Philadelphia, cofounder of *Mrs. Paul's Kitchen*, enjoyed considerable popularity, thanks both to his economic success and to "Project: Pole," a marketing campaign he initialized and sponsored, which aimed to popularize Polish achievements among American society.[50]

This image changed dramatically in the 1980s. With the introduction of martial law, only two periodicals were allowed to be published in Poland: *Trybuna Ludu,* the press organ of the Communist Party, and *Żołnierz Wolności* (The Soldier of Freedom), the press organ of the Polish Army. They contained almost no coverage of the Polish diaspora, in the United States or elsewhere. In 1982 only two articles dealing with Polish Americans were published in the nationwide press, according to the *Content Bibliography of Periodicals* compiled by the National Library in Warsaw, which listed all articles published in Polish periodicals, ranging from weekly to yearly, plus in leading national dailies. There were six such articles in 1983, and four in 1984. In 1985 the number grew to ten and in 1986 it exceeded twenty.[51]

In the post–martial law period, the articles published in Poland were mostly drawing dark, if not entirely bleak, pictures of Polish life in the United States, and in the western countries in general. Unlike the previous decade, journalists did not focus on the achievements of the Polish ethnic community but on the harsh experiences of the newly arrived vacationers. The accounts seemed to be aimed at discouraging further emigration from Poland.

Without research in the archival files of the censorship office, we cannot determine precisely to what extent the censors, per request of the Communist Party leadership, interfered in the texts dealing with vacationers in the communist-controlled press. The authors may have been manipulated by the propaganda themselves, or they might have been paying for the privilege of traveling to or staying in the United States, with their expenses covered by the regime. But they may as well have expressed their genuine worries based on their firsthand observations of specific cases or on the stories that they were told, or that they could read in Polish American sources. The Polish press publications corresponded with vacationers' own accounts published in Polish American outlets. The increased frequency of press articles coincided with the publication of *Wakacjuszka* (1983) and *Dolorado* (1984), and sometimes the articles explicitly referred to the books.[52] Even if the opinions expressed in the two novels were sincere and evidence-based, they supported the anti-emigration tone of the communist propaganda.

Some publications started from the very beginning of the immigrants' stories and focused on detailed descriptions of the difficulties in obtaining entry visas. For example, they made sure readers understood that claiming participation in the Solidarity movement would not be sufficient to claim a political refugee status. They provided accounts of Poles waiting at refugee centers in Europe, where they lived in appalling conditions. The authors also cast aspersions on the moral quality of migrants by reporting on how migrants had to resort to lies and manipulation to avoid that fate. They even reported on the troubles of migrants who traveled to Mexico first and then illegally crossed the land border to enter the United States.[53] The accounts concluded that those migrants were prone to blackmail schemes by their fellow vacationers or other Poles in case of a conflict.[54] Thus, the American (or Western) "adventure" caused problems from the very beginning. A reader could consider whether the adventure was really worth the effort.

The press narratives also told how it often turned out that, contrary to the newcomers' expectations, nobody actually awaited them when they arrived. Even family members or friends offered them only a brief welcome and urged them to find a job, to repay any costs and start independent life as soon as possible. As a result, independence often meant that they shared crowded living spaces with other vacationers. That was something they would never do in Poland, the authors claimed—and readers probably agreed.[55]

The press also advanced narratives that to earn a living, even educated specialists had to take menial jobs in the United States. The reasons were quite simple: lower-paid jobs were widely available and required little or no English language skills, and employers rarely checked for documentation. Polish reporters seemed to enjoy writing the stories of Poles working below their education or skills.[56] One such account featured a physics teacher whose job was to press the button in a garage.[57] Another story told how a well-known surgeon was now sealing cabbage and chicken packages in a factory.[58] In another sensational account, a married couple, both lawyers, went to the United States to visit their alcoholic mother and ended up taking factory jobs, only to be fired just before a salary raise took effect. They then had to switch to cleaning house, an even more menial occupation. Although they ultimately earned enough to afford a home mortgage in the United States, the story still featured disappointment directed at their lower-class employment. Even though they allegedly claimed that their American occupations were a matter of their free choice, the author regarded their explanations as excuses that rationalized their social degradation. America could offer some kind of well-being but deprived the immigrants of chances for personal development and prestige.[59] Redliński would probably add that they could not achieve their life goals in Poland either while the official press focused only on the drawbacks of Polish American life.

The articles can be interpreted as one-sided voices in the debates on emigration. The debates indeed must have been happening in many Polish homes at that time, yet they could not go public in their entirety because the main argument in favor of emigration was the critique of the communist system, while voicing such critique was prohibited by the censorship control. Therefore, unlike *Wakacjuszka* and *Dolorado,* the Polish press provided only various arguments against the decision to emigrate.

Like the novels, the 1980s press presented Polish life in America with very little appreciation or kindness. The authors seemed to assume that the myth of America as the land of milk and honey was taken for granted among the Polish people, but the articles did not analyze it in any detail, as if merely mentioning positive details of life in America could bring unwanted comparisons with the political and economic situation in Poland. Instead, they put a lot of effort into debunking the common beliefs. The prevailing impression in the texts was that of disillusionment.

One of the most basic arguments claimed that, contrary to popular belief, America was nothing extraordinary. As some authors argued, the life of the

Polish immigrants differed little from the realities of their home villages and towns. You traveled to Chicago, and once you arrived there, instead of diving into the American life, you were meeting your former neighbors from Poland and discussing with them the land disputes from your home village. Old conflicts from the homeland were perpetuated in America, and gossip was spread on both sides of the ocean, with the help of friends and relatives. What, then, was the point of all the efforts involved in migration if one ended up with the same people and the same problems?—a reader could (and should) ask.

If a reader, nevertheless, considered some benefits of living with their kin, the reporters explained that such close contacts did not prevent anyone from trying to exploit anyone else. Those who settled down did not help the newcomers but either profited from them or completely ignored them. Most significantly, the Polish press emphasized negative features of Polish American "bosses" and offered potential migrants a cautionary tale about placing their trust in their ethnic counterparts. Many media outlets focused on the abuses that the newcomers faced because they generally worked without authorization. It featured tales of Polish Americans exploiting Polish migrants with low pay, firing on a whim or assigning the most exhausting or the least profitable tasks, also as a form of punishment for real or fake faults. That message resonated with Redliński and Mierzyńska as well.[60]

One could also expect little understanding or support from the established Polish community, according to the Polish press. Polish American organizations' staunch anti-communism was emphasized. It was said to divide Polish Americans from Polish newcomers. It might indeed be the personal experience of the authors—as representatives of the regime press, they were treated with utmost suspicion by the Polish American leaders. At the same time, criticizing Polish American anti-communism helped them meet the regime's expectations.

Some articles suggested that the best a new immigrant from Poland could do was to leave their Polish neighborhood, since it offered little to the newcomers and instead deprived them of the benefits of the "real" American experience. Thus, if only their language skills allowed it, they should have looked for a job outside the Polish community, which very few did, according to the Polish press. Such remarks apparently contributed to the negative side of the media portrait of both the Polish diaspora—who exploited rather than protected their "compatriots"—and of the newcomers who had left Poland unprepared, basing their plans on unrealistic expectations and lacking basic skills and mental capabilities.

However, Polish commentators also lamented the loss of a "Polish" identity among migrants. Their children Americanized quickly—they did not even want to speak the Polish language and preferred to have American friends and spend time in American ways. Thus, both options evoked criticism: staying in the

Polish ghetto limited immigrants' opportunities and may even make immigration pointless, while entering mainstream American society put their personal integrity in danger, and it deprived the Polish nation of its people.

Nationalist arguments were raised quite often in migrant news coverage: many regarded leaving Poland as a drain on the country's (and nation's) social capital. Two contradictory arguments were used in this regard in the communist-controlled press—which most likely corresponded with the views of other Polish commentators, also originating from the Catholic Church, as Mary Erdmans has pointed out in relation to the Polish immigrants of the post-communist Poland of the 1990s.[61]

On the one hand, prioritizing one's own personal development over the country's and nation's common good was regarded as morally dubious. Moreover, as one of the letters to the editor claimed, the alleged "poverty" of Poland under communism was nothing compared to the prewar levels. In those old times, emigration had been justified, but in the 1980s it only served to fulfill artificially created and ever-expanding needs.[62]

On the other hand, taking menial jobs in the United States was regarded as harming the "national dignity." In the same vein, vacationers' misbehaviors were said to harm the image of Poland and the Poles in the United States.[63]

A recurring element in the immigration stories was extramarital affairs, so-called "American marriages," that lasted only as long as one stayed in the United States and were hidden when a legal spouse from Poland visited.[64] In accordance with the message of *Wakacjuszka*, such affairs could be used cynically to secure a better job or a better place to live.[65] If legalized, a marriage with an American citizen could help obtain a legal resident status.[66] But in most cases, as some immigrants were allegedly explaining it, an American marriage (formal or informal) was a matter of "personal hygiene," meaning that it provided psychological support and helped satisfy sexual needs.

The psychological burden of migration was addressed quite frequently. Immigrants' nostalgia was not only directed toward the home country but also more personally toward family and friends. Many texts drew readers' attention to the feelings of loneliness experienced by both the vacationers and their families back home, with special emphasis on the children who grew up in Poland not really knowing their parent.[67] Immigrants missed not only intimate contacts with their spouses but also genuine personal—not only business-driven—relations with others, with whom they shared both memories and everyday problems. In America, immigrants constantly competed with one another for jobs, accommodation, and other goods. Everybody's preoccupation with work and money did not help build positive interpersonal relations.

Several journalists emphasized how detrimental excessive work was, not only to migrants' personal development and interpersonal relations but also even to their physical and mental health.[68] Working overtime, taking night or weekend shifts, or working two full-time jobs were presented as common strategies that vacationers used in the United States to build wealth.[69] One of the reporters deplored immigrants' lack of entrepreneurship when he found out that the only services offered in Polish classifieds were cleaning, housekeeping, remodeling, fortune-telling, photography, and teaching a foreign language or how to play a musical instrument. Others, he wrote, preferred twelve-hour-a-day toil. How he distinguished new immigrants' announcements from the rest, and the ones by vacationers from those by political émigrés of the 1980s, is not clear. Since immigrants' businesses on his list also included restaurants, shops, hairdressers, doctors and lawyers, most likely, he simply did not reflect on the various cohorts of Polish immigrants while expressing his disillusionment.[70]

In the context of vacationers' work, their experiences in Poland were mentioned as a point of reference. The Polish press sometimes insinuated that vacationers had never worked as hard in Poland. Some even went on disability in Poland, while in the United States they worked full-time, seven days a week, without any medical care or social benefits—the articles claimed.[71] The implications were twofold. First, had vacationers worked as hard in Poland as they did in America, their economic situation could have improved without the need to leave the country (Redliński claimed that it would not, due to the nature of the communist system). The second implication was that by focusing on work and prospective wealth, vacationers had no time to engage in any meaningful social activities or to develop fulfilling hobbies. Their entertainment was portrayed as primitive and often immoral. Commentators lamented migrants getting hooked on "trashy" American television programs like World Wrestling Entertainment (WWE), drinking in excess, and partying at disco clubs on weekends.[72]

Alcoholism was presented as a common problem. Excessive alcohol consumption was described as one of the few forms of entertainment, but also as a popular, yet in the long run inefficient, way of dealing with troubles.[73] One reporter noted that he encountered a former Polish ski jumping master as well as a rock music star among Chicago's alcoholics.[74] The press did not mention in this context, however, that alcoholism was a serious social problem in Poland, too, and that drinking habits could have been developed before migration.

Media accounts wanted their readers to understand that because visa overstayers lacked legal standing in the United States, they often were denied access to the types of state-provided social services that could help them in such situations.[75] Some accounts asserted that unless migrants fabricated or illegally acquired a social security number, they were largely prevented from acquiring even basic medical care. According to one of the reporters, some migrants even lost their teeth due to both stress and the lack of affordable dental care.[76] If they got sick, they were fired, since there was always someone else waiting for their job. In severe cases, such circumstances might lead to nervous breakdowns. If they got seriously sick, they should go back home to Poland, or they could lose all their money and fall into debt.[77] Alcoholism, illness, disability, or divorce might lead to debt or impoverishment.[78] Hence, stories were published of suffering Poles who had to borrow money to buy a ticket home, or of those who could not afford even that and died in the United States.[79]

Coverage of unauthorized Polish migrants to the United States, in the official media controlled by the communist regime, was apparently aimed at preventing further emigration. Although vacationers' conditions usually improved as time passed, and many of them managed to legalize their immigration status in the United States, the Polish press preferred to concentrate on the tough beginnings and examples of failure. It also kept presenting migration as "a loss" to both the migrant and homeland and emphasized the distance between the migrants and their homeland.

By leaving Poland, the migrants entered the new world, which brought experiences and emotions that only other vacationers could understand. As mentioned in the context of "American marriages," the relations between the migrants and those who stayed in Poland were presented as lacking mutual understanding, honesty, or genuine support. The media also stressed that Polish relatives did not realize how much it actually cost to send remittances that they took for granted and sometimes spent on luxuries that remained beyond the reach of their American donors.

Portraits of returnees or migrants who returned to Poland for a visit reflected little appreciation or sympathy from the Polish journalists.[80] Returnees were presented as good-looking products of their hard but nasty work back in the United States. They were charged with bringing only financial capital, but not social or cultural benefits, to Polish society when they returned. They learned no English (since Polish sufficed for functioning in the Polish community in the United States) and had seen nothing outside a Polish neighborhood.[81]

Some portrayals insinuated that migrants returned with the intention to provoke envy among those who stayed behind.[82] Some accounts decried how returnees often showed a lack of good taste in sporting their wealth or their newly acquired American manners. The very fact that they dared to live off the savings they accrued from their work in the United States and not return to work in Poland, where the cost of living was comparably lower, was regarded by some commentators as immoral.[83] Stories also frequently lamented the loss of morality among migrants who were reported to experience higher rates of financial fraud, alcoholism, broken marriages, and other undesirable behavior.[84]

The chasm between the vacationers and their Polish homes could not be bridged easily, according to the press accounts, and the migrants were blamed for any difficulties in this regard. This image corresponds with the accounts of migrants returning to other societies from America, such as to Sicily at the turn of the nineteenth and twentieth century, and to contemporary Mexico.[85] American experiences change perspectives, habits, and relations, so that returnees find practices prevailing at home incompatible with the American way of life that they had a chance to enjoy, even if in a distorted, non-ideal form.[86]

In the context of Poland under communism, Dariusz Stola goes beyond negative aspects of discrepancies between America and the Polish homeland. He claims that the American (and Western European) experiences of the Polish migrants contributed to the fall of the communist regime. Not only did the migrants' experiences prove that life outside the regime's control might bring more benefits than drawbacks, but also, the profits gained from migration, including remittances and know-how, opened opportunities to develop careers and secure well-being beyond the frameworks provided (or imposed) by the regime. To cite Stola: "Besides meeting material needs, foreign earnings made it possible to achieve a variety of life goals, from helping one's children in their careers and social advancement (through better education or purchase of a flat that made it possible to move to a city) to continuing prestigious but underpaid academic work . . . to expensive hobbies and exotic travel. They could even buy time, by hiring a 'stander' (a person who stood in queues for others), and avoid the nuisance of waiting in the ever-present long queues."[87]

Toward the Collapse of the Regime and a More Positive Image of Migrants

In the last years of the 1980s, positive voices about Polish life in America could be heard more often in the Polish press. Without detailed research in the archival files of the censorship office and other sources documenting the information policy of the Warsaw regime, one cannot tell if it was due to the regime's goodwill and relaxed control over the press—or to the depth of the economic crisis and the calculation that profits of remittances from the West could outperform losses from population drain, or to yet other factors.

For example, the material aspects of the decision not to return to Poland were explained in one of the articles: one needed about six months to earn enough to buy a car in Poland, three to four years to buy an apartment, and about five years to be able to start a business back home. But after five years, an immigrant usually had enough money and know-how to live a normal life in the United States. Why return to Poland at that point, then? Especially because middle-class life in America was better, nicer, and more comfortable than the life of a millionaire in Poland, the article admitted.[88]

In 1987, Ewa Berberyusz from the Catholic weekly *Tygodnik Powszechny*, who had previously published a series of articles discouraging emigration, and even expressed her aversion toward vacationers—whom she regarded as indicating their Polishness as a burden, not as an asset—ultimately admitted that it was not the whole truth about the Polish migrants.[89] She acknowledged that the cases described in both the Polish and Polish American press were the extreme ones, as nobody is interested in those who improved their living conditions and were spending their time happily either in America or in Poland. She claimed that Polish migrants, especially women, were known to be hardworking and resourceful, which helped them adapt easily to the labor landscape in the United States. In an about-face, Berberyusz eventually concluded that once migrants learned English and other skills for resettlement in the United States, their prospects were actually quite bright. The only thing that Berberyusz still lamented was that the young generation neglected the Polish language and culture.[90]

In 1988 the *Kierunki* weekly, also claiming to promote Catholic viewpoints, published the findings of Danuta Mostwin, a Polish American psychologist and sociologist, who immigrated to the United States shortly after World War II and remained interested in Polish immigration throughout her career. Like Berberyusz, she had previously criticized vacationers in a London weekly, where she lamented the frequency of extramarital affairs, psychiatric problems, and excessive drinking among migrants.[91] But in 1988 she claimed that negative opinions of new immigrants were based on the behavior of a "noisy minority," while the vast majority of migrants in fact profited from their stay in the United States. Although they indeed prioritized work among their values, they generally pursued "decent" (*godna*) work that would bring both profit and satisfaction to their lives, rather than only pursuing "hard work" that had been available to the Polish migrants of the nineteenth century. They also valued Poland, but because it did not provide satisfactory living conditions, they chose to emigrate, and the text did not label their choice as morally wrong.[92]

On the whole, however, successful stories of vacationers were still few and far between.

The negative portrait of Poles who left for "vacation" in the United States did not significantly change even after the communist regime collapsed. Mary Patrice Erdmans pointed to the contradictory ("schizophrenic") images of Polish migrants in the local press from southern Poland in the early 1990s: with a mixture of pride in their achievements and laments on failures and misbehaviors.[93] So was the tone of the articles published by Jan Latus, a representative of the new generation of Polish migrants, in the Polish language press in New York, and the accounts of Polish residents of Greenpoint in the 1970s and 1980s collected by Ewa Winnicka in the 2010s.[94]

As for literary works, Redliński wrote a follow-up to *Dolorado,* titled *Szczuropolacy,* which literally means "Rat-Poles," but following protests by the Polish American community, he changed the title into *Szczurojorczycy* ("Rat-Yorkers").[95]

The book, which illustrated the same negative features of the new illegal Polish immigrants as *Dolorado* and *Wakacjuszka*, was subsequently put on stage and on screen as *Szczęśliwego Nowego Jorku* ("Happy New York").

In the twenty-first century, Adam Lizakowski, another well-known Polish writer and poet who immigrated to the United States, ridiculed the dreams of new immigrants, narrowing them down to being a millionaire and dominating over those on whom they previously had to depend.[96] This critical genre was not limited to the life of the Polish migrants in the contemporary United States. Malcolm XD's *Emigracja* ("Emigration") portrayed the Polish community in London, formed as a result of waiving immigration restrictions that followed Poland's accession to the European Union.[97]

Conclusions

While the origins of the immigration cohort of Polish vacationers in the United States received little publicity, genuine problems of this group, as expressed in the two novels that were written in the United States, *Wakacjuszka* and *Dolorado*, were used in the Warsaw regime's propaganda in the 1980s, with the apparent goal to discourage further emigration. The specificity of the literary genres of the sources used in this chapter (the novels and the censored press addressed to general readership) should be taken into consideration while drawing conclusions. They prioritize emotional narratives of exaggerated or extreme cases. One cannot deny, however, that they referred to a dilemma that many Poles faced in the 1980s: whether to emigrate or not.

Wakacjuszka and *Dolorado* argued that there was no right answer to this question, since no decision could bring satisfaction or happiness. Although life in Poland was hopeless, life in America meant incurring high costs, not so much in financial terms—they improved quite quickly—but rather in moral, psychological, social, and personal ones. The official Polish press analyzed only those costs. Its arguments remained in line with the narratives of Mierzyńska and Redliński. However, since the critique of the decision to stay in Poland was ignored (probably to meet the censorship regulations), readers could conclude that it is emigration that leads to situations with no good solutions.

The tone of the publications seems to correspond with and support what sociologist Michał Garapich calls the "sedentarist metaphysics" of the Polish people who regard migration as unnatural and potentially dangerous to individuals but also to the Polish nation as a whole, for it challenges social ties and an established system of values.[98] However, even though the publications constantly questioned the American dream, they did bring it to the fore. As a result, images of Polish migrants that Mary Erdmans calls "schizophrenic" were provided. On the one hand, emigration was said to offer opportunities and the pride of achievements, but on the other hand, the laments on failures and misbehaviors could be heard.[99]

Altogether, like many other messages of the regime, the messages about the nasty vacationers' life in America proved to be ineffective. They did not discourage Polish people from emigration, particularly to the United States, which was reflected in the record numbers of Diversity Visa program (green card) applications in the 1990s.[100] Among the factors that contributed to this phenomenon were the power of the American dream (and myth), the prevalence of the migration strategies laid out by predecessors, and the contacts between the diasporic Polish communities and their hometowns and villages, with constant human and capital flow—contrary to what some press articles suggested. The success stories of the migrants that reached homeland communities were noticed even by the Communist Party activists, who lamented in the internal party documents on their effects as migration boosters.[101] Their effectiveness multiplied when combined with the Poles' general disillusionment with the communist regime, which suffered from permanent crisis—and later, with the economic difficulties of the post-communist transition period.

Notes

1. See e.g. Helena Znaniecka-Łopata, *Polish Americans: Status Competition in an Ethnic Community* (Englewood Cliffs, NJ: Prentice-Hall, 1976), 36–42, 89.

2. Anna Jaroszyńska-Kirchmann, *The Exile Mission: The Polish Political Diaspora and Polish Americans, 1939–1956* (Athens: Ohio University Press, 2004), 108. The book provides a detailed presentation of this immigration cohort.

3. Dariusz Stola, "Opting Out of Socialism: For-Profit Mobility from Communist Poland," *East European Politics and Societies* 35, no. 4 (2021): 1139.

4. Stola, "Opting Out of Socialism," 1141.

5. For post–World War II history of Poland, including the issues of the 1970s and 1980s referred to in this chapter, see: Andrzej Paczkowski, *Spring Will Be Ours: Poland and the Poles from Occupation to Freedom* (University Park: Pennsylvania State University Press, 2010).

6. Stola, "Opting Out of Socialism," 1141–42.

7. Stola, "Opting Out of Socialism."

8. Cf. Joanna Kulpińska, "Multigenerational Migration Chains of Families from the Village of Babica—an Attempt to Create a Typology," *Polish American Studies* 75, no. 2 (2018): 77–94.

9. Dariusz Stola, "Opening a Non-Exit State: The Passport Policy of Communist Poland, 1949–1980," *East European Politics and Societies* 29, no. 1 (2015): 96–119.

10. Maria Konwicka, *Byli sobie raz* (Kraków: Znak, 2019), 212. She attributed a positive decision regarding her parents' application in the 1980s to the possible intervention of Mieczysław Rakowski, then a prominent activist of the Communist Party, whom she met at her friend's apartment in New York and complained that the passport office did not let her parents visit her in America (252).

11. Dariusz Stola, *Kraj bez wyjścia? Migracje z Polski 1949–1989* (Warszawa: ISP PAN & IPN, 2010), 147.

12. According to the Polish passport officers, up to 90 percent of trips to the United States involved employment. Stola, "Opting Out of Socialism," 1148.

13. Stola, "Opting Out of Socialism," 1149; Edward Redliński, *Szczurojorczycy* (Warszawa: Muza, 2000), 8.

14. Undated memo, file no. BU 3171/15/1, pp. 104–5, AIPN, discussed in Joanna Wojdon, "A Portrait of the Intelligence Officers of the Polish People's Republic in the United States," *Polish American Studies* 75, no. 2 (2018): 55–76.

15. Cf. the collection of correspondence of Jan Nowak-Jeziorański at Ossolinski Institute, Wrocław.

16. Jerzy Wlazło, Katarzyna Rij, *Lubomir Tomaszewski. Portret w płomieniach* (Warszawa: Agora, 2021).

17. Wlazło and Rij, *Lubomir Tomaszewski*. On the variety of motives and strategies of emigration, see Magdalena Wnuk, *Kierunek Zachód, przystanek emigracja. Adaptacja polskich emigrantów w Austrii, Szwecji i we Włoszech od lat 80. XX w. do współczesności* (Toruń: UMK, 2019), 56–88. Cf. Karol Jackowski, "Saksy. Kierunek—Ameryka. Początek drogi," *Kultura* 2, no. 16 (1986): 6.

18. Stola, "Opting Out of Socialism," 1148.

19. Frank Mocha, *American "Polonia" and Poland: A Sequel to Poles in America: Bicentennial Essays* (Boulder, CO, and New York: Columbia University Press, 1998), 31–32.

20. Anna Sosnowska, *Polski Greenpoint a Nowy Jork. Gentryfikacja, stosunki etniczne i imigrancki rynek pracy na przełomie XX i XXI wieku* (Warszawa: Scholar, 2016), 175.

21. Sosnowska, *Polski Greenpoint*, 140–41. Cf. Polish & Slavic Federal Credit Union, https://en.psfcu.com/overview accessed March 24, 2023.

22. Ewa Winnicka, *Greenpoint. Kroniki Małej Polski* (Wołowiec: Czarne, 2021); Polish and Slavic Federal Credit Union, History, https://www.psfcu.com/about-us/history, accessed March 24, 2023.

23. Winnicka, *Greenpoint*.

24. Danuta Piątkowska, "Polsko-Słowiańska Federalna Unia Kredytowa sukcesem amerykańskiej Polonii," *Przegląd Polsko-Polonijny* 3–4 (2016): 11–55.

25. *Protokół ósmej krajowej konwencji Kongresu Polonii Amerykańskiej odbytej w dniach 14, 16 i 16 sierpnia 1970 roku w Chicago, Illinois* (Chicago: PAC, 1971), 68; H. Gordon, "Polish American Congress (Michigan Division) Reviews Activities," *Naród Polski* no. 12 (June 18, 1981), 8.

26. Joanna Wojdon, *White and Red Umbrella: Polish American Congress in the Cold War Era 1944–1988* (Reno, NV: Helena History Press, 2015), 317.

27. Wojdon, *White and Red Umbrella*, 314–17.

28. Wojdon, *White and Red Umbrella*, 315, note 173 provides references to the PAC documents reporting on this issue.

29. Sosnowska, *Polski Greenpoint*, 155–259.

30. See the story of Andrzej Pityński in Winnicka, *Greenpoint*.

31. Agenda: Meeting of Polish American Congress, April 28, 1981 (an attachment to the letter of May 15, 1981), Papers of Edward Tomasik, Box 1, Immigration History Research

Center Archives (hereafter cited as IHRCA); Walter Conery to Mazewski, August 23, 1980, Papers of Aloysius Mazewski, Box 110, Folder 7, IHRCA; Statement of the Polish American Congress to Democratic Platform Committee, June 13, 1980, Papers of Aloysius Mazewski, Box 110, Folder 7, IHRCA. Cf. Wojdon, *White and Red Umbrella*, 316.

32. Report of President Aloysius A. Mazewski from October 25, 1980, to October 20, 1981: Board of Directors Meeting October 30, 1981, Washington, DC, in Minutes 1981, 19. Cf. Wojdon, *White and Red Umbrella*, 316.

33. Minutes of the Executive Committee and Board Meeting of the PAC, December 6, 1968, Papers of Edward Tomasik, Box 2, IHRCA (in Polish).

34. *Protokół ósmej krajowej konwencji Kongresu Polonii Amerykańskiej odbytej w dniach 14, 16 i 16 sierpnia 1970 roku w Chicago, Illinois* (Chicago: PAC, 1971), 66.

35. Wojdon, *White and Red Umbrella*, 314.

36. See Mary Patrice Erdmans, *Opposite Poles: Immigrants and Ethnics in Polish Chicago, 1976–1990* (University Park: Pennsylvania State University Press, 2010); Joanna Wojdon, "Polish Americans' Reception of the 'Solidarity' immigration cohort," *Studia Migracyjne-Przegląd Polonijny* 44, no. 4 (170) (2018): 31–43.

37. Lynda J. Oswald, "Extended Voluntary Departure: Limiting the Attorney General's Discretion in Immigration Matters," *Michigan Law Review* 85, no. 1 (1986): 152–90.

38. Wojdon, *White and Red Umbrella*, 318–19.

39. Stola, "Opting Out of Socialism," 1148.

40. For statistics, see Donald Pienkos, *For Your Freedom through Ours: Polish American Efforts on Poland's Behalf, 1863–1991* (New York and Boulder: University of Colorado Press, 1991), 204–5.

41. Wojdon, *White and Red Umbrella*, 319–20.

42. See e.g. Wojdon, "Polish Americans' Reception"; Andrzej Krajewski, *Region USA. Działacze 'Solidarnści' o kraju, o emigracji, o sobie* (London: Aneks, 1989).

43. Stanislaus Blejwas, "Old and New Polonias: Tensions within an Ethnic Community," *Polish American Studies* 38, no. 2 (1981): 55–83; Erdmans, *Opposite Poles*.

44. Zofia Mierzyńska, *Wakacjuszka* (Chicago: Z & L Song & Publishing Co., 1983; first edition in Poland 1990, after the collapse of the communist regime); Edward Redliński, *Dolorado* (Chicago: Contemporary Images, 1984; first edition in Poland: 1985 by NOWA—independent, illegal publisher, beyond the censorship control).

45. Andreea Deciu Ritivoi, *Yesterday's Self: Nostalgia and the Immigrant Identity* (Lanham, MD: Rowman & Littlefield, 2002); Dominica Radulescu, *Realms of Exile: Nomadism, Diasporas, and Eastern European Voices* (New York: Lexington Books, 2002); Susan J. Matt, *Homesickness: An American History* (Oxford, UK: Oxford University Press, 2011).

46. A detailed analysis based on the articles listed in the "Content Bibliography of Periodicals" (*Bibliografia zawartości czasopism*) can be found in Joanna Wojdon, "Polish Americans in the Press of the People's Republic of Poland (1952–1989)," *Polish American Studies* 59, no. 2 (2002): 29–78.

47. Cf. Marcin Zaremba, *Communism—Legitimacy—Nationalism: Nationalist Legitimization of the Communist Regime in Poland* (New York: Peter Lang, 2019).

48. Joanna Wojdon, "Myths Pertaining to Polish Americans in the Press of Communist Poland," *Ad Americam: Journal of American Studies* 15 (2014): 81–89.

49. Hieronim Kubiak, "Saga Gromadów," *Przekrój* 1745 (1978): 10–11.

50. On Piszek's biography, see Edward Piszek, *Some Good in the World. A Life of Purpose: A Memoir by E. J. Piszek As Told to Jake Morgan* (Boulder, CO, and New York: Columbia University Press, 2001). For a list of Polish articles on Piszek, see Wojdon, "Polish Americans in the Press," 39.

51. See Wojdon, "Polish Americans in the Press," for a detailed bibliography.

52. Wiesław Łuka, "Bez darmowych obiadków," *Prawo i Życie* no. 11 (1986): 16; Zygmunt Wójcik, "Kartki z Dolorado (1)," *Argumenty* no. 35 (1988): 4.

53. Jackowski, "Saksy. Kierunek—Ameryka. Początek drogi."

54. Piotr K. Domaradzki, "Żadnej pracy się nie boję," *Przemiany* 20, no. 12 (1989): 3.

55. Karol Jackowski, "Saksy. Kierunek—Ameryka. No problem," *Kultura* 2, no. 18 (1986): 6.

56. Lidia Zawistowska, "Jak u Mrożka," *Przemiany* no. 3 (1989): 9; Domaradzki, "Żadnej pracy."

57. Jackowski, "Saksy. Kierunek—Ameryka. No problem."

58. Zygmunt Wójcik, "Kartki z Dolorado (2)," *Argumenty* no. 37 (1988): 4.

59. Łuka, "Bez darmowych obiadków," 15. Cf. Krystyna Zielińska, "Zielona karta," *Przegląd Tygodniowy* 6, no. 29 (1987): 10–11 (elderly care).

60. Karol Jackowski, "Saksy. Kierunek—Ameryka. Jak zostać robolem?," *Kultura* 2, no. 17 (1986): 6. Cf. Łuka, "Bez darmowych obiadków," 16; Elżbieta Szołucha, "Gra w zielone," *Rzeczywistość* 6, no. 32 (1986): 5; Ewa Berberyusz, "Emigracja marzeń," *Tygodnik Powszechny* 40, no. 50 (1986): 5; Zielińska, "Zielona karta"; Domaradzki, "Żadnej pracy."

61. Mary Patrice Erdmans, "Portraits of Emigration: Sour Milk and Honey in the Promised Land," *Sociological Inquiry* 69, no. 3 (1999): 337–63.

62. Zielińska, "Zielona karta"; Wójcik, "Kartki z Dolorado (2)." Cf. Zawistowska, "Jak u Mrożka."

63. Adam Rzęsa, Letter to Editor, *Przegląd Tygodniowy* 6, no. 31 (1987): 5. Cf. Berberyusz, "Emigracja marzeń"; Wójcik, "Kartki z Dolorado (5)."

64. Ewa Berberyusz, "Z punktu widzenia sprzątaczki. Korespondencja z Nowego Jorku," *Tygodnik Powszechny* 40, no. 32 (1986): 1, 4; Wójcik, "Kartki z Dolorado (1)"; Zygmunt Wójcik, "Kartki z Dolorado (5)," *Argumenty* no. 49 (1988): 4; Zawistowska, "Jak u Mrożka"; Olbromski, "Samotność."

65. Jackowski, "Saksy. Kierunek—Ameryka. No problem"; Karol Jackowski, "Saksy. Kierunek—Ameryka. Kwestia higieny osobistej," *Kultura* 2, no. 20 (1986): 6; Wiesław Łuka, "Wędzenie na zimno," *Prawo i Życie* no. 28 (1986): 12–13.

66. Zielińska, "Zielona karta"; Zawistowska, "Jak u Mrożka."

67. Numerous testimonies from both the parents who emigrated and the children who stayed in Poland can be found in Winnicka, *Greenpoint*.

68. E.g. Zygmunt Wójcik, "Kartki z Dolorado (6)," *Argumenty* no. 35 (1988): 4; Wójcik, "Kartki z Dolorado (2)"; Olbromski, "Samotność"; Zielińska, "Zielona karta"; Wąsewicz, "Ameryka zaułków."

69. Zielińska, "Zielona karta"; Domaradzki, "Żadnej pracy."

70. Karol Jackowski, "Saksy. Kierunek—Ameryka. Załatwią każdą sprawę," *Kultura* 2, no. 19 (1986): 6.

71. Zielińska, "Zielona karta."

72. Zawistowska, "Jak u Mrożka"; Olbromski, "Samotność."

73. Mieczyslaw R. Olbromski, "Samotność," *Rzeczywistość* 6, no. 51/52 (1986): 18; Adam Wąsewicz, "Ameryka zaułków," *Przegląd Tygodniowy* 6, no. 31 (1987): 15; Wójcik, "Kartki z Dolorado (1)."

74. Wąsewicz, "Ameryka zaułków."

75. Jackowski, "Saksy. Kierunek—Ameryka. Jak zostać robolem?"

76. Wójcik, "Kartki z Dolorado (2)."

77. Jackowski, "Saksy. Kierunek—Ameryka. Jak zostać robolem?"

78. Szołucha, "Gra w zielone"; Wąsewicz, "Ameryka zaułków."

79. Karol Jackowski, "Saksy. Kierunek—Ameryka. Znowu w domu," *Kultura* 2, no. 21 (1986): 6.

80. Zielińska, "Zielona karta."

81. Jackowski, "Saksy. Kierunek—Ameryka. Znowu w domu"; Berberyusz, "Z punktu widzenia sprzątaczki"; Zawistowska, "Jak u Mrożka"; Domaradzki, "Żadnej pracy."

82. Zawistowska, "Jak u Mrożka"; Domaradzki, "Żadnej pracy"; Olbromski, "Samotność."

83. Rzęsa, Letter to Editor.

84. Ewa Szczukajtys, "Amerykanie zza Buga," *Kontrasty*, no. 8 (1985): 7–9.

85. David Fitzgerald, *A Nation of Emigrants: How Mexico Manages Its Migration* (Berkeley: University of California Press, 2008); Linda Reeder, *Widows in White: Migration and the Transformation of Rural Italian Women, Sicily, 1880–1920* (Toronto: University of Toronto Press, 2003).

86. Winnicka's interviewees, depicted in her *Greenpoint*, no matter how traumatic their American experiences had been, claimed that they would never like to return to Poland.

87. Stola, "Opting Out of Socialism," 1151.

88. Jackowski, "Saksy. Kierunek—Ameryka. No problem"; cf. Zawistowska, "Jak u Mrożka."

89. Berberyusz, "Emigracja marzeń."

90. Ewa Berberyusz, "Przywiążcie mnie sznurami," *Tygodnik Powszechny* 41, no. 35 (1987): 1, 4.

91. Cited in Jan Krawiec, *Od Bachórca do Chicago* (Warszawa: IPN, 2015), 288.

92. Danuta Mostwin, "Milcząca większość," *Kierunki* no. 34 (1988): 1, 5.

93. Erdmans, "Portraits of Emigration."

94. Jan Latus, *Stąd widać najlepiej* (Warszawa: Nowy Świat, 2004); Winnicka, *Greenpoint.*

95. Edward Redliński, *Szczuropolacy: Podsłuchowisko* (Warszawa: Prószyński i s-ka, 1994); Redliński, *Szczurojorczycy* (Warszawa: BGW, 1997).

96. Adam Lizakowski, *Kuzyn Józef albo emigracja loteryjna po roku 1989 do Ameryki, czyli wyprawa po złote runo* (Toruń: Adam Marszałek, 2003).

97. Malcolm XD, *Emigracja* (Warszawa: W.A.B., 2019).

98. Michał Garapich, "Odyssean Refugees, Migrants and Power—Construction of 'Other' Within the Polish 'Community' in the UK," in D. Reed-Danahay and C. Brettell,

eds., *Immigration and Citizenship in Europe and the US: Anthropological Perspectives* (New Brunswick, NJ: Rutgers University Press, 2007), 124–44.

99. Erdmans, "Portraits of Emigration."

100. U.S. Immigration and Naturalization Service, *Statistical Yearbook of the Immigration and Naturalization Service, 1996* (Washington, DC: U.S. Government Printing Office, 1997), 19; U.S. Immigration and Naturalization Service, *Statistical Yearbook of the Immigration and Naturalization Service, 1997* (Washington, DC: U.S. Government Printing Office, 1999), 44.

101. See Stola, "Opting Out of Socialism," 1152.

Contributors

DANIELLE BATTISTI is Associate Professor of History at the University of Nebraska at Omaha, where she specializes in U.S. immigration and ethnic history. Her first book, *Whom We Shall Welcome: Italian Americans and Immigration Reform* (Fordham University Press, 2019) examined both the liberal and conservative elements of Italian American efforts to influence American immigration policies in the 1950s and 1960s. It won the First Book Award from the Immigration and Ethnic History Society in 2020. She is currently researching American involvement in the creation and operations of the Intergovernmental Committee for European Migration, an international organization created in 1951 and charged with resettling European displaced persons to receiving states in the Americas and Oceania. Battisti has also published articles and chapters in the *Journal of American Ethnic History, The Italian American Review, Making Italian America: Consumer Culture and the Production of Ethnic Identities* (Fordham University Press, 2014), and *Ethnic Families in America* (Prentice Hall, 2011).

ASHLEY JOHNSON BAVERY is Associate Professor of History at Eastern Michigan University, where she teaches courses on U.S. immigration and ethnic history. Her book, *Bootlegged Aliens: Immigration Politics on America's Northern Border* (University of Pennsylvania Press, 2020), received the First Book Award from the Immigration and Ethnic History Society for its examination of unauthorized European immigration to Detroit before World War II. Her articles have been published in the *Journal of American History,* the *Journal of Urban History,* and *Mashriq & Mahjar: Journal of Middle East and North African Migration Studies.* She is currently working on a book that draws on oral histories and mosque records to explore Muslim immigration, race, and industrialization in the American Midwest during the first half of the twentieth century.

MARY PATRICE ERDMANS is Professor of Sociology at Case Western Reserve University. She received her PhD in Sociology from Northwestern University. Her areas of interest include immigration and ethnicity, with a focus on contemporary Polish migration. She is the author of *Opposite Poles* (1998), *The Grasinski Girls* (2005), and *On Becoming a Teen Mom* (2015), and her articles have appeared in such journals as *Sociological Quarterly, Journal of American Ethnic History, Studia Migracyjne,* and *Polish American Studies.* Her current research project is an oral history of Polish return migration among activists from the Solidarity movement.

POLINA ERMOSHKINA is a doctoral candidate in the Department of Sociology at Case Western Reserve University (CWRU). She earned a law degree from the Bashkir State University Institute of Law in Russia. She holds three master's degrees in diverse fields: family and child studies (Miami University, 2012), gerontological studies (Miami University, 2014), and sociology (CWRU, 2021). Ermoshkina is a medical sociologist and a critical gerontologist, who uses qualitative methods to study caregiving in Eastern Europe. Her dissertation examines the lived experiences of only daughters from single-parent households taking care of their aging mothers in the metropolitan city of Ufa in the Ural Mountains of Russia. For her contributions to gerontological research and exemplary performance at CWRU, she was awarded the prestigious Marie Haug Award. She is an Editorial Assistant for the newly established *Journal of Elder Policy* (Editor-in-Chief Eva Kahana, PhD), published by the Policy Studies Organization and housed at CWRU.

TORSTEN FEYS has worked at Flanders Marine Institute (VLIZ) since 2020, where he conducts research on tourism, migration, and maritime history. He also teaches on these subjects as a guest professor at the University of Antwerp. He obtained his doctorate at the European University Institute, with a thesis on the commercialization of transatlantic migrant transport during the long nineteenth century, published as *The Battle for the Migrants* (2013). His postdoctoral research at Ghent University (2010–2017) zoomed in on how shipping companies influenced the enactment, enforcement, and evasion of U.S. migration laws and was published in the *Journal of Migration History,* the *Journal of Modern European History,* and the *International Migration Review.* A sequel to the chapter in this volume focusing on deportations during the First World War, titled "Deportation at All Costs?," was submitted to the journal *Immigrants & Minorities.* Feys also worked at the Free University of Brussels (2015–2020) on the IMMIBEL-project, where his research focused on expulsion practices and uncovered how the bureaucratic apparatus to control foreigners developed in Belgium. This work has been published in the *Journal of Tourism History, Journal of Transport History,* and *Diasporas.*

CARLY GOODMAN is Assistant Professor of History at Rutgers University–Camden. Her book *Dreamland: America's Immigration Lottery in an Age of Restriction* (University of North Carolina Press, 2023) received the First Book Award from the Immigration and Ethnic History Society. She is a Senior Editor for Made by History at *TIME* Magazine.

S. DEBORAH KANG is Associate Professor of History in the Corcoran Department of History and John L. Nau III Associate Professor of the History and Principles of Democracy at the Karsh Institute of Democracy at the University of Virginia. Her first book, *The INS on the Line: Making Immigration Law on the US-Mexico Border, 1917–1954* (Oxford University Press, 2017), traces the history of U.S. immigration agencies on the U.S.-Mexico border and earned several awards, including the Henry Adams Prize from the Society for History in the Federal Government, the Theodore Saloutos Book Award from the Immigration and Ethnic History Society, the Berkshire Conference of Women Historians Book Prize, the W. Turrentine Jackson Award from the Western History Association, and the Américo Paredes Book Award for Best Nonfiction Book on Chicano/a, Mexican American and/or Latino/a Studies. It was also recognized as a finalist for the 2018 Weber-Clements Book Prize by the Western History Association. She is currently preparing law review articles on the criminalization of undocumented immigration and a second monograph on the history of immigration legalization in the United States.

E. KYLE ROMERO is Assistant Professor of History at the University of North Florida. He writes and teaches on the history of U.S. foreign policy, immigration and global migration, and humanitarianism and human rights. He received his PhD in 2020 from Vanderbilt University and has previously served as a postdoctoral fellow at the Dickey Center for International Understanding at Dartmouth College.

RANDA TAWIL is Assistant Professor of Women and Gender Studies at Texas Christian University. Her research interests include histories of empire, gendered migration, and mobility in the twentieth century. Her forthcoming book, *Race in Transit: Mobilities between Greater Syria and U.S. Empire,* traces the mobilities of people from Ottoman Syria to the United States to reveal the messy relations between local and global constructions of race and gender, and the consequences for migrants who straddle racial categories. She has published articles in journals such as *Amerasia, Frontiers: A Journal of Women's Studies,* contributed essays to media outlets such as *The Washington Post* and *Open Democracy, Palestine Square,* and appeared on numerous podcasts. The research for her chapter was supported by the Cokie Roberts Women's History Fellowship at the National Archives in Washington, DC.

JOANNA WOJDON is Professor of History at the University of Wrocław, Poland. Her research interests focus on history education, public history, and Polish American history. Her recent publications include *Polish American History after 1939* (Routledge, 2024), *Communist Propaganda at School: Reading Primers of the Soviet Bloc, 1949–1989* (Routledge, 2021), *Public History in Poland* (Routledge, 2021), and *Public in Public History* (coedited with Dorota Wiśniewska, Routledge, 2021).

Index

The University of Illinois Press
is a founding member of the
Association of University Presses.

———————————————

Composed in 10.5/13 Minion Pro
by Lisa Connery
at the University of Illinois Press

University of Illinois Press
1325 South Oak Street
Champaign, IL 61820–6903
www.press.uillinois.edu